TITAN SCREWED

TITAN SCREWED

LOST SMILES, STUNNERS, AND SCREWJOBS

James Dixon
Justin Henry

with RD Reynolds & Benjamin Richardson

whatculture.com

Copyright © James Dixon 2016. All Rights Reserved.

Published by WhatCulture.com

All rights reserved. This book may not be reproduced, in whole or in any part, in any form, without written permission from the publisher or author.

This book is set in Garamond.

10 9 8 7 6 5 4 3 2 1

This book was printed and bound in the United Kingdom.

ISBN: 978-1-326-68559-1

Bret made a very, very selfish decision. Bret is going to have to live with that for the rest of his life. I have no sympathy whatsoever for Bret.

- Vince McMahon

Dedicated to the memories of Kris Travis and Brian 'Axl Rotten' Knighton

FOREWORD
by RD Reynolds

NINETEEN-NINETY-SEVEN. AS A man obsessed with pro wrestling, simply typing that number gives me chills. While other twelve-month periods had better single matches or better individual feuds, nothing could ever top this one. It had everything a fan could ever want.

When folks get all teary-eyed and start babbling like love sick teenagers about the Monday Night Wars era, the year the battle was most engaged – and the most fun – was this one. The fight for supremacy was intense, and led to some of the greatest one-upsmanship ever witnessed not only in professional wrestling, but in any entertainment medium. Those in charge of the WWF, WCW, and ECW did everything in their power to not only assist their own company but to damage the others, and that insanity drove everyone in the industry to better their game, be that wrestlers, bookers, even the fans themselves.

So many legendary events occurred during the calendar year. Sting in the rafters, finally descending to battle Hulk Hogan at Starrcade. ECW's first pay-per-view event, Barely Legal. And of course, the biggest moment of the year, perhaps in the history of pro wrestling itself: Sid pooping his pants at WrestleMania.

Oh come on now, surely that is just some urban legend, a myth from the bygone days of RSPW and Compuserve forums with crackpot sysops. That couldn't have really happened....right?

This book might tell you.

And yes, it will also definitely tell you the full story of what I probably should have added as the third point in the paragraph above instead of defecation-centred humour: Montreal. The Montreal screw-job and the entire sordid story leading up to it. It's like something out of the craziest motion picture you can imagine, and even its title ("Sunny Days and Lost Smiles: The Shawn Michaels Story") sounds completely fictional. But it happened, and it all played out with real human beings who were so utterly obsessed with the business they were in that they lost sight of everything outside the squared circle.

Such fervour led to so many positive moments, though, and the Shawn Michaels-Bret Hart feud was just one of them. We got to see the rise of many who would become the foundation for the industry for years to come, including "Stone Cold" Steve Austin, The Rock, Triple H, Kane, and the most despicable heel fans had ever seen, Mr. McMahon. Great matches weren't an annual occurrence; they happened weekly as the world's top performers climbed over each other to be featured on Raw and Nitro. And then there was ECW, lurking in a bingo hall in a skanky part of Philadelphia, breaking rules that had never been broken, generally for good reason.

Many fans believed it could never get any better.

They were right.

And now you get to relive it through the eyes of two of the best young writers in the world today, James Dixon and Justin Henry. James has done an incredible job with the first two titles, chronicling the low ebb that was mid-nineties WWF in his previous releases, and it's great to see him continue on now with the rise of WWF's fortunes. As for Justin, I've never met anyone who has his combination of dry wit and keen reflection. As I've told him several times, talent cannot be held back, and this book is proof of that. Whether you lived through this era or are just learning about it now, you cannot possibly have better tour guides.

So take it away, Mr. Dixon and Mr. Henry.

But do me a favour, will you? Please leave out the parts about Sid's bowel movements.

Some things are best left unknown.

RD Reynolds
May 2016

ONE

FOR SIXTEEN MONTHS, WAR HAD raged throughout the wrestling industry. This epic clash was not a violent yet well-orchestrated ballet contested between two muscled performers within the confines of a wrestling ring, rather a battle fought between two global corporations via the medium of cable television. At the forefront was World Championship Wrestling based out of Atlanta, an entity bankrolled by billionaire mogul Ted Turner. The group had long been considered North America's number two wrestling promotion, languishing in the shadows as Vince McMahon's mighty World Wrestling Federation dominated the industry. WCW's arrival on Turner-owned network TNT in September 1995 with *Monday Nitro* changed all that. The company enjoyed widely unexpected success in a weekly head-to-head television war against the WWF's flagship broadcast *Monday Night Raw*.

With WCW prospering, the misconception was that the publicly humiliated WWF was floundering, struggling to stay afloat thanks to its frequent defeats in the weekly ratings battle. It was a myth that brazen WCW Vice President Eric Bischoff was more than happy to perpetuate. Bischoff repeated the fallacy with such frequent gusto that many in the industry began to accept it as gospel. Moreover, WWF staff, officials, and performers believed the notion too, with some switching sides to apparently greener pastures after seeing the writing on the wall.

The reality of the WWF's standing was much different to the Bischoff-led allusions of their impending demise. The weekly ratings battle was a war of perception, existing purely to fuel bragging rights between networks TNT and USA about which of them was number one on cable. While there was some financial motivation behind the broadcasters vying for top spot – more viewers meant greater advertising revenue – the effect of the war was far less detrimental to Titan's bottom line than WCW propaganda, and indeed the WWF's own propaganda, implied.

There was no doubt that WCW's business had improved across the board since the advent of *Nitro* and particularly with Bischoff's creation of the New World Order storyline in mid-1996, but the belief that the ticket buying public had deserted the WWF was simply not the case. The WWF's performance on Monday nights had surprisingly little bearing on their prosperity in other avenues, for while McMahon watched his ratings plummet into the low 2s[1], his house show business was growing at a phenomenal rate. By the end of 1996, the WWF's average house show attendance for the year was almost 5,000 fans per show – 1,500 higher than the previous year's average – whereas WCW's was under 3,500. The numbers were so bad for WCW that all house shows were money losing ventures, resulting in many members of the large talent roster having to take substantial pay cuts.

The statistics told an interesting story. The casual television audience who watched *Nitro* on a Monday night rarely parted with their cash for live events, whereas the hardcore fan base who were willing to spend money on wrestling favoured the WWF. Numbers on pay-per-view, the real litmus test that showed how a company's product was resonating with its audience, were almost identical. The WWF's average over the year was a 0.62 buyrate[2], whereas WCW had a 0.64. The difference was almost negligible. However, the WWF presented two more paid broadcasts than WCW in 1996, thus generating more revenue throughout the year via the medium. Removing the WWF's two lowest drawing PPV cards would have seen them ahead in the yearly average.

The WWF also dominated WCW in terms of both licensing and merchandise agreements, with the WWF making a healthy profit on sales of shirts (largely down to the success of the incredibly popular 'Austin 3:16' tee), action figures, and various other branded products. While still generating strong revenue, by comparison WCW was lagging far behind. Other than the supremely popular 'nWo' shirt, little else was selling. It was clear that the nWo had become the 'in' thing with both the live audience and the armchair fan, and it was they rather than WCW as a whole that were making the difference.

Internationally the WWF was leagues ahead of WCW in its global reach. WCW was limited to non-live late night shows on secondary cable channels in Germany and the United Kingdom, and rarely toured outside of the United States. Conversely, the WWF enjoyed enduring relationships with many large international broadcasters, and frequently ventured overseas to promote shows across four continents in front of loud, often sell-out crowds. While there was

---

[1] In 1997, a 1.0 Nielsen rating equated to approximately 970,000 homes. Thus a 2.0 rating meant around 1.94 million households were tuned into a program. Each 0.1 increment was worth around 97,000 homes.

[2] A pay-per-view buy rate is calculated by sharing the total number of homes with the capacity to buy the event, shared by the number of actual buys. The WWF's 0.62 average was around 160,000 buys.

no doubt that WCW was the market leader on television, the WWF's supposed demise was significantly overstated.

Often overlooked is that WCW had *always* beaten the WWF on cable television, even during the final throngs of Titan's Hulkamania boom period at the beginning of the decade. At a time when WCW was struggling to bounce back from losing company icon Ric Flair to McMahon, with house show attendance often falling under 1,000, their average cable rating remained superior to the WWF's numbers. The pattern remained right up until the onset of *Nitro* in 1995, a year which actually saw the closest gap between the sides in yearly average ratings (2.04 to 1.97, or approximately 63,000 viewers) since 1992. It had always been that way, only it was never factored as important or even particularly relevant before because television ratings had little bearing on revenue.

The observation that a seismic shift had occurred underfoot, sending the balance of power to Atlanta, was fanciful at best. Unquestionably the terrain had changed, and WCW was in the ascendancy, but the WWF was hardly a dead brand clinging on to the final vestige of its past success. The significant difference was that WCW was now beating the WWF directly on Monday night prime time cable, rather than in a non-direct Saturday afternoon slot. It was only after Ted Turner's decision to run *Nitro* in the same timeslot as *Monday Night Raw* – an intentional assault on the WWF brand designed to settle a longstanding personal feud with McMahon – that anyone started to take notice of ratings.

While *Nitro* was handily beating *Raw* in the weekly Nielsens, the newfound competition did not harm the WWF as Turner had hoped; in fact, the opposite occurred. The dilution of the industry that many had predicted when *Nitro* launched – alongside a significant increase in pay-per-views from both companies – did not come to pass. On the contrary, the heightened level of competition had lit a fire under both sides to produce stronger television output, dragging the outdated business into a new era of reality-based programming featuring more modern characters.

By 1997, both groups were enjoying a general uptick in business across the board, with WCW posting a record company attendance for *Nitro* in New Orleans on January 13 (10,000 paid) and obliterating it the following week in Chicago (17,000). Meanwhile, WWF house show business was the strongest it had been in half a decade. Regardless, McMahon was dejected that WCW was defeating his company so handily on Monday nights. By nature, he despised losing at anything, so clawing back ground on *Nitro* in the overstated ratings battle began to consume him. In late 1995 he had begun laying the groundwork for a new look WWF, an edgier and more violent production than he had ever presented prior. However, he was frequently quelled in his desire to rebrand due to a combination of talent departures, sponsor concerns, network squeamishness, and cold feet. When Bischoff unleashed the nWo and began winning the Monday Night War more and more comfortably each week, by the end of 1996 he no longer cared about the reservations and restrictions – he was going to market the WWF towards an adult audience regardless.

AMONGST THE first directives McMahon implemented was a new syndicated television show airing live on Saturdays at 11 p.m. called *Shotgun Saturday Night*. The broadcast was McMahon's direct interpretation of Paul Heyman's Extreme Championship Wrestling, the veritable third wheel in the Monday Night Wars. ECW had risen from low-budget independent group to national entity in little over three years, making waves with its vocal hardcore fan base, daring programming, and copious violence. McMahon yearned for the WWF to be as contemporary, so decided to channel the key elements that he believed made ECW successful: risqué characters, shocking angles, and an intimate setting.

He aired the first episode on January 4 from the Mirage nightclub in New York, and rather missed the point entirely. The show came across as ECW-lite, with the WWF trying far too hard to be cutting edge and modern. On the inaugural broadcast there were aspects where Vince seemingly tried to set the tone for the future of his programming, only for events to take a turn for the outrageous or unintentionally comedic. The whole thing seemed like a twisted cartoon version of ECW, a garbled misinterpretation of what McMahon believed the ethos of the company to be. It was widely panned by critics.

The next week aired from the All-Star Café, also in New York, in front of a small but rowdy crowd of 150 people. The intimate setting meant a handful of vocal fans could dictate the tone of the broadcast, and they wilfully cheered the heels throughout the show. It was an act of defiance that would become a nationwide epidemic throughout the year, with increasingly large numbers of fans rejecting the antiquated black and white notion of good guys and bad guys, instead determined to vociferously boo and cheer whomever they liked.

One man who took the brunt of the audience's abuse more than most was Dwayne Johnson, still learning his craft only two months into his WWF run. His Rocky Maivia persona became the poster boy for fan vitriol against force-fed characters they shared no affinity with. McMahon had pushed him too hard, too fast. Soon, crowds across the nation spat verbal barbs Johnson's way, screaming "Die, Rocky, Die" at the top of their lungs, or bellowing "Rocky Sucks" at the rookie because of their hatred for his cloying babyface act.

The appearance of ECW regular and industry veteran Terry Funk on the January 18 broadcast finally gave *Shotgun* the much-needed edge that it had been sorely lacking. Funk unleashed a volley of profanity directed towards McMahon, who was situated as a commentator at ringside, before brawling around the building with Steve Austin. It was a well-received and memorable segment, something the already foundering *Shotgun* had been crying out for. However, the show's Long Island syndicator was put off by the coarse language Funk used, resulting in *Shotgun* being pushed back an hour to a midnight time slot. McMahon was furious, vowing to never use the grizzled Texan again.

The new midnight slot caused significant strain on an already overworked production team, with the efforts of creating a live Saturday evening broadcast, live editing a *Superstars* taping on Sunday morning, and then *Raw* on Monday evenings causing many to become severely fatigued and rapidly jaded. The competitors frequenting *Shotgun* felt much the same way, with many complaining about the low payoffs, unsociable schedule, and cost of weekly road expenses in New York. Many felt it was not worth their time and effort to be working in small, badly-lit venues in front of a largely bored crowd, on a show that no one had anything positive to say about.

Jim Cornette, then a member of the WWF creative team, recalled the weekly ordeal. "It was a trip for us every Saturday night right into the middle of the freaking city. It meant we had to fly talent in from wherever they were on tour, we had to rebook weekend cards to make people available. It was one of those ideas that Vince loved, but that quickly changed when other things came along and took priority."

McMahon continued to plug away with *Shotgun*, though it was becoming evident with each passing week that he was rapidly losing interest in the experiment. Little over a month after it started, *Shotgun* was dead in the water. The live concept was shelved following the February 8 broadcast, which aired not from a nightclub, but from Penn Station. *Shotgun* continued following that, though rather than going out live it was filmed a week in advance prior to, and occasionally following *Monday Night Raw*.

Though *Shotgun* was an unmitigated disaster, McMahon was now so far into his bold new WWF vision that there was no turning back. His thirst for a more daring product had not been quenched with the failed Saturday night venture as some expected it might be, and he decided to continue plunging headfirst into the violent brand of meta-fictional programming that he had deemed would be the company's saviour. Soon, he would transplant the ethos of *Shotgun* onto *Monday Night Raw*.

WHILE ON the surface WCW appeared to be riding *Nitro's* wave of momentum to hit previously unseen heights, their onscreen triumph hid the truth of a company struggling to cope with its own success. Behind the curtain, WCW was tormented by an ever-present internal conflict raging between the two most politically powerful entities in the company: Hulk Hogan and 'the Outsiders', Scott Hall and Kevin Nash. Both parties possessed an unhealthy amount of stroke in the promotion, with their fat salaries giving them a direct line to Eric Bischoff's ever-willing ear. Even the once-untouchable WCW kingpin Ric Flair had been reduced to simply another member of the roster as a result of their vast collective influence.

Since their vaunted arrival in May 1996, Nash and Hall were proving to be increasingly difficult to work with for many of the boys in the back, and executives in the office. It was a reputation they brought with them to Atlanta from their time in the WWF, where they had been part of the notorious backstage power troupe The Kliq. Their lax attitudes towards work and contempt for the majority of their peers was already starting to cause internal problems.

Chris Jericho – at the time an undercard aerialist on the low end of the guaranteed contract pay scale – recounted how Hall confronted him backstage and berated him following a house show match with Jerry Lynn. "You guys are going way too long and doing way too much. Nobody is paying a dime to see you. Do a short match and hit the showers." Jericho was furious. He felt like slapping the taste right out of Hall's mouth. After contemplating it for a moment, he thought better of it. He was new to WCW and Hall was a powerful opponent; striking him would spell the end of his time with the company.

He was in the same boat as fellow Canadian Chris Benoit, who like Jericho had been determined to give Hall a beating after a behind-the-scenes incident. In Benoit's case, he found out that Hall had urinated in his cowboy boots while in a drunken stupor and he was apoplectic about it. Again, calmer heads prevailed when Benoit reasoned that Hall was only lashing out against he and others out of jealousy, because he was lazy in the ring and did not like having to follow them on the card.

Even though lucrative contracts had lured Hall and Nash to WCW, they found out fairly quickly that what they were dealing with was a wholly different operation to the one they had left behind in New York. In their first week they realised that the landscape was far more relaxed in Atlanta, when they turned up to work fifteen minutes early and were the only ones in the building for the next hour. Hall and Nash were accustomed to the WWF's rigorous time-keeping and strict rules, and immediately figured out that they could get away with whatever they wanted in their new home. So that is exactly what they did.

"Nash and Hall were both massive prima donnas," attested Jericho, "One night there was a problem with the sound system, so they refused to go to the ring. They kept complaining that it was 'jojo', which was their term to mean bush league. They complained, 'We always had music in New York. If there's no music, we're not going to the ring'."

"When Nash and Hall arrived in WCW, it was like somebody threw a couple of vipers into the dressing room," remembered Eddie Guerrero, "It went from being reasonably content to a full-blown snake pit. They acted as if they were the only reason for WCW's success. And since they were the company's saviours, they could treat it as if it was theirs and theirs alone. Nash is one of the most arrogant people I've ever had the displeasure to know. He'd walk right past you and not acknowledge your presence unless he thought there was something he could get out of you. I don't say this lightly, but I genuinely feel Nash is evil. He's never done anything for this business. The only person he cares about is himself. He became a rich man from this business and then shit on the people that really cared about wrestling. From the day they arrived in WCW, he and his clique saw me and my friends as second tier. They used to call us the Vanilla Midgets, which was hugely insulting."

When it came to Nash and Hall, Bischoff paid little attention to the distrustful grumblings and petty quibbles of his underneath talent. The duo were numbers movers, which in his ratings obsessed world made them untouchable. Almost. There was one man whom the Outsiders were not able to run political carte blanche over: Hulk Hogan.

'The Hulkster' had professed much displeasure upon first learning of the pair's arrival in WCW, publicly undermining his boss by complaining that he would have rather seen the money Bischoff had used to acquire the pair spent on bringing in other names who had a proven record drawing money. However, upon seeing their immediate success in WCW he was quick to change his mind and jump on the Nash and Hall bandwagon. Hogan was inserted into their burgeoning invaders storyline, then revealed as the 'third man' in the newly-christened nWo thanks to an industry-shaking heel turn. As had been the case in his career for over a decade, Hulk Hogan was again the most talked-about name in the business.

Hogan's torpedoing of the angle did not sit well with Nash and Hall, who resented the massive amount of sway he possessed over Bischoff. They felt Hulk was greedy and no longer relevant, desperately looking to elongate his legacy by feeding off their success. Conversely, Hogan felt the Outsiders were far too full of themselves as two performers who had never drawn a dime between them (WWF business was at its lowest ebb when Nash was WWF Champion in 1995), and he resented them coming in from New York and getting over immediately with an audience that had constantly rejected him.

HOGAN WAS renowned for his ego. Since arriving in WCW he had caused the writing team chagrin by demanding to be consulted on all aspects of WCW programming, a request afforded to him by virtue of his loaded contract. Such had been Eric Bischoff's desire to sign Hogan in 1994 that he had acceded to his every demand, which included unprecedented creative control of his own storylines – as well as everybody else's.

The result was that WCW quickly turned into The Hulk Hogan Show, with the veteran grappler using his considerable influence to secure jobs for his friends or those who he felt he was owed a TV win against. Once an alternative to the WWF, within months of Hogan's arrival the Atlanta group became a retread of the WWF's 1980s heyday, with aging, stale acts populating the card. It caused many long-time WCW performers to lose their jobs entirely. One such case was Steve Austin, who was refused a program with Hogan by Bischoff because he was not deemed to be on the same level, and was punished for his apparent insolence by being forced to put over 1980's relic 'Hacksaw' Jim Duggan in under a minute. Austin was fired soon afterwards.

Austin's tag partner Brian Pillman was also frustrated at the Hogan-led circus dominating the WCW main event scene, and created his notorious 'Loose Cannon' persona as a direct counter to that. He hoped his off-the-wall antics and elevated reputation as a result would catapult him into the headline mix. It did, though only because Hogan wanted to pin Pillman, kill his momentum, and get over on his newfound persona. Pillman was smart enough to realise Hogan's plan and bailed on WCW before it could happen.

Former multiple time WCW Champion Leon 'Vader' White also lost his job thanks to Hogan's machinations. The super-heavyweight had been in a program with Hogan throughout 1995, but the aging 'Hulkster' was not thrilled to be in the ring with a performer who worked as snugly as Vader did. When Vader was involved in a real-life scuffle with Hogan's ally Paul Orndorff, he leaned on Bischoff just enough that he was able to get him fired.

Hogan's presence in WCW had caused whole-scale changes across the board, with booker Kevin Sullivan admitting that he spent half of his job trying to appease Hogan's ego, and the other half trying to book storylines and opponents in a way that made Hogan comfortable. Thus outrageous gimmicks such as the Dungeon of Doom, a Devil-worshipping stable fronted by Sullivan full of oversized or out of shape performers from the WWF's past, were born. They were all ex-foes of Hogan's, men he had wrestled before and was comfortable sharing the ring with. They could all perform 'Hogan's match', with the ability to work at his delicate pace and do so without hurting him. All that mattered to WCW was that their key money-drawing figure was satiated, even if their television output had to suffer creatively as a result

Hogan had been the same in the WWF, even though he did not previously have it in writing that he could run roughshod over the talent base both onscreen and behind the scenes as he now did in WCW. So big a star was Hogan for Vince McMahon that he was allowed to control his programs, angles, and dates in the Federation. He would exert his power frequently, such as in 1990 when he decided he wanted to win that year's *Royal Rumble* event, taking away an accolade that had been reserved for Curt Hennig's 'Mr. Perfect' character. Hogan's win cut the legs off Hennig as a viable contender for the WWF Championship down the line, thus giving Hogan's eventual successor The Ultimate Warrior no one to work with when he dethroned him. It was a conniving double whammy of rival burial, executed in one fell swoop.

In his last WWF run, Hogan had refused to drop the WWF Championship to Bret Hart at *SummerSlam* in 1993, decreeing that Hart was too diminutive in stature to realistically defeat him. It caused tension between Hart and Hogan, not to mention the pair and Vince McMahon, who eventually cut his losses and decided to let Hogan walk away, believing his time as a viable headline draw had passed. As far as he was concerned, Hogan was simply not worth the hassle anymore.

THE COMBUSTIBLE elements of Hogan, Nash, and Hall made for many headaches for Eric Bischoff and his WCW staff. Hogan and the Outsiders both yearned for absolute power, even though their position on the card made no difference to their earnings potential due to them all receiving guaranteed money. Their lust for top billing was purely ego-driven, and the constant one-upmanship led to a palpable tension that began to tear WCW apart from the inside.

"It was almost comical," recalled one former WCW enhancement talent. "There was a booking sheet taped to the locker room wall at television tapings, and throughout the course of the day, Kevin Nash and Hulk Hogan would take turns coming into the room and changing it. Without consulting anyone, Nash would fix something he didn't like, then Hogan would wander in with his big black pen and cross out whatever Nash had written and make his own changes. After that, Randy Savage would come in and do the same thing! They would go back and forth like that all day long, resulting in none of the boys having a clue what they were supposed to be doing. It was farcical."

"Nobody was on the same page," remembered Jericho. "Bischoff was supposed to be in charge, but he was a marionette that did whatever Hogan and his lackeys puppeteered him to do. Terry Taylor was one booker, Kevin Sullivan was another, and others like Hall and Nash did whatever they wanted to do no matter what the bookers said. It was hard to tell who the boss really was."

While the constant bickering over largely inane matters would usually only cause frustration, sometimes the mistrust and the warring cliques' mutual dislike would lead to the tensions spilling out in physical confrontations. One such incident occurred on January 4, 1997 in Shreveport, Louisiana between the Outsiders and two of Hogan's close friends, the Nasty Boys, Brian 'Knobbs' Yandrisovitz and Jerome 'Sags' Saganowich.

THROUGHOUT THEIR tenure in the business, the Nasty Boys became well-known for their party-going lifestyle and public spats with their peers. The duo - notorious for their belligerent attitudes and brazen personalities - had rubbed many the wrong way during their career.

One such incident cost Knobbs $7,000. During a WWF European tour in 1992, Knobbs was stood in front of then-WWF Champion Randy Savage, who was with his wife Elizabeth Hulette, whilst queuing to check in at the airport. As he had a tendency to do in public, Knobbs loudly broke wind, though he did not realise who was behind him. "Knobbs was always trying to earn his 'Nasty Boy' name," quipped Savage's brother Lanny Poffo. The notoriously intense and fiercely-protective Savage flipped. "How dare you do that in front of my wife!" he screamed. Savage was spitting feathers and called up Vince McMahon, demanding something be done about the insult. Left with no choice, McMahon levied Knobbs with the hefty fine to appease his infuriated champion.

Status and reverence made little difference to the cantankerous duo, who would cross swords with anyone who challenged them. One cold January night in Manhattan in early 1993, they were involved in a drunken altercation with industry legend Ric Flair. Following a *Monday Night Raw* taping at the Manhattan Center, the majority of the boys and Vince McMahon were gathered a mile from the evening's venue at the China Club. Flair was in attendance with his friend Robert Kanoff, a former senior vice president of sales at toymakers Lewis Galoob - the one-time manufacturers of WCW action figures. Kanoff was celebrating a new job in the toy industry with the recently formed Original San Francisco Toymakers,[3] and was having a great time cutting promos and joking around playing wrestler for the evening.

The Nasty Boys had been mercilessly tormenting Kanoff all night, and it was becoming too much for Flair to take. When Knobbs grabbed the defenceless toymaker's sunglasses and crushed them under his boot, Flair decided to step in. "Hey, leave the poor son-of-a-bitch alone," he warned. Knobbs took offence, furling his face into a sneering snarl and yelling, "Fuck you, Flair".

Flair responded with a swift, hard slap across the face, catching the drunken Knobbs by surprise. His attempts to fight back were futile. Knobbs was saved by his tag partner, who leapt out of his seat and dived through the air with a flying punch that connected on the side of Flair's face. The pair scuffled until Vince and the boys broke them up. The China Club threw Flair out of the bar and charged the damage to his credit card. He was furious. "They threw *me* out of the bar! I had to leave, but the Nasty Boys stayed in! What is wrong with that picture?"

When they felt the numbers were in their favour, the Nasty Boys were not afraid of confronting anyone. They even tussled with future UFC Hall of Famer Ken Shamrock, roughing him up in a violent motel brawl. The altercation took place in 1990 while both parties were working for small-time promotion South Atlantic Pro Wrestling, based in the Carolinas. Following the evening's show, Shamrock - who worked under the ring name Vince Torelli - was sat at a local bar called Funk Crazies with a friend from the ring crew and his girlfriend. Brian

---

[3] When Flair left for WCW shortly afterwards, his friendship with Kanoff played a part in WCW striking a deal with OSFT to create a new line of action figures for the company.

Knobbs was sitting at the table next to them. "I started it," admitted Knobbs, "We were drinking, and I was drinking a lot. Maybe a little bit too much. I was drunk."

"Knobbs kept reaching over and grabbing my buddy's girlfriend's tits," recalled Shamrock. "He did it three or four times and she kept slapping his hand away. My friend - who wasn't a big guy - was saying, 'Come on, brother. Please, man.' Knobbs refused to listen, putting his hand in his face and yelling, 'Shut up dude.' I jumped up and said, 'You know what? That's it. Dude, next time you touch her, I'm breaking your hand.'"

Knobbs, who grew up as a barroom fighter, was eager to test the youngster's mettle. "Oh, so you're a tough guy, huh?" he sneered, before pressing his face aggressively into Shamrock's. Seeing red, Shamrock threw his drink at Knobbs, only to be immediately grabbed by one of the club's bouncers and hauled into the bathroom. "Calm down brother, they're out of here. We kicked them out. Go back out there and be cool," he was advised. When Shamrock returned to his table, as promised the Nasty Boys had been ejected from the venue.

Shamrock was so angry that he could not let the issue drop. As the SAPW performers were all staying in the same motel that evening, he decided to knock on every door until he found the pair. By the time he reached the door of Robert 'Colonel Parker' Fuller, Shamrock was so worked up that he screamed, "What room are the Nasty Boys in? I know you know where they are!" Fuller could do little but point in the direction of their door.

Shamrock had hardly been subtle in his quest to find the tandem, and they were waiting for him when he kicked down their motel room door. He was greeted with the sight of a wasted Knobbs apparently unconscious on his bed, and Sags waiting behind the door. There was a brief skirmish, in which Sags was knocked over the television set and Shamrock began pounding on Knobbs, leaving him sporting a black eye the next day. Then Sags caught Shamrock from behind and knocked him out cold.

"I saw Knobbs lying on the bed, passed out. That's all I remember," said Shamrock. "From the medical reports and the police report, from what I understand, Sags hit me in the back of the head with a steel phone. They started putting the boots to me, both of 'em. Knobbs was pretending to be asleep, but it was some kind of set up. They broke my sternum, broke my eye socket, put me in a concussion. They almost killed me. I actually died in the ambulance going to the hospital. It took me almost a year to recover."

"Ken was in bad shape. His head was swollen to the point that it almost didn't look human," remembered SAPW booker Frank Dusek. "His entire face was a mass of purples, greens, and shades of yellow." For his part, Sags denied that Knobbs had any involvement, or that he assaulted Shamrock with a phone. "I never hit him with anything but my hands and feet," claimed Sags. "I was on the phone when he burst into the room, and he knocked me over the television set then jumped on top of Knobbs. I punched him in the face and we went at it."

"Their version of the story turns them into superheroes," dismissed Shamrock. "I walked into the room, I didn't jump on him and start beating on him, that's ridiculous. I looked over, I yelled at him, and that's the last thing I remembered."

After Shamrock had knocked on his door, Robert Fuller had a suspicion about what was going to transpire. He heard and saw the commotion from his room down the hall and realised he needed to intervene, for the sake of the Nasty Boys' future as much as Shamrock's health. With assistance from The Pitbulls, Gary 'Spike' Wolfe and Anthony 'Rex' Durante, Fuller was able to talk the Nasty Boys out of throwing the prone Shamrock off the hotel balcony and onto the concrete below, averting certain death.

Eight years later when the two parties encountered each another for the first time since the fracas in a chance airport meeting, Shamrock was a bona fide Ultimate Fighting legend and an active WWF performer, and the Nasty Boys had recently been fired from WCW. Despite the time that had elapsed, Shamrock had not forgiven the duo for what they did to him. He was stood in line with Billy Gunn waiting to check in, when he spotted Knobbs sidling up next to him. Shamrock saw red immediately and was determined to avenge the beating he had taken nearly a decade earlier.

The situation between Shamrock and the Nasty Boys was well known throughout the industry, with many of the WWF performers getting a kick out of playfully ribbing Shamrock about the incident. "World's most dangerous man? Jerry Sags..." they mocked, which irritated the proud Shamrock no end. Billy Gunn realised there was a situation brewing immediately, warning through gritted teeth, "Don't do it, dude." Shamrock was shaking with rage and did not pay the advice any attention. Instead, he leaned in close to Knobbs and calmly whispered to him, "I'm gonna kill you." Gunn stepped in and grabbed Shamrock to prevent him ruining his career, and potentially his life, while Knobbs realised he was in a precarious situation and high-tailed it out of the vicinity.

"Talk about the biggest wimp you have ever seen," observed Shamrock, "He had been bragging for years about how they beat me up, and now he was running away from me." Knobbs caught up with his tag partner, who was at the gate catching up with old friends from the duo's time in the WWF. He told him the situation, and Sags loudly voiced, "Hey, what's up with Shamrock? Man, someone needs to give that guy a chill pill. He had better watch himself." Sags did not realise that Shamrock was stood right behind him. In a flash, Shamrock jumped over a chair and spun Sags around, yelling so all the boys could hear, "I'm standing right here, you little bitch. What are you gonna do now? I'm gonna kill you. I'm gonna *kill* you, you son of a bitch."

Sags realised an airport was not the smartest place to be fighting, and tried to calm the situation down. "Dude, chill out man, it was years ago. If you have such a problem with it, fly to my house and fight me there." Shamrock was not interested in reasoning with him, and responded, "Yeah, for you it was. For me it feels like it just happened, and I haven't forgotten about it." Sags simply turned away from him and warned, "If you hit me, it is a federal offence." Instantly, the situation calmed down. "At that point, all the anger left my body. He was totally sickening," said Shamrock. "He pussed out in front of everyone, in front of all of the boys. He was like a little child shitting his pants. What do you do with a guy like that? I'm not a bully. When he did that I was like, 'You know what? I'm good with that'. It was kind of satisfying. It was better than anything I could have done to him."

THE ROOT of the eventual blow-up between the Outsiders and the Nasty Boys in Shreveport can be traced back to an episode of *Nitro* broadcast November 18, 1996 from Florence, South Carolina, which opened with the aftermath of a storyline Nash and Hall assault that had taken place during the show's dark match. Representing renegade outlaw faction the New World Order, the duo hit the ring and took out both of the Nasty Boys with folding steel chairs. Hall was swinging for the fences when he teed up Sags' head and almost decapitated him with a brutal shot, causing his already damaged neck to compact.

While the injury was an accident, it did nothing to help pre-existing tensions between the tandems that had arisen due to Nash and Hall's large guaranteed salaries. While other performers, including the Nasty Boys, had been forced to take pay cuts because of WCW's unprofitable house show business, the Outsiders were raking in $750,000 per annum apiece. After the altercation the friction escalated backstage when Sags walked in on the end of a conversation and caught Hall laughing with Nash about the chair shot.

Worked up from the incident, Sags assumed that Hall was laughing because he had taken liberties with him in the ring. Hall was actually telling Nash he had no idea he had potatoed Sags, stating with a nervous laugh that it was a good job he did not hit him again because he thought Sags was *feeding*[4] for him after the first shot. It was this nervous laugh that Sags heard out of context, and he was so furious that he intended to fight Hall right there and then in the locker room. When Hall apologised and cleared up the situation, Sags decided it would be in his best interests to let the matter drop. After all, in wrestling circles Hall was a dangerous man politically to be making enemies with.

---

[4] In wrestling terms, 'feeding' is presenting a part of your body to an opponent so they can throw a worked blow, apply a hold, or perform a move. In this case, if Hall believed Sags to be feeding for him then he was under the impression the performer was willingly preparing himself for another blow.

Sags' neck injury was so severe that he immediately told the WCW office he would require time off to recuperate. However, he was already booked for and advertised to be appearing on WCW's forthcoming *World War 3* pay-per-view in a triangle tag match opposite the Outsiders, and the pairing of Meng and The Barbarian. Sags protested to booker Kevin Sullivan and new talent head J.J. Dillon, both of whom insisted that he make the date due to the bout's billing as a 'marquee match'. "J.J. said to him, 'Just go out there and work,'" recounted Nash, "He basically forced him to work. I witnessed that."

Sags agreed to work the show and the subsequent sequels on the house show loop, under the agreement that he was strictly off limits with regards to any moves that might further damage his neck, specifically chair shots. "Kevin Sullivan said [Sags] would just stand on the apron and not even get touched," recalled Knobbs. It was during one of these matches in Shreveport, Louisiana, that a second incident occurred between Sags and Hall that ultimately led to the Nasty Boys leaving WCW. The bout was another rematch from *World War 3*, and as had been the case on previous cards around the horn, the finish called for interference from nWo member Sean 'Syxx' Waltman. What the participants were not aware of was that Waltman was incapacitated from an injury he had sustained earlier in the evening.

When Syxx failed to show up as scheduled, the six participants hurriedly began to improvise. The Nasty Boys tried to distract the crowd to make the unplanned finish look like part of the organised chaos, and began hurling plastic chairs into the ring. As they were doing so, Nash cold-cocked Sags in the back of the head with his WCW Tag Team Championship title belt, completely forgetting about his opponent's neck injury.

"I didn't know what hit me," remembered Sags, "I went down and I was seeing stars. I felt like there was a cut on the back of my neck, but I was feeling back there and there was no cut. I looked around and I didn't know who had hit me from behind." In another case of incriminating timing, Sags looked up as Hall was grabbing one of the chairs that he and Knobbs had thrown in the ring. Incorrectly assuming that Hall had blasted him in the back of the head again, Sags angrily stomped up the steel steps and into the ring, where Hall, chair in hand, stared directly into his eyes. Hall had no idea that Sags was legitimately furious; he simply thought he was playing his character. Giving him what he thought was a mutually understood knowing glance, Hall hurled the chair towards Sags and hit him squarely in the face.

Sags could hardly believe what had happened. This time he was convinced that Hall was intentionally stiffing him. Losing all semblance of professionalism, he charged at the bewildered grappler, bruising and bloodying him with a flurry of non-worked punches to the face. "I didn't wanna fight him, it just happened," said Sags, "Something was building up there from the first time he hit me."

"He thought I was taking liberties with him," assessed Hall. "He thought I was messing with his income and his family. He started hitting me with live rounds, he was hitting me for real. You see, in the ring, that's not how we do it. If you want to fight me, fight me in the locker room. Fight me in a parking lot. Don't fight me in the ring, because I think its fake. I'm leaning my face out there and he's hitting me with everything he has. And by the way, he's a big bad fucker. He knocked my tooth out and it went like five rows back."

The match concluded, and the disorientated Hall turned to his buddy Nash and simply asked, "Is my face alright?" It was a mess. The attack had left Hall with a black eye, a missing tooth, and a damaged ear drum. "I turned around and Scott was just pouring with blood," remembered Nash, "I was livid." He stormed into the Nasty Boys' dressing room armed with a baseball bat and started furiously smashing it into the wall above Knobbs' head. Sags was still showering at the time though he still clearly heard Nash yelling, "We'll see who has the stroke in this company!" "I was gonna kill 'em," Nash later revealed. "Scott was my boy, but he said, 'No man, he thinks he's right.'"

"That was pretty much Kevin telling us we were getting fired," said Sags. "At the time they were practically booking, and I had just knocked the booker's teeth down his throat." After the show, Hall was sat in his hotel room with an icepack pressed up against his swollen face when the telephone rang. It was Eric Bischoff, who had received a report on the show from an agent. He immediately told Hall that he would fire Sags on the spot for his unprofessional behaviour. It was Hall's decision, but he rejected the notion, imploring Bischoff, "No man, he's got kids." Hall was also acutely aware of the Nasty Boys' relationship with Hogan, mindful that should they be fired because of him it would create a further significant rift between them. Bischoff agreed not to fire Sags, but he had no plans to use him again, instead content to let him collect his paycheque as he convalesced. Hall too was sent home, not on reprimand but rather to undergo oral surgery because of the injuries he sustained. He missed the following night's episode of *Nitro* because of them and returned the following week.

Because of his injuries, Sags could not work for WCW again, and Bischoff had no intention of paying him to sit at home doing nothing. The fact was, he had been waiting for a good excuse to cut the team from his roster for a while. A few months earlier in Cleveland, Sags had infuriated him during an nWo skit by bellowing, "I wanna show you guys something," then bending over and spreading his buttocks to do an impression of the WCW Vice President; the less than subtle intimation was that Bischoff talked out of his ass. The executive was so infuriated that he stormed off the live broadcast and drove straight to the hotel where the skit was being filmed in order to admonish the Nasty Boys for their insolence. It was clear the duo were in hot water in subsequent segments, as they were buried at all opportunities as means of punishment.

For Bischoff, the incident in Shreveport with Hall had been the final straw. Even though he risked riling Hulk Hogan and upsetting the delicate balance of power at the top of his card, he did not care. He was fed up of the Nasty Boys' unprofessional attitude, and once the furore died down he terminated their contracts. Seeing as Sags had essentially retired, he felt he was justified in releasing the pair.

The Nasty Boys disagreed. Sags was furious, immediately filing a lawsuit against WCW that claimed the company had been wilfully negligent in scripting Nash and Hall to hit him with a chair in the first place. Sags won the case and collected a healthy settlement from the ordeal, but he still regretted everything that had happened.[5]

"I wish I could take that punch back a million times," he lamented. "When I watched the video I saw that it was Kevin Nash who had hit me the first time, so Hall had taken the beating for Nash. I don't know why Kevin would even hit me when he was told not to touch me. They fired me and Knobbs because of that incident, which was bullshit. The second time I shouldn't have even been in the ring because I was hurt. When they fired us I was only in my thirties - in the prime of my career - but my neck was hurt. It cost us millions of dollars."

WITH THE cacophony of chaos taking place beneath him, it was becoming increasingly apparent that behind the bravado the effort of the Monday Night Wars was beginning to have an adverse effect on Eric Bischoff. He was blindly arrogant, so unrelentingly driven to put Vince McMahon out of business that he was both alienating his staff, and losing sight of what WCW was producing onscreen.

By January, 1997, Bischoff was utterly drunk on the nWo's success. Such was the renegade faction's seemingly unstoppable momentum that he had a brainwave: he would give the nWo their own show. Not just a free television show either, rather a full three-hour pay-per-view broadcast, which was to be styled and themed around the invading stable.

To capture the essence of the New World Order, Bischoff instructed his production team to create a completely different feel to the broadcast, named *Souled Out*. The usually vibrant presentation was instead bathed only in the nWo's black and white, WCW performers on the card were stripped of entrance music and ring introductions, instead mocked and insulted by a disembodied pro-nWo announcer as they traversed the aisle. Bischoff handled commentary duties himself, alongside fellow nWo member Ted DiBiase, and the pair spent

---

[5] Irrespective of his best friend's lawsuit against the company and his own ill-feeling towards the way they had been released, Brian Knobbs returned to work for the company in 1999 as a singles competitor, competing mostly in WCW's "hardcore" division.

the majority of the broadcast ignoring the in-ring action in favour of discussing motorcycles and stroking Hogan's ego.

"*Souled Out* was designed to be the nWo's version of what a pay-per-view should look like - an attempt to give pay-per-view a different feel," defended Bischoff. "Everything about it was designed to reflect the renegade, counterculture anarchy that defined nWo. It had a stark, industrial feel, and we tried to do things in keeping with that. At the same time, I hoped to explore and possibly lay the foundations for separating WCW into separate brands: the mainstream of older WCW brand and the rebel nWo. Each would have its own roster of wrestlers and, eventually, its own show. That way, I could have my own war. I knew competition was the key to our success. Us versus them was the formula that had gotten us to the top of the ratings. Everyone had always fantasised about an event pitting the WWF and WCW wrestlers - a Super Bowl, if you will. That was never going to happen. But I thought that, by creating two brands, I would get as close as possible. We were so far ahead of the WWF that they were not even really competition, at least not in my mind."

"The nWo is the James Bond of wrestling identities," equated Kevin Nash, "Most of the James Bond movies I have watched don't start in Hong Kong or Berlin, they usually start in some place like… Cedar Rapids. Why would [*Souled Out*] not be in Vegas? Then you take that and fly us in the night before and have us ride the streets in garbage trucks at minus twenty? Then you have the Miss nWo contest… it should have been the *Maxim* top twenty-five girls. If [nWo] guys were gonna do jobs, it was because they were coming back from the locker room with their hair messed up… It was Eric's vision. He had the concept, but we created the [nWo] image. We were cool. I remember Scott and I thinking, "Let's just shut up, we'll use it against them later. This is their vision, not ours."

The whole experience was unquestionably different, but within a few minutes the novelty value wore off and the joke began to wear thin. The 5,120 capacity crowd at the Five Seasons Center in Cedar Rapids, IA soon realised that this was not a professional wrestling show, it was a three-hour long ego trip. Dave Meltzer wrote in his *Wrestling Observer*:

> *Souled Out,* which came off to outsiders as the brainchild of someone intoxicated by his own success to the point of all perspective being lost, was the single worst PPV show in the history of pro wrestling. You may call it the night that the nWo gimmick was fully exposed. Maybe it'll even go down as a turning point in an ever changing wrestling war at the very worst. There have been shows where the quality of the matches was worse, although this would be a bad show by that criterion. There have been shows with less heat and worse atmosphere, although this would be a bad show by those criteria as well. But there has never been a show with such poor announcing and

outside wrestling skits, combined with the bad wrestling, lack of heat and bad atmosphere.

The pay-per-view numbers told the story. *Souled Out* pulled a dismal 0.47 buyrate, or approximately half of what WCW's previous event, *Starrcade,* had drawn in December. It was proof that while the nWo were the hottest thing on free television each week, as a standalone brand that could sell tickets, they were not at the level Bischoff had pegged them to be.

"The numbers told me that we hadn't built the nWo up yet to the point where it could sustain its own weekly show," he assessed. "As strong as the concept had been up to this point, we didn't quite have the infrastructure in terms of story and talent to sustain it. The buzz was starting to weaken."

The failure of *Souled Out* caused some who had previously been optimistic about WCW's chances in the Monday Night Wars to question whether Eric Bischoff knew what he was doing after all, or whether he had lucked into WCW's turn around. Bischoff had let the success – and the power it afforded him – go to his head. He felt the strong *Nitro* numbers and his creation of the New World Order made him untouchable, and that because WCW's momentum was so strong he could do no wrong. He was invincible.

"There was no-one in higher management who looked over Bischoff's shoulders to see if he was doing a good job or not," recalled J.J. Dillon. "I kind of liken it to being on the Titanic and sitting up there in the bridge and suddenly seeing a blip on the screen, and seeing a huge iceberg and trying to get everyone's attention to tell them we're facing a disaster, but nobody's listening. They thought it was a vessel that couldn't sink and I think a lot of people thought that."

With the benefit of hindsight, Bischoff was able to look back at his time in charge of WCW and assess it with a more honest critical eye. "We were doing so well that no one, myself included, recognised the problems brewing," he said. "We were operating at the limits of our capacity, maybe even beyond. As much as I hate to admit it, I was going too fast."

That frantic pace and cloudy judgment caused Bischoff and WCW to make countless small but significant mistakes over the next year, beginning a slow and painful demise for a company sitting atop the wrestling world. It was a death from a thousand paper cuts, and *Souled Out* was the first miniscule slice.

TWO

IN 1996, SHAWN MICHAELS HAD been handed the WWF Championship at *WrestleMania* and given the mammoth task of carrying the WWF on his back in the ongoing fight against WCW. He was positioned as Vince McMahon's leading quarterback, the man solely relied upon to help the company retake the lead in the Monday Night Wars. Shawn's failure to do so caused him significant emotional turmoil, with the strain increasingly evident as the year progressed. McMahon eventually realised that his champion was in danger of a breakdown and had him drop the title to 'Sycho' Sid at November's *Survivor Series* pay-per-view in Madison Square Garden. The intention was to rebuild Michaels, removing the elements of his persona that had caused many Garden fans to gleefully boo him, despite his positioning as the babyface underdog against an unbeatable monster.

The *Royal Rumble* in Shawn's hometown of San Antonio, TX was long-pegged as the maligned performer's reckoning, simultaneously his glorious homecoming, and re-ascent to the Federation throne. Michaels' quest to reclaim Sid's ill-gotten gold was the crux on which the Rumble was sold. Selling out the building would require significant work, because Vince had decided to run the card in the 75,000 seat capacity Alamo Dome. It was a venue few believed the WWF would be able to fill. "Vince was trying to make a point of drawing a big crowd like the WWF used to," said Jim Cornette. "I questioned San Antonio because it was not a place that a lot of people would travel to. He was relying on it being Shawn's hometown."

Vince looked to add a further emotional slant to the Shawn-Sid program by adding sixty-two-year-old Texas wrestling legend José Lothario to the mix. Lothario had seconded Michaels since *WrestleMania* and had been involved in Shawn losing the WWF Championship at *Survivor Series*, when Michaels became side-tracked by the health of his mentor after Sid assaulted him with a television camera. Lothario had been absent since the attack, and the *Royal Rumble* was promoted as the final time he would accompany Shawn. Vince, even though he was not aware of it, was recreating a storyline directly out of Sylvester Stallone's *Rocky* movies.

McMahon also had another trick up his sleeve which he felt would help the WWF fill the cavernous stadium: a link up with Antonio Peña's Mexican *lucha libre* group Asistencia Asesoría y Administración (AAA). The promotion was formed in 1992 when Peña broke away from Consejo Mundial de Lucha Libre (CMLL) along with their headline attraction and former World Heavyweight Champion Charles 'Konnan' Ashenoff. The progressive-thinking Peña was annoyed that CMLL owner Paco Alonso favoured the more introverted Juan Herrera as his booker, and thusly quit. Both he and Konnan desired more freedom in their creative operations, so they formed AAA as a direct rival to their ex-employers.

To fund the new entity, Peña struck a deal with television channel Televisa, who agreed to finance the wrestling group and feature it on their station in return for owning the rights to the AAA name. Peña and Konnan brought with them a number of jaded CMLL performers who favoured Peña's methods over Herrera's, and AAA quickly built up significant momentum. Enjoying a period of great success, AAA peaked with a show held in the United States in 1994 called *When Worlds Collide*, which received universal critical acclaim.[6]

Konnan eventually began splitting his time wrestling and booking in AAA with dates for WCW, as Eric Bischoff scoured all corners of the Earth trying to fill out his undercard. Konnan assisted Bischoff in bringing over other *lucha libre* stars, many of whom quickly became regular attractions on *Nitro*. Bischoff's motivation was the freshness the unknown aerialists brought to his product, because they were significantly different from anything the WWF had.

The situation in Mexico turned sour shortly afterwards when relations between Peña and Konnan started to break down. Konnan had split the locker room by phasing out traditional *lucha libre* wrestling in favour of a hardcore style reminiscent of ECW in America and FMW in Japan, which many of the long-time wrestlers resented. The other bone of contention related to the performers Konnan was booking in WCW. Peña was annoyed that many of his bigger stars were increasingly missing AAA dates in favour of WCW bookings. For the wrestlers, deciding who to work for was an easy choice; they were earning in the region of $2000 a night in WCW, compared to a miserly $140-$280 per match in Mexico.

Peña wanted a rotating policy with the names Konnan booked in WCW, thus reducing the impact on his promotion and keeping his locker room happy

---

[6] *When Worlds Collide* was co-promoted in the United States with WCW. When the WWF purchased WCW in 2001 it also bought the rights to the event. However, outside of the odd match making it to DVD, they have rarely used the footage. It is one of only a handful of pay-per-view events owned by the company not available on the WWE Network.

as all would be profiting from WCW's generosity. What Peña failed to understand was that WCW wanted a specific group of AAA performers so they could establish them as regular features. Mexican performers generally struggled to get over in America due to the differences in wrestling culture and the visual similarities between a number of the masked grapplers. Keeping a small, specific group with clear identities helped fans to differentiate them from one another.

Peña began reducing Konnan's power in AAA, with the final straw that brought their fractured relationship beyond repair coming when Peña took away the profitable Tijuana territory away from Konnan. The two fell out for good soon afterwards, and Konnan quit AAA in October 1996 to form his own offshoot promotion Promo Azteca, which he intended to promote while juggling WCW dates.

Konnan's departure left Peña the captain of a sinking ship, because much like the CMLL stars had three years earlier, many of the AAA wrestlers followed Konnan out of the door, knowing they would lose their well-paying WCW jobs if they did not. Peña was in need of a boost, so when the WWF came calling in late 1996 with a business proposal, he was all ears. The deal was brokered by part-time WWF wrestler and creative team advisor Jake 'The Snake' Roberts, one of few on the WWF crew who had spent time in Mexico and had a pre-existing relationship with the AAA honcho.

His proposal to Peña was that his AAA wrestlers would be involved in the *Royal Rumble* pay-per-view broadcast, giving them exposure in return for their part in helping to draw the house. Peña was also promised that prior to the main televised broadcast, AAA would run a number of other 'dark' matches for the live audience only, making the entire presentation a combined WWF/AAA affair as far as the San Antonio crowd was concerned.

The WWF wanted AAA on board due to San Antonio's large Hispanic population, believing that AAA would draw well for them in the city as the group had on their own merits in other largely Hispanic hotbeds such as El Paso, TX and San Jose, CA. What Titan did not realise, or that no one in the company had bothered checking, was that AAA at their peak had booked a show in San Antonio and cancelled it because of poor ticket sales. Peña himself knew that AAA likely offered little to the draw in the city, though he was hardly about to let anyone in New York in on that little detail.

He was eager to do business, realising that the mainstream international exposure and big brand tie-in would be a significant boon to his decimated group. Desperate to seal the deal, he told Roberts that he still owned many contracts of former AAA workers now wrestling for Promo Azteca and WCW, giving the impression that the bigger name stars such as Rey Misterio Jr., Psicosis and Juventud Guerrera would be willing to jump ship and compete for the WWF, leaving WCW's popular cruiserweight division in tatters.

This revelation was music to McMahon's ears. He was always eager to partake in any venture that would grant him a victory over Bischoff and WCW. Except Peña was not entirely honest in his portrayal of the situation. While it was true that most of the Mexican workers in WCW were under contract to AAA, there was a catch. In 1995, Televisa had sold the AAA name rights to Peña in an attempt to stay afloat during the Mexican peso crash, and Peña formed a new holding company known as Promociones Antonio Peña S.A. or PAPSA, though still promoted cards under the AAA banner. AAA in its pre-PAPSA form no longer existed, and thus the contracts that the WCW performers had worked under were invalid.

That did not stop a paranoid Eric Bischoff responding in a typically knee-jerk manner. Opting for the "better safe than sorry approach" in lieu of some quick research or a frank conversation with Konnan, the mistrustful Vice President suspected he was being used as an unwitting deal facilitator in a similar manner to how Brian Pillman had played him like a fiddle to snare a job with Titan earlier in the year. Prior to November's *World War 3* pay-per-view, Bischoff gathered up the Mexican contingent and strong-armed them into signing WCW contracts to prevent McMahon getting his hands on them.

McMahon had more than simply selling out the Alamo Dome and irking Bischoff in mind when he signed off on the idea of co-promoting with Peña - he also had designs on running WWF cards in Mexico City, one of the most densely populated agglomerations in the world. With the Mexican wrestling scene already overflowing with promotions, he realised he would need to embark upon a joint venture – at least at first – to make that a reality. He had tried something similar before with Genichiro Tenryu's Super World of Sports in Japan, a group the WWF ran cross-promotional shows with from 1990-1992. The agreement saw WWF talent competing on SWS shows in Japan, and Japanese talent working on McMahon's cards in the United States. Vince's reason for entering into the deal was to learn the unique Japanese market so he could eventually run it without any assistance, much as he had done with the Canadian scene several years prior. It did not come to pass as a result of SWS folding in 1992 because of the economy in Japan crashing and the financial backers of the company pulling out. The key difference between that failed venture and McMahon's attempts with Peña's group was that SWS had been a start-up organisation, whereas AAA was well-established. McMahon was willing to give a foreign partnership a second go around.

WHILE THE Sid and Michaels issue created local interest in the *Royal Rumble*, and the link-up with AAA seemingly had the Hispanic population covered, neither were significant enough to shift all the Alamo tickets at usual WWF prices. Realising as much, McMahon slashed the entry fee and offered a significant portion of the event at only $10 per head, with some tickets available for as little as $5 when Taco Bell and Dr. Pepper discount coupons were redeemed. Vince gave thousands more tickets away to various local schools, newspapers and businesses, and blacked out the pay-per-view in southeast Texas to ensure anyone in the state who wanted to see their hometown hero prevail had to attend the event in person. All the concessions combined with a strong local media campaign made *Royal Rumble* the most heavily advertised non-*WrestleMania* card that Vince had ever promoted.

The hard work paid off in getting bodies through the door. *Royal Rumble* pulled 60,525 fans, though only 48,014 paid (totalling $480,013), with a staggering 12,511 comps. Despite the heavy papering, the show was still the second largest paid attendance in the history of United States pro wrestling, trailing only *WrestleMania III* at Pontiac's Silverdome in 1987. Federation officials were delighted with the number, which far surpassed everybody's realistic private expectations. Only a week earlier the draw looked like it was going to be considerably less, with an unprecedented 20,000 tickets sold in the final days leading up to the event.

AAA talent featured heavily on the undercard, with McMahon living up to his promise and giving two dark matches and a *Free for All* bout over to the company, in addition to a contest on the pay-per-view broadcast. However, the general response to the promotion was widespread indifference. McMahon had miscalculated the market; the AAA performers were all considerably less known than his own WWF stars. Far from being the WWF's answer to WCW's exciting cruiserweight division, the AAA wrestlers featured were more ground-based in style, and generic in appearance compared to WCW's imports.

The Mexican group's wrestlers in the *Royal Rumble* match itself struggled to make much of an impact either. The exception was Mil Mascaras, a thirty-two-year veteran and one of Mexican wrestling's "big three" all-time stars. Mascaras entered the bout twenty minutes in, refused to sell for anyone, and eliminated himself from the contest due to a career-long aversion to doing anything that might get someone else over on his name.

McMahon, thoroughly unimpressed with what he was given by Peña's operation, opted out of the deal shortly after the event. His track record working with others was patchy at best due to his inability to allow his playmates to compete on an even keel with WWF talent, so the split came as no surprise. Vince had clearly been trying to recreate what Bischoff had with WCW, but he almost entirely missed the point. AAA felt like a guest slot rather than an entity tied in with the WWF product, and the group ultimately achieved little from the AAA union.

There were some beneficiaries to the AAA deal however, namely struggling WWF stars Rick 'Razor Ramon' Bognar and Glen 'Diesel' Jacobs. Having outlived their usefulness on all levels attempting to recreate two of Vince's most popular stars, they looked destined for the unemployment line. Both were sent packing to AAA, where they gained a new lease of life. Curiously, they were used as another Hall and Nash parody act, this time as the "mWo", a send-up of the New World Order.

THE REAL draw in the Alamo Dome was unquestionably Shawn Michaels. That much was evident when he headed to the ring for his main event showdown with Sid and received a gigantic sustained ovation. What few in the audience realised was that Michaels' participation in the match had been in some doubt throughout the day, due to Shawn battling against a flu bug that was sweeping its way through the locker room.

Having spent the afternoon curled up in Vince McMahon's office trying to sleep off the virus, Michaels managed to pull himself together enough to go on. Ever the perfectionist, he was disappointed with what transpired. "The match wasn't very good," he remembered truthfully. "The combination of my physical condition and Sid was too much for me to overcome."

The match quality mattered little to the San Antonio crowd, whose only concern was seeing Michaels reclaim the WWF's top prize. When he pinned Sid to commence his second reign as WWF Champion, the mood in the building was vastly different to the negative Garden response at *Survivor Series* which had haunted him for the past two months. Michaels was revered as a hero, the underdog hometown boy done good who had slain his giant foe.

Even Bret Hart was impressed with Michaels' performance in the face of adversity and under the burden of heavy pressure. He made a point of seeking out Michaels in the locker room after the match, telling him that he was proud of him and pleased that he was WWF Champion once again. Shawn, showing a rare moment of graciousness, humbly thanked Hart and told him he appreciated the support.

Hart had endured a strange evening of his own competing in the pay-per-views titular showcase. For months he had been scripted to win the thirty-man contest, though plans had recently been changed due to a bout of overzealous reporting from the WWF's Saturday morning wrap-up show presenter Vince Russo. Hosting *Livewire*, the loud-mouthed New York native fancied himself as a modern day Nostradamus, predicting with some conviction that Hart was going to win the match.

Vince McMahon was furious. The unwritten rule in the WWF was for such predictions to be way off the mark so as to keep the identity of the winner a surprise. It was bad enough that WCW were gleefully giving away his pre-taped television results, McMahon mused, never mind his own staff revealing the outcomes of major pay-per-view encounters.

Paranoia caused McMahon to change course. In an era of reactionary booking short-termism, McMahon responded with a kneejerk directive. Instead of Hart, he opted for 'Stone Cold' Steve Austin, whom he had win the match via nefarious means. His intention was to make another star. While content with his crop of established headline acts, McMahon realised that WCW's main event scene was full of mainstream names, and in that regard the WWF was falling behind. Giving Austin the win would catapult him to the upper-echelons of the promotion. However, McMahon was not yet confident in Austin as his *WrestleMania* headline act, so had him lose the *WrestleMania* title shot the Rumble victory granted him in the weeks preceding the supershow.

HART WAS not happy with what he perceived to be a demotion, wondering what the payoff was going to be for his character. McMahon assured Hart that he still intended for him to compete in the *WrestleMania* main event, working a long-awaited rematch with Shawn Michaels. It was a bout that had been mooted since *WrestleMania XII* the previous year, though it was one fraught with problems due to the respective egos and reservations of the three parties involved. Sure enough, that plan began to change above Hart in the following weeks.

Back in 1996, during his extended time away from the WWF, Hart spent a few days in New York working on a video game. By this time, WCW had landed a devastating one-two combo across McMahon's protruding jaw in the form of Scott Hall and Kevin Nash's hostile disruptions. Beginning June 10, *Nitro* would win the Nielsen ratings war for the next twenty-two months, with the factor of unpredictability tempting the maw of the intrigued fan base.

With Hart's WWF contract expiring later in the year, McMahon was not about to take any chances on another one of his hand-crafted generals ending up in the Atlanta army. In between recording sessions in New York for the video game, Hart was whisked away to the chairman's palatial Greenwich, Connecticut home, where McMahon and Jim Ross attempted to hammer out the details of a tempting twenty-year deal. While Hart would not sign on the dotted line for another four months, he did toss delectable chow to his salivating bosses in the form of a storyline suggestion. Per the work, Hart would go over on Michaels either at or around *WrestleMania 13*, likely for the WWF Title, but just as importantly it would level the series of their blurred-line rivalry. An even series opened the door for a rubber match, in which Hart volunteered to not only put over Michaels, but to shake his hand in the ring as a concrete endorsement, theoretically instilling the respect in Michaels that some fans found hard to foster. That twist of the screw was absent from their *WrestleMania XII* contest, where a disconsolate Hart tore a malevolent path to the locker room after losing in the famed Iron Man Match's surprise overtime period.

In a curious piece of happenstance, on the flight back home to Calgary, Hart ended up seated next to Michaels, who at this time was bearing the weight of the world on his weakening shoulders. Not only had Michaels lost best friends Nash and Hall to the unlocked bank vault that was World Championship

Wrestling, but now their striking of creative oil had relegated Michaels' run at the top to a visible second-place. As Michaels was the champion over on *Raw*, carrying the flag of the 'inferior' show took a hard mental toll. No matter how much Michaels flung his deteriorating body around the ring trying to captivate viewers, racking up classic matches like carnival tickets, his own drinking buddies from the Kliq were inadvertently applying pressure to his crumbling frame. The champion is only as strong as the company he represents, and if WWF was number two in the ratings, so too was its athletically-gifted yet emotionally-fragile hero. As Hall and Nash raised hell, Michaels could only watch with a half-smile. His friends were succeeding without him, and to his continued detriment as well.

The weathering effects of what had become a wrestling war did not deter Michaels from talking the lighter side of life with Hart. After amiably comparing notes about their professional and personal lives, Hart let slip the details of the angle he had laid before McMahon, noting that it would conclude with Michaels winning the tiebreaker at some undetermined point down the line. Michaels, for his part, did not express much joy at the idea, instead getting hung up on the crux of the second match, where he would return Hart's job from *WrestleMania XII*.

"I saw the colour drain from his face," said Hart when he informed Michaels of how the first return bout would conclude. "He clearly didn't like the sound of any of this."

History paints Hart both as an expressionless sceptic and imaginative optimist at different times, the latter to the point where he could see an enthralling endgame to a wrestling conundrum, but would also have difficulty imagining why his contemporaries might not be willing to follow his lead in getting there. Despite Michaels' obvious discomfort at being asked to lay down at *WrestleMania 13* with nine months' notice, Hart mostly dismissed it. After all, Michaels would reign supreme in the end anyway – what was one pot hole on the road to immortality?

Eight months later, on the night of a special Thursday edition of *Raw* titled *Thursday Raw Thursday* which aired live the night before Valentine's Day, the pot hole was filled to the brim. The jaunt toward the *WrestleMania* Mecca would send the best laid plans hydroplaning into rocky terrain.

Ten days earlier, Hart engaged in a tense phone call with McMahon, where he was stunned to learn that his highly-anticipated rematch with Michaels at *WrestleMania* would not have the WWF Championship at stake. Instead, the new plan was that Michaels would drop the belt on the Thursday special to Sid, where a scornful Hart would run interference. Three nights later at *In Your House: Final Four*, Michaels would then prevent Hart from winning the *Royal Rumble* restart match, leaving Undertaker as lone survivor to challenge for Sid's gold.

"It's too predictable now. I'm changing it," McMahon told Hart of the title match plans when pressed for the decided implications. McMahon went so far as to suggest that Hart's match with Michaels would be a ladder match in which Michaels would put his hair on the line, and would subsequently be shaved bald in defeat. For Hart, juvenile public humiliation at the expense of his professional rival was a lousy stand-in for an epic showdown with the title up for grabs. With Hart earning $1.5 million per year for the next three years from a company that was not in its most solvent times, the *WrestleMania* demotion seemed counterproductive.

In the end, Hart did not even get the match with Michaels, belt or no belt, no ladder to climb, and no hair to shave. Dropping the title back to the unreliable, lumbering Sid en route to an even more high-profile loss to Hart at *WrestleMania* was the sort of one-two wallop that Michaels had no interest in enduring. At his wit's end from a fracturing body, the pressures of being the face of the promotion, and a loss of seventy-five percent of his Kliq co-conspirators, Michaels dropped a bomb on the WWF office: he was handing in the WWF Championship belt, and removing himself from the ring for the foreseeable future.

OVER A stretch of seventeen years, from 1992 through the end of 2009, Michaels would be booked to win championship gold on thirteen occasions under McMahon's eye. In total, that haul included three WWF Championships, one World Heavyweight Championship, three Intercontinental Titles, one reign as European Champion, and five runs as some form of Tag Team Champion.

Michaels' second reign as WWF Champion in 1997 marked his seventh piece of gold attained under McMahon. Among those prior six reigns, only two of them were ended inside a wrestling ring. On the other four occasions, some form of divine intervention would prevent Michaels from counting arena lights in the time-honoured tradition of passing 'rub' down the line.

While Michaels did drop his first Intercontinental Title to former partner Marty Jannetty in a spirited clash on the May 17, 1993 edition of *Raw*, Michaels would regain it three weeks later at a house show in Albany, NY. That reign unceremoniously ended on September 27 of that year, the kayfabe reason claiming a lack of title defences from a villain presented in the classic mould of a coward. The real story was much darker for a World Wrestling Federation under the public microscope: Michaels was informed that one of his drug tests came back positive for steroids, a charge he claims is false to this day. Michaels makes a valid point to the observing eye - his body in 1993 displayed a billowing gut and little of the muscle definition that would complement his nuanced role of smarmy womaniser. By Michaels' account, he was overindulging in beer and junk food with Nash on a nightly basis, and the proof was in his accumulated blubber. Nonetheless, even if Michaels' theory that somebody had spiked one of his drinks could be proven true, there would be no appealing. With an indictment for steroid distribution looming for McMahon, a hard-line stance took precedent, and Michaels was unseated as champion.

Michaels' next three tenures with WWF gold would end just as abruptly. At *Survivor Series '94*, Michaels terminated his lengthy union with Nash after accidentally superkicking him during their elimination bout. Michaels fled from the supercharged, furious Nash, and conveniently forfeited his belt to confirm the dissolution of the duo. The idea was to free up both for *WrestleMania XI*'s WWF Title bout, a belt Nash would take from Bob Backlund three nights later. It could be argued that both men needed to remain as strong as possible heading into a cloudy *WrestleMania* season, and there were no teams on the roster strong enough to make a pinfall on either top guy feasible.

If that abdication of gold was executed to preserve two workers requiring an infallible sheen, their next hand-back was a frustrating parallel. At the third *In Your House* pay-per-view in September 1995, Intercontinental Champion Michaels and WWF Champion Kevin 'Diesel' Nash, on-screen allies once more, joined forces against Tag Team Champions Owen Hart and Yokozuna in the first match of its kind: a 'Triple Header'. All the championships were at stake, though jaded fans could see a bait-and-switch coming from a mile away.

Indeed, Davey Boy Smith substituted for the younger Hart, who was legitimately late arriving to the event after the birth of his daughter, Athena. Hart, in his gear, stormed the ring late in the bout, only to be immediately powerbombed and pinned by Diesel. The win meant that every male-exclusive belt in the WWF belonged to Michaels and Diesel. However, the two were stripped of the Tag Team belts the following day, with Hart deemed ineligible to take the pinfall as a story explanation. The belts were merely returned to the original champions, only to have them drop the straps to the Smoking Gunns that night. As for Michaels, it was another championship handed in without the expense of personal indignity.

One month later, indignity would become too overwhelming to simply bat away for the troubled Michaels. One week before a scheduled championship loss to Troy 'Dean Douglas' Martin at the fourth *In Your House* pay-per-view, an inebriated Michaels was assaulted outside Syracuse's Club 37 by twenty-three-year-old Corporal Douglas Griffith, following a misunderstanding involving a club waitress that Griffith had once dated. Michaels sustained significant damage to his face, including a torn eyelid and two black eyes, having been kicked in the face by the steel-capped boot clad Griffith.

Long before the nightclub incident, Martin had run afoul of Michaels and his Kliq allies. His stock plummeted following a 'litmus test' match with Sean '1-2-3 Kid' Waltman at the August 28, 1995 *Raw* tapings. One month later, citing a legitimate herniated disc, Martin balked at wrestling at the hallowed Madison Square Garden, which drew the ire of McMahon. For the *In Your House* match,

Michaels was pulled from the booking due to his injuries, a reason that Martin disputes. According to the former multi-time ECW Champion, he had gotten wind that Michaels had openly called him an "embarrassment" in front of a locker room court of performers. Michaels was allegedly fearful that Martin would work exceedingly stiff with him once those comments had made the rounds, and according to Martin, had used the nightclub attack as an excuse to take time off. Michaels, for his part, claims McMahon made the decision out of concern for his condition.

That night in Winnipeg, a melancholy Michaels surrendered the Intercontinental belt to a cackling Martin, who would go on to drop the strap within the hour to Michaels' comrade Scott Hall. Within a month, Michaels was wrestling at *Survivor Series*, as spring-loaded and bouncy as he had been before the sordid headlines were written.

Science fiction author Emma Bull wrote, "Coincidence is the word we use when we can't see the levers and pulleys." The Kliq indoctrination, perhaps infestation, of mid-1990s WWF gave numerous wrestlers an idea of who had their hands on what rope, and who tugged the strings of the corporate marionettes. No wrestler has lost more championships in the WWF outside of the ring than Michaels.

AROUND SIX o'clock the night before *Thursday Raw Thursday*, little more than twenty-four hours before his scheduled loss to Sid, Michaels informed the office that he was taking time off for medical reasons. Michaels claimed that his doctor, noticing the lack of an ACL in his knee (which Michaels said he had wrestled for years without), told him his wrestling days were over.

"He took an MRI, looked at the results, and then said to me, 'You will never wrestle again,'" claimed Michaels. "I was devastated. He was a doctor, and I thought his word was final. I thought my career was over."

At the time of Michaels' revelation, he was coming off a house show loop through Pennsylvania and New Jersey where he had worked tag team bouts with Steve Austin against Sid and Hart. Because of the timing, as well as the circumstances of the immediate booking that would not benefit Michaels, scepticism ran rampant.

"The Undertaker looked at me like this was all bullshit and said, 'I'll believe it when I see the scar. The little fucker doesn't want to drop the belt'," recalled a bemused Hart. "I'd worked a tag team match with Shawn at the Meadowlands only three days before, and there was nothing wrong with his knee. He hadn't wrestled since. I found myself agreeing with Taker - I'll believe this bullshit when I see the scar."

Jim Cornette concurred, adding, "A bunch of people were pissed - all of the agents, Gerald Brisco, Jim Ross, Vince himself. At the same time Shawn was pissed off about something, he conveniently got this knee injury and couldn't drop this fucking belt."

The setting inside the Memorial Auditorium in Lowell, Massachusetts was not quite as caustic as the attitudes toward Michaels behind the scenes, but there was little sympathy to be felt either. With on-air President Gorilla Monsoon standing by, McMahon began to introduce Michaels for the forfeiture. Setting the stage with plain-spoken bombast, McMahon implored the crowd to, "Please welcome, the most flamboyant, the most charismatic WWF Champion, perhaps of all time," a request met mostly with sustained jeers. The negative response understandably remained when McMahon added that Michaels would be surrendering the championship in a matter of moments. In an attempt to change the energy of the room, McMahon transformed into full-blown ringmaster, introducing Michaels by name in his patented throaty growl, knees bent as he swiftly gestured with his arm toward the entranceway.

Enter Michaels, dressed business-like in a sport-coat and dress pants, flowing mane of hair tied back conservatively in a ponytail. Michaels' gait did not so much demonstrate a limp as it did a slow, shambling glide, almost half-walk, half-skate. Cameras zoomed in on females in the audience snapping photos of the resident teen idol, as well as children brandishing signs of encouragement toward their wounded hero. As Michaels slowly stepped through the ropes to the upbeat riffs of *'Sexy Boy'*, it was commentator Jim Ross who declared in a benign monotone, "If you love him or if you hate him, if you're a wrestling fan, you have to respect him." Continuing the apparent spin-doctoring, Jerry Lawler, a sworn heel in WWF canon, followed Ross' declaration by adding just as flatly, "I don't care for him professionally, but this is a stand-up thing to do as soon as he gets word from the doctor. I think I would've hung onto the belt as long as I could."

Michaels began his remarks by cracking to McMahon with a wan smile, "It seems like we've done this before." As Michaels related his doctor's purported belief that he should never wrestle again given the condition of his knee, undecipherable catcalls showered him, turning into a sustained chant of "We want Sid." Michaels laughed a nervous giggle before looking down towards the mat to collect himself. Sensing Shawn was losing it, McMahon took over the interview, trying to get Michaels' thoughts back on track by putting over the calibre of the fighting champion he had been portrayed as over the previous year. Michaels acknowledged the chants and took a transparently conciliatory tack by responding, "In spite of what people may think about me, all I've wanted for all of these people is for them to have a good time, for them to enjoy themselves." As he further explained that all his work was for the enjoyment of ticket-paying customers, the negative reception from the fans in Lowell did not abate one bit.

After Michaels' further claim that he, "had no toughness" for anybody in the WWF, he simply turned to Monsoon and said, "Here ya go; here's your belt," and handed over the strap. Hollow as that moment played out on television, that was a passing breeze compared to his next statement, one repeated in the ensuing years as a punch line by those who saw the entire ordeal as unintentional comedy writ large: "I know that over the last several months, I've lost a lot of things, and one of them has been my smile," Michaels rasped to near silence.

Michaels later claimed that the statement was coined by his mother a month before the surrender. She commented on his apparent physical burnout by telling her son, "You don't even smile anymore. You always had such a sweet smile. You've lost your smile." Whether or not Carol Hickenbottom uttered those words, and no doubt there's genuine sentiment of a mother's love in there if she had, Michaels' use of the phrase only earned him more derision from those who felt he was weaselling out of doing business the right way.

By now, Michaels had gotten worked up to the point of legitimate tears, and the production team began zooming in on the faces of select women in the audience who were thoroughly emotionally captivated by his story. He made his exit after hugging both McMahon and Monsoon to more boos than cheers, as the cameras once more cut to two crying women, who began snapping photos of Michaels despite their apparent grief. There was a farewell lap around ringside, with Michaels tagging hands and sharing hugs with less-jaded audience members. Lawler called him, "the most resilient champion ever." Ross referred to him as a, "franchise player," adding, "Takes a man's man to do what he just did, folks," as Michaels hobbled toward the entrance set. A few days later in his *Wrestling Observer Newsletter*, Dave Meltzer grumbled:

> It wound up only to have noted orthopaedic surgeon Dr. Jim Andrews say Michaels' knee injury wouldn't even require surgery at all, and that after four to six weeks of rehab, he may be able to return. The irony was just last year, the last time they played this game and teased Michaels never wrestling again, it set him up for the biggest run of his career. Perhaps he forgot, or hoped people wouldn't remember that when he talked in the interview about a doctor telling him he may not be able to wrestle again for the first time in his life, that it may have been the first time a doctor actually said that to him, but it wasn't the first time that story had been told about him.

One week later, Meltzer provided a concrete take that confirmed many scepticisms by noting:

> More likely than not, Michaels' leaving had to do with being burned out from all the travel and pressure and needing a break, combined with the timing of having to put over Sid for the WWF title on the 2/13 special and knowing he was going to follow it up in his next high-profile match having

to put Bret Hart over at *WrestleMania*. By leaving before doing the job and giving that interview, Michaels made himself the man of the hour in a positive way, plus avoided losing the title in the ring and put off the inevitable favour for his legitimate rival. There is little dispute that he had a knee injury, but the belief is that it was something he could have continued to work on had he wanted to, although it was bad enough that any doctor would have recommended taking time off and this was the opportune time.

THREE

BY MID-JANUARY 1997, IT had been three months since Bret Hart signed that loaded twenty-year contract as a pledge of loyalty to Titan. The security of the deal promised to bolster Hart's bank account like nothing before it, yet there was a deep sense of melancholy in his gut. The nature of the job continued to provide jitters, and Hart remained as persistently uneasy at the backstage machinations of Shawn Michaels and Paul 'Triple H' Levesque as ever. However, a new jagged concern was beginning to burrow firmly into his stride. Since breaking out as a permanent singles performer in 1991, Hart balanced WWF cards with a blend of humility and earnest confidence. The ever-reliable technician, now in his thirteenth year of employment under McMahon, had long served as the modestly-human contrast to tooth-gnashing gargoyles such as The Ultimate Warrior and The Legion of Doom, among other prismatic crazies. Hart's placidness resonated with his worldwide fan base just as much as his strong work ethic and crisp athleticism. One of the strongest elements of Hart's on-camera avatar was his dignity, a quality he relished enormously. The 'Hitman' character played it smooth. Barely cracking more than a confident smile from time to time, Hart exuded the softer charisma of a cool customer with absolute mastery of any situation, only sweating in the context of his many physical battles.

That was why Hart could only take on the newest shift of his character with an uneasy wince. The normally-civil sheen that Hart had honed for much of his career was slowly coming undone in the gust of the WWF's programming shift, in which every main character displayed more boundless vigilance than ever. The latest drastic transformation of Hart's persona came on the January 20 episode of *Raw*, one night after his tainted *Royal Rumble* match loss. Appearing early in the broadcast that aired live from Beaumont, TX, Hart verbally ran down all the wrestlers that had unjustly "screwed" him since his return, even chipping at the long-standing fourth wall by blaming commentator McMahon for his on-camera misfortunes. Hart then emphatically 'quit' the company, kicking off a show-long thread where he was eventually coaxed back by Gorilla Monsoon, who bluntly nullified Austin's *WrestleMania* title match.

Although Hart's character was justifiably irate about the *Royal Rumble* conclusion, the long-time babyface was deeply disturbed by his designed actions. He worried that this latest public seething would cause his fans to sour on him. "It all seemed quite real, too real, but I did as Vince told me," Hart said of the meltdown, which he claimed was "carefully scripted". Hart believed that the only factor keeping him grounded on the babyface side of the fence was the virulent Austin. That is, when crowds could actually bring themselves to boo Austin's minacious 'Stone Cold' act.

Through his physical and verbal work over the prior eight months, Steve Austin had been cultivated into an indispensable weapon in Titan's ongoing battle with WCW. For Austin, the breakthrough moment of his career was his improvised "Austin 3:16" promo at the 1996 *King of the Ring*. The idea to subvert scripture in mocking fallen opponent and born-again Christian, Jake 'the Snake' Roberts came spur of the moment, not from the pen of a staffer. It was this from-the-heart tenacity that allowed Austin to break from an aimless pack, leaving a midcard filled with occupational characters and technicolour cheese in his torrential wake. Not only did Austin connect with audiences that wanted a detestable villain to root against, he also struck a chord with the rebel-minded viewers that relished having an unvarnished anti-hero to get behind. For an American society that was now feasting on blood-stained Quentin Tarantino films, sophomoric MTV fare, and disassociative alternative rock with much gratification, Austin struck this more distorted zeitgeist with a firmly clenched fist.

Despite the proliferation of excited fans charmed by Austin's injection of danger into WWF broadcasts, McMahon seemed determined to keep him securely rooted as a heel. Austin recalled an instance in 1996 when he had verbally tore into undercard babyface Peter 'Aldo Montoya' Polaco, whose trademark was wearing a yellow mask that looked unmistakably like a jockstrap. Later, Austin would notice that some of his more venomous barbs, specifically ones that called out the mask for what it resembled, were edited from the TV broadcast. At another taping shortly thereafter, an obstinate Austin took McMahon aside and pointedly queried his boss as to why his quips were not making the airwaves. A steadfast McMahon responded to Austin that his comments were, "making the people laugh back in the studio. We are concerned because, as a heel, we want the fans *not* to like you." A contentious Austin held his ground, noting that while he could not compete with the company's giants and monsters on a physical level, if he was allowed to display his unique personality he could, "compete with anybody. I guarantee it."

Vince had gotten the message. Drawing laughter or not in his most diabolical moments, he was still drawing a reaction, nothing short of a miracle in front of the endless slogs that were the monthly four-hour television tapings throughout the remainder of 1996. For McMahon, the revelation of Austin's spurt in popularity was almost impossible to fathom. He'd spent the previous two years sanding most of the serrated edges off of Kevin Nash and Shawn Michaels, packaging them with do-gooder smiles that betrayed the cool factor each had exhibited as heels, ones who were on the cusp of inevitable babyface runs. Both men's lengthy reigns as WWF Champion had failed to jumpstart Titan's dull vitals. There was a painful irony in place, one not lost on McMahon: the Monday Night Wars were being won by the side that proudly hawked Nash as a whimsical mercenary with mean-spirited comedic bite. The team trailing the battle was the one that took away the smarm-with-charm that shot Michaels into stardom, and repackaged their stud with a reverent choir-boy attitude that was only sometimes upstaged by something closer to Dennis the Menace than to Axl Rose. The influx of New World Order t-shirts being worn by fans attending WWF events could only make a weary McMahon defer to Austin's forceful instincts, whether or not he could understand their place in the pro wrestling reality he had once shaped.

It was not only the production workers at McMahon's Stamford television studio that ate up Austin's act with glee. The Monday night wrestling audience was comprised of far more than engineers and video editors, and the majority of TV viewers were tuning into WCW's *Monday Nitro* to keep up with the nWo's lawless exploits. Whether Nash and his band of renegades were disrupting an innocuous match to attack the participants, or commandeering the announcer's table to preach their glib rhetoric, fans were watching - and cheering on rebels like Austin. As the children who dreamed of being like Hulk Hogan reached their teenage years, their tastes had changed. Titan was losing its grip on the Hulkamania-era fans that saw no attempts for cradle-to-the-grave appeal. Nash wielding a baseball bat with a shit-eating smirk was just the tonic the post-pubescent crowd had been waiting for. McMahon's failure to understand the potential of Austin, especially with the juxtaposition of the nWo on the Monday night split-screen, was especially galling if one assumed he had learned any lessons from the 1995 *King of the Ring* pay-per-view.

The WWF Chairman shuffled uncomfortably on his usual commentary perch that night, seemingly caught off-guard at the hostile reaction from the Philadelphia Spectrum onlookers during the tournament's final match, which pitted the unheralded Juan 'Savio Vega' Rivera against purple-clad monster Nelson 'Mabel' Frazier. When Vega and Mabel's glacial exhibition trudged into an endless bog of motionless bear hugs, the Philly crowd responded with what would soon become a time-honoured chant of three locally popular letters: E-C-W. "Listen to this!" yelped a startled McMahon, interpreting the sudden spark as a show of support for underdog Vega. Once clear that the rebellious fans were throwing their support behind a local independent wrestling outfit, McMahon scrambled, more stunned than hurt by the verbal right cross, quickly trying to shift attention to Vega's roll-up on the looming Mabel. Those same fans pelted Mabel with beverage cups and other assorted debris during his subsequent coronation as 'King' of the WWF, providing the image of an explicit microcosm: the common man was staging an uprising against an oblivious monarchy.

THE DENIZENS of the ECW Arena, a repurposed bingo hall tucked beneath Interstate 95 in south Philadelphia's warehouse district, had been revelling in a much different wrestling product on virtually a tri-weekly basis for much of the previous two years. Eight nights before Mabel's much-derided ascension, ECW Champion Jim 'The Sandman' Fullington went over on Mick Foley, in his Cactus Jack role, after garrotting him with barbed wire. Such was usual of life in ECW circles. The Arena patrons had for years gotten their wrestling fix from the exploits of violent booze hounds like Sandman, in addition to other unique sociopaths in Tommy 'Dreamer' Laughlin and the messiah of such sadism, reckless mute Terry 'Sabu' Brunk. Offsetting the Thunderdome-like insanity were hearty courses of world-class grappling from the likes of Eddy Guerrero, Chris Benoit, Charles 'Too Cold Scorpio' Scaggs, and Dean 'Malenko' Simon. After watching Dreamer smash breakaway cookware over the heads of opponents, those same fans would applaud feverishly as Guerrero and Malenko completed a mat-based stalemate with a ballet-like flourish. Rarely could you spot a fan inside the ECW Arena younger than high school age. These consumers merrily traded in Hulkamania bandanas and Bret Hart's Mylar sunglasses for black t-shirts emblazoned with ECW's barbed logo, an "extreme" rite of passage.

Billing his programming with the exclusionary tagline, "It's not for everyone!", ECW head booker Paul Heyman fed the maw of the fan far removed from the technicolour circus that the World Wrestling Federation had become. If Austin's anti-heroism was a revelation to the mainstream wrestling world, especially Vince himself, it was hardly a novelty to Philly's underground fringe. "Vince's curiosity with ECW started at the *King of the Ring* in Philadelphia," claimed Heyman years later, not that the event was McMahon's first harsh dose of reprisal in one of his territorial strongholds.

In early 1993, when McMahon launched *Monday Night Raw* as a successor to studio-based *Prime Time Wrestling*, the show's campaign promised to be as its name suggested, with its "Uncut, Uncensored, Uncooked," tagline. The first year of *Raw's* existence featured scantily-clad women holding up brand-centric placards between matches, not at all dissimilar to round-card women in boxing. McMahon brought in Brooklyn-born comedian and radio personality Rob Bartlett to serve as boisterous colour-commentator, a tenure that lasted only thirteen weeks as Bartlett felt out of place, citing his low wrestling acumen. While these elements failed to add any precarious zest to what was still larger-than-life New York-style pro wrestling, the intimate New York setting provided *Raw* its edgy feel in its day.

For much of 1993, *Raw* emanated from New York City's Manhattan Center, a box-shaped ballroom with balcony seating and blood-red velvet carpeting. The venue was configured with upper-crust cultural elitists in mind. Once McMahon came up with the idea to set up a wrestling ring and some steel barricades centre stage of the midtown hall, the audience dialled toward the opposite direction. Caustic young adults replaced the action figure-wielding youth that populated house shows and B-town television tapings, offering up a brutally-different response to the circus that Titan had become. Months before Philly's ECW Arena earned its unofficial name, wrestling's most vociferous fans cackled heartily as one heckler screamed, "Kill yourself!" at a downtrodden Ed 'Brutus Beefcake' Leslie. Michaels, honing his act as mulleted sexual dandy, was met with unflattering homosexual assertions from the blue-collars and beer-bellies that packed the hall like vitriolic sardines.

This was the precursor to those smartened-up ECW Arena crowds, one of wrestling's earliest 'too hip for the room' audiences. McMahon sat ringside through those raucous *Raw* airings, no doubt fully capable of hearing every heckle directed at the terrible gimmicks and flavourless has-beens. He continued to push forward with his youth-targeted carnival well into 1996, long after the Manhattan Center had been replaced by small-scale civic centres and convention halls, primarily in the north-eastern US. Although ECW's syndicated shows reached many of the subsequent regions, *Raw's* loudmouthed crazies had mostly been replaced by the families that McMahon aimed his product toward.

Through telescopic arms, Extreme Championship Wrestling beamed its brand of mayhem into Florida via The Sunshine Network (today part of the FOX family as Sun Sports), among other scattered American syndicates in Chicago, Boston, and Los Angeles. The crown jewel outside of its Tuesday night airings on hockey-centric SportsChannel Philadelphia was late Saturday night placement on the MSG Network in New York City. The weekly program provided market penetration in the WWF's home base, during the lean years when Titan struggled to rebuild from the post-steroid trial fallout, and when its once-deep fan base was coming of age. ECW's appeal as a macabre alternative played admirably into the New York market. From December 1995 through April 1996, Heyman booked four shows at the Lost Battalion Hall in the Rego Park neighbourhood of Queens, drawing between 1100 and 1300 per house, comparably matching the capacities of its jam-packed Philly nest. Through the remainder of 1996, Staten Island and Middletown, NY became regular weekend stops for the growing touring brand.

New York, namely the crowds that filled Madison Square Garden, remained

McMahon's barometer – his alpha-constituency. "If the fans responded to a performer in MSG, it went a long way with the McMahon family in determining who would get pushed as a star," Chris Jericho stated, affirming a long-held industry belief. When that home crowd ferociously booed white-meat champion Michaels out of its doors at the 1996 *Survivor Series*, McMahon knew he had to reconsider his approach. The ECW uprising within the north-eastern region of the United States was becoming undeniably influential. "By the winter of 1997, they regularly bought up the tickets for the first few rows of seats at all Vince's TV shows on the east coast just so that they could be heard on TV around the world booing the babyfaces and cheering the heels," claimed Bret Hart. "The general TV audience had no idea that it was the same group of ECW fans showing up everywhere. Instead they thought a trend was developing, and as a result hating the good guys and loving the heels actually started to catch on." Whether it *was* a trend or simply a change in preference, McMahon longed for his product to appear as hiply dangerous to those same fans. It would begin with a strategic alliance, in the hope of gaining some of that coolness through osmosis.

THE WWF-ECW connection had begun producing sparks in the fall of 1996. Titan's September pay-per-view offering, entitled *In Your House: Mind Games*, emanated from the same Philadelphia Spectrum in which Vega and Frazier were unknowingly thrown to the jackals. Knowing the locale, McMahon capitalized on a chance for connection by discreetly contacting Heyman with an offer for the two sides to work together. "Obviously, we had such momentum at the time, it would behove McMahon's business to acknowledge ECW," declared Heyman. The plan would need to serve two masters: the ECW contingent that wanted a forum to appear belligerent on a larger stage, and a musty Titan that had a chance to benefit from a memorable brush with wrestling's new wave.

However, it was imperative that the two sides appeared to be anything but in cahoots. "It was not going to help us to be embraced and endorsed by Vince McMahon," Heyman wisely reasoned. The solution was presented during *Mind Games'* opening bout, a 'strap match' pitting Savio Vega against future WWE Champion John 'Bradshaw' Layfield, at the time cartooned as one-note Texas varmint Justin 'Hawk' Bradshaw. The brawl spilled to ringside, where Heyman sat behind the guardrail, flanked by ECW regulars Sandman and Dreamer. Suddenly, to a palpable cheer from knowing spectators, Sandman spewed a geyser of beer into Vega's face. Feigning restrained indignance, McMahon, in between shooting dirty glares at middle finger-offering Heyman, muttered about a "local wrestling group" attempting to score free publicity at the WWF's expense. With most incidents involving bad fan behaviour, the producers would pan away from the ruckus to avoid encouraging future acts. Here, McMahon's faint allusion betrayed any chance of Sandman's actions being real, but that hardly mattered. "Heyman played it right," Dave Meltzer noted. "His audience will know about it on their television as he'll play it up big. It gets his group over as a renegade group, exactly how it has positioned itself, particularly with the much more high profile nWo around and he no longer has the monopoly on that market."

The designed guerrilla tactics were carried out again one night later at the *Raw* tapings in nearby Hershey, PA. It was here that mohawked, squat-bodied Peter Senerchia, billed professionally as Taz, leapt over the guardrail during a tag team match, brandishing a sign that read, "SABU FEARS TAZ". Announcer Ross largely glossed over Senerchia's presence, coarsely dismissing the ECW entity by noting that the performers wrestled in a bingo hall. The disruption provided a segue into a commercial, with nothing post-break to indicate the act of invasion, save for some scattered chants of, "We Want Taz." *Nitro* won the ratings battle for the night by a whopping score of 3.4 to 2.0, indicating that virtually no buzz was provided from the prior night's intrusion. Meltzer felt McMahon was being short-sighted with this strategic alliance, writing, "Emotion of being in a war replaced analysis of business and looking at simple numbers. This has been the WWF's downfall as it is spending more energy competing in a war it can't win on Mondays because of WCW's one-hour jump on them, than focusing on areas that are and can be successful."

IN LATE February 1997, the WWF roster was halved for touring purposes. To call the divide an even split would be woefully off the mark, for most of the bigger names were ushered across the Atlantic for a tour of Europe. The likes of Bret and Owen Hart would be joining Davey Boy Smith, Mick Foley, Vader, and others for an extensive trek through Germany, while a veritable skeleton crew struggled to fill out live events in the north-eastern United States. Aside from The Undertaker (who headlined most of the houses against Ron 'Faarooq' Simmons) and Dustin 'Goldust' Runnels, nobody else on those comparative 'B-shows' was proven anywhere near the top of WWF cards to that point.

If Faarooq was not the default number three draw, then blonde bombshell Tammy 'Sunny' Sytch, at her peak as America Online's most downloaded celebrity, filled that slot by taking part in arm-wrestling matches against Goldust's wife, Terri 'Marlena' Runnels. As an example of the dearth of talent on the American shows, undercard tag team The Headbangers were set apart for the live events, working singles matches against curtain-jerking forgottens in Barry Horowitz and Tracy 'Freddie Joe Floyd' Smothers, both of whom were in their final lap as Titan regulars. This half of the roster would be the ones combating *Nitro* on the night of February 24, 1997, a full eight months into the one-sided beatings that the Monday Night Wars had become. A troupe led by Undertaker with an array of misfits would surely be trounced against a red-hot *Nitro*, with the New World Order still flexing its daunting muscle. On that night, *Raw* was set to take place in the Manhattan Center for the first time in three and a half years, and for the first time since ECW firmly embraced 'extreme' as part of its identification. Thus, the next chapter in the barely-scratched WWF-ECW rivalry was about to be written, capitalising on what promised to be an extremely vocal crowd in mid-town New York.

Knowing that the majority of patrons inside the ballroom venue would likely jeer most non-ECW endeavours, save for possibly Undertaker and the half-clothed precursors to the company's 'Divas', announcer Jerry 'The King' Lawler was positioned as designated heat magnet. One week earlier, with *Raw* airing live from Nashville, Lawler sat ringside with the stoically-focused Jim Ross, and careened off on a seemingly-unprovoked, lesser-refined tangent of the Dennis Miller stock. If Ross and McMahon had previously hinted at ECW with vaguely disparaging labels, then Lawler was about to explicitly butt heads with the nuisance. Lawler noted the presence of a number of signs in the arena, before turning his attention to an obvious plant behind the retaining barricade, waving an "ECW RULES" sign in his direction. Lawler jerked it from his hands and abruptly began a monologue on the subject of Extreme Championship Wrestling. "Ninety-nine percent of the people in the world have never heard of ECW," seethed Lawler, holding the sign aloft as an object of ridicule. He then compared ECW to John Carpenter's *Escape From New York*, noting the degenerative lawlessness of the outlaw-themed brand, before dismissing their weekend warriors as, "a bunch of misfits and a bunch of has-beens that couldn't make it in the WWF!" Instead of potentially casting the WWF as a spoon-fed villain against the *Delta House*-like interlopers from Philadelphia, Lawler was made token agitator, ensuring the heat would be transferred solely to him.

Lawler concluded the tirade by inviting anyone from the ECW roster to show up on *Raw* one week later at the Manhattan Center, although he personally had reservations about the purpose of the story. Lawler could not understand why McMahon was giving such valuable air time to a rival group. Strategic alliances with Lawler's own USWA promotion, as well as Jim Cornette's Smoky Mountain Wrestling, had taken place on a smaller scale, but nothing with the corrosive nature of a WWF-ECW holy war had ever been attempted, especially with almost a month to go before the annual *WrestleMania* extravaganza. McMahon was so consumed with image enhancement in the Monday Night Wars that he was allotting valuable television space to outsiders that would have nothing to do with Titan's flagship pay-per-view.

An hour later, Paul Heyman called into *Raw* during a technically-sound match pitting then-Tag Team Champion Owen Hart against former ECW mainstay Flash Funk, an edgeless hybrid of George Clinton and Dolemite. While Hart and Funk ate up quarter of an hour with solid wrestling, Lawler and Heyman traded schoolyard barbs to hype up the following week's showdown. As Hart and the former Scorpio executed an elaborate spot where the two exchanged monkey flips out of a double knuckle-lock, Lawler began running down stars like Sandman and Brian 'The Blue Meanie' Heffron by name. Heyman responded by hitting below the belt, claiming that as long as "the neighbourhood watch doesn't have to be informed," Lawler would be in New York (a reference to Lawler being indicted on statutory rape charges against an underage teenage girl in 1993)[7] Heyman would see him there.

Days later, with Lawler genuinely incensed by the remarks, Heyman was informed by WWF officials of what he was not permitted to say in regards to Lawler during the February 24 broadcast. If the Brian Pillman-Steve Austin gun incident was crossing the line, at least Pillman and Austin were the best of friends. In the case of smart-assed, vociferous Heyman, for whom some of the disdain between he and Lawler was authentic, coaching was required. Not even four months had passed since the USA Network recoiled at the sight of a gun-wielding Pillman, and the proceedings needed at least a modicum of control. As the ECW portions of the New York *Raw* were a nationally-televised infomercial for their first pay-per-view, *Barely Legal*, the last thing Heyman needed was for Lawler to sabotage the promotion's credibility, or personally paint Heyman as any kind of fraud or shyster. The ECW honcho would have to work cordially with Lawler in regards to what pot-shots they took towards one another.

No such restrictions were placed on over a thousand patrons cramming the venue, the 1993 charm restored with all inhibition checked at the door on West 34th Street. Throughout the course of the night, Heyman's ECW was allowed three exhibitions from his talent pool, interspersed between WWF's fare, and the boss himself sat in on commentary for those matches with Lawler and McMahon, who played it irascible and disquieted respectively. "A lot of the Extreme Championship Wrestling fans have inundated this arena," stated McMahon benignly, taking a sort of neutral role, not without a hint of perplexity at the brazen screams of, "Nitro Sucks," from the gallery. Heyman made his grand entrance following the first fifteen minutes, accompanying ECW Tag Team Champions Perry 'Saturn' Satullo and George 'Kronus' Caiazzo, known collectively as The Eliminators. The duo laid out a planted ring crew member with their double roundhouse kick known as Total Elimination, as a lit powder keg hit its inevitable boom. "Your challenge has been accepted," screeched Heyman in Lawler's direction. "ECW is in the house!"

The matches themselves were simple squashes to get across ECW's primary stars. Michael 'Stevie Richards' Manna, accompanied by his chums from the offbeat Blue World Order, was in the midst of his first serious push after a long spell as the company's clueless comic relief, and went over on scrappy James

---

[7] The rape and sodomy charges were dropped in February 1994, at which time Lawler pleaded guilty to a lesser charge of harassing a fourteen-year-old witness. He received a twelve-month sentence, discharged to two years of probation.

'Little Guido' Maritato. Brooding ECW World Champion Scott 'Raven' Levy appeared at one juncture to confront Richards, his former lickspittle, giving their rivalry a simple nod. Ironically, at WWF's last tapings at the Manhattan Center in 1993, Levy performed as manager Johnny Polo, a loud caricature of an over-privileged snot that was far more hyperactive than Levy's icier Raven character, whom Heyman boldly referred to as "the David Koresh of wrestling." The juxtaposition of the Polo and Raven gimmicks, to anyone aware, only further summed up the divide between the anodyne WWF that McMahon had carved out, and the intoxicating pump that he now wanted his product to tap into.

From there, Taz systematically suplexed and stretched out plucky underdog John 'Mikey Whipwreck' Watson, en route to his highly-anticipated showdown with Sabu at *Barely Legal*. Sabu famously made his presence felt by appearing on *Raw's* entrance way, a ten-foot-tall cut-out of the letters R-A-W, diving onto a cell of obedient Taz trainees that doubled as his silent followers. The final match saw Dreamer defeat Devon 'D-Von Dudley' Hughes, with the most basic weaponry (steel chair, frying pan) coming into play. Heavyset Italian Mark 'Bubba Ray Dudley' LoMonaco made the save for his African-American 'half-brother', before Sandman stormed the ring to even the odds alongside Dreamer. In all, it was little more than an elementary primer into ECW rather than a demonstration of its core insanity, though the New York crowd swallowed it up like the heartiest of meals.

Ironically, those diehards missed the real 'hardcore match' of the evening, which pitted commentators Heyman and Lawler at their snarkiest. Lawler took every opportunity to lambast anything that could be perceived as an ECW shortcoming, whether it was Maritato's smaller body, or the general uncouthness of the 'guests'. "The first thing I remember when I saw these guys were how small they were," Lawler stated years later. "Everybody looked like miniature wrestlers running around, and I remember commenting after looking at Taz, to Vince, 'He looked a lot bigger on the Lucky Charms box, you know, McMahon?'" If Lawler was galled by the size of the wrestlers – ones that would struggle to break out of the jobber caste in a Hogan-ruled WWF – he had to be further puzzled by the fans cheering this tableau on. Maritato's introduction alone received bigger cheers than four larger performers from WWF's match just prior, a tag team contest featuring one anachronistic gimmick (Arkansas hog farmers Henry and Phineas Godwinn) against another (Stetson-wearing cowboys The New Blackjacks). When Heyman grunted, "Man, has this show sucked without ECW, or what?" over a live microphone, Manhattan screamed their affirmation.

McMahon, in his neutral role as disaffected host, could hardly hide his bewilderment, while enduring some pokes to the ribs from Heyman. Moments after McMahon errantly referred to Stevie Richards as "Stevie Ray" (a WCW tag wrestler who partnered with his brother Booker T in Harlem Heat), the inimical Heyman snorted, "You impress me as an announcer. If this WWF thing does not work out for you, we could actually give you a job in ECW." McMahon, under his breath, could only reply, "Thank you, I appreciate that." Lawler fired back, eagerly trampling over McMahon's response, "I've seen your shows - you need an announcer."

It may have been hard for McMahon to immediately process the proceedings, but that did not stop him from displaying his gracious side. One member of Taz's entourage was twenty-three-year-old Daniel Morrison, a student of Taz and Saturn's at the House of Hardcore training facility who would go on to become eventual ECW Tag Team Champion 'Dastardly' Danny Doring. Morrison remembered that McMahon took time to personally acknowledge every visitor from ECW, including the unknowns in Taz's crew, saying, "He met with us all actually, one by one. Looked us all in the eye, shook all of our hands, thanked us very much. All in a row."

Despite all the hoopla surrounding the promise of a hell-raising intrusion on WWF turf, the novel drama failed to end the eight-month streak of ratings wins for the coasting WCW. *Nitro* won the night 2.97 to 2.43 on the heels of a quality *SuperBrawl VII* pay-per-view the night before. Perhaps making matters a bit harder to swallow for the vigilant McMahon was the fact that the only quarter hour won by *Raw* featured ECW content. The first-hour match-up between Manna and Maritato drew a 2.7 to *Nitro's* 2.6. In that timeframe, *Nitro* had offered up glorified C-show fodder in the form of 'Hacksaw' Jim Duggan squashing luchador Galaxy (Damien 666), and Dungeon of Doomer Bill 'Hugh Morrus' DeMott pummelling Joe Gomez. Dave Meltzer in the *Wrestling Observer* wrote after the fact:

> There is no question the appearance, even if it was a let-down in many ways, was a positive for ECW in that more people saw the product than ever before and they were allowed to plug their PPV. It is both amazing and mind-boggling to see a television show four weeks before *WrestleMania* have more hype for a supposed rival promotion's PPV than for their own biggest show of the year. Still, ECW came off as a minor league promotion on big-time television since Vince McMahon didn't even know who the wrestlers are, and when the fan at home sees that arguably the most powerful man in the industry and the voice they recognize in wrestling doesn't even know or seem to much care about these guys, how important can they be?

AS CLUELESS as McMahon was toward the nuances of each ECW visitor, there was one returning act that evening whom every wrestling fan instantly recognised. No matter what promotion that the Road Warriors, Michael 'Hawk' Hegstrand and Joseph 'Animal' Laurinaitis, stormed into, the *Mad Max*-inspired musclemen popped crowds. They were an easy duo to recognise, having collectively honed their act for a decade and a half with little deviation from their macabre war paint, spiked shoulder pads, finely-shorn Mohawk hairstyles, and high volume growling bluster.

The formative years of Road Warrior lore saw the duo presented as unmovable villains, in spite of the undeniable adulation that their nonchalant mayhem evinced. Fans quickly migrated to Hawk and Animal's bandwagon, no matter what babyface ended up getting military-pressed with ease. Predating Sting and The Ultimate Warrior, not to mention eventual doppelgängers Demolition and The Powers of Pain, the Road Warriors were an epiphany in professional wrestling - some wrestlers got over with their bodies, while others with costumes. Hawk and Animal took the opportunity to shoot themselves into the stratosphere by hitting hard on both fronts.

The Road Warriors officially ended the paradox of ironic cheers by becoming good guys once and for all. On July 6, 1985, the then-AWA World Tag Team Champions battled NWA titleholders Ivan Koloff and Krusher Khruschev in a unification bout at the first ever *Great American Bash*, held by Jim Crockett Promotions (overseer of the NWA belts). With anti-Soviet sentiment a major part of the American climate, there was no way that Hawk and Animal would receive a single boo from the 27,000-strong crowd at the American Legion Memorial Stadium in Charlotte. It was easier to believe that the shoot-Canadian Koloff and legitimate American Khrushchev could be Russian than it was that Animal and Hawk could be heels. The match ended with a double-disqualification, which proved to be a career victory for the Warriors.

By this point the pair were in demand more than ever, and the Warriors enjoyed a financially-rewarding tour through Crockett's territory at the end of that summer, but wanted to dip their cup in for much more. In early September 1985, Laurinaitis, Hegstrand, and manager Paul Ellering – an intellectual, wiry menace with a booming Shakespearian bellow – sought guaranteed deals that would make the Road Warriors contractual property of Crockett's, providing the kind of six-figure security that Laurinaitis in particular coveted for his young family. Together, they sat down with NWA President Crockett, where the team was given an estimated assurance of $500,000 annually for their full loyalty (dates in Japan aside). The normally stoic Laurinaitis almost collapsed in ecstasy upon hearing the figure. However, Crockett would not offer a guaranteed deal, which only emboldened Laurinaitis. Instead of intently holding his ground in Crockett's luxurious office, he paid a visit to McMahon.

Ellering arranged a meeting for the Minnesota monsters with the WWF chief not long after, and the trio took a flight into New York's JFK Airport, followed by a short limo drive up to McMahon's tucked-away home in a wooded section of Stamford. McMahon greeted the three at his doorstep in attire that Laurinaitis describes as, "out of an L.L. Bean catalogue," with khakis and a sweater draped around his neck. The group shared a house tour and a gourmet lunch before getting down to business. McMahon made it clear that he did not offer guaranteed contracts, instead emphasising the plum that was merchandising. Laurinaitis was hardly disappointed, for his intent with the Connecticut trip was to "put pressure on Crockett and get our contracts." The chatter soon spread about the Warriors' round-trip flight; thus the business move was well-executed. "Jimmy would have to 'shit or get off the pot' in regards to signing us to contracts," Laurinaitis said. For the next five years, save for some international excursions, the Road Warriors were well-paid property of Crockett.

By the summer of 1990, Hawk and Animal finally did return to the gates of Titan, fed up with what was by now Ted Turner-owned World Championship Wrestling, in particular the oft-maligned leadership of former Pizza Hut manager Jim Herd, who had worked as WCW's Executive Vice President since early 1989. After being reduced to disbelieving cackles at the sight of film character RoboCop saving Sting from the clutches of the Four Horsemen at the *Capital Combat* pay-per-view, Laurinaitis told Hegstrand, "Let's get out of this dump", leaving the venue behind, as well as WCW.

McMahon could only offer a similar deal to his 1985 pitch, but the newly-branded Legion of Doom happily took it, reasoning that merchandise and pay-per-view payoffs would fill their bank accounts as good as any guarantee. For the next two years, the 'LOD' continued their pantheon-level run as wrestling's most indomitable tag team, capturing the WWF World Tag Team belts from the Nasty Boys at the 1991 *SummerSlam* in Madison Square Garden. This made Hawk and Animal the first and only team to hold the AWA, NWA/WCW, and WWF Tag Team belts, a tribute to their endurance as a high-demand act. Their physical endurance, however, was another story.

The notoriously-rough travel schedule took its toll on two wrestlers known for being impervious to pain, with Hegstrand resorting to illicit drug use to keep moving. "Hawk and some of the others would just say, 'Fuck it,' and snort lines of coke to stay up all day and night long," Laurinaitis lamented. He would frequently have to answer for Hegstrand's lack of dependability, particularly what state he was in, and whether he would be punctual for shows. Laurinaitis claimed that his partner would fail random drug tests administered by Titan, which still did not change anything. "For the most part, they'd turn the other cheek and let him off the hook with a warning or a fine, but I wondered for how long," mused Laurinaitis. Hegstrand would end up suspended for sixty days for one violation in May 1991, though upon return, the LOD's path to the titles continued uninhibited.

One year later, the Legion of Doom disintegrated. Hegstrand endured a second suspension in January 1992 that led to the end of their title reign the following month. By the time of the Wembley Stadium *SummerSlam* in late

August, Laurinaitis claimed, although he did not know it at the time, that Hegstrand had failed yet another test before the cross-Atlantic flight to London, and was anticipating another suspension or perhaps even termination. Loading himself with sedatives before a tag team match with Ted DiBiase and Mike 'Irwin R. Schyster' Rotunda in front of 80,000 lively fans, Hegstrand was in enough of a physical lull that McMahon noticed at ringside. "After the show, Bobby Heenan came up to me and said that Vince had been cursing Mike off camera the entire match," Laurinaitis remembered. That would be Hegstrand's last WWF appearance for over four and a half years, as he quit shortly after the pay-per-view. Laurinaitis likewise would take time away from the business for several years himself to deal with serious back injuries, collecting on a Lloyd's of London insurance policy during his convalescence.

By early 1996, following several years of mending both personal fences and their aching bodies, Animal and Hawk were reunited in WCW, with Animal taking part in his first matches since leaving WWF in the fall of 1992. Their tenure rekindled some of the old magic as they participated in matches involving old Turner notables Sting, Lex Luger, and the Steiner Brothers. However, it would only last less than four months. Laurinaitis claimed the Warriors flew the coop after a long-term deal with Bischoff was unable to be reached. Wanting full-time work in the United States, Laurinaitis called McMahon to seek another go-around. He assured the curious boss that Hegstrand had put his demons behind him, and just like that, a three-year deal was hammered out. Considering the diminished talent pool as a result of the touring split, no one would argue that the roster did not need a boost. "They were the Road Warriors, and you should at least give them a try, because talent was in short supply," Cornette reasoned.

Once again dubbed the Legion of Doom, they re-debuted to their familiar power rock theme music (preceded by Hawk's patented grunt of "What a Rush!") that night in the Manhattan Center, with even the most vociferous smart-asses in the crowd popping at the surprise. The "LOD" chant showed that the duo's act, even by Hegstrand's fortieth birthday the previous month, still retained its magic. McMahon silently let the reintroduction play out before yelping, "Unbelievable!" with excited enunciation. Their opponents that night were a relatively new team to the WWF fold in Monster Factory-trainees Mosh and Thrasher, The Headbangers. It seemed like the opportunity for Animal and Hawk to re-establish themselves as no-nonsense enforcers against two lighter-weight tackling dummies (Thrasher had previously served as WWF enhancement talent under his birth name Glenn Ruth), but there were other plans.

McMahon informed the returning team that Jake Roberts would be the agent for their match, and Roberts in turn broke the news that the match would end up a double count-out. Laurinaitis was already annoyed that Roberts presented the Headbangers to him and Hegstrand by saying, "They're kind of like the new Road Warriors." Now he was wrapping his head around going fifty-fifty with an undercard tandem that held zero momentum at the time, recalling, "As Jake tried to slither away, I caught up to him to verify the finish. 'Are you sure that's the way our return's supposed to go? That doesn't really make any sense, Jake.' 'Don't worry. You'll make it up. There's big plans coming for you and Hawk. This is the way Vince wants it.'" And so it played out, without any further fuss, a standard tag team bout with a double count-out, drawing a mixture of silence and unhappy murmurs. As a parting shot, the Legion of Doom walloped Mosh with their dangerous and awe-inspiring finish, the Doomsday Device, to put a collective smile on the audience's face. It was a weirdly ominous sign for the Legion of Doom, despite Roberts' reassurance, that their return was afforded more uncertainty than decisiveness.

VINCE MCMAHON has been known to go to great lengths to disguise any sign of weakness, particularly worry or exhaustion. One imagines the fearless Titan commander staving off any zombie-like body tics as he flew across the ocean to join the other half of his roster in Berlin for a *Raw* taping less than forty-eight hours after the ECW gathering in New York. The Berlin event was the seventh WWF show in Germany over a nine-day stretch, and was the site of a tape-delayed *Raw* that would air in its normal time slot five nights later. Five of the nine stops drew less than 3,000 fans, the most dismal being the 1,473 paid that attended on the first night in Aschaffenburg. Not one of the dates had sold out.

The *Raw* taping featured the conclusion of a tournament to crown the inaugural European Champion, the company's first non-weight and non-gender-based secondary belt since the Intercontinental belt's introduction in 1979. The championship looked like little more than a token for long-standing European draw Davey Boy Smith, giving the chiselled Brit a prop to tote around during future tours of the continent. Smith's brother-in-law Bret Hart believes the belt was designed to mollify Smith, who had signed a five-year contract with Titan eight months earlier, stating, "Vince had made promises to Davey when he signed him, but he hadn't lived up to them and was trying to appease Davey by putting the European Title on him."

Smith's triumph for the gold took place before 6,373 fans at Berlin's rectangular Deutschlandhalle, a building that seated approximately 10,000 for concerts and other exhibitions, prior to its 2011 demolition. Smith's win came over tag team partner Owen Hart after twenty-three minutes of what was perhaps the best match to take place on either Monday night broadcast since the wrestling war began. In contrast to the superb grappling display from two gifted veterans hearkening back to their formative junior-heavyweight days, the tape-delayed program as a whole lacked polish. The Monday Night Wars had seen both sides use production value among their ammunition, but the Berlin *Raw* was poorly-lit, coming off as grainy as the company's lower-budgeted television tapings of their pre-national expansion era. The taped nature of the show combined with the bland video quality to give *Raw* an abysmal 1.9 television rating to *Nitro's* 3.4, triple the gap of the previous week.

The chaos of the parallel tours, shoehorning of the ECW infomercial, and having to dictate and keep peace for two shows 4,000 miles apart in person, in less than two days, would make any promoter wander aimlessly. With somewhat-controlled anarchy kicking up dust into his face, how far was McMahon off the beaten path toward *WrestleMania*?

Jim Cornette was working at the studios in Stamford on Monday, March 3, remaining steadfast that the show was a bad idea. Despite Cornette's concerns and protestations, McMahon could not be deterred from running it. "It was a series of matches shot with one or two cameras, badly lit with no stories, and then we voiced it over after the fact," Cornette bitterly rasped. "It was rotten! I knew it was going to be rotten when they planned it, but they thought, '*Raw* will come from Germany! That'll be a big deal!' No, it wasn't a big deal. It did like the worst rating in the history of fucking ratings."

McMahon and fellow announcers Jim Ross and The Honky Tonk Man provided live commentary from the studios for the broadcast. This was done in a vain attempt to make *Raw* appear anything less than pre-recorded, a common practice for taped episodes of the show since its inception. Oftentimes, announcer McMahon and his colleagues would reference unrelated news events from the day of the airdate to give their 'rasslin' show some sort of topical relevance, misleading less-savvy viewers into thinking that taped matches from upwards of three weeks earlier were indeed airing in real-time. In this case, with Germany situated six hours ahead of New York on the time-zone map, that meant McMahon was giving the impression that a show airing in Germany could possibly be 'live' at 2 a.m. Tuesday morning in local Berlin time.

The morning after, a furious McMahon summoned his inner circle to the office for an emergency meeting. Cornette, who had slept in Tuesday morning after arriving home past midnight, recalled groggily receiving a message from fellow executive and close friend Bruce Prichard to get to the office. Arriving late to the meeting only exacerbated McMahon's sour mood, which quickly degenerated into the mother of all chew-outs. "Vince was fucking mad at everybody!" Cornette recalled. "He's mad at everybody for showing a fucking show that most people thought was going to suck to begin with if they told the fucking truth about it."

As McMahon breathed fire at the likes of Cornette, Prichard, and Jim Ross, fast-talking thirty-six-year-old New Yorker Vince Russo added his own voice to the fray. Only five years earlier, Russo was hosting *Vicious Vincent's World of Wrestling*, a radio program on Freeport, NY's WGBB station. By 1993, Russo, who was personally plunking down somewhere around a thousand dollars a week to keep the show going, found himself financially in the red. While Russo claimed to have made a strong living wage as an appliance salesman in conjunction with his radio work, the pipe dream of making it in the wrestling business through a niche broadcast was draining his nest egg. With a wife and three young children relying on the breadwinner to come through big, Russo penned a letter to Linda McMahon in the hope of securing work.

"Whereas Vince was running the show on the stage, Linda was directing traffic behind the scenes," Russo reasoned for choosing to contact her instead of her husband. "It was a longshot, but what did I have to lose? I sat down and penned Linda a heartfelt letter. I told her of my trials and tribulations in the wrestling business; my dreams, goals, and aspirations; and that I was literally hanging on by my last Washington."

In the spring of 1993, Russo received a phone call from Linda's assistant, Liz DeFabio, who patched the Titan matriarch through to the desperate radio jock. "This was my opportunity," Russo said of the call. "I sold like a salesman one percent short of his commission with only thirty minutes left in the month. I sold, sold, sold, and sold some more. I barely let Linda get a word in edgewise, but from what I can remember, she mentioned to me that they were looking for freelance writers for the *World Wrestling Federation Magazine*, and that someone would be getting in touch with me shortly after *WrestleMania IX*, that weekend."

Not long after, Russo took on the gig, writing two articles per month for $150 apiece. By early 1994, Russo had secured the magazine's editor job, following the sudden firing of long-time editor, and Russo mentor, Ed Ricciuti. From there, the then-thirty-three-year-old Russo left his fingerprints all over *WWF Magazine* not only as editor, but with a monthly 'insider' column called *The Bite*, written under the mordant pseudonym Vic Venom. His printed copy served as an extension of the stereotypical brashness of his New York ilk, frequently displaying entire sentences in all capital letters, the indication of an in-your-face speaker that could blow out a stereo system, even in text.

All the while Russo's vision for the magazine amounted to a jarring shout, he found himself at odds with the slide-whistle humour and rudimentary storylines of WWF television. Embarrassed by the litany of characters and happenings that he was tasked with writing about, Russo began to shoot his own angles for the publications, particularly *Raw Magazine*, which launched in 1996 as an edgier sibling to its predecessor. *Raw Magazine* not only featured shoot-based articles that peeled back the curtain on WWF's own gritty underbelly, but would break through partitions, referencing competitors by name. Russo recalled interviewing Bret Hart for the newer publication, explicitly discussing WCW and Eric Bischoff. That decision prompted a beckoning from an angry McMahon.

"I remember he had the magazine and with one arm, he cleared everything that was on his desk," relates Russo. "He screamed at me, 'What the hell are you trying to do? Are you trying to put me out of business?' I vividly remember the moment and should have been scared to death and fired on the spot. Something made me say, 'No Vince, I'm trying to help you.' It just came out, and I wasn't fired."

Not only was Russo not let go, but he would join the company's creative team later in 1996, despite a lack of experience at that particular level. Several months after holding his ground over magazine content, Russo persisted to McMahon, imploring that he be allowed to join creative in an attempt to help wash the mildew off the product. Russo recalled telling McMahon, "'Listen, if [the magazine] is all I'm capable of, I need you to tell me, because I know I'm capable of more.' Vince McMahon got hot at me, red in the face. I don't think anybody ever did this to him before. I remember him getting red in the face at me and I'm thinking, 'Bro, I don't want more money, I want to help you.'" Days after that particular push, Russo was once more summoned before the boss, this time with an audience. Lagging in the ratings war with *Nitro*, McMahon had made the decision to go in a new direction with his product, and had called Russo into a conference populated with his closest confidants. "He had the magazine in his hands and threw it down in front of everybody and said this is what our show needs to be," claimed Russo.

McMahon's blunt declaration heralded Russo's official ascent into creative, the writer's confidence bolstered by the Chairman's faith. Because of this, and despite his status as freshman in a room filled with decorated seniors, Russo had no qualms about speaking up during McMahon's brimstone sermon on March 4.

"Russo's like, 'I told you so,' and Vince goes, 'Well this guy must know what he's talking about, because he's the only one that wasn't involved in it!' And that's when he started taking Vince Russo's ideas," recalled Cornette. "So McMahon starts listening to knucklehead, because knucklehead's like, 'See, all those phony cartoon characters like Honky Tonk Man, and all this other shit...' Well, that's the goddamn deal that I'd been screaming about; there's too many phony cartoon characters. So he has 'real life' that goes into his insane, bizarro-world version of real life, and off we go into a different direction that's equally as maddening. That's when Russo got influence, because Vince just got mad one day, and went off in a 180-degree direction - as he does sometimes – that everybody else was the shits because of this one show that nobody fucking liked in the first place."

Russo's quarrel with the programming extended beyond taped shows recorded beneath a meagre lighting grid. His views had not wavered from his time running the magazine, particularly with how characters came off before the audience. One of his tasks on the creative staff was to write dialogue for Shawn Michaels, a job that quickly opened his eyes to McMahon's apparent shortsightedness. "It wasn't that Shawn wasn't capable of writing his own shtick, because he was," Russo said. "It was just that Shawn wasn't capable of coming up with the verbiage Vince wanted him to say. At that time, Vince wanted Shawn to be this sappy, make-you-want-to-puke babyface - the total opposite of who he was."

"I had to write such vanilla promos for Shawn - we both questioned it, but Vince was the boss. No offence intended, but at the time, Vince seemed so far out of date it wasn't even funny. Eighties wrestling just wasn't working. All the old rules were breaking down day-by-day."

ON OCTOBER 8, 1996, two weeks after the release of his breakthrough album *Antichrist Superstar*, uninhibited shock rocker Marilyn Manson dropped the LP's first single out of necessity for superficial success: *Superstar's* second track, '*The Beautiful People*', which lyrically dealt with wilful slavery to the distortions of a propaganda machine. The words hardly mattered; most fans of the song fell in love with the rhythmic drums and supercharged aggressive guitar slashes, entranced by Manson's whispery intonations. '*The Beautiful People*' was more metal than metal, a call-to-action that displaced the strained lamentations of the recent Seattle grunge phase. Manson's macabre image and nightmarish shrieks frightened parents and enraptured teenagers, a marketable divide fit for the second MTV generation.

Not since the Rock 'n Wrestling era had the World Wrestling Federation run parallel with the tops in contemporary music. If Cyndi Lauper and Queen had their music licensed out to underscore the bohemian camp of 1980s WWF, Manson would pack punch for any entity needing to display edge. With Titan now seeking a youthful audience that yearned not to be treated like babies, '*The Beautiful People*' would be an appropriate welcoming siren for viewers to professional wrestling's newest dawn.

At eight o'clock eastern time on Monday night, March 10, 1997, that song kicked into thudding gear, bedding the anarchic visuals of *Raw's* new opening. A bombed-out warehouse served as the battleground for a no-holds-barred fracas in proximity of oil barrels that sent dangerous explosions into the air. Barking German shepherds dotted the dystopia as Steve Austin walked nonchalantly in the direction of twin fireballs the size of sports utility vehicles, unmoved as they careened into each other. Ahmed Johnson slammed a two-by-four against a chain-link fence in his stomp toward the fray. They joined Hart, Michaels, The Undertaker, and Sycho Sid in duking it out inside a make-shift ring as the explosions continued, several of the ropes catching fire, all while Manson screeched the song's chorus. This was not 'Cool Dad' trying to prove he was still hip: this was the WWF aesthetically triumphing in spite of itself.[8]

---

[8] '*The Beautiful People*' would only last for the first three episodes of *Raw is War's* lifetime, quickly

ENTER RAW *is War*, a rebranding that came equipped with a relentless fireworks opening atop a grated-steel stage and entrance ramp, which was overlooked by an elephantine video screen that later became known in wrestling parlance as the 'Titan Tron'. The nearly-7,500 fans at the Centrum in Worcester, MA were immediately whipped into a frenzy beneath the pyrotechnics, for this sort of demonstration was like nothing they had seen before.

For the first three weeks of its new life, through the night after *WrestleMania 13*, *Raw is War* was set to air live. After that, a cycle would begin in which there would be back-to-back tapings of a live *Raw* on Monday night, and the following week's episode recorded on Tuesday night to save on a number of costs, including travel for the ring and production crews. It was a far cry from the marathon TV tapings undertaken on a monthly basis, where the audience members would be slapping themselves awake during heatless squash matches near the end of the line. The increased frequency of live showings gave *Raw* what *Nitro* had, and was all too quick to rub in Titan's face: the anything-could-happen aura.

Night one of *Raw is War* featured another visit from Paul Heyman and his ECW rowdies. This time, Heyman and Lawler took part in an in-ring debate concerning the merits of ECW's very existence. After Lawler ran down the lower attendance figures for the ECW Arena, Heyman made another vicious insinuation toward Lawler's legal history by asking, "How ya doing at the see-saws in Louisville, Jerry?", before screaming that Lawler's sons (wrestlers Brian Christopher and Kevin Christian) refused to use the Lawler surname out of shame. Lawler retorted by accusing Heyman of still living with his parents, adding that they financed Heyman's wrestling endeavours. Several ECW notables had Heyman's back, including Tommy Dreamer, who promised to "start an effin' war" if Lawler wanted to fetch some of his WWF allies. Four months after Brian Pillman dropped an uncensored "fucking" during the Austin home invasion, rambunctious Dreamer bellied up to the standards and practices safety line.

While Dreamer refrained from crossing that line, The Sandman barrelled through a few long-standing edicts when he busted open his own forehead with a partially-filled can of beer – one of his rituals. It was not even the first bloodshed of the night; Mick Foley took that 'honour' by punching himself in the face until drawing red during an interview. Only fifteen months earlier, WWF Vice President of Distribution Michael Ortman watched horrified as Bret Hart wrestled through a haemorrhaging wound at the December 1995 *In Your*

---

replaced for licensing reasons. Its substitution, several edits of a mercenarial in-house heavy metal song entitled *'Thorn in Your Eye'*, would persist as *Monday Night Raw's* main theme for five years. Interestingly, Titan would unearth *'The Beautiful People'* in August 2001 as the theme for *Raw's* sister show, *SmackDown*.

House pay-per-view (the result of a secretive blade-job). At that point, Ortman was cleaning up the WWF of anything violent while the United States Congress was mulling a crime bill affixed with a rider that targeted violence in the entertainment industry. Ortman feared that with passage, wrestling could have been relegated to later time slots if it fell into programming deemed unsuitable for children.

Ortman had already confronted McMahon after Hart and Kevin Nash attacked each other with weapons at *Survivor Series* a month earlier; this time, Linda McMahon quickly called Ortman to assure him that Hart's bleeding was simply a freak accident. Shortly thereafter, a memo passed through WWF's headquarters, justifying the employment of "elements which are consistent with the time period," on WWF programming, contradicted by the reminder of responsibility toward the younger audience. Sometimes accidents can happen, wink-wink, especially when there is a ratings battle to be won.

While the shedding of blood could be questioned as to whether or not it was pre-meditated, a profanity-laced tirade was harder to defend. Hart continued his character's newfound crutch of excessive whining on the maiden *Raw is War*, sowing the seeds of a forthcoming heel turn by crying foul over his recent WWF Championship loss. One week later, with six days to go before *WrestleMania*, Hart worked the main event with Sid inside a steel cage for the gold. Their respective *WrestleMania* opponents, Austin and Undertaker, were involved in the latter stages, each ironically and intentionally running interference for their nemeses to preserve (in Undertaker's case) or gain (for Austin) the title shot at *WrestleMania*. Hart once again endured a storyline injustice when Undertaker slammed the cage door in his face, ensuring that Sid retained the belt.

Moments after a commercial aired for Karate Fighter action figures, undoubtedly targeted at elementary school-aged boys, McMahon took to the ring to interview the disconsolate Hart. The 'Hitman' accurately portrayed the picture of silent rage, pacing the ring during the deconstruction of the blue-barred cage, similar to a jilted prom-goer that sulks long after the last dance. After McMahon noted over the microphone that Hart was likely frustrated after the turn of events, Hart simultaneously swiped the mic and shoved McMahon to the canvas. "Frustrated isn't the goddamn word for it!" Hart screamed, immediately following up with, "This is bullshit!" With no seven-second delay in place, Jim Ross humbly blurted out an apology as Hart's verbal rampage continued. Lost among several more uses of "goddamn" and an emphatic "tough shit" to the booing crowd was Hart screaming his, "Best there is, best there was, and the best there ever will be," catchphrase, minus the plain-spoken confidence that his entire babyface run up until 1997 could be identified by.

Hart was told to curse if he so desired, in an effort to make the promo feel as real as possible. "He may have gone a little far, farther than what anybody thought he would have," Jim Cornette admitted, "but the general gist of it was intentional."

The show went off the air with a four-way brawl between Hart, Austin, Undertaker, and Sid to hard-sell the forthcoming *WrestleMania* one last time. The west-coast United States airing replayed Hart's entire speech just as nakedly uncensored as the original live telecast, although the WWF did issue an apology on its America Online home page for Hart's language. While Hart was questioning the direction of his own character, the ironic truth was that Titan itself had finally found some semblance of a linear direction, even as it voyaged deeper into what were still uncharted waters.

FOUR

TRADITIONALLY, THE VERY NAME WRESTLEMANIA carried a certain austerity. But in financially and creatively leaner times for the World Wrestling Federation, and with a pay-per-view calendar ballooned to monthly offerings that diluted the specialness of supercards, the lustre of the event had dulled somewhat. Yet the show remained propped-up through the genuflection of Titan's power brokers. Once the original incarnation beamed out to over a million pairs of eyes on closed-circuit television in March 1985, there would forevermore be a landmark coda on the WWF calendar. The florid mayhem could criss-cross in perpetuity throughout the year, especially at *WrestleMania* itself. But for one night, an overstated formality would blend with such zaniness. Through celebrity involvement, glossier production values, and posh video packages, *WrestleMania* had to resonate above the grunting din. The thirteenth incarnation would be no different. It was the first *WrestleMania* to emanate from Chicago's Rosemont Horizon since one-third of tri-mulcast *WrestleMania 2* took place there in 1986. On March 23, 1997, over 16,000 fans paid $837,150, a then-record for any wrestling event in the Windy City, to see the show.

The home viewer was immediately confronted with majesty begetting malice. Under black and white tint, a roll call of past *WrestleMania* celebrities, including Ray Charles and Muhammad Ali, faded into each other over soft violin music. "A magical night where dreams become reality, where legends stand immortal," rhapsodised the voiceover. Shawn Michaels descending gracefully from atop a ladder at *WrestleMania X* was interspersed with the montage, as was a triumphant Bret Hart holding the WWF Championship aloft from the same event.

The music cue turned foreboding. A brief spot of darkness faded into the bitter glare of The Undertaker, while the same speaker ventilated that on this night "a tempest engulfs utopia." Threatening whomps and squawks of trumpets and trombones accompanied violent images of The Nation of Domination stomping Ahmed Johnson in gangland fashion, and Undertaker chokeslamming a referee during a fit of rage. One year removed from the quaint saga of Michaels achieving his noble boyhood dream to become the WWF Champion, Titan's personal Super Bowl was now presented as a battleground for appeasing one's angst with balled-up fists. All pretences of outworldly characters engaging in hyperbolic competition lay dead under the weight of the parting line, "It's supposed to be a night of celebration, a time to rejoice. But tonight, none of these men are smiling." This was no longer the *WrestleMania* of anyone's youth.

TRADITIONALLY, THE event had served as a platform for, among other endeavours, showcasing the promotion's silver medal, the Intercontinental Championship. Long thought of as "the workhorse belt", *WrestleMania* had been a haven for memorable clashes over the strap. By 1997, debates over what was *WrestleMania*'s greatest match of all time had come down to two magnificent candidates: Ricky 'The Dragon' Steamboat's vengeful victory that ended 'Macho Man' Randy Savage's fourteen-month reign with the gold at *WrestleMania III*, and Michaels' marvellous showing in defeat to champion Razor Ramon in a ladder match at *WrestleMania X*. The former battle featured an endless stream of false finishes that enthralled a purported 93,000 fans[9] at the Pontiac Silverdome, and is oft cited as Titan's best match of the eighties, while the latter set the standard (thanks to Michaels' spring-loaded efforts) for future high wire stunt shows under the WWF banner. To put it another way, both matches were undeniably ahead of their time. Despite the changes made in 1997 to remain on the cutting edge, there were still elements that situated the WWF behind the times, one of which provided guest commentary for this year's title bout.

The Honky Tonk Man was a throwback to Rock 'n Wrestling's second act, when the boisterous Elvis impersonator shocked fans by felling Steamboat to capture the Intercontinental Title in June 1987 on syndicated TV. For nearly fifteen-months, a record that has never come close to being shattered, Honky dodged all babyface challengers, retaining the title through divine intervention, or irksome disqualification losses. While Hogan headlined A-shows as superhero champion, Honky worked the second-tier cards, barely warding off the likes of Steamboat, Savage, and Brutus Beefcake through the skin of his corn-fed teeth. The act of the cowardly champion proved a remarkable draw, as fans plunked down good money in the hope they would witness an annoyance be dethroned. That would not happen until the inaugural *SummerSlam* in 1988, when twenty-nine-year-old Jim Hellwig, under the face-painted guise of The

---

[9] This is a fabricated number generated by the WWF for "entertainment purposes". The real paid attendance was 78,000.

Ultimate Warrior, ripped Honky to shreds in under thirty seconds to take the gold.

From there, Honky's WWF run continued largely without relevance, returning jobs to Warrior, and working tag team bouts alongside weather-beaten roughneck Jonathan Wisniski, better known as Greg 'The Hammer' Valentine, prior to quitting the company shortly after Christmas 1990. Close to six years later, Honky would return, Brylcreem and jumpsuit intact. There lay the palpable difference between promotions: Hogan and Savage were on the other channel, wardrobe updated with blackened garb, and were leading on the unpredictable hooliganism of the New World Order. Honky, save for a reduction in metabolism, looked exactly the same as he did in 1988. The anachronistic villain was now in his mid-forties, bringing his conceited musings to guest commentary roles, and a storyline search for a blue-chip wrestler to take under his wing.

Honky had nothing new to say. In his defence, he was only guilty of extending the life span of a successful role that was quite long in the tooth, but also enriched with warm memories. The combatants for the Intercontinental Title, on the other hand, were gifted young wrestlers that had yet to find authentic voices. Instead, they were portraying the embodiment of the one-note pap that the newer-vision Titan sought to flee. The challenger was thirty-one-year-old Solofa Fatu Jr., formerly Headshrinker Fatu, one of many branches on wrestling's Anoa'i Family Tree. The business, Titan in particular, had long portrayed Samoans as unintelligible savages that would probably cannibalise their opponents if not for some managerial handler talking them out of such barbarism.

Indeed, Fatu took on that savage simpleton role for many years, but a few scribbles of the booker's pen now wrote him in as The Sultan, a Middle-Eastern menace whose face was half-concealed by a Bane-like mask, allegedly covering up a mouth that was missing its tongue (in story, the tongue was cut out after he refused to speak when prompted by captors). Factor in genie pants and a hat that critics believed resembled a Hershey's Kiss, and off Fatu went, carrying out a gimmick that lacked motivation and was laughably outdated. The presence of former WWF Champions Bob Backlund and The Iron Sheik as his handlers did not help his case.

If The Sultan was a forgettable midcard occupier, his opponent had it worse as a duplicitous poster boy, lauded by the firm and hated by the masses. Fatu's real life cousin Dwayne Johnson was only twenty-four-years-old when he became Rocky Maivia, a name that paid homage to his wrestling elders, father Rocky Johnson and grandfather 'High Chief' Peter Maivia. After a respectable showing in his first televised match at the 1996 *Survivor Series*, the highly-athletic Johnson ascended the card, winning the Intercontinental gold from Hunter Hearst Helmsley at the *Thursday Raw Thursday* special on February 13. Despite his clean-cut appearance and sharper wrestling instincts (for his age and experience level), Johnson found it onerous to win over the fans. His put-on smile was just as gag-inducing as his uplifting, synthesizer-heavy theme music, narrow-mindedly titled, '*Destiny*'. Johnson played the role of ardent do-gooder that wanted nothing more than to add on to his family's proud legacy, which only fuelled frequent chants of, "Rocky Sucks," from unimpressed scores of fans. By *WrestleMania*, he had scrapped his unusual entrance attire, a neck-dress that came adorned with lengthy, streamer-like frills.

Maivia's offensive tray was quickly emptied out on Sultan, an entire 1980s diet of dropkicks and theatrically-fiery right hands, before Sultan applied a nerve hold mere minutes into the contest. The pedestrian proceedings provided an opportunity for anti-Maivia sentiment to echo from the annoyed fans at the Rosemont Horizon. "This Rocky kid's blown up, he's out of shape; he's not as strong as you say he is!" goaded Honky at McMahon on commentary, ostensibly a heel diminishing a babyface before his inevitable comeback. Nonetheless, the inexperience of Johnson at the top level was abundantly clear, given that Fatu was working in the match's second rest hold, a chinlock, during Honky's taunts. The chinlock was of such length that McMahon, rarely one to impart Wrestling 101, explained the psychology of the hold as the crowd grew restless. When Maivia held his arm aloft to indicate a lack of surrender, the fans' boos grew in volume. It was a minor improvement when Maivia's comeback dance into the Ali Shuffle (appropriated from his father's bag of tricks) drew more silence than jeers. Some snappy-looking DDTs and piledrivers turned the crowd to a small degree, and fans did pop when Maivia won with a schoolboy roll-up, but the writing was on the wall for Johnson's push. "A lot of folks resent him getting pushed to this degree because he's not there yet," noted Dave Meltzer in his review of the match.

A post-match attack on Maivia by Sultan, Backlund, and Sheik was broken up by fifty-two-year-old Rocky Johnson, who saved his defenceless son from the clutches of two middle-aged former champions and a character destined for near-immediate scrapping. There would come a day where no one could fathom Dwayne Johnson needing to be rescued by his aging father, but March 23, 1997 certainly was not it.

IT MAY have actually been more dignifying had Johnson been rescued by the accompaniment now afforded to Hunter Hearst Helmsley. At *In Your House: Final Four* in Chattanooga the previous month, Helmsley had lost a rematch for the Intercontinental Title against Maivia, following interference from Goldust, who had entered into a feud with Helmsley in late-1996. The crux of the story was set around an apparent sexual pass that Helmsley had made to Goldust's valet, and real-life spouse, Marlena, driving Goldust mad with rage. Helmsley won the first battle, retaining the belt at January's *Royal Rumble*, where Dave

Meltzer remained underwhelmed by Helmsley's push, saying that he, "has potential, but at this point, he's being pushed only on potential and politics, and because he's got a good head of hair. His work is only slightly better than average and his interviews and persona are below average." Nevertheless, with the political connection with Michaels and the deeper immersion into company machinations, there was little danger of Triple H being shunted down WWF cards any time soon.

Helmsley desperately needed some kind of hook to better justify his placement on Titan's pecking order. Beginning in early 1996, the character of privileged aristocrat was fleshed out a little more by having buxom escorts in evening-wear walk Helmsley down the aisle for TV matches, beginning with former *Playboy* centrefold Shae Marks. The idea seemed to be that if fans did not care enough to boo a spoon-fed gentleman of leisure, they would be incensed by his ability to bag statuesque models thanks to his privilege. Reactions to Helmsley remained mostly lukewarm throughout the year, even after he ditched the dames and fell under the brief tutelage of 'Mr. Perfect' Curt Hennig. That alliance, which is what yielded the Intercontinental reign, fell through within a month. Hennig had bitterly departed the company for WCW, following a situation where he held the WWF accountable for his failure to receive a six-figure disability sum from his Lloyd's of London insurance policy. At January's *Royal Rumble*, Helmsley debuted the imposing, sneering Curtis Hughes, known better in wrestling circles as 'Mr. Hughes', as his ringside butler/bodyguard. That union was also short-lived, because Hughes was side-lined with a serious medical crisis involving his heart and kidneys that saw the goliath wrestler end up in intensive care.[10]

Wladek 'Killer' Kowalski played a wrestling menace of notorious renown between the ropes, but outside of it Kowalski was a gentle giant that strongly advocated vegetarianism, and trained a number of notable wrestlers, including Helmsley. It was through Kowalski that another one of his protégés and Hunter's next bodyguard entered the WWF's scope, with far-reaching implications for the future.

At a WWF house show in Miami later in 1996, Kowalski introduced this student to Vince's son, Shane McMahon. Kowalski performed scouting duties for the McMahons, as his connection to New York wrestling could be traced all the way back to Vince's father, and this time he had what looked like an easy sell. The impressive specimen that Kowalski had brought to Titan's attention had a chiselled body, granite jaw, puncturing eyes, and boasted a cultured athletic background that included flawless handsprings. While that doesn't sound too unusual for some diamonds in wrestling's rough, the fact that Joan

---

[10] Hughes recovered, and later returned to the WWF in 1999, in tremendous shape, as the bodyguard of Chris Jericho. The union was again a brief one, with Hughes gone within a couple of weeks.

Marie Laurer was a woman that combined imposition with grace like no other female in wrestling made her a unique attraction.

"I tried to explain to Shane that on my answering machine at home I had received a message from Kevin Nash of World Championship Wrestling," Kowalski said in 2001. "Nash said, 'Paul Levesque called us to take this here girl that you've trained and try to hire her. That she might be pretty good.' I told Shane McMahon the whole story and I said, 'WCW is interested in this girl. Why don't you guys take her?' I talked to him twice again and he said, 'We will hire her.'"

Michaels recalled meeting Laurer earlier that year with Levesque, and claimed to have advocated for her hiring, but Vince was non-committal. "She was a big strong girl, and from the moment we saw her, we wanted to bring her in as a bodyguard," Michaels remembered. "We pitched the idea to Vince, but he didn't like it. 'Nobody is going to buy a woman beating all these guys up.' Shane was into it. He and Hunter went back and eventually sold Vince on the idea."

Chyna, as would become Laurer's impartible professional name, would debut moments after Goldust cost Helmsley his match with Maivia at *Final Four*. While Helmsley and Goldust goaded each other with fighting words, Chyna sprang into action, reaching over the guardrail, snaring Marlena in something close to a rear-naked choke. The unmistakable height difference (Chyna was listed at 5'10 to Marlena's five feet flat) was just as jarring as the fact that Marlena's neck was completely obscured by a forearm the size of a flower pot. While consultant Hennig and muted Hughes were turns on old ideas, the idea of a convincing female bodyguard held potential. The new wrinkle would focus on how Chyna would insinuate herself into Helmsley's matches, because her character showed no hesitation toward locking horns with the men. This was made clear on the first edition of *Raw is War* during a pre-*WrestleMania* pull-apart involving Helmsley, Goldust, and their respective seconds. With multiple referees involved, Chyna gorilla pressed diminutive referee Harvey Wippleman into two other officials, drawing disbelieving cheers.

Helmsley went over on Goldust at *WrestleMania* after a respectable fourteen-minute match, all of which was overshadowed by Chyna snatching Marlena in a bear hug during the final minute, horrifically whiplashing her lithe, frail body in such a way that she resembled a Jack-in-the-Box contorting violently on its spring base. While his previous pushes had been mostly met with indifference, Helmsley was now supported by a side act that defied all prior wrestling logic. In other words, it was different, and in this era, 'different' was most definitely conducive to opportunity.

THE LEGION of Doom's return to Titan in the last week of February came with added convenience: the duo proudly hailing from the unforgiving streets of

Chicago would perform in that same city come *WrestleMania*, teaming with Tony 'Ahmed Johnson' Norris to combat the militant Nation of Domination, led by Ron 'Faarooq' Simmons, still invoking a virulent blend of Huey Newton and Louis Farrakhan in his forceful rhetoric. While the African-American Simmons led a group that featured bowtie-wearing followers not unlike that of the Nation of Islam they were caricaturing, Simmons' two partners were anything but black.

For one, white Brian 'Crush' Adams traded on his real-life 1995 arrest for possession of anabolic steroids and unregistered firearms by dressing like a self-appointed kingpin of a prison yard, complete with temporary forehead tattoo. That Adams was rehired in the summer of 1996 during his probation period is mystifying in and of itself, but his kayfabe alignment with a black-power faction looked bafflingly out of place. Same for Savio Vega, who was not only born in Puerto Rico, but for almost two years had his Latin heritage put to use as the entirety of his gimmick, complete with lively trumpet-and-bongo theme music. Vega traded in the colourful sleeveless shirts for a full-length leather trench coat and matching skull cap, at least looking the part of dangerous hoodlum, if not a staunchly militant soldier.

Simmons stood between his partners and tuxedoed adherents shortly before the match, billed as a 'Chicago Street Fight', promising bodily harm for, "that punk coloured boy, Ahmed Johnson," and the LOD. Ironically, it was Simmons who would suffer the brunt of the damage during the eleven-minute donnybrook, separating his shoulder after being jerked from the middle rope by Hawk, while he held one end of a nylon rope. The rope's introduction into the match came minutes earlier, when Vega placed the end of a carefully-tied noose around Ahmed's neck, while a normally animated McMahon lowered his voice, wincing, and said, "Don't do that!" over his headset. The only thing diluting any racial overtones is that once the noose was wrapped around Johnson's neck, the slack was taken out by two other black performers, Nation legal representative Clarence Mason, and yet-to-be-named disciple in a tux Accie 'D'Lo Brown' Connor.

The entire spectacle came to an end after Crush was clotheslined with a two-by-four, one of the many weapons littering a fray that never stopped to catch its breath. Fire extinguisher clouds persisted about ringside, giving the impression that a towering inferno had been finally brought under control. While literal debris scattered about from the fracas, the wrestling world was still preoccupied from the metaphorical dust settling from the match that had preceded it.

IF FANS of the National Football League remain in awe of the sculpted physique of Ed Hochuli, the impressively-muscled middle-aged attorney that has worked Sundays as a head referee since 1990, they would freeze deer-like at the walking gun show that was Ken Shamrock. Only one-hundred odd days removed from choking out future New Japan grappler Brian 'Fury' Johnston at

UFC's second annual *Ultimate Ultimate*, Shamrock more than looked the part of evolutionary fighting machine, with bulging biceps and pillar-thick thighs stretching the stitch work of his attire, a sleeveless pinstriped referee shirt and spandex shorts. Just getting his arms through the sleeve holes likely required some degree of contortionism.

In February 1997, at the height of his popularity, inaugural UFC Superfight Champion Shamrock signed a three-year, seven-figure contract with Titan, spurning the opportunity to wrestle IWGP Heavyweight Champion Shinya Hashimoto at the Tokyo Dome in the spring. Five days before Shamrock put the ink to McMahon's paper, New Japan had made the grave mistake of announcing that the Hashimoto-Shamrock title bout was official. The Ultimate Fighting Championship at the time was declining in pay-per-view revenue, drawing a mere 120,000 buys for the December 1996 event where Shamrock choked Johnston out. In the fight, Shamrock sustained a broken hand, rendering him unable to continue in the evening's single elimination tournament. Shamrock saw the writing on the wall and took the WWF's financially-loaded offer out of deference to economics. "If I do something I like and can support my family, I will continue to do it. The minute I can't, I've got to do something else," Shamrock told the *Dayton Daily News* shortly after signing with Titan.

Hard to miss in most settings, Shamrock's task for the night of *WrestleMania 13* was to be inconspicuous, to remain tucked no deeper than one layer into the scenery, save for one moment of shine. Until that moment, the most blazing-hot angle in the territory was about to have the heat turned up even more in an unforgettable way.

After McMahon and co-announcers Ross and Lawler affirmed Shamrock's status as duly lethal, their attention shifted toward 'Stone Cold' Steve Austin, walking with purpose through a backstage corridor toward the entrance curtain. Barely audible in the din alongside his thudding *'Bulls on Parade'* derivative music, Austin commanded toward the backtracking cameraman, "Get your ass out of the way." Only seven and a half years into his wrestling career, the determined Texan could already see the apex, the penthouse where the industry giants congregated without fear of relegation. No longer would political speedbumps, nor a dutiful cameraman, cut off Austin's destined ascent.

The signature sound of shattering glass affixed to Austin's urgent entrance music brought to mind a home invader, with no meek subtlety of a cat burglar. The 'Stone Cold' genre of invasion was more akin to Genghis Khan in Wranglers and Timberlands, and the more boisterous the arrival, the more fitting it was. At *WrestleMania 13*, not only did the glass break in Austin's custom theme song, but an actual pane of blackened glass fitted over the entrance way, with 'AUSTIN 3:16' painted onto it, was shattered into jagged drops of sharpened rain. Austin strode over the shards, calling to mind Bruce Willis' painful walk across broken glass in *Die Hard*. Willis' John McClane character was saving hostages from violent German thieves. Austin was about to save a ho-hum *WrestleMania* from its own stirred-and-served tedium.

Typically breathing verbal fire in his south-eastern Texas grunt, Austin was more subdued in this instance. He parked himself in the far corner, wrists laid on the intersecting ropes while gazing out pensively into the crowd. Standard bluster for the cameras was side-tracked by what looked to be a contemplative moment, perhaps collecting his bearings or even a silent prayer. So much had rode upon Austin's broad shoulders since the previous June in his undeniable standing as the territory's top villain. By the match's end, provided everything hit their marks, Steve Austin was due to become the WWF's number one hero. With Hart due to swap seats with Austin, in effect turning heel for the first time in nine years, McMahon was gambling that two of his most reliable professionals would make the double-transition seamless. It was a tall order nonetheless, and Austin needed a beat to collect himself.

Hart entered second to a largely-positive response, the previous months of detrimental character actions leaving only flesh wounds on his credibility. Stepping over the glass remnants of Austin's entrance facade, there was a symbolic crossing of the tracks, immediately evident to the long-time do-gooder. "I got a strong cheer, but there were enough angry signs and boos for me to see that my days as a babyface were truly over," Hart recalled, making his post-match fate an easier pill to digest. McMahon further stoked those flames of change, noting, "A mixed reaction for a man who unquestionably has a legacy here in the World Wrestling Federation. But as of late, that legacy has somewhat taken a turn."

The bout was billed as a 'submission' match, where the victor would be the one to force his opponent into an unconditional surrender, by whatever means. The announcers noted the contrast in each man's working style, that Hart would be more likely to try winning with his world-class scientific grappling, while ornery Austin seemed more inclined to bludgeon and batter 'The Hitman' until he quit. True to type, Austin began the match with a lunging double-leg takedown, leading to a rambunctious schoolyard-style slugfest with Hart returning volleys in lockstep. The first cringe-inducing incident took place outside the ring, when Hart sent Austin careening into the ringpost front-first, the smack of flesh and bone-on-steel echoing through the Rosemont Horizon. There was no rest for the wicked; Austin responded shortly thereafter by reversing a suplex so that he crotched Hart onto the crowd-retaining steel barricade.

The spot took place right in front of yesteryear icons Captain Lou Albano and 'Mr. USA' Tony Atlas, whose collective astonishment was clear. They thrived in an era where Bruno Sammartino and Sgt Slaughter engaged with others in bloodbaths and anything-goes brawls, but rarely did such mayhem spill into the seats. Austin joined Hart among the frenzied audience, together stalking toward the back of the arena exchanging strikes inside of an amorphous sea of screaming humanity. Those rowdy onlookers prevented the home audience from seeing the harrowing conclusion to one particular move: Hart backdropping his way out of an Austin piledriver on a staircase, with 'Stone Cold's' exact landing a mystery, save to those who saw it first-hand. For Austin, the chaotic scene was an appropriate add-on for the match.

"Sometimes, fighting out in the crowd can be a real pain in the ass," Austin later explained. "But everyone was cooperating with us, giving us a couple slaps on the back. People were very excited to see this action come right by them, because man, when you're about a hundred yards from the ring, and all of a sudden the action is right next to you up close and personal, it's pretty fun."

Back at ringside, Hart, for probably the first time in his two-decades-long career, leapt from atop the guardrail to land a pedestrian elbow smash onto a prone Austin. Though far from the unfettered daredevilry that the forthcoming era would promise its paying customers, the gesture on Hart's part was the upping of a personal ante in its own way. Seconds later, Hart would be sent careening hard into the ring steps, dislodging them from their ringpost mooring. The tit-for-tat evenness, the notion that Hart could lose his most high-profile bout in a year, gave McMahon the opening to further paint his workhorse with smeary colours.

"If Bret Hart loses this match," McMahon uttered, "you wonder what he's going to come up with as an excuse, because he'll have one - in my view." Those final three words were tacked on rivet-gun style after a sustained pause, reminding those listening that what he was saying was simply one man's editorial. To that point, it was rare for broadcaster McMahon to ever chastise an established hero, or even to be so absolute against one's character. As if the initial pop for Hart's entrance laid to rest any doubt the direction he was headed was understood by the masses, McMahon sharply turned the wheel back on the intended course. For his part, Jim Ross vehemently disagreed with McMahon's assessment, treading along a curious stream of existence in these times where the identity of the 'good guy' was not always apparent.

Onward the match rolled with Hart getting back to basics, working over Austin's left knee with inalienable focus. The textbook display of quad-stretches and seated cannonballs across the knee joint played as an instant throwback, the Hart of old, but not *too* old, frozen in his ideal time. That allowed Austin to carry out his own typecasting, throwing up double-middle fingers in Shamrock's direction for daring to ask if Austin wanted to give in. The rebellious act sharply contrasted Hart's bread-and-butter wrestling style, and the subtle juxtaposition could not have done more to draw a line between the trite New Generation and the ungovernable fashionings of this bold new era.

"I was just watching the transformation while we were in the ring," remembered Shamrock, "You could feel the atmosphere change from this pro wrestling attitude to this bad ass attitude. You felt it change that night."

McMahon made further note of this sudden continental divide, continuing to repurpose his Canadian trump card by adding, "You would hope that maybe after this match, maybe 'the Hitman' Bret Hart would settle down and return to the great legacy that he has had before in the World Wrestling Federation. Maybe something, hopefully, would bring him back to his senses." Austin disrupted Hart's methodical dissection by pulling his leg away from another seated cannonball attempt, before following up with his patented Stone Cold Stunner to a rising cheer. There was no notable follow-up to the move in this submission match, though the standalone moment of judging the aftermath to the Stunner revealed lots of potential in its status as a pay-per-view ender, the violently-abrupt answer to Hulk Hogan's Superman finish.

As the Stunner had yet to gain its 'Game Over' stature, Hart was back on offence shortly thereafter, snaring Austin in his new pet move, a figure-four leglock wrapped around the ringpost. Austin appeared courageous as he hung in there despite the torturous pain that viewers assumed was being applied. At this point, line-walking Hart stumbled back toward underhanded and desperate, fetching the ring bell. He placed the weapon conveniently on the ring apron before recovering a metal folding chair. Though it seemed that Hart had decided the bell was not appropriate for the havoc he was fixing to wreak, the action was an ingenious plot device. Austin noted, "This was a plan to be able to use the bell later in the match. We're introducing the bell to be used later... that was my idea because Bret had a different idea to get into that final Sharpshooter which I didn't like. I needed something to put me at a weakened state."

With the chair, Hart attempted to snare Austin's lower leg into the fold as a call-back to October 1996, when Austin put former ally Brian Pillman out of commission by stomping his leg while it was wrapped in a steel chair. Known to fans as 'Pillmanizing', Hart delicately laced Austin's foot through the groove between the backrest and seat before ascending the ropes. A rejuvenated Austin removed the chair and struck quickly, whacking a precarious Hart across the back with the weapon, sending him rolling to the canvas in a heap. Austin followed up with several more strikes with the chair before stomping the groin of his nemesis. That act was followed by a camera pan to Hart's eight-year-old daughter Alexandria holding her hands over her eyes in the front row, unable to watch her father be thrashed by a sociopath in black tights. Exploitative? Ross urgently declared, "It's not for the weak at heart!" while Lawler dementedly cackled at her discomfort. In an era where a home invasion was used as a ratings stunt, the bundling of familial pain fit the changing narrative. Hart's elderly father, legendary grappler and promoter Stu Hart, was also shown at ringside with a worrisome expression across his weary face.

Austin switched up the assault, transitioning from streetwise malevolence to traditional technical wrestling by applying a version of an octopus stretch out of a Russian leg sweep. Proving his resourcefulness, a failure to draw Hart's surrender there led to a Boston crab from the defined brawler. Hart forced a break by snaring the bottom rope, a provision that made zero sense in a match with no disqualifications. Divinely, Austin only broke that hold when Shamrock nearly accosted him in an act where the official quite literally threw his weight around. Otherwise, the sadistic Texan's acquiescence would have been entirely out of place. Not that Austin's stock was in danger of plummeting; seconds later, he attempted to wrap Hart in his own Sharpshooter leg grapevine. Led to the raging stream by Austin's irresistible act, the Chicago hordes let out a mixture of cheers and astonished gasps at the gesture. Other than Yokozuna vanquishing Hulkamania with his own thunderous leg drop almost four years prior, using a wrestler's own gun against him was extremely uncommon.

Hart prevented being flipped into the hold with a deft rake of the eyes, giving giggly Lawler occasion to unintentionally foreshadow history by crowing, "Wouldn't that have been the greatest of all time - to have to submit to the Sharpshooter?!" Desert-dry, McMahon responded, "Hey, it could happen. It's just that painful!" Austin deposited Hart to the floor, sending the crumbling pillar crashing down in front of his immediate family with rancorous callousness. That too only boosted the swelling pro-Austin sentiment, drowning out any sympathy that time-tested family man Hart would customarily receive. Ironically, Austin would be the one soon eliciting sympathy from the 18,000-plus in attendance, because unbeknownst to McMahon, his two all-stars were about to break company ordinance to spike the drama.

"I looked Steve right in the eye and said, 'What would really make this a great match would be for you to get a little juice,'" Hart remembered, convincing Austin that the loss of blood would elevate his career in defeat. "Steve uneasily admitted that he'd never done that before, but he offered to try."

"Bret said, 'Steve, if you're going to pass out in the Sharpshooter, you need to have colour,'" confirmed Austin. "What he was saying was it would make me look weak if we didn't have colour; the visual would be better. He was a hundred percent right. It was very unselfish of Bret, because he was not looking out for Bret Hart; he was looking out for 'Stone Cold' Steve Austin."

Hart similarly gambled with getting one over on McMahon's seasoned eyes five years prior at *WrestleMania VIII*, discreetly cutting his own forehead during a skirmish for the Intercontinental Championship with Roddy Piper. Hart and 'Hot Rod' played off the breaking of skin as an accident, fooling everyone with the authority to punish them, including McMahon himself. The same could not be said for Ric Flair and Randy Savage in that night's WWF Championship contest, as Flair carved his own forehead with a ringside camera trained on him.

According to Hart, both of those men were fined for their wilful violation of the no-blood edict. Austin complied with Hart's suggestion, trusting they could pull it off expertly. While Hart lay selling the tumble outside the ring, he subtly spat a small blade into his hand, knowing the focus would be on Austin's unrepentant gloating between the ropes. Once Austin joined Hart outside the ring, the match took its famous turn.

"When I leaned down to pick up Bret... I'm telling him, 'judgment call,' meaning we've got these people hook, line, and sinker - I don't care if you cut me or not," Austin remembered, indicating that his hesitance came roaring back in a climactic moment. "As we slugged it out on the floor, I said, 'It's time!'" Hart remembered, "I faintly heard him say, 'Maybe we shouldn't.' I reversed his throw and told him, 'It's too late!' I hurled him crashing hard into the timekeeper, and he barrelled into the steel barricade. I calmly stepped over Steve, with Vince looking right at me and screaming fans only inches away. I grabbed his head and beat him with my fists like rubber hammers. Then I cut him perfectly, less than a half-inch long, and as deep as a dime slot. No one saw a thing."

"That cut was only about a quarter-inch long, maybe an eighth-inch deep," Austin estimated. "It was just the placing of the cut that allowed it to bleed so good. Sometimes people get overdone with the colour, and it's too much. This was just an absolute perfect blend. Me being bald-headed, no hair with a goatee, blood looks good on my skin tone."

The amount of crimson spilling from over Austin's left eye stained the ringside area, dark red dots contrasting on blue gymnastic mats. Through his unfocused stumble, Austin managed to spill blood all over Lawler's notes, noting that 'The King' kept those papers as a grim souvenir, not that the announcer could ever fathom forgetting the spectacle. It was also a testament to how approximate the blade-job was to McMahon, walking a pun-not-intended razor's edge. The rate of spillage became at once alarming, coating Austin's left wrist when he subconsciously wiped away the bothersome flow. Rivulets of blood were running down Austin's face as Hart slammed him into the guardrail and ring post to firmly gain control of what now resembled a fight to the death. By the time Hart rolled his messy opponent into the ring, the fans were clued in to how bad the damage was from an extended camera shot, letting out a collective gasp when they realised that Austin's brow and his left wrist could pass for two of the five Great Lakes. In a 2014 lookback upon the match, Austin narrated this part by saying, "I'm draining, I'm draining, I'm draining - I've got cottonmouth like a son-of-a-gun here, blood pouring off the temple of my head."

"Bret and Steve wanted to challenge themselves," said Shamrock. "They wanted to bring this thing to the point, that fine line where people couldn't see the difference whether it was [real] or it wasn't. I was refereeing the match and even *I* couldn't tell."

Austin was left bare, thoroughly vulnerable and compromised for the first time since forging his own hell raiser mantle nine months earlier. The brash and unapologetic outsider was getting unforgettable comeuppance from the cocksure sheriff, but the townspeople had no desire to see Austin run out on the rail. As a hell-bent Hart grabbed the folding chair to inflict further damage, fewer fans than before were egging on the attack. McMahon too pledged sympathy for the devil with as much journalistic neutrality as he could, calling Hart's use of the chair, "uncalled for." The harsh drop in his voice was still resonating with home viewers as Hart stabbed the lip of the back-rest into Austin's wounded knee on compulsive loop.

Austin avoided a subsequent Sharpshooter attempt by receipting Hart the earlier eye rake, and then staved off a beat down against the turnbuckles by explicitly kicking Hart below the belt. 'The Hitman' sold the punt on his back, knees curled subconsciously off the mat, while McMahon stripped away all semblance of impartiality by referencing the kick to Hart's testicles, noting, "Not so sure it wasn't deserved." Blood-soaked Austin soon sprang back to life with a Hogan-like second-wind, swinging the pendulum back to deafening cheers. McMahon's tone morphed yet again, declaring, "Austin, back up on his feet!" in a clipped, Howard Cosell-like frenzied delivery. Ross concurred, gushing, "Austin's a stud," personal admiration oozing through his professional call.

In Austin's gassed-up comeback, Hart was sent careening into the turnbuckles, sprung backward with car-crash force. Through some form of whiplashing diffusion, Austin began shaking his head violently, the adrenaline rush overwhelming. "Austin is ready to rock and roll!" Ross bellowed, as Austin took to stomping a drained Hart against the bottom turnbuckle pad. At the same volume, Ross took a practice swing with another potential call for babyface Stone Cold: "Austin is one tough S.O.B, and he is kicking a mud hole in Bret Hart!"

The coda to this particular flurry was an Austin superplex, punctuated by more 'oohs' from an enthralled crowd following a close-up of Austin's mug, now reddened and soaked to Carrie White on prom night levels. It's here that the final act began, Austin recognising his banana peel lying in wait. Hart was tossed onto the apron to ground him so that Austin could fetch an extension cord from the timekeeper's area. With a hint of an uncontrolled stagger in his step, Austin climbed back between the ropes and wrapped the cord around Hart's neck three times. To counter, Hart lifted the conveniently-placed ring bell from earlier and slammed it into unsuspecting Austin's head, sending him sprawling back to the canvas. After the fans had a moment to digest the swift turn of the tide, Hart snared the flailing Austin into his Sharpshooter, ostensibly cranking the injured knee, and leaving a pain-ravaged Austin to swim against the imaginary current, ominously-dark blood spewing from the wound near his left temple.

While Austin let out phlegmy, guttural groans that only seemed to hasten the loss of blood, referee Shamrock wanted an answer. There was none; Austin's sole focus was escaping this long-unbroken hold, no time to waste in even saying, "No." The babyface turn was hereby completed by this struggle against the odds, without any overt declaration necessary. There was much to be identified with the surly roughneck as he pressed up onto his palms, eyes clenched shut, blood descending in streaks down his face in what would become the defining image of the forthcoming age. Austin used his remaining strength to send Hart onto his face, seemingly breaking the Sharpshooter, only for Hart to keep his arm around Austin's left leg, resetting himself with little effort. Hart suggested precisely this finish as a parallel to Jack Nicholson in *One Flew Over the Cuckoo's Nest*, trying like hell to remove an indelibly-bolted sink so he could chuck it through the window of the mental home, and escape to go watch baseball's World Series. The incorrigible Nicholson failed at this task, to the bemusement of everyone watching. Austin's failure to break the Sharpshooter was to produce the same heart-breaking effect, turning antagonist into protagonist after a well-crafted build. Hart won, but Austin did not quit. No other ending would have worked.

With Hart cinching back up on Austin's legs, the mangled ruffian softened and became stationary. "Steve! Do you give up?!" Shamrock screamed. "If you do not answer me, I will stop the fight!" With Austin lulled into a physical abyss, Shamrock waved off Hart to end the match, the initial cheers underscored by the wailing guitar riff of 'the Hitman's' entrance music. At this point, it was not clear if a bad guy existed in that blood-stained ring. The only question lay in which of the two combatants, the winner or loser, was more heroic.

Hart killed two questions with one answer, celebrating only briefly to respectful adulation before returning his focus back to motionless Austin. Not satisfied with a hollow victory, a persistent Hart began kicking the leg of his unconscious opponent, a credibility-killer in light of Austin's resolve. Hart even attempted another Sharpshooter to his defenceless foe before being strong-armed away by Shamrock, via a magnificently-elevated waistlock throw. Shamrock assumed a stiff-armed stance, imploring Hart to fight a grappler with his full faculties if he was really a man. With the crowd firmly behind vigilant Shamrock, a disgusted Hart walked away, stepping through the ropes to the loudest chorus of boos he had received since he and brother-in-law Jim 'the Anvil' Neidhart teamed under the leadership of Jimmy Hart a decade earlier. Pausing a beat to survey the fans that he would come to view under a heel's eyes as turncoats, Hart modestly stepped down from the ring and began his jaunt back up the aisle, tagging hands with some fans, before pausing to flip off a goateed, college-age fan who offered his own middle finger initially. This was a dualism that Hart would come to know for the remainder of his time with Titan, but in the moment, his pride was showing.

"I loved it. The match. Everything," wistfully assessed Hart. "If I ever wanted my fans to remember just one picture of me, it would be that moment, as I was walking back to the dressing room."

The match itself received acclaim and accolades like few matches before it. Dave Meltzer of *The Wrestling Observer* graded it with a perfect five-star rating, only the third WWF match to that point to ace his personal rating system. Jim Cornette, never a particular fan of Titan's model of match presentation, gave the submission match high praise, stating, "That was my favourite WWF match because it felt like an old-fashioned NWA wrestling match. It wasn't a sports-entertainment match. It wasn't *clean* like Shawn Michaels' great matches with the ladders. It was dirty, it was real, it was more like a Mid-South or a Mid-Atlantic match. You felt it, you believed it. The blood, the people were into it. I loved that fucking match. That's the one I pick if I have to pick a WWF match that I really, really liked."

"I remember laying there with my eyes closed in a pool of blood, and it was probably the deepest sense of satisfaction I had in the ring," said Austin. "I knew all the chips were on the line, it was the semi-main, and the task at hand was to do a double turn, and we executed it with perfection."

For all intents and purposes, despite the magnitude and importance of the match as a whole, Hart was firmly on the backburner the second he disappeared behind the curtain. One week after *WrestleMania*, Hart made quick use of his heel turn through a reunion with brother Owen and in-law Davey Boy Smith, convincing the reigning Tag Team Champions to drop their petty squabbles and join him in his crusade against the ugly maw of Americana. Owen masterfully worked himself up to the point of tears as Bret professed his brotherly love, ending a three-year feud that had occasionally been fetched from the back of the fridge for a quick nuking.

For the first time since 1991, the Hart Foundation name had active relevance. It was not the New World Order, rather a cell whose membership was contingent on blood or marriage. A united family front against debauchery and skulduggery would have been a babyface troupe in any other era, but not in the American wrestling scene of 1997. In fact, the Hart Foundation would be babyfaces everywhere except for America, a precarious duplicity that called for a world war waged on stubborn pride.

LESS THAN six weeks after declaring that he had forfeited the WWF Championship on account of a purported career-ending knee injury, Shawn Michaels made a grand entrance preceding the night's main event, complete with in-ring pyrotechnic display. Performing his trademark double-bicep pose while deeply bending the injured right knee seemed to betray the tear drops in Lowell, especially as he hammed it up with boyish whimsy beneath the sparks. On the way down to the ring, Michaels was mobbed by fans, some of whom flashed the 'Kliq' hand gesture his way. Michaels returned the gestures with his own Kliq signal, which by this time had been usurped by the New World Order as their own form of fraternity handshake. On the apron prior to stepping through the ropes, Michaels flashed the signal once to the camera, at shutter speed quickness. Twenty-four hours later, Michaels' spit-brother Kevin Nash performed the gesture at a TV camera during *Monday Nitro*, yelping, "Right back 'atcha, HBK!" With Michaels unhappy at being asked to lay down for Sid and Hart days apart the previous month, his loyalty to Titan had every right to be questioned.

Michaels bellied up to the commentary table in time for the sixth WWF Championship switch in the previous four months, including Michaels' February abdication. This time, Sid would do the honours for The Undertaker after a long, plodding bout that was seemingly changed on the fly to a no-holds-barred match to allow for some elements of chaos in an otherwise pedestrian battle of monsters. The announcement of said stipulation would not be made until the match was six-minutes old, and only because McMahon told the home viewer exactly that while the two leviathans brawled by the security railing. Undertaker seemed to have made peace with the idea that the match had little ambition towards academia; Hart claimed that following his match with Austin, Undertaker told him, "Helluva match, man, not a chance in hell me and Sid are ever gonna top that!"

As for Hart, his night was far from over, despite leaving it all in the ring just an hour earlier. As the main event combatants came nose to nose, Hart stormed down to the ring to a wave of boos, selling obvious discontent. "Oh, imagine that; Bret being resentful of not being in the main event or being the man," spewed Michaels. Over the house microphone, Hart referred to Michaels as a, "phony little faker," as McMahon, in a peculiar visual, stood behind Michaels, apparently restraining him from getting out of his chair. While Michaels feigned fear against the tide of Hart's words, the focus turned to 'the Hitman' furthering his heel turn by berating Undertaker and Sid. The tirade ended with a Sid powerbomb to Hart, to both cheers of approval from the crowd, and a braying hyena-like laugh from Michaels.

Finally, ten full minutes after Michaels strutted down the aisle, the championship bout commenced. Within minutes, the limits of what Sid could do without technicians like Hart or Michaels to spring off of his mighty slams was apparent, as the champion worked a prolonged bear hug hardly two minutes into the headline match. At one juncture, the director switched to a split-screen of Michaels as he exchanged verbal haymakers with an agitated Lawler. At least the home audience had a soundtrack to keep them from falling into a lull. Later, Lawler further disparaged Hart for his whinier tone, to which Michaels added, "I've got an update on him too: I hear he doesn't like me!" For his part, McMahon huffed out a silly chuckle, trying to keep the mood light.

Another Sid rest hold prompted an excuse to cut to a wide shot of the expansive crowd, while Ross put over the attendance, and promoted the next pay-per-view - during the World Championship contest. After a spot where Sid planted Undertaker with his own Tombstone piledriver, Hart stormed the ring, striking Sid twice in the back with a steel chair as a receipt for the powerbomb. With the heel turn laid on doubly thick, Michaels rabbit-punched at Hart some more from behind the table, taunting, "He's bitter! He can't take it, the spotlight's not on him!" The storyline was that Hart's turn was expedited by an increase in legitimate injustices done to his character, and his confusion toward the fan base that now favoured outlaws, meaning Michaels' criticisms were completely off-script, and firmly on the side of personal attacks. Lawler, under his breath, grunted, "There's the pot calling the kettle black."

The monotonous exhibition finally ended with yet another Hart run-in, this time throating Sid across the top rope before the champion could perform his finishing powerbomb. Undertaker immediately Tombstoned Sid to a highly-favourable reaction and his second WWF Championship. In the aftermath, the commentators, Michaels included, put solely Undertaker on the pedestal as focus, save for Michaels' not-so-vague comment, "There've been a lot of men who've held that belt undeservingly, but I can say with all truth, that man deserves to be exactly where he's at!"

So ended the most anarchic *WrestleMania* to date, both on camera, and away from prying eyes. Undertaker's simplistic celebration took place beneath a light show that created the sensation of thunder and lightning inside of the Rosemont Horizon. There were indeed storm clouds forming overtop of the World Wrestling Federation, and only those aware of the impending squall had an inkling of the hazardous days ahead.

FIVE

AFTER THE SHOW, A GROGGY Austin used the ropes to pull up his battered body, re-establishing his dangerous streak by attacking assisting referee Mike Chioda by spiking him with the Stone Cold Stunner. After that brief assault, Austin returned to understated nobility, easing back to the dressing room with a pronounced limp, caked in his own blood. For his well-played poise, the fans offered up a round of applause that gradually increased in volume before it served as a musical bed to a thunderous chant of "AU-STIN, AU-STIN".

"I recognised and I let them in just a little bit," Austin said of the chants. "I didn't want to over-milk that part of the process yet, because there was still work to be done. I didn't want to say, 'Yeah, I'm a babyface,' or 'Yeah, I'm on board with you cheering me,' because I never needed anybody's support from the get-go. I always believed in myself."

Austin did not need to open the door to fan support; McMahon cut the ribbon himself as Austin hobbled away without assistance, stating for all to hear, "I've never seen anyone so gutsy that he wouldn't submit. So obstinate, so stubborn, so proud that he would not submit under that kind of pain - his body gave out on him. He passed out. I've never witnessed anything like that, ever. And refusing help! Refusing help from anyone. He'll go back and he'll take his pride with him back to the locker room. Have you witnessed anything like that in your life?"

Following an explicit zoom-in on the blood-spattered canvas, McMahon relayed a somewhat-wincing disclaimer to the home audience, plainly offering, "That was not a pretty match, and quite frankly, one that we're not necessarily proud to show you." But it was down this uncharted path with an insurrectionary character – one now firmly positioned in Titan's penthouse tier as a good guy.

It seemed like overkill to follow Austin's stretch on the crucible with the unquellable Chicago Street Fight, like following up a hearty steak dinner with fiery buffalo wings. The excessive violence that played out over the real-time duration of forty minutes was like nothing else in *WrestleMania*'s storied lore. If the WWF had become too 'fake' for its audience, Austin's gutsy limp back up the entrance aisle was more emphatic than any middle finger he could hold aloft.

He no longer had to sell his pronounced limp once he reached the end of the locker room tunnel. With "AU-STIN" chants still ringing in a chorus muffled by the sanctuary of the wrestlers' haven, Austin's ability to walk would only be hampered by any coagulated blood crusting over his eyes. Bearing literal scars of war, Austin had collaborated on the work of a lifetime with Bret Hart in a gritty submission match that held up a generation later as one of the greatest matches in wrestling, not just *WrestleMania*, history. Any burning streaks of crimson flowing down his face were downright chilly compared to the warmth of pride in his gut. As if co-assembling a violent performance for the ages was not enough of a convincing work for Austin, once backstage, he and 'the Hitman' immediately slipped into the second part of their wholesale pitch: convincing any inquiring minds that the blade job which had unleashed torrents of Austin's blood was merely a strike too snug from an amped-up Hart. Intentional bloodletting was still a no-no in a World Wrestling Federation that sought to stretch tight parameters, but even if Austin had copped to the blading conspiracy, it's unlikely that Austin would have experienced any wing-clipping during his undeniable breakout performance.

Austin found himself in a fortunate situation, not discrediting the hard work that had gone into shaping his career to this point. At the top of the card, his alignment swap with Hart placed Austin in a babyface class with Shawn Michaels, new WWF Champion The Undertaker, and Sycho Sid. Sid's general unreliability made him unlikely to assume the mantle of long-term babyface hero, along with his unfavourable standing with the influential Michaels. Undertaker faced an uncertain future as champion, largely untested in the role aside from a six-day transitional reign in 1991 that existed primarily to draw interest in a rematch with the dethroned Hulk Hogan at an experimental pay-per-view, *This Tuesday in Texas*. Since that time, Undertaker cemented his lot with Titan as the latter-day Andre the Giant, a towering novelty act that could perpetually anchor the cards. Logic dictated that a WWF pay-per-view guaranteed two noteworthy bouts: a WWF Championship contest, and Undertaker's match. How Undertaker would fare as literal golden boy was to be determined.

Austin's only other competition was Michaels, whose instability was continuing to manifest itself, only excusable by his unmatched ability to string together incredible in-ring performances, no matter his mental or physical state. The "lost smile" incident of the prior month was a deep gash in his long-term viability, and with the office and locker room alike tired of his frazzled, thin-skinned insecurities and antics, Michaels embodied the rock-star conundrum: a consummate show-stealer like no other, but with more baggage than an international airport. As real-life tensions between Michaels and Hart continued to boil, the flamboyant dynamo that had ascended Titan's apex one year earlier was continually looking like more trouble than his immense worth could balance.

As truculent Michaels antagonised heelish Hart from the safe distance of a commentator's chair at the end of *WrestleMania 13*, and Undertaker and Sid lumbered through a dull World Title closer, a physically-spent Austin could only become more eager about his future. It seemed with each ounce of fragmentation and uncertainly that plagued the rest of the main event scene, his path to the top was opening up.

Fifteen nights later, on April 7, Austin returned to the ring in the most inauspicious of ways: a singles bout against rudderless Billy Gunn during a live *Raw is War* in front of 3,500 fans in the industrialised city of Muncie, IN. With Hart off touring South Africa with half of the roster, there would be no rally for revenge, or settlement of unfinished business, on this night. Instead, an oddly-subdued Austin worked his first match as a full-fledged babyface, stomping out the kinks of what was to become a transcendent act.

One good sign: though the pop for Austin's glass-breaking intro was lukewarm at best, once Austin stepped through the entrance curtain, the cheers picked up to a more-than-acceptable level while he swaggered down *Raw's* steel-grated ramp. The cheers from the sparse crowd were downright convulsive when one realises Austin had to win them back moments after The Godwinns flung hog slop across The Legion of Doom's chests.

In this block of television, the Muncie crowd was charmed by every Austin comeback, even roaring for an intentional low blow delivered via a backward mule kick. Those cheers grew louder following referee Tim White's admonishment, when Austin flipped him off with both hands once the official's back was turned. "Stone Cold certainly doesn't know the words 'sportsmanship' or 'fair play'; he just likes to whip people's you-know-what!" Ross exclaimed on his headset, earning McMahon's patented yuk-yuk laugh, the Chairman's own ringing endorsement. Austin finished the extended exhibition with his Stunner following a missed Gunn clothesline. Post-match, Ross reinforced Austin's fortitude for refusing to quit at *WrestleMania*, while McMahon acknowledged that Austin, "impressed this capacity crowd."

That was more than could be said for Shawn Michaels, who delivered an extended in-ring monologue along the lines of self-serving character assassination against Hart. The fans in Muncie remained mostly silent as wild-eyed Michaels, the hand-selected babyface of the story, accused Hart of exploiting his own family for storyline purposes, receiving sustained jeers for flatly stating that Hart would sell out his own mother if he could. This was no 'fun' for a crowd that had enjoyed Austin's spirited exploits less than half-an-hour earlier, and no airing of dirty laundry, especially the type that exposed scripted immortals as dirty-faced angels, was as fun as watching a fresh new character run through a bag of tricks never before seen on a WWF stage.

MCMAHON DEEMED Austin heroic enough to be introduced in his customary phlegmy bark on the April 21 episode of *Raw* in Binghamton, NY, a table-setter for Austin's street fight with full-fledged heel Hart. One night earlier, Austin went over on Hart via disqualification to close out an innocuous *In Your House* pay-per-view in Rochester, and the workmanlike match was not quite on the level of their *WrestleMania* game-changer. In what would become the norm of the forthcoming age, a pay-per-view wrestling match was to be relegated into history's recesses by the mayhem on a free television show. To that end, Austin eschewed McMahon's proclamation of an Austin-Undertaker WWF Championship match for the following *In Your House*, ordering McMahon to shut his mouth while he began a steely tirade against Hart, a grudge that involved no gold. Austin was now the poster-child for mainstream wrestling's Age of Aquarius, the right-damn-now-generation that made week-to-week promotional vehicles in syndication even more obsolete. The pay-per-views would still be scheduled, but there would be no guarantee of the volatile powder kegs going unlit in the meantime.

By those terms, the story elements of April 21 *Raw* went off like a chain of proximity mines following Austin's opening spiel, in which he demanded that the ailing Hart show his face for a no-holds-barred street fight. The two pieced together a simple clash in t-shirts and jeans, concluding with Austin walloping Hart's leg with a steel chair several times before twisting him into a crude application of Hart's own Sharpshooter. The pain was legitimately searing: Hart was set to have overdue knee surgery days later, and the brawl would be the story impetus for side-lining him physically. "We'd forgotten to calculate for no knee wrap: the damage and pain were very real," Hart later said pertaining to Austin's initial chair strike, while conceding he could not tape or brace his knee beneath constrictive denim.

Needing a further touch of mayhem, in what history recorded as a signature 'Stone Cold' moment, Austin hid in the driver's seat of the ambulance set to transport the writhing Hart to the local hospital, viciously seizing control of the vehicle once the gurney was loaded into the rear. The attack found a sensible groove: not as far-fetched or controversial as the story of the Pillman home invasion, but far enough above the confines of wrestling-as-usual that the audience would still be astounded. On-screen President Gorilla Monsoon, a soft-spoken gentle giant from the rose-tinted old guard, was scripted to loudly berate Austin for his vigilance, ordering him out of the arena with an uncharacteristic cry of, "I want you to get your ass out of the building, right now!" The curse was sharply emphasised, giving the impression that Austin's cloud of influence was capable of infecting the stern morality of yesteryear. The fan tastes had turned rogue, and golden agers were not immune either.

A shade over 200,000 homes parted with $19.95 to watch Austin unsuccessfully challenge for Undertaker's WWF Championship on May 11 at a secondary *In Your House* subtitled *Cold Day in Hell*. That number of homes was up roughly 25,000 purchases from *Revenge of The Taker* a scant three weeks earlier at the same price, indicating some early returns for Austin as a headliner. The fans in Richmond, VA at the pay-per-view seemed confused as to who to cheer between the two fan favourites, since neither was particularly fit to be jeered. Austin's beef with the Harts, and Undertaker's long-running saga with former manager Paul Bearer, had dominated television leading up to the B-show, so there was no clear reason to cheer one man over the other. With these circumstances in mind, a fourteen percent increase in home buys largely on the merit of Austin challenging for Titan's biggest prize spoke highly of his increasing magnetism.

As for the match itself, Austin was given a visual win over the largely-protected Undertaker by delivering his Stone Cold Stunner, clean as a whistle. The necessary chicanery that cost him the match was Brian Pillman, firmly associated with Hart, clanging the ring bell before a fall could be rendered. After the confusion cleared, Austin was allotted another moment of gleam: he reversed a rejuvenated Undertaker's attempt at a Tombstone before having that table turned back on him, taking the loss to the unsustainable piledriver. Rendering WWF's 'Phenom' vulnerable at two critical passes was no coincidence, as evidenced by Austin cleaning house of an invading Hart Foundation in the aftermath, including toppling over wheelchair-bound Hart, and running off the rest of the extended family with one of his crutches. For good measure, Austin concluded the night by laying out Undertaker with another Stunner, telling everyone watching who the winner ought to have been.

Determined to keep Austin a main eventer without actually putting the top belt on him just yet, Austin and Michaels went over on Owen Hart and Davey Boy Smith at the Memorial Day *Raw* to become WWF World Tag Team Champions. The belt was Austin's first physical piece of recognised gold with Titan, although his partnership with Michaels overshadowed his afforded token. In storylines, the only commonality that loner Austin and emotionally-inconsistent Michaels shared was their compulsion to drive the Hart Foundation into ruin. Beyond that parallel, Austin was still balking at allies, further clouding the notion of concrete babyface and heel alignments. The two would brawl with one another in the interim weeks before the title match, which itself was thirteen minutes of frenzied activity. The crowd in Evansville, IN bought into the entire evening's drama with their own frenzy of excitement, sustaining nuclear levels of response for the main event, in which Austin pinned Smith after 'The British Bulldog' had been floored by Michaels' superkick.

WHILE AUSTIN'S stock had never been higher between the ropes, his health was becoming a concern. In early June, Austin sought a second opinion for neck pain after the first doctor he consulted had suggested retirement. A second doctor warned Austin that while he could continue to wrestle, the pain he felt stemmed from erosion in his neck vertebrae, and that he would have to work through residual pain.

Work he did, tearing down the house at the 1997 *King of the Ring* in Providence, RI with Michaels in a twenty-two-minute slugfest, the first of its kind on pay-per-view amongst reigning Tag Team Champions. Pundits wondered who would take the fall amid two company trump cards on seemingly divergent paths, the answer to which was a resounding "neither". Fans chanted "bullshit" for a non-finish that saw both performers disqualified for separately attacking officials, but the road to that dud ending was wild. If Providence was a barometer, it could accurately rate each man's general standing with WWF crowds at large: the talented-yet-tumultuous Michaels received a mixed reaction of cheers and boos, accentuated by the screams of charmed females. Austin did not receive that sort of rock star-groupie adulation, but his reception could be termed as sustained positivity nonetheless.

After Michaels went AWOL again the next night, Austin continued to accept partners only under protest, continuing his streak of standing on his own two legs unless numbers needed to be made up. One detour from that image came in filling Michaels' void as tag title co-holder, and it seemed as though it were an attempt to humanise Austin to a palpable degree. Revealing Austin's beating heart was Mick Foley, who had been lobbying to be 'Stone Cold's' new partner in his Mankind guise, only for Austin to violently reject him in disgust. When the time came for Austin to wrestle Hart and Smith for what were essentially the vacant belts on July 14, Foley interjected himself into the match not as Mankind, but rather Dude Love, the jive-talking flower child that Foley had invented as a Long Island teenager, a caricature of the high hopes he had held for himself as a debonair wrestling personality.

A month prior in a sit-down interview with Jim Ross, Foley had outlined the character with the use of some grainy home movies filmed in the early 1980s, drawing the line between Dude Love's resonant self-confidence and flair, opposite Mankind's grim outlook and dishevelled appearance. Dude was immediately well-received. The endorsement grew when Austin, initially wearing a look of perplexity, merrily tagged Dude into the match. The duo took the win after Austin planted Smith with his Stunner, allowing Dude the pin, Foley's own first championship in the territory. Though Austin soon went back to his bewilderment at Foley's hammy duplicity, especially as Dude gyrated with a pair of mini-skirted revellers that scuzzy Mankind would never get a second look from, something became clear: Austin possessed Teflon-qualities. Something as silly and potentially inane as Mankind's metamorphosis into a tie-dyed pacifist could have been groan-worthy, but an endorsement from Austin only galvanised the audience further. Austin would never be caught dead frolicking in the meadows with an acoustic guitar and some incense, but as a physical juxtaposition, he possessed the power of respected authority. As an ironic voice of the village, Steve Austin was bulletproof.

Bulletproof was one thing, but shatter-proof was another. On August 3, at an unusually early *SummerSlam* in terms of calendar placement, everything that Austin had built for himself was nearly wiped out in the blink of an eye.

From the signature shatter of glass, the fans in East Rutherford, NJ, skirting the shadows of WWF's New York City barometer, loudly heralded Austin's arrival at the summer's cornerstone pay-per-view. On commentary, McMahon mixed equal parts befuddlement and pride when he said of Austin, "Don't ask me why they love him, but they sure do - he's as ornery as a rattlesnake!" While Hart and Michaels paced the locker rooms like paranoid carnivores on the Serengeti, fixing sideways glances to compound each other's personal mistrust and angst, Austin remained free from political snares, above the sabotage of others, and without the desire to sully his hands in it. Instead, those hands were put to use raking in cash: *SummerSlam* that year topped over $200,000 in merchandise sales at the Meadowlands, much of that going toward white-print-on-black 'Austin 3:16' t-shirts, the counterpunch to the pool of nWo merchandise revenue that Eric Bischoff was doing backstrokes in.

That night, Austin was working with Owen Hart for Hart's Intercontinental Championship, with an additional wager: confident Austin decreed that he would literally kiss Hart's buttocks if he could not capture the gold. Logic dictated that an Austin win was inevitable with the company rightfully unwilling to subject their new cash cow to any form of mojo killer. The two worked a spirited match, more in line with consummate wrestling than what would become Austin's trademark roughhouse brawling. Knowing the heel tropes as second-nature traits, Hart keyed in on Austin's neck as a methodical interlude. "Austin, in his career, has had neck problems," Ross enunciated as a plot point, while Hart built his heat by working over the neck with wear-down submissions, as well as a majestic-looking German suplex.

Austin began a comeback close to fifteen minutes into the bout, striking back after a rest hold. He flung Hart into the ropes for the next spot: a gutwrench lift, which Owen would counter into a seated Tombstone piledriver, a move with especially dire consequences if not done safely. Prior to the bout, Austin suggested the Tombstone spot to Hart as a means for creating a dramatic false finish, and claimed a disagreement was had over Hart's preferred method of execution.

"I said, 'You're going to drop to your knees, right?' And he said, 'No, I'm going to drop to my ass.'" Austin would later state. "When he assured me I'd be okay, I took his word that I'd be okay. I didn't think twice about it. I had mentioned my concerns to him twice. But in an inverted Tombstone piledriver, done the way Undertaker does it, it's always knees, not ass."

After Hart flipped out of Austin's lift, he elevated his opponent into the piledriver hold, but held him critically low. The top of Austin's skull was level with Hart's kneecaps when Hart started into the jump, and a significant portion of Austin's head was visible when Hart extended his legs horizontally for the landing. "There was a little bit of cushion and impact on my thighs. His neck was just so vulnerable that it kinked, and he just went numb," remembered Owen. After the thudding impact, Austin ended up on his back, unable to move his legs. His arms rested on his elbows, hands barely waving like front porch wind chimes. Hardly able to lift his head, Austin clearly informed Hart that something had gone horribly wrong, leading Hart to noticeably and awkwardly stall for time.

"I knew then there was something wrong," Hart said. "Austin said, 'I can't feel my fingers.' My first concern was, 'Is he paralysed? Is he done?' It's funny - in that twenty seconds, it felt like forever. You know, slow motion, what do you do? Do I look at the promoter and tell him, 'This isn't part of the match?'"

"There was nobody safer to work with than Owen Hart," Jim Cornette attested. "It was like a Tombstone, but Austin's feet weren't straight up, they were over Owen's head, and when he jumped, he didn't drop to his knees, he jumped and did the sit-down thing. We immediately knew something was wrong, because Austin wasn't getting up, and Austin had to win!"

"I remember when it happened, I was going to kick out on two and a half or two and three-quarters," Austin recalled. "I was going to sell the piledriver, but I was going to kick out of it at the last second. When my head hit the mat, it was as if a big gong went off in my body. I remember kind of picking my head up from the mat and telling the referee, Earl Hebner, 'Tell him not to fucking touch me, I can't move.' I said, 'Tell him to buy me some time.'"

"Now he's gonna kiss my ass!" a perplexed Hart yelled at the equally-confused audience as Austin began to flail his head and hands in an attempt to execute some type of movement. Hart paced the ring, alternating between taunting the fans with a hasty "Canada" chant while helplessly peering down at Austin's horrifying predicament. After a long minute, Austin finally rolled onto his stomach at a turtle's pace. Knowing this was as good a go-home cue as there was going to be, Hart turned his back. Austin, crawling as though the canvas were covered in tacks and broken glass, painfully made it to Hart, tugging his right leg with minimal strength until the titleholder fell backwards into a threadbare school-boy roll-up. Hart allowed himself to be pinned and the crowd erupted at the result.

"My two-year-old daughter could have rolled me up better," noted Owen, "He didn't have the strength to do anything else." Austin has his own take on the final seconds of the bout. "I meant for that to be the end of it, but Owen kicked right out after three," he complained. "Why? To make himself look strong, like he was barely beat. That kick-out hurt me like hell too, and could easily have injured my neck further."

Bret Hart recalled that his younger brother was "beside himself with guilt and dread" after the accident. Though he noted that Owen held his emotions together during the agonising stretch, once behind the curtain, Owen staggered past him, "crushed and in a daze."

"I watched that damn tape over and over and over again," recalled Austin, "I cannot tell you how many times I watched that match, well not the match, but the accident." Austin could barely roll back over in the aftermath, needing Earl Hebner's assistance to get back to a seated position, which was only temporary as he slumped back to the canvas. Officials Jim Korderas and Tim White rushed to the ring to help Austin to his feet, and unlike at *WrestleMania*, there was no macho posturing in the form of a violent rebuke toward authority. Hebner managed to wedge the belt into Austin's hand, but the new champion could barely hold it aloft, his body contorting like a Slinky against the bracings of the referees.

The temporary paralysis sent a wave of panic through Austin, one of few rushes he was capable of feeling in the moment. In truth, an MRI conducted days later revealed damage to the C-4 and C-5 vertebrae, level with the lower jawbone. The injuries were consistent with what's known in medical vernacular as a *stinger*, a neurological injury that can cause precisely the numbness that Austin endured. The first specialist Austin met with recommended retirement, but with fat cheques waiting to be cashed, that was not an option. Austin vacated both the Intercontinental and Tag Team Championships while letting his spine heal, and as with the physical gold it seemed his momentum could dissipate as well. After all, what good was 'Stone Cold' if he was not engaging in knock-down, drag-out brawls befitting of his cultivation?

"I was out for three or four months after that, and I didn't really think I was going to get back in because my doctor was saying, 'No, no, no,'" Austin revealed. "He wasn't going to clear me. That was my first experience with an injury of that magnitude. I had all these red flags going, warning me not to get back in the ring."

As upsetting as the physical jeopardy was for Austin in a multitude of ways, adding to his mental burden was his claim that Hart did not once call him during his convalescence, or even offer any form of apology for nearly ending his career.

"When he didn't call me at my house afterward, that kind of upset me a bit," Austin lamented years after that fact. "It was like, 'Hey, if I damn near paralysed someone, I'd be calling them every damn day of the week!' I don't remember him calling. I just figure you fuck a guy up like that, you say 'Hey man, my bad', or whatever. I think he might have said something in the dressing room, I don't remember, that was such an emotional blur of a time backstage"

Austin also admitted the missed opportunity for contact carved an irremediable rift between he and the youngest Hart brother, noting, "It was never the same between us. I didn't think he was as funny as I used to think he was. When we'd pass in the hall or in the back, I'd say hi, but we never really spoke much after I came back. I could never figure that out. Did I hate Owen? No. That's just the business and we weren't really friends to start with. Did I want to work with him after that? No, I didn't. I didn't want to do business with him again. Right or wrong, that's how I felt."

MAKING THE most of the awful circumstances, Austin was put to use in the sparing role of human lightning strike, delivering a quick beating with little physical risk. Not only was the role safe for Austin to handle, but it would also keep him fresh. A little nibble for the desirous audience would keep them begging for more, only enhancing his value as a prime time player.

After five weeks off the road, Austin appeared in person alongside Dude Love at *In Your House: Ground Zero* on September 7 to officially abdicate the Tag Team Titles. Austin, portraying his usual agitation, delivered his Stone Cold Stunner to Jim Ross during the belt handover. In the conclusion of a four-way tag team bout to fill the vacancy, Austin continued his saga with Hart by planting him with another Stunner, allowing the Headbangers to win the belts. The swathe of destruction continued two nights later at a *Raw* taping, where the angle consisted of Hart filing a restraining order against Austin. Jerry Lawler, presiding as interviewer during the segment, would be the recipient of a Stunner to continue the random acts of violence.

On September 22, *Monday Night Raw* emanated from New York City's sports mecca Madison Square Garden for the first time ever. For decades, the McMahon family's business of athletics and soap opera intertwined romantically with the pillars of Pennsylvania Place. New York's cultural melting pot was the ethnicity of the WWF itself: colourful characters from across the globe herding into the Garden as though it were wrestling's Ellis Island – opportunity awaited between those walls. If Austin, limited as he was by his present impairment, was going to make the time during his injury layoff count, something had to go down inside MSG.

Reinforcing that point, just as McMahon and company finished running down the evening's card, Austin made a grand appearance in the cheap seats with a live microphone. Almost drowning in a sea of exuberant humanity, he bellowed, "Ain't no way you can have a *Monday Night Raw* in New York City without 'Stone Cold' Steve Austin!" The camera happened to be focused on a mostly-placid McMahon when Austin made the vow that somebody "would get their ass whipped" that evening.

Austin's next strike came at the conclusion of a match within the tournament to fill the Intercontinental title vacancy, with Owen Hart defeating on-and-off camera ally Brian Pillman by disqualification after Goldust interjected himself. Goldust ran Pillman off, leaving Hart to gloat proudly over the victory. Naturally, that was the setup for Austin to pummel him from behind before getting swarmed by a gaggle of police officers assigned to enforce Hart's kayfabed order of protection. Austin engaged in a stand-off with the club-wielding cops, leading to McMahon, still very much a benign announcer when the red lights were on, hitting the ring to try restoring order.

Acting as a concerned father, McMahon attempted to appeal to Austin's senses, saying that nobody wanted to see Austin end up paralysed from pushing through his limits. The hipper New York crowd saw the segment for its apparent ending, and began buzzing en masse for Austin to draw the conclusion for them. Moments later, Austin feigned appreciation for McMahon's goodwill, before grunting, "You can kiss my ass!" With that defiant cry came a hallmark Stunner, the first of many for McMahon. Laying on the canvas, twitching as though Austin lodged a stun-gun into his torso, McMahon could hear the fever pitch that the New York crowd was whipped into, only turning to boos when the rent-a-cops slapped handcuffs on Austin and took him away. The ensuing "Austin" chants sounded like the cries of protestors railing against the injustice suffered by their cult personality of choice. Austin was clearly that choice, the flavour of the new age, and McMahon's constituency had made that resoundingly clear.

SIX

EYEBROWS WERE RAISED WHEN ECW'S maiden pay-per-view *Barely Legal* pulled in a 0.26 buyrate, equivalent to around 104,000 purchases. Considering that no other wrestling outfit had penetrated the pay-per-view market so effectively outside of WWF and WCW, the lure of the unvarnished ECW product was a startling revelation. By comparison, in late-1988, the eroding pillars of what had been Verne Gagne's American Wrestling Association cobbled together their only attempt at a pay-per-view through a consortium of other promotions. What was known as *SuperClash III* drew a dismal estimated 40,000 buys, and the AWA would cease running shows within the next two years.

But the AWA, through Gagne's stringent view on what wrestling should always be, changed so little with the times that calling the company an 'alternative' would be misleading. As ECW caught the eyes of weary wrestling fans in the mid-nineties, the Philadelphia outfit was precisely this alternative to stale New York wrestling, as well as the manifestation of Hulk Hogan's self-indulgence that had infested WCW. Accordingly, Vince McMahon and Eric Bischoff began to dial their own products toward incorporating unpredictability, as well as blighting danger to what were previously comparable to live-action Saturday morning cartoons. That 104,000 households sheltered at least one person willing to spend their Sunday evening taking in the pandemonium that was ECW *Barely Legal* spoke of a considerable demand. Certainly, ECW's pseudo-infomercial on the February 24 edition of *Monday Night Raw* elevated their profile to an even wider cult.

While Titan tapped into ECW's essence, WCW began to make plays for the principals involved. Ten days after *Barely Legal* aired, Scott 'Raven' Levy, who had dropped the ECW Championship to fifty-two-year-old Terry Funk at the pay-per-view, let Paul Heyman know that he would be leaving for Atlanta after signing a three-year deal worth $225,000 per annum. Levy had spent the previous two years repurposing himself with the Raven character that deftly displayed manic and morose characteristics, a far cry from his pestiferous 1992 turn in WCW as Scotty Flamingo, a Florida-based surfer bedecked in popular neon colours of the time. After bringing those obnoxious qualities to his managerial role of Johnny Polo in the WWF shortly thereafter, the invention of Raven was downright startling. His monotoned poetic ramblings, delivered with crimped hair shrouding his disinterested eyes, read like a malevolent hybrid of Kurt Cobain and Jack Kerouac, and suited the disconnect of Generation X. If any character aside from Austin was the ideal affront to pro wrestling's antiquated model, it was Levy's Raven.

The weekend of *Barely Legal* made for an interesting situation. The pay-per-view took place from the company's home base, Philadelphia's ECW Arena, while WCW's *Monday Nitro* the following evening emanated from Philly's CoreStates Spectrum. On Saturday, April 12, WCW ran a house show in Pittsburgh, and a number of talents had made the cross-state trek, arriving in Philadelphia well before nightfall on Sunday. As such, a number of WCW performers paid visits to their industry peers on their ascendant night. Both Dean Malenko and Rocco Rock, vital parts of the ECW championship scene throughout 1994-95, hoped to catch up with old friends before the show went on the air. Kevin Sullivan attended the festivities after the show, flanked by former Dungeon of Doom ally Bill 'Hugh Morrus' DeMott, as well as ring announcer David Penzer.

The arrivals of Malenko and Rock, as well as WCW referee Nick Patrick, were cause for concern among a locker room that had spent much of the previous few weeks with their collective stomach in a knot. "There was a lot of anxiety, a lot of nerves," recalled Danny Doring. "I remember Paul probably being one of the worst. Even Taz, who never showed any emotion whatsoever, seemed nervous." While the WCW contingent was looking to be nothing more than peaceful and well-wishing, their presence could well have been a vigorous shake to the hornet's nest that were the boys and girls that comprised ECW. In Heyman's recollection of the night, he remembered that the mere word of the WCW talents hanging by the back gate almost led to a confrontation which he quickly had to quell.

"We can't even let friends in tonight from other organisations because we can't trust anybody," Heyman said he told the outsiders, snuffing out a fuse before it could be lit.

At the time, only four men that were scheduled to wrestle on that night's show had ever wrestled on an American pay-per-view, three of whom were ECW Champion Raven, ECW Television Champion Shane Douglas, and crowd favourite Sabu. The fourth was former NWA World Champion Terry Funk, the sentimental choice for a two-match parlay on the card. The woven yarn was that if Funk could outlast The Sandman and Stevie Richards in a triple threat match, he would have an immediate shot at Raven's ECW title. Anyone that knows the Disney formula by heart, and was also aware of a banquet held in Funk's honour the night before the pay-per-view, could have seen the ending a mile away.

Besides the four veteran wrestlers of differing renown, the pay-per-view depths were unexplored terrain for everyone else working a match that night. With this in mind, Heyman gathered the entire roster backstage before show time to give his rendition of William Wallace's "freedom" speech. Standing on a staircase in the back of the repurposed bingo hall, Heyman looked down upon his graciously-loyal subjects, and delivered an uplift that was famously immortalised on Barry Blaustein's documentary *Beyond the Mat*.

"Seventeen million homes that have availability for this show tonight," began Heyman softly, "and will pay twenty dollars, hopefully, for the privilege to see you guys do what you have done for three and a half years. Thank Terry Funk for all he's done for this company. For [his] help putting us on the map. For being unselfish in selfish times. For taking the young guys and showing them a better way."

Heyman's inflection began to rise for the heart-pumping flourish, continuing, "Tonight we have a chance to say, 'Yeah, you're right. We're too extreme. We're too wild. We're too out of control. We're too full of our own shit.' Or we have a chance to say, 'Hey - fuck you, you're wrong! Fuck you, we're right!' Because you have all made it to the dance, 'cause believe me - this-is-the-dance!"

"They all had lumps in their throats, even Paul E.," remembered Funk, who sat in front of the gathered horde while Heyman rhapsodised in his Scarsdale grunt. "They knew they had truly been a part of building something and having it become at least somewhat successful."

Even if the talents had worked their matches with nothing but ice water coursing their veins, the trouble spots that popped up were beyond their control.

Moments before *Barely Legal* beamed out to the pay-per-view audience, announcer Joey Styles took to the ring for his customary welcoming of everyone watching. Ordinarily, Styles would stand in an otherwise empty ring while all the rowdies in attendance hooted and hollered at the top of their lungs, spontaneously breaking in an "E-C-DUB!" chant. Then after the noise would slightly subside, Styles would energetically welcome everyone to the event in question.

Styles readied himself to count down the arena crowd to show-time, the entertainment equivalent of a "T-minus" from ten. As he went into the count, it was quickly apparent that his microphone was completely dead. Sensing trouble, the ECW Arena crowd began counting down in his stead, knowing their cue and filling the awkwardness while Styles was handed a working microphone.

The home audience never would have known there was a problem.

Other crises were also well-disguised from the home viewers. A blood-soaked Funk's miraculous victory over Raven in the finale had to take place as quickly as possible, when it was realized that the cut-off time for the pay-per-view was closing in. Funk duked it out with Richards and Sandman in the semi-main, all the while Heyman panicked backstage, realising that the hourglass of air-time was running low on sand. As the portly producer shed a gallon of sweat at the possibility of his show ending unceremoniously, the outgoing ECW Champion was the precise opposite.

"Raven was as cool as the other side of the pillow, like Joe Montana in Super Bowl XXIII," Doring remembered. "He had no time to finish the match with Terry. The pay-per-view was going to end; they were going to cut it off at a certain time. Paul's screaming, everyone is nervous, and Raven just says, 'Paul - I got it.' It had no bearing on him whatsoever, and that was pretty cool to see. He went out there and he did it."

After barely seven minutes, the main event concluded with weary Funk cradling Raven, pinning him for the feel-good ending, and setting off an explosion of cheers inside the ECW Arena. Funk held the title aloft among a sea of ringsiders, hugging protégé Dreamer right before the second explosion - this one, technological.

The overworked power supply had blown out, less than thirty seconds after Funk folded up Raven and held his shoulders down for the count. The lights inside the ECW Arena were a victim of the power failure, shrouding the jubilation under darkness. Had the generator blown a minute earlier, nobody at home would have seen the emotional conclusion, and it would have cast a shadow on ECW's big night – literally and figuratively.

"Fifteen seconds after we went off the air, the generator blew," Heyman recalled. "And the backup generator blew with it. The blowout was so bad it got both generators."

Despite the book-ending of technical gaffes, Extreme Championship Wrestling had done it. No matter what anyone had said before, or would say on future days, they had made it to pay-per-view. They did the impossible. All that was left to do as the calendar rolled over to April 14 was celebrate their unlikely triumph.

WHILE BARELY *Legal* begat a celebration for the ECW militia, a victory of sorts against some type of mainline conformity, there was one name among the group that was not feeling so harmonious. For twenty-six-year-old Robert Szatkowski, known professionally for the limitless elasticity he routinely displayed under the name Rob Van Dam, his résumé upon arriving in ECW in early 1996 spoke for itself. Risky dives and flips, combined with action-hero roundhouse kicks, quickly placed him into the tier with Chris Jericho and Rey

Misterio, Jr, as the wave of talent that adequately replaced the departures of Chris Benoit, Eddy Guerrero, and Dean Malenko. Where ECW needed finesse as buffer between comedy and carnage, Van Dam was part of the unit that could provide it. Misterio would bolt for WCW by spring 1996, and Jericho would follow right behind him later that summer. By the end of 1996, Too Cold Scorpio headed north to Titan, joined by recent ECW imports from All-Japan Pro Wrestling Doug Furnas and Philip 'Dan Kroffat' LaFon. Through all the constant changes to the roster, Van Dam remained a dependable bright spot throughout 1996, first warring over respect with real-life comrade Sabu, and then teaming with him in feverish battles with Furnas and Kroffat, as well as the Eliminators. In spite of his portrayal of a petulant, disrespectful snot, Van Dam was turned babyface on the merit of his enthralling work, which had become an indelible part of the ECW allure long before the end of the year.

It was curious, then, that Van Dam was not originally scheduled for *Barely Legal*, in spite of his value to the company. There were seven billed matches, including three championship bouts, the long-awaited Taz-Sabu showdown, and a six-man tag featuring dynamic talents from Japan's Michinoku Pro organisation, but no room for the man that would soon bill himself as, "The Whole Fucking Show." One of the matches for the card pitted two gifted technicians that had been with ECW for less time than Van Dam had put in. Among the duo were recent Titan exile Chris Candido, who had fled his WWF role of Bodydonna Skip in the fall of 1996, and Jericho's training partner and stoic counterpart Lance Storm, who had only debuted on February 1, 1997 with ECW. Van Dam ended up working the pay-per-view anyway, after Candido sustained a bicep injury in the final week of March, and thus 'RVD' would step in with Storm. In spite of the sudden opportunity, Van Dam's ego was still ailing.

"I was a little irritated that I wasn't originally going to be on *Barely Legal*," Van Dam mused. "I ended up going on as a substitute for Chris Candido, and I was upset about that. I usually 'listen to the universe', and I thought it was telling me that this might be something that's good for my career, to get the hell out of here where I'm not appreciated, and go where someone's trying to take care of you better."

One month before the pay-per-view, a jilted Van Dam strategically appeared backstage at the March 17 edition of *Monday Nitro* in Savannah, GA, seeking the graces of appreciation. While watching such one-time ECW talents like Misterio and his professional nemesis Dionicio 'Psicosis' Castellanos take to the skies with unmatched virtuosity, Van Dam wondered if it was time to join the next graduating class of ECW performers.

"I was there to say 'hi' to some friends, as I lived in Savannah at the time," Van Dam recounted of the night. "I also did want to be seen there, to stir up the gossip for business purposes. I was legitimately considering leaving ECW for WCW."

That evening, the estranged Van Dam spoke with Eric Bischoff. Bischoff quietly took Van Dam aside and quickly put together an offer to bring the Michigan-born grappler's talents on board. By Van Dam's accounts of the meeting, the offer presented to him was worth 'substantial money.' It was enough to strongly weigh the possibility of plying his trade with a company that a number of ECW forebears now worked for.

By the end of March, Van Dam had informed Heyman that he was considering leaving ECW to head south. Heyman held a lengthy meeting with the roster after the Easter Sunday show in Monaca, PA, a sleepy borough northeast of Pittsburgh in which Shane Douglas used his local pull to help promote events. There, Heyman urged unity, because the biggest night of ECW's existence sat merely two weeks away. Reportedly, Heyman told his talent that if any of them attended the April 14 *Nitro* in Philadelphia, he would consider their professional and personal relationships with him severed. He also stressed that if anybody wanted to leave ECW, then they could come to him and he could either arrange a meeting with McMahon, or give them a release to legally contact anyone at WCW. Van Dam's situation was not brought up during Heyman's extended monologue, but word would soon leak out anyhow.

On April 5, Van Dam worked a match with Anthony 'Pitbull #2' Durante at the Lost Battalion Hall in Rego Park, NY, in what would be the last show prior to *Barely Legal*. News of Van Dam's apparent break for Atlanta, and the gist of Heyman's talent meeting, appeared in the dirt sheets three nights earlier, and savvy readers got the word out in time for 800 New York fans to serenade Van Dam with chants of "You Sold Out!"

It was more of same come the second televised match of *Barely Legal*, when Van Dam received those same chants to go along with some appreciative cheers from the home crowd in Philadelphia. None of the near-1,200 fans on hand were damning him when he executed a picturesque somersault dive to the outside onto a waiting Storm. The spotty exhibition trucked along, mostly sound tracked by amazed cheers, though there was still audible derision. After Van Dam hit a low chair-assisted dropkick into a cornered Storm's face, a segment of the crowd attracted Van Dam's attention with a chant of "Sell out!" Late in the contest, Van Dam slipped off the ropes while attempting a springboard kick, barely salvaging the move with an improvised back-elbow. Both men lay in a heap while Philadelphia unleashed a heavy "You fucked up" chant, less mercy for the apparent defector. The annoyance turned to Storm, who struck Van Dam in the head with a chair so lightly that the Canadian was almost booed out of the venue. Van Dam spun the finish toward satisfaction by roundhouse-kicking the chair into Storm's face (an act known in wrestling jargon as "The Van Daminator"), and immediately executing a standing moonsault for the pin.

The chants of, "You Sold Out!" started up once more in the post-mortem. Van Dam picked up the house microphone and began with a simple heel promo, proclaiming that he did not need the respect of Storm or the fans, before weaving in real sentiment by declaring, "I don't give a shit about respect from any of the boys back there in the ECW dressing room, including Paul E.!" Van Dam then directly addressed his consternation at being an alternate for the show. "I sold out to myself by putting my boots on and getting in the ring tonight," Van Dam raged, before justifying the reversal of his real-life principle by noting that the match with Storm put him on the map to not only demand more money from ECW, but, in Van Dam's precise verbiage, "elsewhere". This was not a crafty bit of storytelling designed to cast Van Dam as a mercenary that would ultimately wind up staying with ECW; for all intents and purposes, Van Dam would be out the door by mid-June, working the story as an unsympathetic turncoat to make his eventual exit an easier pill to swallow. Later in the show, Van Dam appeared again, assisting Sabu in a post-match beat down of Taz, and again milking his own predicament by goading the crowd, informing them that he loved to "work Mondays."

By late-April, Van Dam had blown off his WCW offer. The heat had been so incredible at the pay-per-view that Heyman had found value in Van Dam as an anti-ECW property, similar to what Jerry Lawler had been portraying on WWF programming. At this time, Heyman presented Van Dam with a plan that seemingly more than made up for his initial omission from *Barely Legal*. He was going to portray Van Dam as wrestling's most talked-about freelancer.

"Through some talks at this time with Paul, I discovered that Paul had some connections with WWF," Van Dam remembered. "It was actually his idea to have me appear somehow on WCW, then pull a switcharoo and appear on WWF. I knew this was a chance to really have the spotlight of the entire industry on me jumping fences from promotion to promotion. It sounded like a great idea if we could pull it off."

The WCW part of the plan would never come to fruition. After Bischoff had worked himself out of Brian Pillman's contract during Pillman's attention-seeking "Loose Cannon" phase, there was simply no way he would let Van Dam appear on his programming without a concrete deal in place. With that element of the idea a no-go, the wheels were set in motion to have Van Dam work for both WWF and ECW simultaneously, during this stretch of *detente* between the northeast-based companies. Van Dam, with egotistical musings that smugly laid bare his willingness to leave behind blue-collar ECW for the transparent glitz of mainstream wrestling, was exactly the contemptible asshole that the black t-shirted customers could rally against. While ECW fans were already booing Van Dam heartily, his presence on Titan's programming would only turn up the flames of wrestling's latest war, this one waged through precarious cooperation.

On Saturday night, May 10, ECW ran in Philadelphia for the first time since *Barely Legal* four weeks earlier. Van Dam and Sabu lost to Taz and Candido in the semi-main, with Van Dam taking the fall from Candido. After heated rivals Sabu and Taz brawled up the aisle, Van Dam feigned disconsolation, spitting out another rant toward the ECW Arena crowd. "Rob Van Dam does not belong wrestling in front of 1,200 drunken, screaming idiots," he whined over the boos. "I've got millions and millions of fans all over Earth that are requesting my presence!" Those 'idiots' serenaded Van Dam with a time-honoured ditty reserved for any hated wrestler that chose to leave ECW for greener pastures: a mocking rendition of Steam's sixties ditty, '*Na Na Hey Hey Kiss Him Goodbye*'. It would be Van Dam's last ECW appearance for almost a full month.

IT WAS less than an hour's drive from Philadelphia to the Bob Carpenter Center in Newark, DE, home of the post-pay-per-view edition of *Raw* that was held two nights after Van Dam's curtain call. With an audience more than triple the number that Van Dam disparaged in the ECW Arena, "Mr. Monday Night" made his entrance during *Raw*'s second hour. If there were any doubts about the authenticity of the Van Dam/ECW split, they were confirmed when the brash superstar entered to the theme from ECW's weekly television show - a spacy, doomier instrumental sound-alike of White Zombie's, '*More Human than Human*', complete with Heyman himself rasping the promotion's full name during the opening bass licks.

The initial reaction was mostly silent, but once Howard Finkel shouted Van Dam's name, segments of the audience performed a double-take, cheering mostly out of dumbfoundedness. Then the angle kicked up, as ECW detractor Lawler snatched the microphone and trekked down the familiar road of burying the promotion's tenets. Van Dam did the same when prompted, giving a cleaner version of the testimonials that he once routed before ECW crowds. This produced an amusing irony when several fans renewed the "you sold out" chants formerly lobbed his way in the other promotion, when the ones conducting the chant had purchased tickets to see a WWF show in the first place. Heyman was on hand to make sure the angle played out smoothly, working with WWF official and noted ECW fan Bruce Prichard to make sure that Van Dam came off as a big-time player. There was little need for worry; the signature acrobatics were on full-display against nineteen-year-old crash dummy Jeff Hardy, several years before Hardy's signature style would manifest itself into one of wrestling's induplicable performers. Until that day, Hardy was Van Dam's safety net, breaking his fall on a wild flipping dive to the arena floor, in which Van Dam's heels caught the security railing. Back inside the ring, Van Dam finished with a form-perfect split-legged moonsault, executing the pinfall with his face arrogantly propped on his own fist, exhibiting the toothy smile of a matinee idol that knows he's made it big.

Soon after, on ECW's weekly program, an extended montage played, with members of the roster taking their own pot shots at the defector. While those fighting words were simply building blocks to the next stage of Heyman's plan, the reprisal from within the WWF locker room became palpably thick. For expendable WWF veterans who understood that a date with the chopping block could be imminent, they wondered what all the hubbub was about this aerodynamic outsider.

"Certain wrestlers were exceptionally cool and came forward, like Owen Hart," Van Dam recounted. "The longer I was there, the more I felt they didn't appreciate us as an outside company being on their TV, and us beating their guys. So if I was building up a winning streak, it was something that I knew wasn't going to last too long."

Van Dam reported that this was especially the case at the June 9 *Raw* in Hartford, where he was given a victory over former ECW opponent Too Cold Scorpio, now treading water in his frilly but one-dimensional Flash Funk role. "I don't think Scorpio was happy about the match we had," he recalled. "He wasn't going to say it, but it had more to do with his own direction at the time, what was going on with his character. They were picking him to put over an outside company, and I totally get his view."

In accordance with that direction, Scorpio was nothing more than an afterthought in the exhibition of Van Dam, quietly taking the fall to a split-legged moonsault after mere minutes. The match itself was simply a convenience to have Van Dam in the venue, so that he and Lawler could be attacked by a caustic Heyman and Tommy Dreamer, who were situated at front row ringside. The fray was a logical continuation of the defection angle, which spiked to awesome heights two nights earlier at the ECW Arena.

It was that Saturday night at ECW's *WrestlePalooza* taping that Dreamer ended his two-year feud with Raven by pinning him in a loser-leaves-ECW match. The win marked the first time Dreamer had ever gotten to pin Raven, a quirk oft-mentioned in storyline canon. The result was hardly in doubt once it became public knowledge that Raven was on his way to WCW, and his final match was moved up to June 7 from its original planned date of August 17, the night of ECW's second pay-per-view, *Hardcore Heaven*. The story continued into the denouement, with Dreamer emitting cathartic tears in the wake of his futility's end.

The reality had hardly set in when the lights in the ECW Arena went out, re-illuminating seconds later to reveal Van Dam, clad in a black *Monday Night Raw* t-shirt, standing in the ring. In his first ECW appearance in a month, Van Dam, flanked by obnoxious second banana Bill Alfonso, waylaid Dreamer with his Van Daminator kick before calling attention to his choice of attire. The battle resumed with Dreamer turning the tables, only for the lights to cut out a second time. This time, Sabu was the intruder, flinging a steel chair straight into Dreamer's face when the reveal was made. Once more, Dreamer took a beating, only to shift momentum by DDTing both villains. That is when the lights went out for the third and final time.

Through camera flashes and the dim flicker of lighters held aloft, many fans solved the mystery before the lights officially came back on, collectively shouting, "Lawler!" once they saw the red-topped crown amidst the strobe light-style effect. Indeed, Jerry Lawler had invaded the ECW Arena, braying and cackling mightily as Van Dam and Sabu beat down not only Dreamer, but an entire brigade of ECW Stormtroopers that hit the ring, from Axl Rotten to Chris Chetti to Balls Mahoney. "This bingo hall oughta be built outta toilet paper, because there's nothing in it but shit!" screamed a dismissive Lawler over the microphone. Fans alternated between role-playing jeers and incredulous cheers, knowing they were witnessing the hottest occurrence to hit the promotion since Shane Douglas threw down the NWA Championship in 1994.

"They had seen the ECW guys invade *Raw*, but I could tell by the reaction that they never thought a WWF guy would come to the ECW Arena," Lawler explained years later.

"The heat was phenomenal," recalled Danny Doring. "A lot of us didn't even know what was happening, and just watched on the monitors, just like the fans, completely into the moment. But we also knew this was big for the company."

Van Dam remembered there being some tension backstage from the boys when they were informed of Lawler's participation in the story, but also indicates that once Lawler was at the building, it was all business, and business was good.

"It felt special when we were in the ring getting booed, the heat from the crowd was something else," Van Dam wistfully related. "We felt like this would get us a lot of attention for ECW, and us as important members of the program. I think Jerry got out of there quick afterwards; I don't think he hung out and played cards in the back or anything. There may have been tension on his part, but I could not say."

Lawler's only apprehension came from the fans on hand, who were whipped into a frenzied cauldron, relating that it was "sheer pandemonium" while surrounded by the arena-goers, adding "I don't often get scared for my safety, but that night I was."

Further attempts to quell the onslaught from The Sandman, The Gangstas, and even plain-clothed Heyman were met with violent resistance from Van Dam and Sabu. The pro-WWF contingent bailed when Taz made a dynamic entrance, as though he were a pugnacious stand-in for RoboCop. From there, Lawler was quickly whisked out of the venue, and began his journey to Titan's *King of the Ring* pay-per-view taking place less than twenty-four hours later, 275 miles northeast in Providence.

The buzz from the angle was tremendous. *The Wrestling Observer* reported in the aftermath that a tag team match for the forthcoming *SummerSlam* in East Rutherford was tentatively set, pitting Van Dam and either Lawler or Sabu against Dreamer and Sandman. Lawler would also work one-on-one with Dreamer at ECW's *Hardcore Heaven* pay-per-view in Fort Lauderdale two weeks after that. The latter match would take place as planned, with Dreamer toppling meddlesome Lawler in grand fashion, but the former bout did not come to pass. By the end of June, the ECW element on WWF telecasts would evaporate entirely.

AT THE June 23 *Raw* in Detroit, Flash Funk would once again be working with one of his former ECW colleagues, this time Sabu. In his time as Scorpio, he and Sabu tore down the house at ECW's *CyberSlam '96* with a thirty-minute draw, contested over Scorpio's Television title. The match on *Raw* would be another stalemate between the globetrotting daredevils, this time a double count-out after less than five minutes. Sabu did get to put Funk through a particularly-sturdy table after the match, maintaining his image as a persistent sadistic, but the actual finish was a bone of contention.

Sabu bristled loudly behind the curtain about doing the non-finish. A year earlier, Sabu may not have grumbled about going fifty-fifty with a renowned peer possessing a similar résumé, but this was not braggadocios Too Cold Scorpio he was breaking even with; it was zoot-suited afterthought Flash Funk. What good was Sabu if he could not invade a territory and knock off a designated low man on the totem pole, regardless of his talent?

"Toward the end, I didn't want to put their guys over, either," Van Dam admitted. "I mean, I'm here to get ECW exposure, not to go on your TV and show that your guys are better than us."

At this stage of the game, Flash Funk had more residual credibility than Brian James, youngest son of the legendary 'Bullet' Bob Armstrong who was now hopelessly floundering as good-hearted country crooner 'Double J' Jesse James. That same night, Van Dam, sixteen days removed from playing antagonist in a watershed storyline for ECW, was asked to lose via disqualification to James on the company's secondary broadcast *Shotgun*. The match did not happen, because Van Dam walked out that night with Sabu and Heyman, dissolving the working agreement.

"Paul was involved in it and was like, 'Well, James doesn't beat anybody; he's on the opening match for the WWF, and Van Dam is my top guy!'" remembered Jim Cornette. "Well, it's a DQ, just go ahead and do it. It's political. It's bullshit. Everybody knows that. They made a big stink, so they all fucking went home."

"There was a lot of tension on the last day," Van Dam acknowledged. "We were in Detroit, and Paul had put all the pressure on me. He told me it was up to me whenever I wanted to pull the plug, mention the word, and we're out of there. The time came where I was asking him for advice, and I said, 'Paul, do you think I should do this? Should I do what they're asking?' He says, 'Say the word, and we'll go.'"

Van Dam, whose relationship with Heyman and ECW had gone from rocky and icy three months earlier to broadly enriching with the line-crossing story, had his own theories as to why Heyman authorised the walk-out that night in Detroit, and it paints Heyman as the manipulative genius that many claim he is.

"Paul made sure that we felt uncomfortable by filling our head with a bunch of bullshit about how the other boys are jealous, they don't want us there. You know, make sure you don't leave your bags unwatched in the back, things like that, so we stuck together pretty tight."

"His whole thing was he wanted me to go to WWF so I wouldn't go to WCW, capitalise on it by getting ECW some exposure, and he wanted me and Sabu to bury ourselves, so he didn't have to worry about us leaving ECW. Everything was accomplished for him."

Van Dam salivated at the thrills of exposure and the comfort of respect, but those lures were far from the only reasons a wrestler would consider packing up the tights and bolting for either Atlanta or New York. Money was wrestling's greatest motivator, a hard commodity to come by working for a company whose sole television exposure was in the form of pay-to-play syndication slots.

"The problem with syndicated TV was they were paying for the time slots," offered Dave Meltzer, "You're paying so much for the TV, you've got to make that back in profit on the house shows, and that became pretty difficult."

Heyman's quixotic dreams of expansion into the pay-per-view market looked like a rallying cry for the legitimacy that the undisputed number three promotion desperately needed, but the lack of viable television time slots made it difficult for Heyman to turn a profit, no matter how well he promoted blood feuds, or what bar-raising insanity he promised his mostly-niche audience.

WHEN TOD Gordon founded ECW in 1992, the Philadelphia-based independent picked up the pieces of its recently-passed doppelgänger, Joel Goodhart's Tri-State Wrestling Alliance. Goodhart's ambitions led to him throwing good money at good ideas, but with little return. Tri-State beckoned 1,200-plus fans to a May 1991 Philadelphia card that featured recognisable names in Rick Rude, The Honky Tonk Man, Paul Orndorff, and Jerry Lawler, for a gate of $22,311. Four months later at the same Penn Hall venue, over 1,500 patrons paid a combined $27,000 to see Abdullah the Butcher rip flesh with the legendary Ed 'The Sheik' Farhat inside a steel cage, as well as Terry Funk doing battle with fellow in-ring sociopath Kevin Sullivan.

By the time Gordon ran the first ECW card in April 1992, Tri-State had been dead for three months, crushed beneath the weight of debt. An announced card for January 25, 1992 that promoted All-Japan regulars Steve Williams, Terry Gordy, Doug Furnas, and Dan Kroffat, as well as New Japan standouts Chris Benoit and Shiro Koshinaka, did not happen. The highlight would have been a battle of the "Nature Boys", with latter-day barnstormer Buddy Landel squaring off with seventy-year-old grappling treasure Buddy Rogers, the first WWWF Champion in 1963. A week before the planned supercard, Goodhart dissolved the operation and took himself off the grid.

Gordon, whose full beard and soft-but-gruff voice gave him an authoritative presence that served him well as the fan-friendly kayfabe commissioner, hired journeyman heel Eddie Gilbert to serve as head booker in 1993. While Gilbert quickly booked himself as headliner, he would not be on top long, as 'Hot Stuff' cut a burning swath out the door that autumn.

As Gordon remembered it, "Eddie had demons. Oh, did he have demons. He just wanted to show up when he wanted to show up – he's trying to run a TV show for me. He got really paranoid about Paul, because Paul was working with [Jim] Crockett. One day, he was at the studio with me where we did the TV show, and he did his usual tantrum where he threatened to quit, and I said, 'Well, go ahead and quit then. The company's not going to go under today if you tell me you're going back to Tennessee.' And he did, he quit. I brought Paul in to do the next show, and I brought in Kevin Sullivan to be [Eddie's] replacement in a match. Eddie *hated* Kevin. My God, did he hate Kevin. About three or four days before the show, he called me up, 'Hey man, I'm sorry, I don't why I said that. I wanna come back and I don't want to leave you high and dry like that.' I said, 'I've already replaced you.' He said, 'With who?' and I told him Kevin, and I thought you could smell the smoke coming through the telephone. The next day, he called me back and said, 'How about this: can I at least come in and say goodbye? Me and Funk are running this big angle down in Amarillo, and we'd like to get some stuff on tape that he can use and I can use, so can I come in and do something with him as kind of a sidebar thing?', and I said 'Yeah.'

"At the time, Paul's running his first show. When Eddie took the mic, Paul's not aware that he was gonna take the mic. He got very upset that he took the mic, because he thought he might say something that would undermine what he was trying to accomplish there. He started making comments like, 'Who the fuck told him he could take the microphone?!' and that's when Doug Gilbert got all upset, 'What are you talking about, you motherfucker? After the way you treated him?' And then he took a baseball bat and started smashing all the glasses on a table. He wasn't coming towards Paul or anybody, he was just pissed off and acting out."

Gordon found himself enamoured with the creative mind of the young Heyman, who had recently come aboard to assist backstage, and continue his trusty work as a ringside manager. Gilbert's vision for ECW amounted to "Lawler's Memphis, but in Philadelphia." Heyman wanted to foster something else entirely.

"I asked Paul to assist me with *UltraClash '93* since he was already assisting me anyway with promos and things like that," said Gordon, "But I didn't give him the book at all that night; we hadn't talked about anything like that. At the time, he was supposed to be starting a company with Jim Crockett, the WWN[11], so we never looked at it as a possibility. It wasn't until we did a show together that he started to make a play for it. He saw an opportunity. Kevin Sullivan wasn't making a play for it. Funk didn't want it, because I'd talked to him about it, and he said, 'No no no, you can't afford me as a booker *ana* a worker.' I turned to Paul, and I asked if he would take on that job."

In 1995, Gordon sold his majority interest to Heyman, but claimed that he held onto fifty-one percent of the voting stock to Heyman's forty-nine. Other than that arrangement, Heyman called the day-to-day shots for the promotion, while Gordon remained mostly hands-off. According to Gordon, Heyman's spend-thrift habits were as short-sighted, if not more so, than Goodhart's.

"You can't spend a hundred thousand dollars in a month without any return," Gordon contested. "When I got an offer from the Sunshine Network in Florida, it was three thousand dollars a week. The MSG Network was also three thousand a week. I said we can't afford that in addition to what we're paying now. Paul said it's not a problem, I've already got the advertisers lined up. There wasn't one advertiser. All of a sudden, I'm locked to a contract, and to go backwards from that would've made us look terrible as a company. Perception is reality in the business. We're losing money hand over fist because Paul wanted to be on TV in New York."

Heyman's bullish strides were following a similar pattern to Goodhart's previous excesses, and Gordon claimed that the talent was not getting paid for their time and effort.

"Paul had basically lost the entire locker room," he noted. "He had gotten to the point where all of these people that had put their blind faith into him found out that they were not being rewarded accordingly. They were getting lied to, they were getting their checks bounced. He'd pretty much lost the Philly guys. He was starting to lose the New York guys a little bit, and he was in trouble."

---

[11] WWN, or World Wrestling Network, was founded by Jim Crockett, Jr., the former NWA promoter that had sold his business interests to Ted Turner in the autumn of 1988. After adhering to a three-year no-compete agreement stipulated in the sale, Crockett finally got back into wrestling by launching the NWA-affiliated WWN in 1993, with Heyman helping out with booking. The venture ran only a handful of shows from August 1993 through February 1994, the last of which was a TV taping which included a number of ECW talents, as well as Jake 'The Snake' Roberts, Road Warrior Hawk, and 'Cowboy' Bob Orton. Heyman and Crockett's union was short-lived, and the two butted heads over content and direction. "He wanted to go back to 1986, but you had to be progressive, not retro," Heyman would later say.

To clarify, according to Gordon the 'Philly guys' were the ECW employees closest to him: The Sandman, Raven, Stevie Richards, Too Cold Scorpio, The Pitbulls, and Bill Alfonso. Scorpio was gone by the end of 1996, and Raven had agreed to his lucrative WCW deal. Richards would be following Raven south by mid-June. The Pitbulls, Gary Wolfe and Anthony Durante, were fired in the early summer of 1997 after pleading guilty to supplying an undercover federal informant with steroids and marijuana.

The "New York" crew of wrestlers included the likes of Tommy Dreamer, Taz, The Eliminators, Mikey Whipwreck, Little Guido, and The Dudley Boyz among others, those more aligned with Heyman. These men also held several key jobs in the organisation that entailed more than simply wrestling. Taz designed logos and t-shirts for company use, while also training students at the ECW House of Hardcore wrestling school alongside Perry Saturn. Dreamer would process t-shirt orders and help book the shows. Bubba booked venues for which the shows would run. ECW was powered by the faith and sweat of its strongest links, but without the earnings to show for their tireless work, their faith in Heyman's word was beginning to wane.

Meltzer explained, "Paul's deal was he would promote a pay-per-view, and then he would have to come back and promote another pay-per-view and spend the money to promote it, but the money from number one hadn't come back by the time number two came. So Paul would borrow money from this guy to fund number two. And then number three would come and it was always one of those things where you have to borrow money to do the next one based on the revenue that you should have already received but you haven't gotten."

"It had gotten to the point where I couldn't do business with him anymore, quite honestly," said Gordon. "Unlike the other guys, I didn't make a living because of him. I didn't depend on him, so I couldn't be like they were and say, 'That's alright, you can lie to me and lie to me, what am I going to do? It's the only place I've got to work.' That wasn't the case with me. It just got to the point where I knew we were going to end up becoming enemies if we didn't do something."

Gordon's mind was made up. He was leaving ECW in September 1997. On top of the irritation of seeing the company flounder under Heyman's optimistic whims, he had a young family at home that he wanted to spend more time with. Knowing that he did not need wrestling to pay his bills, he gave Heyman, the man he had hired four years earlier, his notice. By Gordon's account of the story, it was his wilfulness to look out for enterprising employees that would later be used against him on the way out, and remains part of an ongoing slice of wrestling lore.

In 1995, Gordon had gotten jobs in WCW for Theodore (Ted) 'Rocco Rock' Petty and Mike 'Johnny Grunge' Durham, two wisecracking hoodlum caricatures that ascended to the top of ECW as The Public Enemy, and became multiple time ECW Tag Team Champions. After Heyman gave the two his blessing to jump to the WWF, Gordon found out that the long-time Philly favourites had not even spoken to WCW, and worked to get them the best possible deal. Kevin Sullivan worked in WCW's office, and was enthusiastically keen on signing Petty and Durham, impressed with their act after briefly working with them in ECW in 1994.

With that in mind, Gordon became the liaison for other ECW performers that wanted to seek comfortable deals with the bigger companies. Gordon maintained that he would only reach out for other wrestlers if personally asked, and the arrangement would prevent said wrestlers getting heat from Heyman if the ECW owner found out they were looking elsewhere.

"Nothing else was more than an exploratory phone conversation," Gordon insisted.

History has painted Gordon as a turncoat, attempting to leverage himself a job with WCW by promising booker Terry Taylor that he could procure him a litany of ECW wrestlers for yet another invasion angle, a New World Order baptised in blood and guts.

"Tod Gordon calls, and has this big plan," claimed Taylor. "He calls me up and it was an invasion angle, like the nWo that had started to wind down. He goes, 'I can bring you this number of ECW talents. We can do an invasion.' These guys were all working for ECW at the time, and I said, 'You clear that with Paul E, and we'll talk. If I hear Paul E tell me [okay to] the list of everyone that you have, then we'll talk.' He goes, 'I can't do that. We're going to take this group of people and come down there.' I said, 'We're going to be up front about it or we're not going to do it.'"

Gordon insisted this was a lie, saying, "There were no mass invasion plans. I would read these stories and be like, 'What? What mass invasion, what are you talking about?!' Then all of a sudden, there's Shane Douglas walking around the locker room, saying, 'They offered me three hundred thousand to be a part of the package.' Again, I'm like, 'What?' I didn't even discuss this with Shane Douglas! Everybody was just trying to use this to their advantage."

Gordon claimed that he only ever called Taylor on behalf of three wrestlers that were looking to explore their options: Sabu, The Sandman, and Perry Saturn. Saturn was the only one of the three at the time that ultimately made the jump, exiting in August 1997, mere weeks before Gordon's planned final weekend as an ECW employee.

As the world recoiled in shock at the gruesome car accident which claimed the life of Princess Diana, Heyman was readying himself to shock his most loyal employees with news that would hit much closer to home. Gathering Dreamer, Taz, and others, Heyman reportedly had procured some damning audio that painted Gordon as an undermining force. Or as wrestling parlance would have it, a 'mole'.

"Heyman broke into Tod Gordon's cell phone and played all the messages of all the guys calling him," Dreamer recalled. "Me and Taz were at Paul's house, and we couldn't believe it was going on. It was Terry Taylor. It was Bill Alfonso. They were just talking, 'Great deal, man, we can bring this all in.' They were going to do an ECW invasion."

"As he's losing the New York guys, he needs something to draw them all back in," Gordon countered. "Paul being Paul, he loves to create a storyline. He got the guys together in the studio, saying, 'Listen, we got a problem, there's a mole,' and he kept building it and building it."

Despite whatever audio the wrestlers may have heard, Gordon believed that none of it should be interpreted as an attempted coup, but rather one professional looking out for colleagues that had asked him to play middleman in the search for greener pastures on their behalf.

"I'm getting out of the business, and I told Heyman I was. The 'invasion' angle wouldn't make any kind of sense for me - I wasn't trying to sign a contract with anybody."

As to why Taylor would tell a much different story, presenting Gordon as shady, Gordon theorised that Taylor would not want to burn any bridges with Heyman by looking unscrupulous, stating, "He just decided it was more important to have an ally in Paul than to have an ally in me."

Gordon's ultimate claim was that Heyman needed to win over the boys once more during the times of financial uncertainty. By presenting ECW as being in a war with WCW over talent, the wrestlers that swore loyalty to ECW, and had put in overtime with the various odd jobs, would feel more galvanised to dig their heels in and fight for the smaller army. Even with the elevation in paranoia that surrounded Gordon, and ultimately his exit, Heyman reportedly had asked his long-time associate to keep hush.

Gordon's recollection of Heyman's words were, "I'm trying to get these guys to rally around me; I need you not to ever say anything. Promise me you're not going to say anything. Otherwise, I'll lose whatever I have left in the locker room."

"Next thing you know, he's got all the New York guys together and says, 'Here's what I know about Tod,'" Gordon added.

"I remember when it all happened, when it was first breaking, we were training at the House of Hardcore," recalled Danny Doring. "Taz called us all into the office and told us that someone put a rumour in the dirt sheets that Chris Chetti was leaving to be a part of The Flock. I actually suspect this was Raven, just to kinda fuck with Taz. I can't imagine anyone else who would put this out there except Raven, because he was connected to the sheets. We were called in and asked if we knew about it, and Chris is like, 'Taz, I'm your cousin - why wouldn't I tell you if I was planning on leaving?' It caused a lot of paranoia back there, with who was going and who wasn't, and it was definitely a weird time. Depending on the person, if they were mad, they were mad that people left, or were mad that they didn't get the call themselves to go."

"We all had to be paranoid, because we had WCW and the WWF breathing down our necks to try and take our talent," asserted Dreamer. "Everyone was trying to knock us down, and Paul is very paranoid."

"Paul was, and probably still is, one of the most paranoid people in the world," noted Gordon. "Someone's out to get him, someone's out to work him. He didn't trust any of the boys or anybody, really. It was a shame."

The 'mole' story took on a life of its own within the dirt sheets, which lapped up the tale with flickering tongues, and among the boys who suddenly felt more inclined to carry the ECW banner, with payoffs or without.

"In his own way, he bought himself six to eight months of goodwill with the boys," believed Gordon. "My friends, the Sandmans and Sabus and Bill Alfonsos, they were all a privy to what was going on with me. Nobody thought that I was trying to undermine anything. Just try to tell that to Dreamer, who was Paul's boy. He never saw the forest for the trees. Paul was manipulating, sold the dream, and they all bought it."

"I don't know if it's fair to say that Paul was losing the locker room, because people kinda always knew that Paul was full of shit," contended Doring. "You knew he was full of shit, but you always wanted to believe him."

After the first weekend of September 1997, Gordon departed from ECW as he had originally intended. Although Heyman was still playing him up as a traitor to all of his overworked subordinates, he did take time to give Gordon a respectful send-off on an edition of *ECW Hardcore TV* that aired the second week of the month. Heyman's speech concluded the one-hour broadcast, filmed in front of a lone camera with canned arena chatter employed as a sound bed. Heyman humbly spoke before the camera:

> My name is Paul Heyman, and I am the executive producer and talent coordinator of Extreme Championship Wrestling. It's a job that was given to me on September 18, 1993, by the founder of this promotion, Tod Gordon. It is, therefore, my responsibility to inform the public with a heavy heart, earlier this week, ECW accepted the resignation of Tod Gordon as commissioner of Extreme Championship Wrestling. Citing increasing pressures as father of four children and running a family business, Tod could no longer assume the responsibility of being ECW's commissioner. We here at Extreme Championship Wrestling wish Tod nothing but the best in all of his future endeavours and want to let him know that we intend to make him proud as we carry on his version of ECW.

As the coming months would reveal, paranoia in the professional wrestling world was far from confined to just one locker room.

SEVEN

THE ESCALATING TENSIONS BETWEEN BRET Hart and Shawn Michaels, the two men whom McMahon was schizophrenically bouncing between as his would-be top dog, were becoming increasingly strained as 1997 unfolded beyond *WrestleMania 13*. Michaels remained convinced that Hart wanted to usurp him and reclaim the headline spot that he had vacated in 1996. Bret on the other hand merely yearned for Shawn's respect and for him to change his defiant behaviour behind the curtain. With each passing week it became increasingly clear that peace was a pipedream. The two proud lions were ready to go to war in the ultimate battle to become the WWF's alpha male.

While working the house show circuit with rising star Steve Austin in early February, Hart was troubled to learn from his opponent that Shawn and Kliq ally Triple H were calculatedly trying to cause a rift between them. Having worked the main event of a matinee show in Montreal on February 2, Hart was tardy arriving at the Corel Center in Ottawa for the evening's card. With Hart not there to oppose them, Hunter and Shawn pulled Austin aside and told him, "Bret doesn't want to put you over. You were supposed to go over in Quebec, but he refused." Austin - who had witnessed the prior year's infamous Curtain Call first-hand - knew exactly what sort of shenanigans the pair were capable of, and responded to their claims with silent trepidation.

When Hart eventually arrived at the arena two hours before he was set to go on in the semi-main event, Austin led him into a private room and informed him of what he had been told. Hart soon realised that despite his best efforts to get along with Shawn and Hunter, they appeared determined to sabotage him regardless. Hart told Austin that he had nothing but respect for him, and vehemently denied refusing to lose to him. Austin believed him, then told Hart that Michaels and Hunter had also been stirring up the agents by complaining about Bret being late to the show. Shawn's point of contention was that he too had been part of the main event in Montreal, yet he had shown up on time.

The pair had created enough of a fuss that road agent Pat Patterson soon came to Hart with a request: he wanted him to put over Hunter that night in their triple-threat bout with Steve Austin. "Vince wants you to do it, just to show the boys," Patterson informed him. Hart knew immediately that "the boys" in question were only Shawn and Hunter, because few others if any in the locker room were on the side of the Kliq. Hart told Patterson as much and agreed to a compromise; he had no problem not winning, but he would not put Hunter over directly. Instead that job fell to Austin, who took the loss after falling victim to a Hart belt shot.

Unhappy that Hart had not allowed himself to be beaten by Hunter, the Kliq double act - whom McMahon had recently permitted to be in attendance at private booking meetings - were determined to make him do a job for them. Three weeks later in Berlin, Germany, it was Gerald Brisco who delivered the news to Hart that Hunter was going to beat him via pinfall that night on *Raw*. Hunter was sat directly opposite Hart in the dressing room, and shot an irritated glance in his direction when he overheard Bret complain about the result. "I calmly said that I didn't see any sense in Hunter beating the most over guy they had in Europe less than a month before *WrestleMania 13*, when 'Stone Cold' and I were being relied upon to carry the pay-per-view," Hart recalled. Rather than argue with middleman Brisco, Bret sought out McMahon directly. He informed him of his take on the match, questioning why Vince was paying him so much to be the WWF's most expensive jobber. The chairman agreed with his assessment and a compromise was reached when McMahon changed the finish to a disqualification win for Helmsley, allowing Hart to remain strong by shoving the official in the heat of the moment. Once again, Hart had avoided the Kliq getting one over on him between the ropes or politically.

When Shawn learned of Hart's refusal to comply, he was fuming. He decided to take matters into his own hands and deal with Hart the only way he felt he could: by degrading him on the microphone. Michaels knew he would likely be creamed by Hart in a genuine fight, but he also believed that behind the stick, Hart could not come close to him.

On an episode of *Raw* filmed in early April, Hart was away doing Federation promotional work in Kuwait, giving Michaels - again, under the orders of McMahon - free reign to rip the 'Hitman' to shreds. In a long diatribe umpired by McMahon, Michaels tore into Hart for among other things, having an obsession with the WWF Championship, only returning to the company for money, and for his desire to be in the limelight irrespective of who he had to tread on to get there.

Hart did not learn of the interview until Owen Hart and Davey Boy Smith arrived in Kuwait and detailed what Shawn had said. Hart immediately called his close friend and personal assistant Marcy Englestein for further information, clenching his fist into a white-knuckled grip as she played him the full audio from the tirade over the phone. Hart was irate about some of Shawn's entirely fabricated claims, and dismayed that McMahon had stood idly by as Michaels removed the veil of kayfabe enshrouding the Bret Hart character, while lifting the lid on Bret Hart the man.

Hart called McMahon, who immediately tried to soothe him with promises that Shawn would be severely reprimanded for his unauthorised tirade. Hart ended the call believing him, but still felt uneasy about the situation. What he did not realise was that McMahon saw Hart's very personal, real-life rivalry with Shawn as television gold; he was eager to mine every bit of it. Vince was the puppet master, constantly pitting his two favourites against one another for the sake of driving higher ratings, encouraging them without the other's knowledge to cut close to the bone during interviews. McMahon was paying little care or attention to the damage he was doing to locker room morale in doing so, and soon the uneasiness of the Hart-Michaels relationship turned to an outright dislike.

RELATIONS BETWEEN the two were hardly helped when Shawn Michaels returned to the ring only three-and-a-half months following his controversial "career-ending" knee injury. As far as Hart was concerned, it proved that Shawn had been lying the whole time, with 'the Hitman' now utterly convinced that the entire story was hokum designed to absolve Michaels from doing a job for him.

By mid-1997, the relationship between Michaels and Hart was frayed beyond repair due to an ongoing series of scathing promos they were cutting about one another. Encouraged further by the new excitable shock TV writer Russo, and goaded by the rest of the locker room, Shawn and Bret pulled no punches in their weekly verbal diatribes. Bret had made sure to clear with Shawn much of what he intended to say about him on the air, and Michaels in turn had consented to him saying whatever he wanted. However, Bret delivered his verbiage with such intensity and venom that it nevertheless wounded Shawn emotionally. "We worked ourselves into a shoot," admitted Hart. "I did it in such a realistic, nasty way that Shawn thought I wasn't being legit with him."

While Michaels was convinced the promos were thinly disguised personal attacks, Bret was under the impression Shawn knew they were working an angle. "Anything I ever said about Shawn was always about Shawn Michaels the wrestling character, I never attacked the real life guy," defended Hart. Shawn did not see it that way. "I didn't think it was attacking my character, because there isn't that much difference between the two," he said, "I didn't have the ability emotionally to look at things as just business back then." In return for the perceived attacks on his person, Michaels countered with inciting snipes at Hart, openly questioning his morals on the road, in addition to insulting his family.

For Michaels, his issues ran far deeper than Hart's petty digging at his character for stripping, having young boys dancing with him in the ring, and his decision to pose for *Playgirl*. Instead, it was the insecurities that had plagued him throughout the past eighteen months coming to the fore. Behind the brash façade, Shawn felt deeply threatened by Bret's return to prominence, due to what he perceived as the precarious nature of his own position. He was paranoid, concerned that the prevailing opinion in the locker room was that he had not done an adequate job in the role of top guy. Bret coming back and saving the day condemned him to the annals of history as a failure.

Ever savvy, Hart realised that relations needed smoothing out between the two before the situation became any uglier. "We tried a lot of times to come together and talk, because it was spiralling out of control," he recalled. "The things I was saying were offensive to him, and the things he was saying were offensive to me. We sat down in the spring and had a conversation, promising each other not to say anything about each other without checking first." Michaels explained the situation from his perspective, complaining that Hart had done nothing but bury him for months, while claiming to have said nothing back in return. He warned him that if he did it again, the gloves were off. "The difference between you and me is that I will admit to all the stuff that I do wrong. I don't hide it," Michaels told him, "But, if you keep screwing with me, that's it." The pair agreed to put everything behind them, and shook hands with the intention of starting afresh.

With Bret convinced that Shawn finally trusted him again, the two shared the ring for the closing segment of that night's *Raw* on May 12 in Delaware. Ironically, given Bret's complaints about Shawn's injury in February, Bret was now carrying a knee injury of his own and confined to a wheelchair. The intention of the segment was to hype a match between the two at *King of the Ring*, with Bret's injury having forced McMahon to change it to a stipulation bout that Hart had to win in under ten minutes.

The way the segment was scripted called for Hart to unleash a vicious invective on Michaels, until the point where Shawn could not take it anymore and would shut his rival up with a trademark kick to the chin, sending him careening over his wheelchair. Bret managed the first part with aplomb, ripping Shawn to shreds while the former champion stood there and took it, knowing his retribution was imminent. The scenario did not go according to plan when Hart forgot his go-home line, and in struggling to remember it he failed to realise that he was running out of time to say his piece before the broadcast concluded. Unable to recall the cue, Hart briefly stopped, trying to gather his thoughts. The pause led to a loud "Hitman sucks" chant from the crowd that prevented Hart from hearing agent Bruce Prichard frantically yelling into his hidden earpiece that it was time to take it home.

Unbeknownst to either wrestler, *Raw* went off the air while Hart was mid-rant, meaning Michaels' eventual superkick was completely omitted from the broadcast. When Shawn returned backstage, Prichard came running up to him with the news. "They missed it," he panted, "They missed the superkick!" "What!?" growled Michaels, instantly enraged. "The superkick! It didn't air! Bret was just berating you and berating you, and we went off the air." Michaels, who was often sparked into a frenzied temper at even the most innocuous of incidents, was incensed at the news. He rampaged around the locker room, badmouthing Hart to anyone within earshot. After all the talk earlier in the day of trusting one another and burying the hatchet, Michaels was now convinced that Hart had intentionally sabotaged him, purposely going long with his promo to the detriment of Michaels.

"He went on a tirade and just didn't stop," remembered Michaels. "For the whole time he was talking, viewers saw me standing there looking like an idiot. I was furious. He had done it to me for the last time. He had pushed and pushed and pushed me some more. Now I was going to take the gloves off." Michaels had the remainder of the week off, and spent much of the time drowning his sorrows. He felt Bret had lied to him, and that 'the Hitman' was trying to elaborately work him by saying one thing to his face and then doing something different in his actions. Michaels' coping mechanisms were alcohol and narcotics, two vices which he engaged freely in prior to the next edition of *Raw* on May 19 from Mobile, Alabama.

Michaels turned up at the Mobile Civic Center inebriated, slurring his words and barely able to stand. During a Hart Foundation promo, he appeared on the Titan Tron to interrupt. Bedecked in a black bandana to signify his friendship with and allegiance to Nash, Hall, and Waltman in WCW, he let loose in a drunken flurry. "You couldn't go ten minutes in any situation, if you know what I mean," goaded Michaels, seemingly referring to the proposed *King of the Ring* encounter. "Even though lately you've had some 'Sunny days' my friend, you still can't get the job done."

Hart did not quite catch what Michaels had said, because he was trying to speak over him and the loud crowd at the time. When he returned backstage, the rest of the boys were seething at how unprofessional Michaels had been. The "Sunny days" line was intentionally incendiary, an unsubtle allusion that Hart had been engaging in an extra-marital affair with Tammy 'Sunny' Sytch. "Shawn was a nasty guy," noted former WWF grappler Bam Bam Bigelow, "He used to screw with the boy's wives, just to rub their faces in it, you know?"

When Hart realised what Shawn had implied, he was furious. He decided to bide his time and confront him about it when his knee was healthier, though first he had to face the music at home. "My kids and my father came up and asked me what was going on with Sunny," recalled Hart. "I was really offended by that. That could have caused serious problems for me. We were crossing lines and it was getting ugly."

Ironically, Hart was not one of the wrestlers in the locker room engaging in an affair with the flirtatious blonde temptress. While his two-timing with other women was no secret amongst the boys, Sunny was not among his many extra-marital conquests. She was, however, one of Shawn's belles. Already at the end of his tether with Hart due to the promos, not to mention Bret's far superior – and he felt unwarranted – contract, Michaels was convinced that Bret was also honing in on his romantic territory. He was paranoid, certain that Hart was looking to sabotage him in any conceivable way, including his sexual relationship with Sunny. Shawn felt that by making the rumours of an illicit tryst between them public, it would bring an end to it, returning to him the advantage in their petty feud.

Both Shawn and Bret felt the shaky truce they had agreed to was now shattered for good. Neither was willing to work with the other at all, and there was no way either man intended to lose. The original booking for *King of the Ring* had called for a Hart victory thanks to interference from his Hart Foundation allies, but Michaels refused to comply. Hart firmly felt it was Shawn's turn to stare at the lights in return for the *WrestleMania XII* job he had done for him, not to mention Michaels having dodged losing to him at *WrestleMania 13* due to his brief hiatus. Days later, the *King of the Ring* match was off, ostensibly because of Hart's knee recovering slower than anticipated, but also due to the now palpable tension between them. McMahon realised it was a powder keg pairing them together, so he swapped Hart out with Steve Austin for the bout.

ON JUNE 9, the night after *King of the Ring*, the WWF presented *Raw* from their home state of Connecticut, with the broadcast airing live from the Hartford Civic Center. Both Michaels and Hart were scheduled to be heavily involved, but an altercation forty-minutes prior to the broadcast scuppered all plans, forcing a last minute rewrite of the entire show.

For weeks Hart had intended to confront Michaels about the recent incidents that had occurred between them, detailing his plan that afternoon to Jim Neidhart. Hart's real life brother-in-law was deeply concerned by the news. He had only recently returned to the Federation fold after two years away[12] and was struggling financially, so he pleaded with Bret to reconsider.

Michaels and Hart both spent a significant portion of the evening prior to the broadcast discussing individual issues with Vince McMahon. Michaels' bone of contention related to Hart earning more than him, and how unhappy he was away from his friends in WCW.

---

[12] Neidhart also had a brief spell with the company in 1996, though he wrestled under a mask as 'Who', a short-lived gimmick that lasted only a few months.

When Shawn signed his $750,000 per annum five-year deal shortly after winning the WWF Championship in 1996, McMahon assured him, "Shawn, no one means more to this company than you." Five months later McMahon signed Bret Hart to a twenty-year contract worth $1.5 million per annum for the first three years of the contract, leaving Michaels outraged. He felt that Hart was beneath him as a performer, and certainly not worth double what he was earning. As far as he was concerned, Hart's deal as a snub, a sign that McMahon had lost faith in him and intended to go with Bret as the WWF's saviour, the man to pick up the torch that everyone believed he had fumbled.

That was not the case at all. Rather, McMahon was in a competitive market and had been backed into a corner by Eric Bischoff throwing millions at Hart. With everyone around him advising that Hart was an integral cog in the WWF machine, Vince was left with little choice but to break the bank to secure his signature.

The Hart deal violated a verbal agreement that McMahon had with Michaels which stated he would not be out-earned by anyone on the roster. Michaels had already taken McMahon to task over that fact early in 1997, demanding a new contract that gave him financial parity with Hart. McMahon could not afford to acquiesce and refused. In response Michaels tried to give his notice, telling Vince he wanted to join his Kliq allies in WCW. "Vince, a few years there and I would be set for life," pleaded Michaels. Again, McMahon rejected the request, leaving Shawn miserable and even more temperamental than ever. The same issues came up again on June 9 and once more the outcome left Shawn banging his head against a figurative brick wall.

Hart on the other hand was still seething about Michaels' slanderous "Sunny days" jibe, and was chagrined that no action had been taken against him. Hart had also found out earlier that day from McMahon that the WWF was in financial peril and his lucrative contract was under threat. He suspected Vince was suffering from buyer's remorse, something he had believed to be the case even when they first penned the agreement. McMahon assured Hart that the contract was still valid, but that he might be forced to restructure it so he could make it through the remainder of the year. Hart was sceptical, but McMahon promised him he would still get every penny owed to him.

When Hart bumped into Michaels in a backstage bathroom later in the evening, both were in foul moods as a result of their respective conversations with McMahon. Nevertheless, Hart had decided to heed Neidhart's words and refrain from confronting Shawn. Instead he tried to be friendly, in one last futile attempt at restoring peace between them. "Hey Shawn, I just want to say..." Michaels was in a worse mood than usual and before Hart could finish his sentence, he cut him off. "Fuck you! Don't fucking talk to me. You haven't fucking talked to me in three weeks. Now you've decided that it's time for us to talk? Well, guess what? I don't wanna talk to you."

Hart immediately decided to go back to his original plan of beating the shit out of Michaels, but Shawn had already left the scene and made a beeline for the dressing room. Jerry Lawler, who had heard the initial confrontation while sat in a toilet cubicle, hurriedly finished his business and headed for the locker room to intervene. With decades of experience under his belt, Lawler had seen this sort of thing before, and he knew it was likely to escalate into a violent situation. He was worried that the hatred between the two was so intense that there could be a repeat of a tragic incident in Puerto Rico a decade earlier, where Frank 'Bruiser Brody' Goodish lost his life after being repeatedly stabbed by fellow wrestler Jose 'Super Invader II' Gonzalez following a number of disagreements.

Meanwhile, Hart paced around backstage searching for Shawn. He eventually caught up with him in one of the dressing rooms, where Shawn was bent over tying his boots. Hart shoved him from behind and bellowed angrily, "You got something to say to me? What's your fucking problem?" Michaels knew where the situation was heading, but he was unable to resist provoking the irate 'Hitman' further. "You! You're my fucking problem," he snapped in response.

With all hopes of an uneasy truce having dissipated, Hart now had his mind set firmly on teaching Shawn a lesson. Hart screamed at Shawn for causing problems with his family and threw a shot which Michaels narrowly evaded. Michaels let out a chuckle, amused that Hart had failed to connect, so Hart, balancing precariously on one knee, threw another shot at Michaels that caught him square on the chin, rocking him backwards. Michaels tried to fire back with a weak punch that missed the mark, to which Hart responded by grabbing him by the hair and swinging him around the room. Michaels desperately tried to escape Hart's clutches by going after his injured knee, but Hart saw him coming and his old amateur wrestling instincts took over. He sent Shawn to the floor with a double leg take down which sent them crashing through a nearby partition. Hart then started teeing off on Shawn's head with a flurry of punches.

Jerry Lawler and Pat Patterson desperately tried to pull Hart off the hapless Michaels to no avail. Patterson screamed at Hart's friends Davey Boy Smith and Brian 'Crush' Adams for assistance, but neither were willing to intervene. They both understood that Bret needed to get it out of his system, and privately they also enjoyed seeing Shawn get what they felt had been coming to him for a long time.

"Bret was killing him," remembered Jim Cornette. "Shawn couldn't whip cream with an outboard motor in a real fight, much less Bret Hart." Eventually, with further help from Gerald Brisco, Hart was prised off the now bloody and bruised Michaels. As he was being dragged off, Hart kept hold of Shawn's hair, ripping a large chunk from his scalp. As Michaels' long golden locks fell from his hands, Hart warned him one final time, "Don't fuck with me or my family, you little fucker."

The Honky Tonk Man, Lawler's cousin, was in the room while the fracas was unfolding. He also realised that the fight had been inevitable for some time, and that it needed to happen. "It had nothing to do with professional wrestling, it had to do with a personal vendetta that they had against each other," he said. "These were just two guys who could not co-exist anymore in the same locker room." Word of the scrap between two of the WWF's biggest and most enduring names spread around the locker room like wildfire. "There's nothing like a locker room fight to get everyone talking," said announcer Kevin Kelly. "It's like a schoolyard fight; nothing really happens but everyone loves it."

"I've been around several situations where Bret and Shawn got into fisticuffs," Shamrock recalled. "They were competing against one another for the top spot, and you're going to have those situations, that's just the way it is."

Jim Cornette recalled how long-time road agent Steve Lombardi was flustered and running around in a state of panic, telling everyone in the vicinity what he had witnessed. As a senior road agent and member of the creative team, Cornette decided to take it upon himself to go and inform Vince McMahon about what had transpired. Upon entering Vince's office, Cornette found the chairman trying to catch up on finalising the evening's script, a task that had fell by the wayside following the various interruptions from Michaels and Hart earlier in the day. Cornette picked his moment and told him, "Vince, apparently Shawn and Bret have just had a shoot in the locker room..." As McMahon lifted his head and peered over his glasses, Michaels burst into the room, his eyes puffed up and swollen and his cheeks bruised as a result of the altercation.

"Goddamn this bullshit," screamed Michaels as he slammed a clump of his hair on McMahon's desk. "It's not safe to work here anymore. You've got a goddamn lunatic in there. You've obviously worked him into a frenzy or somebody has. Fuck this shit, Vince, I'll never work for you again." Before McMahon could respond, Michaels turned around and stormed out of the office. With only minutes to go before *Raw* went live, Michaels sought out Kliq sympathiser Peter 'Aldo Montoya' Polaco, one of the few men in the locker room who still gave him the time of day, and convinced him to give him a ride back to the hotel. As he left the building, Michaels loudly yelled – with the intention of being heard – that if he was close enough to Boston where *Nitro* was airing live that evening, he would go there. He had no intention of returning to work for Vince. He planned to fight for a contract release so he could go and be with his friends-cum-bodyguards in WCW.

Meanwhile, the fight and Michaels' subsequent departure from the building had done little to calm Hart. He spent the next thirty minutes loudly arguing with Gerald Brisco about the events, and he was infuriated when the agent reprimanded him for acting in an unprofessional manner. While there was little argument that Bret had thrown the first punch, most in the locker room believed that Shawn was the one to blame for the fight due to his smart-mouthed goading of Hart. Bret was given the rest of the night off by McMahon, leaving the arena thirty minutes into the broadcast without appearing in front of the cameras.

The evening's script had to be rewritten on the fly, with both Michaels and Hart removed. A planned match pitting Steve Austin against Brian Pillman - which had been heavily hyped as the former partners' first collision since the controversial home invasion angle from November 1996 – was scrapped due to Hart's absence; he had been set to play a part in the finish. With Michaels claiming to be done with the promotion, McMahon did not want to risk advertising him for a pay-per-view card he was unlikely to appear on, so removed him from the upcoming *Canadian Stampede* show from Hart's hometown of Calgary, replacing him with Ken Shamrock.

In a different age the backstage scuffle would have remained strictly behind closed doors, but the evolving business was shifting into a reality-based era, and McMahon addressed the fight on the *Raw* broadcast. He explained the absence of two of his top stars with an adapted version of the truth, noting that both had been sent from the arena due to unprofessional conduct. Before the night was out, McMahon used the situation to generate dollars by having Jim Ross shill his premium rate hotline number with the promise of more details about the fracas. On the hotline, Ross revealed that the pair had engaged in a real fist fight that was not part of any angle, and acknowledged that Michaels had walked out of the company.

THE NEXT day, McMahon circulated an internal memo around Titan Towers that read:

> Last night in Hartford, Shawn Michaels breached his contract by refusing to perform. We are hopeful Shawn will reconsider his position and return to work. Shawn has four years to go on his five-year contract. The door is open for Shawn to return under the terms of his contract.

That same day, Michaels was telling friends he would never work for the WWF again, claiming he was quite content to leave the business for four years if that was what it took to escape his contract. With Titan already on shaky financial footing, McMahon had no desire to pay Shawn his $15,000 per week downside guarantee for sitting at home, so he felt forced to take a drastic but unwanted step. Via lawyer Jerry McDevitt, McMahon sent Shawn a letter stating that he had breached his contract by walking out on *Raw* and that he needed to return to work immediately.

McMahon was determined to enforce Michaels' four-year contract. By claiming a breach, it effectively placed Michaels on suspension, so Vince was not obliged to pay him anything until he returned. McMahon felt he had little choice but to take the hard-line approach and keep Shawn tied to Titan, because he believed that losing him to the opposition could be the final blow for his organisation.

Michaels response was to disconnect his telephone so that Federation officials were unable to get in touch, a stalling tactic he used while he consulted his San Antonio-based attorney Skip McCormick. Days later, McCormick sent McDevitt a counter letter denying that any contract breach had taken place, stating that Shawn had left *Raw* because of an "unsafe working environment". He also claimed that Michaels had hurt his knee and neck during the skirmish with Hart, and had missed ensuing dates that he was advertised for as a result of those injuries.

McCormick's approach successfully quashed Titan's attempts to withhold Michaels' pay further, with Federation lawyers realising that Michaels had them over a barrel with regards to the unsafe environment. McCormick advised Shawn to cede a little and soften his stance about working with Vince again, because to refuse going forward would constitute a breach. Under his lawyer's advice, Michaels agreed to return to work for Titan, realising that he was bound by his long-term contract with the WWF whether he liked it or not.

With the Michaels situation still tenuous by the following week's *Raw* broadcast, McMahon decided to keep Bret Hart off television that evening to prevent him from needling at the situation, disrupting the applecart further. The excuse given for his absence was that he and Michaels had been injured in the backstage fight, giving both a valid reason for not appearing. Hart returned to the company the following week, and the ring five days later on the house show loop. After meeting with McMahon and Titan officials on July 3, Michaels finally agreed to come back to work, eventually returning on the July 14 episode of *Raw*.

ON THE same night that Bret Hart and Shawn Michaels were scuffling in Hartford, Michaels' Kliq ally Kevin Nash was enduring similar problems of his own at WCW's *Nitro* event in Boston.

Nash's clash was with veteran grappler and industry icon 'Rowdy' Roddy Piper, a man who shared the responsibility – if not the spotlight or adulation – with Hulk Hogan of making the inaugural *WrestleMania* a success. That was twelve years earlier, and as far as Nash was concerned, he was yet another old-timer clinging on to the final vestiges of his past success. Nash saw Piper as someone getting in the way at the summit of the card, costing him the opportunity to make more money than he already was.

The issue of contention related to Piper's performance in a match the pair had been involved in that evening, which saw Nash teaming with regular partner Scott Hall against the veteran Piper and Ric Flair. The bout was designed to hype an identical return clash at the upcoming *Great American Bash* pay-per-view, and Hall and Nash realised they did not want to give away too much that night so they could save something for the big show. "Scott and I sat down with them before the match and said, 'Whatever we do tonight, let's not jumpstart it, we'll have nowhere to go'," said Nash.

Nevertheless, it was an historic night for WCW, with the group having set a company attendance and gate record at the Boston Fleet Center, and the pressure was on to perform. Piper and Flair, feeding off the electricity of the crowd, could not help themselves but to go against Nash and Hall's instructions, immediately changing the pre-arranged structure of the contest which they had agreed upon backstage. "We got out there and they charged us," complained Nash, "I was pissed. I laid it in out there."

Piper's apparent indiscretion was not an act of malice, rather a generational disparity. In Piper's era, pre-planning spots and rehearsing sequences was not commonplace. He was more familiar with a style that called for a performer to react to the tempo of an audience and call matches on the fly. He felt the audience wanted to see a fast start rather than a heat-driven match that would see Nash and Hall control the pace, so that's what he gave them.

Nash was already riled with his opponent going into the bout. The issue stemmed from an occurrence in the build-up to the main event of the *Slamboree* pay-per-view in May, where Piper had teamed with Ric Flair and active NFL linebacker Kevin Greene against the nWo triumvirate of Nash, Hall and Waltman. Piper and Flair both protested the involvement of Waltman, whom they felt was a good worker but not a big enough name to be competing in a headline match on the card. They wanted him out of the bout because they believed his involvement was purely political, another example of the Kliq looking after their own.

Hall and Nash refused, realising that Waltman was the hardest worker on their team and the man who would be able to carry their side of the bout. Piper suggested that he work with Waltman in a singles bout on the undercard instead, with his transparent motivation being that Waltman would make him look good, quelling locker room disdain towards him for living off his past reputation. WCW management rejected the proposal, determined to run with the six-man tag they had booked.

With *Slamboree* taking place in Charlotte, NC, which in wrestling circles was considered "Flair country", the intention was that Greene would turn on the local icon and side with the nWo, giving the heel trio the victory. Greene, a state hero in his own right due to his time spent playing for the Carolina Panthers in 1996, flat out refused to comply. Piper also rejected requests that his team take the fall, his contractual right due to a creative control clause that Bischoff had written into his deal in order to lure him to Atlanta. The nWo trio decided that for the sake of keeping the peace - not to mention proving to their critics that they were professionals - they would all do the job simultaneously.

By the time *Nitro* from Boston rolled around three weeks later, Nash was still smarting about losing a political power play to the veterans. Thus he did not see Piper's deviation from the script that evening as anything other than an intended snub. In protest, he decided to briefly stop selling. Piper eventually returned to the plan and let the Outsiders throw him around, but his conditioning was poor and his timing off, so he called for the duo to *go home*[13] only halfway into the time the match had been allotted. With six minutes of airtime to fill before *Nitro* ended, a post-match brawl which was intended to last one minute had to be stretched to almost seven.

Nash was furious about Piper changing everything on a whim, in particular because he had been unprepared for Piper's opening salvo and had reinjured his knee during the confusion. Even so, he was content to leave the dispute in the ring, as per the unwritten wrestler code of conduct, until he heard that Piper was in another room running his mouth about him. Egged on by his equally annoyed friends, Nash decided to confront Piper with the intention of putting him in his place.

Piper was with Ric Flair, Eric Bischoff, Randy Savage, and Hulk Hogan in a private locker room, unlacing his boots, when he heard a series of thumping knocks on the door. It was Nash, flanked by Hall and Waltman, who burst into the room yelling, "Motherfucker, if only you would listen." Startled, Piper jumped out of his seat across the room from Nash, readying himself for the inevitable tussle. That only served to rile Nash further, with the seething grappler assuming Piper was squaring up to him. "You think you're running the place around here?" growled Nash, making a beeline across the locker room for Piper. Before he could make it to the stunned wrestler, Piper's bodyguard Craig Malley blocked Nash's path, though quickly moved aside when he realised that Nash was not likely to slow down for him. Nash continued to yell, blaming Piper's refusal to stick to the match plan as the reason he aggravated his knee injury. Piper fired back that Nash was a liar.

By now, Nash had heard enough. He opened up his hand and slapped Piper across the face (he would later claim the openhanded shot rather than a closed fist was a mark of his respect for the aging veteran), sending him staggering backwards into the dressing room wall. Piper quickly shook it off and tried to throw a kick in the direction of Nash's damaged knee, but he came up short. Piper later claimed that he not aware Nash even had a bad knee, but that if he had been, he would have gone for it anyway. He had little time or respect for

---

[13] In wrestling parlance, to "go home" means to end the match.

Nash, whom he felt was trying to run roughshod over the locker room. "They thought they knew better about what was needed for business than the people who ran the business at the time," he grumbled.

As with Hart and Michaels in Hartford, the other wrestlers in the vicinity of the incident acted quickly to make sure the situation did not get too far out of control. Malley and Flair pulled the pair apart, though Nash remained livid about the incident as he was being dragged away.

"Moline, motherfucker, I'll see you in Moline," Nash yelled, referring to the impending *Great American Bash* pay-per-view coming up in the city in six days' time. A few days later, Piper was discussing the altercation with his friend Brad Rheingans, a stocky former Olympic amateur wrestler who had a reputation as a shooter. "What did Nash say?" Rheingans asked, to which Piper told him of the Moline threat. "Yeah, he doesn't wanna fight," assessed Rheingans, "Why wait for Moline?"

He was right. Tempers had significantly calmed by the time the two met again at the pay-per-view. Piper – who claimed not to fear Nash because he had experienced an irate Andre the Giant, noting Nash was not anywhere near as imposing – was still wary. He was older, at a significant size disadvantage, and would be pissing into the proverbial political wind if he attempted to retaliate. Nash too was happy to let the incident drop, explaining, "When you strike a man and see fear in his face, at my size you realise you're playing the bully." The *Great American Bash* match, a repeat of the *Nitro* encounter, passed without incident, and immediately afterwards the pair were separated in the storylines and moved on to different programs.

There was a further incident involving Nash on the Labor Day edition of *Monday Nitro* in September 1997. Nash led several nWo companions through a mockery of the heartfelt retirement speech given one week earlier by thirty-eight-year-old Martin 'Arn Anderson' Lunde, who had been drastically losing the use of his left arm due to accumulated spinal injuries. While Anderson's speech was understandably emotional and bittersweet (his best friend and fellow Four Horsemen lifer Ric Flair wept openly as Anderson spoke), the nWo parody was morbid, with Nash donning a mangy bald-cap and coke-dealer glasses, playing a seven-foot version of 'The Enforcer'. Nash jovially mocked Anderson's purported penchant for overindulgent drinking, while also taking lighter shots at the Horsemen as an aging group of sad-sacks.

"I came up with the idea," admitted Nash, "The Horsemen knew, they all thought it was funny until they called home that night and their wives said they looked like a bunch of boobs. Arn's wife said, 'He made you look like a stupid fucking drunk.'"

"I just assumed and expected Arn would let us weave the reality of what he was going through into a storyline that would benefit others," confessed Eric

Bischoff. "I didn't take into consideration the emotional impact his forced retirement had on him and his family."

"The Horsemen wanted blood," remembered Nash. "It was retributional heat from the wives that caused the heat. I was like, 'I got the okay to do this! You saw me in the make-up chair! I got the cooler [of beer] from Arn's car! It was actually Arn's cooler! It was art imitating life, imitating art, imitating life."

The Horsemen were supposed to run in and assault the New World Order satirists, but agent Terry Taylor was told by Bischoff to nix that part of the plan, allegedly at Nash's request. As a result, an irate Flair refused to cut a promo later in the night against the nWo. After all, where were he and the gang when fallen Anderson's good name was being sullied by the opposition?

Later that night, Anderson confronted Nash about the segment. "We were in Pensacola staying at this nice hotel, and Arn walks over to me with like five beers in his hands, looks up at me and says, 'Why [would] you do that?' I just looked down at his hands, pushed the button, and got in the elevator. I was like, 'Are you fucking shitting me?' It was just like the Curtain Call: Vince said it was fine until all the boys said, 'Oh kayfabe!' and Hunter got his head chopped off. It's always a good idea until everyone bitches about it like a bunch of fucking cunts."

The thinly-spread Kliq was finally being met with resistance. Michaels grumbled openly about Hart's loaded contract, upset that somebody was feasting on a larger piece of the Titan pie. The Wolfpac contingent found themselves politically hamstrung by the stipulations in Piper's deal that allowed him to balk at a loss. Two years earlier, they, along with junior ally Triple H, held McMahon in place over the creative barrel with their iron-strength whimsy, controlling the fates of so many travel-weary men that they never gave a second thought to. Michaels' scalp being ripped out by Hart's vengeful claw was a single window into a wider picture: two locker rooms were standing up against a minified Kliq, fighting against the petulance. Between Hart and Piper's contracts, which still paled to the airtight deal afforded to canonised Hogan, the Kliq ironically found themselves smooshed against a glass ceiling of their own, unprotected backs exposed to fearless reprisal. What good is handsome compensation without absolute power?

OVER IN the WWF, the next pay-per-view *In Your House 16: Canadian Stampede* was set for July 6 from Calgary's Saddledome. It was a show fraught with problems. The initial five match card was wrecked by injuries, and the main event had to be changed due to the absence of Shawn Michaels following the fracas with Bret Hart in Hartford.

On the original bill, The Undertaker had been scheduled to defend his WWF Championship against Ahmed Johnson, who was looking to relaunch his stuttering career, fresh off a heel turn via an induction into black-power militant group the Nation of Domination. However, as had been the story of his WWF tenure, Johnson wound up getting injured for real during a storyline brawl following his inauguration into the group, and resultantly had to be removed from the card. A serendipitous though unfortunate event on June 15 gave the WWF a last minute solution, when Sid Eudy - who was scheduled to wrestle Vader at *Canadian Stampede* - was involved in a car accident en route to Ottawa. Eudy had been driving at 100MPH while struggling to open his sun roof, and the distraction caused him to plough into the curb and flip the vehicle, injuring himself and road partners Doug Furnas, Phil LaFon and Flash Funk. Funk was largely unscathed, though the other three were forced onto the side-lines, with the injuries Eudy sustained forcing him to pull out of the Calgary pay-per-view. The WWF brass simply merged the two cancelled bouts into one, giving them an Undertaker-Vader title confrontation and reducing the card to only four contests.

Going into the event, few had much optimism that it was going to be anything other than a standard *In Your House* broadcast, with interest levels in the botched-together card at seemingly record-low levels. Those fears were assuaged somewhat with a near $230,000 house at the Saddledome, which shattered the previous gate record in the building. Creatively, the four-match show wound up a surprise smash hit, with each contest delivering beyond expectations, and the card's selling point, a ten-man tag team main event pitting the homecoming Hart Foundation against their hated American foes, resonating with both arena and broadcast audiences as a bout for the ages.

The dichotomy for the contest was an unusual one by Federation standards. In the United States, Bret and his allies were despised villains, staunch champions of the Canadian flag, and outspoken in their opinions of American culture. In Calgary it was a complete shift, with the Hart Foundation revered as conquering heroes, Canadians (or rather proxy Canadians in the case of Brian Pillman, who trained at the famous Hart family dungeon, and both Davey Boy Smith and Jim Neidhart, who had married into the Hart family) who had defended their nation by denying its inferiority complex in the shadow of America.

For American viewers it was a curious sight indeed to see the Hart Foundation acting every bit the blue-eyed babyfaces, while their American counterparts - ordinarily good guys in the US - were angrily jeered. It was a riotous atmosphere, unlike anything else the WWF had ever tried previously. With the onset of WWF's edgy new direction, Vince Russo had played a major role in giving the key players on the roster fresh doses of attitude. It meant that the increasingly old-fashioned notion of babyfaces and heels was quickly becoming a thing of the past, as Russo ushered in a philosophy that he liked to call "shades of grey". In other words, babyfaces could be bad, and heels could be good. For a company built on the back of Hulk Hogan telling fans to say their prayers and eat their vitamins, it was a significant shift in ideals.

Due to his knee surgery, the match marked the first time Hart had wrestled a televised bout in three months. Despite having worked a few lower pressure house show bouts to shake his ring rust, he was cautious going into the pay-per-view that his knee was not quite ready for the vigours of the ring. "My knee wasn't healed enough to wrestle safely, and I knew it," he remembered, "But I had waited my entire career for this night, to wrestle at the top of my game in front of the fans who had been with me from the very beginning."

Bret and head road agent Pat Patterson were responsible for formulating the blueprints of the twenty-five-minute match, exchanging suggestions about what spots to include and how best to pace the match in order that the competitors did not blow themselves up too quickly. All ten of the participants in the bout were familiar with what was expected of them, because they had enacted a dry run of the bout in Des Moines, Iowa a week earlier only with the roles reversed. In that contest Steve Austin had pinned Owen Hart to score the win for the American team.

The difference in Calgary was the presence of the vast Hart family, with relations from far and wide turning up for their own fleeting moment of second-hand fame. All the Hart wrestling brothers were there, in addition to Bret and Owen's father Stu, and family matriarch Helen. "I figured since Stu and my brothers were all there, we might as well involve them in the storyline," told Bret, a plan that Vince happily consented to.

The way the match was laid out called for Stu and the brothers to be involved at the conclusion. The plan was for Bruce Hart to throw a drink over Austin, but for Austin to think that Stu had been the one to commit the act, leading to him shoving Stu in his seat. From there the other Hart brothers would get involved, leading to Owen rolling up Austin for the win, setting up a singles confrontation between them at *SummerSlam* the following month.

Bruce was eager to seize the opportunity, and grabbed his moment in the spotlight with both hands. He decided to do more than the script called for, believing that being more heavily involved in the outcome could lead to a potential contract and a place in the Hart Foundation. He also saw it as his chance to share a little of the limelight that his famous brothers enjoyed. Bruce was overzealous, standing up to Austin and brawling at ringside with the American team, taking all the focus away from Owen as he scored the match-winning pinfall. After the show, Owen chastised his older brother for stealing his moment, and Bret similarly reprimanded him for going over the top. Bruce never did receive the contract he had been hankering for.

Post-match, the entire Hart family and their friends entered the ring for a celebration. Little did Bret know that the match would be the last time he would ever wrestle for the WWF in front of his hometown audience. In many ways, *Canadian Stampede* turned out to be his - and the Hart family's - last hurrah.

EIGHT

IT WAS ALMOST 5 P.M. ON October 5, the day of the WWF's *Badd Blood* pay-per-view and everyone had arrived at the building on time except for Bret Hart and Brian Pillman. One of the perks Hart's thirteen-year tenure with the company afforded him was that he could routinely show up late without repercussions, much to the continued irritation of his locker room rivals. Nobody was especially concerned with his tardiness, nor Pillman's for that matter, because officials supposed he had grabbed a ride with Hart. When Bret arrived alone a few minutes later, frustration began to set in. "Where the fuck is Pillman?" grumbled Bruce Prichard to fellow agent Jim Cornette, "He should have been here hours ago!"

Cornette knew that Pillman had worked on a house show in St. Paul, Minnesota the previous night so he asked around some of the boys to find out if they knew of any plans Brian had made to make the show. The boys did not know anything other than that Pillman had missed the WWF shuttle from the airport, and nobody had seen Brian since the previous evening. Searching for more information, Cornette decided to contact the Bugetel Inn in Bloomington where Brian had been staying the night before to try to find out what time he had checked out. Cornette sat in one of the makeshift production offices and punched in the number for the hotel. When the hotel manager answered, Cornette explained who he was and asked, "I'm calling about one of your guests from last night, Brian Pillman. Can you tell me what time he checked out?" The manager immediately asked Cornette to hold, then when he returned to the phone he broke the news: "Sir, Mr. Pillman has passed away."

Cornette struggled to process the magnitude of what he had been told. He heard the words, but his brain could not comprehend how they could possibly be right. Pillman was a thirty-five-year-old in the prime of his life, he had wrestled only the night before and nobody had reported any concerns about him. How could he be dead? Cornette assumed he was being ribbed and suspected that Brian was standing behind the hotel manager egging him on. Cornette probed further and soon it began to dawn on him that this was not an elaborate ruse, but an appalling real-life situation. Cornette yelled out to the only other person in the room Bruno Lauer (better known by his WWF handle Harvey Wippleman) and told him, "Bruno, go get Bruce. Go get him and tell him I said come here right fucking now." In an age before immediate contact via mobile phones or online social media, Cornette realised that he was the only person in the company who knew what had happened to Brian and the onus was on him to deliver the bad news. As he was contemplating how to break it, Prichard stormed into the room annoyed that he had been dragged away from one of the dozen other jobs he was simultaneously trying to manage. "What do you want me to get on the phone for!?" he grumbled, to which Cornette quietly mouthed, "Pillman is dead."

Brian's wife Melanie learned that the de facto father of her five children[14] was dead at around the same time as the news made it to the Kiel Center. Melanie had just come off the phone with the World Wrestling Federation, who had called asking if she knew where Brian was because he had not shown up in St. Louis. She thought nothing of it because Brian had left her a message the night before and she suspected he had simply overslept – likely due to the cocktail of strong medication he was taking to help him battle the excruciating daily pain of an ankle injury he had suffered in a nasty car wreck in early 1996. As Jim Cornette was learning Brian's tragic fate, Melanie received a knock on her front door. It was the police. When they told Melanie that Brian had died in his hotel room, she fainted. Brian's daughter Brittany was only six-years-old, yet she had already experienced more trauma in her young life than anyone her age should have to endure; her mother Rochelle, Brian's ex-fiancé, had committed suicide a few years earlier. When she heard the news that her father was gone too, she let out a blood-curdling shriek of utter anguish and despair, weeping in the arms of the heartbroken policemen.

IT DID not take long for word of Brian's passing to spread to the boys in the back, most of whom were lacing up their boots, making final tweaks to their ring gear, and running through the spots of their forthcoming matches. Del 'The Patriot' Wilkes who was signed by Titan in mid-1997 to work as an All-American babyface in a program with Bret Hart, vividly recalled how he learned the news.

"We were waiting for Bret to get with us to go over our finish, and he just kept putting it off and putting it off. He was very slow getting dressed, which

---

[14] Two of the children, Alexis and Jesse, were Melanie's children from another relationship. Two more were Brian's children, Danielle and Brittany, from different mothers. Brian Jnr., was the only child the two had together prior to Pillman's death.

was pretty typical for Bret; he took his time and moved slow backstage. But I noticed that wow, we were just a few hours away and he's got to come up with a finish, and we've been here all afternoon. So finally, he was ready to get together in a conference room, somewhere in the bowels of the auditorium. It's me, him, Vader, and Davey Boy. It didn't go unnoticed that Brian wasn't there, he wasn't at the building. We had heard from so many people, 'Have you seen Brian?', 'Do you know where Brian's at?' We were in the room going over our finish and there comes a knock on the door. Owen sticks his head in, walks in and says, 'Guys, I'm sorry to interrupt you, but I just wanted to let you know we just found out that they found Brian dead in a hotel room.' It was just utter shock. There wasn't a word spoken for literally fifteen seconds.

"Then Vader, in typical Vader fashion, spoke up and said, 'You know, that's tragic, and I hate it, but we've got an 'effing finish we've gotta come up with, so we can talk about that later?' So we just went back to coming up with our finish." Bret Hart was incensed by Vader's casual dismissal of Brian's death, but Wilkes defended his tag partner's callousness that night. "One thing about Vader that is pretty well known backstage is that he would get bubbled up and nervous before a match. I have seen him throw up before matches, he'd get so nervous and so tense. He was just so nervous about not having a finish down yet." It seemed like denial on the part of the burly Colorado native.

VINCE MCMAHON was sat in a makeup chair when one of his aides quietly whispered the news about Brian. He quickly called an emergency meeting with his closest advisors and immediately engaged damage control mode. Wrestlers had died young before, far too many of them, but not on his watch. This was new ground for McMahon to tread and he had to make a snap decision about how best to proceed. He opted for the truth, or at least an abridged version of it. Made up like a waxwork figure with a face caked in concealer, McMahon broke the news to his audience of Brian Pillman's death during the pay-per-view pre-show:

> Ladies and gentlemen we have some tragic news to report. Approximately five o'clock central time we here in the World Wrestling Federation were notified that Brian Pillman has passed away. Brian Pillman was last with the World Wrestling Federation last night in St. Paul, Minnesota and he was found dead in his hotel room in Bloomington, Minnesota this afternoon. At this juncture we do not have more information other than to tell you that Brian Pillman is dead. We here at the World Wrestling Federation offer our condolences to the Pillman family

By the time the pay-per-view started thirty minutes later, it was as if nothing had happened. There was no further mention made about Pillman's passing on the air, and the vibe given off by announcers McMahon, Jerry Lawler, and Jim Ross did little to indicate that the grave news had any lasting effect. It almost felt as though they had been expecting something like that to happen for so long that they had already come to terms with it. And after all, there was a wrestling war to win, dammit, and real-life had to take a back seat. At least until the next night when McMahon would exploit Brian's death for every penny and ratings point that he could.

DEL WILKES immediately suspected that Pillman's death was drug-related. As he remembered it, "There were a lot of other issues with prescription medication, drugs, it was troubling in the business at that time. It was as much a part of the business as tights and boots." Wilkes decided to make a phone call to Dr. Joel Hackett, Brian's doctor, who also happened to be his supplier. "I knew that Brian used that same doctor, as did a lot of the guys. The first thing I did that night when I got back to the hotel room was call him. I said, 'Look buddy, you better strap your boots on, because I'm sure there were pill bottles in Brian's room with your name on them as the prescriber. You might have a lot to answer for, and I just wanted to give you a heads up.'"

It soon became clear that Brian Pillman's death was at least in part drug-related. When the maid who was sent to clean Pillman's room at 1:09 p.m. found the wrestler sprawled out lifeless on his bed, the accompanying mise-en-scene served as a grim blueprint for the setting of countless future deaths of grapplers not yet in their forties. A bottle of beer stood half-drank on his bedside table and several open bottles of prescription medicine - including wrestler-favourite carisoprodol (Soma) and various painkillers – were dotted throughout the room. The cocktail was enough to suggest on first glance that Pillman had overdosed, although his autopsy later revealed that he had died of a heart attack caused by a congenital heart condition. However, there was little doubt that Pillman's well-known rampant drug use accelerated the condition, with traces of cocaine also found in his system, in addition to later revelations from Melanie that Brian was using ephedrine pills to keep his physique cut and Human Growth Hormone to build muscle onto his small frame.

The majority of the drugs found in Pillman's hotel room were indeed prescribed by Dr. Hackett of Indianapolis, a modern-day Dr. George Zahorian that the boys has christened "Doctor Feelgood" due to the proclivity with which he over-prescribed medication. The boys even used his name as code, quipping, "I just can't Hack-ett anymore" when they were running short on supplies. "He was like some star-struck guy," said Melanie, "I can't imagine putting your heart and soul into medical school and then blowing it because you want to be friends with some wrestlers. I don't know what was going through that man's head. He would just call in five or six pain pill prescriptions for Brian a week." Melanie confronted Hackett over her belief that he was oversubscribing medication to her husband, but he would consistently deny any wrongdoing. Melanie recalled how he would say, "The other doctors don't understand them like I do. They're in so much pain on a nightly basis, and as a doctor, I have to do my duty to alleviate that pain. I can't just let them sit there in pain." Melanie argued that Hackett was prescribing a regulated drug but intentionally failing to regulate it, suggesting that if they were in that much pain then perhaps surgery to repair the damage would be the safer and more sensible option. Despite her pleas, Hackett continued to flagrantly disregard the codes of practice and happily indulged the wrestler's needs.

There were many others besides Brian who called upon Hackett to sate their addictions and the star-struck doctor was only too happy to comply. He became so notorious in wrestling circles that two days after Brian's death, the WWF – fearing a repeat of the costly steroid trial of the early nineties – stepped in and banned its wrestlers from associating with him. "We basically made it clear to all of the performers that he was someone to avoid," said Jim Byrne, former WWF Marketing Vice President. Vince was concerned that the Feds were going to target Hackett with the same vigour as they had gone after George Zahorian, and he realised a second drug trial could be the final nail in the coffin. Hackett tried to save his reputation by playing the race card, claiming the WWF were targeting him because he was African-American, though he had no grounds with which to make such outlandish claims.

The WWF's General Counsel sent out letters to a number of other doctors who had similar reputations to Hackett and would attend WWF cards armed with bags full of medicine, doling out pills to eager open-handed wrestlers like they were kids receiving candy on Halloween. The letters advised the physicians they were banned from WWF locker rooms with immediate effect and warned that dispensing medication should only occur when a wrestler attended their office for an official appointment. Not that any of the boys listened. Del Wilkes openly admitted to having beaten the Hackett drug piñata for every drop of medicinal candy going:

"I'd known Hackett since my days in WCW. He just wrote an unlimited amount of scripts for anything we wanted. It was a joke how easy it was to get Hackett to do anything. I would think to myself, 'There's no way he's going to do this for me this time,' but you'd call him and he'd do it. It even continued after my retirement. Because of my injuries, I could call him up one day and say, 'I need a hundred pain pills,' and he'd call 'em up. Then I could call him the next day and say, 'I needed a hundred more,' and he'd call 'em up. It didn't matter to him. It finally got to the point where he would quit calling them in and every Monday, he would FedEx me out a different written prescription of one hundred pain pills, Somas, Valium, and halcyons.

"I would just shop pharmacies, go to different pharmacies. There was a pharmacist at a Wal-Mart in my hometown that alerted the Indiana State Police, saying, 'Hey, I've got a customer here in Columbia, SC that has had literally thousands upon thousands of pills written to him by a doctor in Indianapolis.' I called Joel one day and said I needed him to refill something for me. He said, 'I can't. The Indiana State Police are waiting to interview me.' He called me back later that day and said, 'We got a big problem. I can't write any more scripts for you. They're onto me.'"

If Hackett thought he had problems after Pillman died, they became significantly worse four months later on February 15, 1998, when former WWF performer and active WCW star Louie Mucciolo (Louie Spicolli) died in his home at the age of twenty-seven. The previous night had been a typical one for Mucciolo, who had spent the evening partying with his friends and washing down somas with bottles of wine. By the time he fell to sleep at 2 a.m. he had consumed two dozen pills, though by his standards that was not a particularly high figure. While still working for the WWF, Mucciolo had once ingested nearly sixty of them, which left him in a critical condition and fighting for his life. McMahon released him soon after that ordeal. That did not stop Mucciolo's drug use, and he built up such a high tolerance for Somas that he could take fifteen of them and feel no effect whatsoever.

On the night he died his friends recall nothing unusual about his behaviour. He was the same Louie as ever and his drug use was no different than normal. That is not to say they were not concerned about it, and at one point they tried to hide the alcohol from Mucciolo, but he soon found it and finished the bottle. They had seen him in far worse conditions before – putting him to bed after he had passed out was a regular ritual - so they were not too worried. Louie's friend John Hannah spent the night, and he awoke at 8:55 a.m. to a foul stench emanating from Mucciolo's room. When he walked in to check on him he found the wrestler lying on the floor face-down in his own vomit, his skin discoloured and his ankles swollen. It was obvious he had been dead for a few hours. The police were immediately called and quickly discovered pills and prescriptions dotted around the room – among them Xanax, Somas and testosterone – all bearing Hackett's name on the labels.

The WWF decided to take the bold step of bringing the issue of Dr. Hackett to the forefront in an effort to paint themselves as the innocent victims of the piece, hoping that by attacking Hackett directly they would absolve themselves of any questions or blame, deflecting the heat onto the doctor. Shortly after Mucciolo's death the WWF wrote to the Indianapolis office of the DEA (Drug Enforcement Administration) to request an investigation into Hackett. Titan promised to cooperate fully and expressed their hope that Hackett's licence would be revoked.

When the authorities investigated further, Hackett's licence was temporarily suspended and the WWF issued a second damage control statement in response:

Since 1995, the WWF has made every effort to keep Indianapolis doctor Joel Hackett out of its locker rooms, backstage areas and away from its performers. The WWF through 1996 and 1997 denied Hackett's repeated requests for complimentary tickets to its events and access to its talent. Hackett was instructed to have no contact with WWF Superstars and talent was requested not to associate with Hackett.

Mucciolo was not the last wrestler with a drug problem linked to Hackett, whose patient list included names such as The Ultimate Warrior and Ahmed Johnson. He was eventually forced to close his practice and was later charged with forty-eight counts of illegally prescribing drugs. As Wilkes recalled, "Once everything went down he sent me a copy of the foreclosure notice, and said, 'Thanks a lot.' I thought, 'You did this to yourself. I didn't do this to you. None of the boys did anything. You were the one; you could have said no at any time!'"

THE MOST tragic thing about Brian Pillman's death was that everybody around him saw it coming and nobody could do anything to prevent it. The warning signs that Brian was running too close to the edge had been there for all to see, since the near-fatal Humvee wreck that had ruined his ankle and derailed his career eighteen months earlier. With his ankle fused into walking position, Pillman could barely get around without enduring searing agony, no less run the ropes and fly around the ring. Pillman was no stranger to living with pain, having suffered from throat cancer since the age of two and undergoing thirty-six operations to remove polyps on his throat, but the pain from his ankle was taking its toll even on him.

Pillman should not have been anywhere near a wrestling ring, but determined to honour the fat guaranteed contract that Vince McMahon had given him in 1996, he felt like he had no choice but to compete in order to provide for his family. Pillman turned to a cocktail of powerful painkillers to numb the pain, though it was so acute they gave him little relief. He took to mixing prescription drugs and over-medicating himself, leaving his eyes red and darting wildly like a junkie.

It began to affect his personal life. Brian was so out of his mind on drugs that he fell into the same trap as many other wrestlers; he could not differentiate between the work of his onscreen 'Loose Cannon' persona and reality. At home he would play his television character when only Melanie and the children were around, which led to constant arguments. Concerned that her husband was going down a one-way path to an early grave, she implored him to check into rehab and change his ways. Brian would have none of it. He resisted her pleas and rubbed the rebuttal in her face by purchasing a "Rehab is for Quitters" shirt, proudly wearing it around the house. Attempts by Brian's friends to convince him to get help were also ignored. Pillman was so paranoid that he became convinced that those looking out for him were actually out to get him.

The incidents continued to pile up. Pillman wrecked three rental cars in the space of a few weeks, two of them on the same weekend, leading to his friends refusing to ride with him for fear a trip with him could be their last. The WWF were hardly oblivious to Pillman's problems and had his long-time ally Jim Ross counsel him several times a week. Pillman resented that, and when Ross asked him to take a drug test he lost his temper. Pillman yelled at Ross that while he was taking pain pills, so was everyone else in the company because it was not possible to be a pro wrestler without them. "What about Shawn [Michaels]?" Brian yelled, "He is fucking worse than me! I have never gone on television so loaded that I can't fuckin' stand up straight, but Shawn has done that twice in the last few weeks. Why is he so goddamn untouchable?" Pillman was furious because he felt he had been singled out for doing something that all the boys were doing, and in his mind he had been betrayed by a man he considered to be a close friend.

Brian was so annoyed with the apparent hypocrisy of the WWF's drug test program that he decided he was going to leave. The night after the argument with Ross, Pillman made a phone call to his good friend Dave Meltzer and told him he was quitting the WWF and planned to go back to WCW where he could slot back into a role as one of the Four Horsemen. Meltzer tried to talk him out of it, realising that the unstructured and anarchic nature of WCW's locker room would not be a positive environment for Brian to be around because he would not be looked after in the same way as he was in the WWF. Pillman argued back that the WWF had caused problems with his marriage by demanding a drug test and causing Melanie to worry that he was a junkie who was going to lose his job.

Brian was pushing Melanie away. She had begun divorce proceedings against him after his anger towards her had driven him to write a graphic and unpleasant letter to their children, in which he viciously derided their mother. Melanie felt the need to get a restraining order against Brian, which he flagrantly disregarded. He violated it with such frequency that he was forced to take anger management classes once a week, causing him to miss all Friday night house shows. By all accounts the couple made up before Brian's death, but their relationship was further strained when Melanie discovered she was pregnant again. Whether Brian knew remains debatable, though his close friends believe that he did, and that he suspected that the child was not his.

Such was the sudden nature of Brian's death that not all of his shattered relationships were patched up prior to his passing. One of his closest friends was well-respected NFL fitness coach Kim Woods, a man he had known since his youth who had always served as a father figure to him, and was the man responsible for coming up with the majority of Pillman's heralded 'Loose Cannon' gimmick. When he noticed Brian playing the character away from the ring he grew concerned that he was no longer able to separate his television character from real life. When Pillman showed up at Kim's house sporting fresh needle marks in his arm, Woods demanded that he leave immediately and never return. It was the last time the two spoke.

Woods cared too much about Brian to sit back and watch him kill himself, and he hoped his harshness would serve as a wakeup call that would set the troubled wrestler straight. But Pillman was in too deep by then. Woods realised as much when a mutual friend came to him with a message. "Paul Heyman told me to let you know that your buddy is on some Mexican Quaalude (a potent hypnotic sedative) and isn't going to last more than a few weeks." Heyman's clairvoyance continued during a conversation with Shane Douglas. When Douglas enquired about the possibility of Pillman being able to work as his opponent at ECW's *November to Remember* pay-per-view as a way to blow off a program they started during Pillman's brief ECW stint in 1996, Heyman responded, "Shane, Brian isn't going to be alive by then."

"It was painfully obvious that Brian was on a very bad path and he was probably going to crash and burn," said Wilkes. "He tried to do a run-in one night during a match, but he was just a mess, bless his heart." Dave Meltzer had similar memories; "I was still in regular contact with Brian and half the time he was still brilliant when it came to business, but the other half, he was scary in the way you knew this wasn't going to have a happy ending."

"Brian was hurting," said Ken Shamrock. "He was kinda getting pushed out at the time. His body was beat up and he was taking a lot of stuff to help ease his pain. He was taking the stuff because he wanted to continue to work. He didn't wanna lose his job. His determination to keep wrestling led to his demise. Most people within the business knew he was going down the wrong path, and that if he didn't start changing things he was going to end up in a bad spot."

Pillman's erratic behaviour was the talk of the WWF locker room, with most having figured out that he was no longer working a gimmick, he was having genuine problems. Some of the boys were planning to hold an intervention of sorts to try pushing him to get help, but nobody could agree on how best to go about it. Others took a different approach, with two of the wrestlers taking Pillman into a secluded spot in the back and roughing him up, warning him, "not to fuck things up for everybody else because he couldn't handle what he was taking." They had no interest in Brian's wellbeing; they simply wanted to ensure that their own addictions would not be put under the spotlight if he were to die.

For all Pillman's imminent self-destruction was evident to those around him, few supposed that his demise was quite so near. "Despite all the wrestlers who had died that I knew, none of whom were as scary at the end, I never fully acknowledged that he could die," said Meltzer. WWF trainer Tom Prichard was in regular contact with Pillman too, having developed a kinship with him during Pillman's frequent visits to the Stamford television studios that housed Prichard's training classes. He recalled how Pillman would often stop by the classes and offer pointers to his students, on occasion battling through the pain barrier to show them a few tricks in the ring. Through his interactions, he did not see anything to suggest that Brian had mere days to live. "He was actually in the studio just two days before he died and he seemed fine," said Prichard, "then the next thing I knew he was dead."

During the WWF house show in St. Paul the night before Brian died, the doomed grappler was in high spirits and shared a few laughs with Hart Foundation ally Bret Hart. As the evening unfolded and the adrenaline from his match wore off, Pillman took a handful of pain pills to counter the onset of agony coursing through his body, and he began to zone out. Veteran Minnesota-based wrestling trainer Eddie Sharkey refereed on the show that night. He remembered seeing Pillman staring into space in the dressing room and by the end of the show noticed that he was curled up in a foetal position on the floor due to his acute pain. Taking pity on Pillman, Sharkey and some of the other wrestlers invited Brian to join them for dinner, but Pillman turned them down and instead headed to a local bar. Far from engaging in a typical night of wrestler excess, Pillman returned to his hotel room at around 10 p.m. slightly tipsy but hardly falling over drunk. He called and left a message for Melanie, the last words he ever spoke, then died sometime between then and the maid finding him the following afternoon.

THE MOOD backstage was understandably sombre the following night at *Raw* in Kansas City's Kemper Arena. While most of the wrestlers could see Brian's death coming from a mile away, most also realised that it could easily have been them. McMahon was circumspect and made a decision, partly influenced by what he planned to do later on the show. He was going to tell his roster that the WWF was changing its ethos, and that the new direction would be to produce more adult-orientated output across the board. Looking out over the assembled throng of teary-eyed wrestlers, road agents, referees and producers, McMahon admitted, "Maybe time has passed me by. Some of the old formulas that have been successful for so long are becoming outdated. From this point onwards, the WWF will be geared towards a more mature fan base." According to Mick Foley, McMahon was true to his word. "That was really the meeting that did away with ridiculous gimmicks and ushered in a new era of realistic human beings that people could actually relate to," he observed.

While perception may well have been that the meeting in Kansas City was the "official" dawn of the WWF's shift in ideals, behind the scenes the pieces had been in place for the move away from child-friendly television since

McMahon's private hotel room meeting in Indianapolis with the Kliq in 1995. McMahon had been on the road to pushing smut and violence at the forefront of his television shows for the past two years, making strategic moves and baby steps towards edgy programming that had caused the new ethos to engulf the company without the majority of his staff even realising it. Now that everyone was finally in on his otherwise unspoken plan of making WWF the wrestling equivalent of in vogue yet vulgar TV broadcasts such as *The Jerry Springer Show, Beavis and Butthead,* and *South Park*, McMahon could forge ahead unimpeded. Brian Pillman's death was a handy excuse for him to finally pull the trigger on the plan and not look back.

"Vince just laid it out: 'We're going to change things. We're going to push the envelope, and we're going to blur the lines'," recalled Wilkes. "It was mixed with some guys being uncomfortable with it, I being one of them," Wilkes continued. "When we got to the arena on Monday nights, there was a big chalkboard with the line-up for the night, so I would call my wife and say, for example, 'I'm going to be on at 9:35 p.m. and I'll be out of the ring at 9:52 p.m., and that's when the boys can watch it. They can't watch it at any other time.' I wouldn't let my kids watch it except for the time their Dad was in the ring, because I knew I wasn't going to go out and flip anybody off, use foul language, grab my crotch, or make any kind of sexual innuendos."

"It was frustrating to watch professional wrestling deteriorate into unrecognizable tripe," grumbled Joe Laurinaitis, better known as Road Warrior Animal. "More often than not, I'd come home and catch [my sons] Joey or James yelling, "Suck it!" all over the house, and I'd want to put my head through a wall."

"Vince had a really good idea about what he wanted to do," Shamrock asserted. "He wanted it to be kick ass. He wanted it to be edgy. He made different types of moves in order to get people's frames of minds to turn towards what he wanted to happen, to alter their mind-set to turn towards what he wanted it to be. It was the only way for it to go. WCW had all the big pro wrestling stars. He needed stars in a different type of atmosphere."

McMahon was so keen to explain the WWF's new direction that day in order to justify a stunt he was going to pull later in the evening – one which he knew po-faced traditionalists would balk at. In a desperate quest for ratings he intended to capitalise on Pillman's unfortunate passing by exploiting the agony of genuine human grief in the coldest, most heartless way possible. He was going to put the widow on the box.

With Vince Russo – Vince's itchy trigger-fingered creative writing lieutenant and trash TV advocate – egging him on, McMahon was about to forge ahead into murky new territory. Coincidentally, he would achieve that by taking cameras into the same home that had set the WWF on the path towards reality-based programming in the first place. Back in November 1996 the infamous angle where Brian Pillman unloaded a gun on Steve Austin was provocative shock TV designed to blur the lines between the fantasy world of wrestling and reality programming more akin to *COPS*. But that had been a well-orchestrated segment designed to get people talking about *Raw's* new timeslot. This time it was different. This time McMahon was crossing a line and using real life tragedy as part of his storylines. The kayfabe era, which had been hanging on by a wavering thread, was now well and truly dead.

That evening's broadcast of *Monday Night Raw* opened with a tableau that would soon become all-too-familiar for wrestling fans; Vince McMahon breaking the news that one of his larger-than-life stars had passed away, punctuated by the sight of the roster assembled on the stage, putting their storyline differences to one side to pay their respects to a fallen comrade. The ring bell was clanged ten times during silence, while the cameras panned over close-up shots of Vince's wrestlers at their grimmest. Less than forty-eight hours earlier they had shared the locker room with Pillman in St. Paul, now they were abruptly coping with his loss. Vader, so insensitive in the dressing room the night before when he first heard the news, was openly weeping. Terri Runnels, Pillman's ex-girlfriend who he had been working a love triangle saga with before he died, hid her grief behind black sunglasses. The Hart Foundation stood front and centre, heads bowed in respect.[15] Notable by their absence were Shawn Michaels and Hunter Hearst Helmsley, who even in these tragic circumstances refused to put aside their professional and personal differences with the Hart clan.

The *Raw* tribute show would become something of a macabre wrestling ritual, one the WWF became far more polished at with practice. The way they handled Pillman's death established a protocol, and the formula remained essentially the same for each unfortunate recipient of the remembrance show treatment. The most notable addition in later versions was clips interspersed throughout the program of tearful wrestlers grieving publicly in front of the television cameras, coerced into sharing private memories of their recently deceased colleague. In due time, the WWF became so accomplished at "doing death" that it became a company trope.

Immediately following that brief moment of reflection it was back to business as usual, with the high-octane, fire and fury *Raw* opening video followed by a promo from D-Generation X, a new boundary-crossing group that were generating more complaints from USA Network officials than any of the stunts McMahon had pulled over the previous two years combined. Ostensibly created as a means to keep Shawn Michaels happy on the road, the

---

[15] The Harts would be forced to endure an even worse tragedy in the same building eighteen months later during the May 1999 pay-per-view *Over the Edge*, when Owen Hart fell from the rafters in a stunt gone wrong, and died in the middle of the ring.

stable's membership was made up of Shawn, Triple H, Chyna and, for a while, retired veteran grappler Rick Rude. DX spearheaded McMahon's directional shift, with their act made up primarily of showing their asses, talking about their penises, delivering crude innuendos, and instructing fans to "Suck it" while pointing to their crotches. It was the sort of thing resident curmudgeon Bret Hart – and a significant sector of the dressing room old guard – loathed.

The controversial troupe cut a promo which followed McMahon's new directive for content on the precipice of decency to the letter. There was no way to deftly segue from stinging anguish into low-brow hijinks, but here were Michaels and Helmsley, adhering to the timeless adage that "the show must go on", with their standard posturing and bravado. Alongside Chyna, the duo gave an exaggerated wedgie to interviewer Michael Cole, before Michaels bragged about his pantheon residence, with Hunter broadly pantomiming to the tune of each boast.

The tone swung from impish to edgy when the Kliq holdovers aired never-before-seen footage of the 1996 Curtain Call incident at Madison Square Garden, while making a mockery of the idea that "good guys" and "bad guys" could co-exist peacefully on the same plane of "reality". This hyper-reality further unfolded with Michaels taunting McMahon at ringside about the kayfabe breach - an incident which portrayed the notoriously-domineering WWF boss as a brittle submissive - rasping in McMahon's direction, "Oh, come on, you were an ass long before I made one out of ya!" If mourning Pillman was a reality that required acknowledgement, then Michaels and Helmsley's revelation of reality may have been viewed as self-indulgence masquerading as a fact-finding mission. In truth, this bending of scripted framework came as an edict, a demand, from the same man being hung out to dry before a perplexed audience.

By the middle of *Raw's* second hour, it was time to visit Walton, Kentucky for McMahon's live interview with Melanie Pillman. Making the situation far more morbid than it needed to be, McMahon had gratuitously promoted the segment throughout the broadcast as if it were a storyline grudge match or a wrestler's rebuttal toward their sworn enemy. Any sense of humanity that the WWF had attempted to put forth lay trampled beneath a huckster's pitch. Those who breathlessly tuned in had previously been conditioned to indulge in make-believe acts of sadism. Now they were whetting their appetites on the legitimate grief of a widow whose suffering could have no miracle payoff.

As the final commercials aired prior to the segment going live, McMahon gave Melanie one final chance to back out. "You know; you don't have to do this if you don't want to. It's not too late to back out," he told her. "No Vince, it's fine," she replied. Melanie felt she had little choice but to comply with McMahon's wishes if she wanted him to live up to a promise of honouring Brian's contract for three months and putting out a tribute magazine celebrating his life, which she would take the proceeds from. "I knew he wanted me to do it," she would later say, "And I knew I would be relying on this man for food."

On the same couch where her late husband had given USA Network executives palpitations by uttering the word "fuck" the previous November, Melanie, dressed in all-black, cut a desolate, desperate figure. She sat cross-legged and ashen-faced with her hand propping up her head, looking thoroughly bewildered and on the verge of a breakdown. McMahon showed little sympathy, immediately probing for a cause of death that would absolve the WWF of any blame.

[Vince McMahon:] Joining us now ladies and gentlemen, in suburban Cincinnati, the wife of Brian Pillman, Melanie Pillman. Thank you so much. I'm sure you're distraught, shocked, dismayed over this news. And we thank you very much for joining us tonight. I wonder... There's a great deal of speculation, obviously, when a thirty-five-year old man who is in competitive condition passes away. Can you please tell us, to end whatever speculation there may be, can you...? What can you tell us about what you have been told as far as Brian's death is concerned?

[Melanie Pillman:] Erm, well, erm, apparently there was a problem with his heart, and apparently his heart was put under a lot of stress for some reason and I can't really, you know, tell you for sure what that reason was, but it was apparently a heart attack in his sleep. And until the test results are back it's kind of inconclusive right now, but apparently, erm, his heart was under a lot of stress.

McMahon needed more than that. He knew that prescription medication had been found next to Brian's deathbed and he wanted Melanie to help him refute reports that the death was somehow related to steroids or a rampant underground drug culture in the WWF. McMahon tried to corner Melanie into blaming Brian for over-medicating himself, simultaneously sending out a message to the rest of his locker room that this developing trend of self-medicating needed to come to an end.

[Vince McMahon:] There was some speculation last night when we spoke, that Brian, because of his injuries, had to take a great deal of prescribed medication. There's some speculation he may have taken too much. If in fact that is proven to be the case, which it is yet to be, is there anything that you would want to say to aspiring athletes who do get hurt and have to resort to prescribed medication, pain killers?

Melanie had been expecting a question of that nature to be forthcoming, but she did not expect McMahon to hit her with it quite so soon. Visibly distressed with the manner of questioning, Melanie realised what McMahon was doing and refused to be corralled into being his chief line of defence against the circling media vultures.

[Melanie Pillman:] Well Vince, I can't comment on whether, you know, well... I know that my husband... Not only was he an athlete but he was involved in a car accident too and he had extensive injuries from that, and after the accident it was a lot harder for him. But I think all athletes, to a degree, experience a reliance on pain medication. And, y'know, I knew it was only a matter of time before it happened to someone. And unfortunately it was my husband, and I just want everyone to know, that I hope it's a wakeup call to some of you, because it could be your husband next, or it could be you. And, y'know, you don't want to leave behind a bunch of orphans like my husband did... [Melanie begins to cry]

That was not what McMahon wanted to hear. Immediately changing tact, he steered the conversation away from the suggestion that his roster were all drug-reliant dope-fiends and returned to his original plan of yanking at Melanie's heartstrings in the hope that his Diane Sawyer-like approach to television would lead to an increase in his ratings.

[Vince McMahon:] Melanie, how are the children taking this news, and do they understand?

[Melanie Pillman:] Well, my four-year old doesn't understand - that's little Brian - he doesn't understand why daddy is not coming home. But Brittany understands, because - she is my adopted child, she is the biological child of my husband and another woman and that woman killed herself two years ago - so Brittany has lost her mom and her dad, biological, and y'know, she just screamed for about fifteen minutes. I dunno Vince, it's hard. It's really hard. It's really hard but I am doing...

Vince cut her off. He was now getting exactly what he wanted; Melanie's battered heart served up for the world to see. If the tone had been dark before, McMahon was far from finished. Beneath his veneer of compassion, he was practically revelling in Melanie's misery, knowing that while he would be condemned from all quarters for deciding to run the piece, that more importantly, it would get people talking. Going far beyond what most would consider acceptable questioning of a widow who had only lost her husband less than twenty-four hours earlier, McMahon continued his bombardment.

[Vince McMahon:] Have you had any opportunity to think about what you, as a single parent, will do to support your five children?

[Melanie Pillman:] Vince, I don't even really know what day it is, so I don't know what I'm gonna do. But I know that the outpouring of support that I've gotten from the fans and the company is helping me go on. I mean, just everyone's calling, and everyone's... the fans on the internet, people are just supporting me from all around. But as for what I will do after this is over? I don't know. I don't even know, Vince, I don't know.

Satisfied that he had achieved exactly what he had set out to, McMahon decided to bring the interview to a close with a question he assumed would not lead to anything damning against the WWF.

[Vince McMahon:] How would you like for Brian to be remembered by WWF fans, and fans all over the world?

[Melanie Pillman:] Vince, I would like Brian to be remembered as one of the most passionate loving men ever and the greatest father in the world, the best father in the world. He also loved this business, Vince. And I guess you could say he lived for this business and he died for this business. I hope no one else has to die.

With that final sentence McMahon inhaled sharply and gritted his teeth. Maybe this had not been such a good idea after all. It almost sounded as if Melanie was in some way blaming him and the WWF for Brian's death, and the last thing he needed after enduring the steroid trial three years earlier was another inquest into what occurred behind the curtain of his dressing room. As Melanie broke down in tears, Vince hurriedly offered her his sincere condolences and ended the call before she could accidentally smear the company further, leaving her a broken wreck alone on her couch.

The critics were quick to pillory McMahon and pan the WWF for running the Melanie interview, with most agreeing that it was tasteless and insulting. Dave Meltzer expressed his take in his *Wrestling Observer Newsletter*, writing, "The segment left a lot of people very uneasy for many different reasons, not the least of which were all the teases and holding it off until late that made it come across as a way to build up ratings." The following week he commented further, "It was too soon. It shouldn't have been done live. Some questions appeared to be asked attempting to garner a close-up of her crying. Given certain realities of the situation, it put Mrs. Pillman – already in an incredibly emotionally-trying situation for both obvious and not so obvious reasons – under a microscope that she didn't deserve to be put under."

Some members of Vince's locker room were far from impressed with the tacky publicity stunt. Bret Hart, who was firmly opposed to the WWF's morally-bereft new direction, commented, "Owen and I felt so sorry for Melanie. The whole thing struck us as a ratings ploy, exploiting this poor girl's misery for all the world to see, as if suddenly the WWF had turned into *The Jerry Springer Show*."

Despite some of the criticisms levelled at him, McMahon remained unrepentant about his decision to run the piece. When asked whether he regretted it by Michael Landsberg on TSN's *Off The Record*, he was bullish in response. "No, not at all. Actually there is very little in my life that I regret. I don't regret that whatsoever because the purpose of having Melanie on, because at the time Brian was known as a real free spirit. He was known from time to time to use recreational drugs. And it was felt at that time by his wife that that was one of the reasons he passed away. So I gave her the forum to say maybe everyone can learn from this, benefit from this tragedy in some capacity and that's why we had Melanie Pillman on. As it turned out he had a heart attack, he had a diseased heart."

AS WINCE-INDUCING as McMahon's line of questioning toward a grieving widow may have been to a locker room of wrestlers that worked with and dressed beside Brian Pillman, the introduction of sweeping changes across the product provided a new lease on life for many talented individuals.

Mick Foley understood full well the benefit of offering fans a genuine look at the person beneath the costume. In the role of Mankind, Foley was little more than a leather-masked variant of his pre-WWF alter ego Cactus Jack, performing all of Jack's moves, albeit watered down. While Mankind had made some impact on WWF crowds in 1996 through his self-sacrificing ring work and immutable charisma, he had yet to reach this audience on a soul-baring level the way he had in ECW two years earlier. While in Philadelphia, Foley still flung himself into strands of barbed wire and dove onto concrete floors with as much zest as ever, but he was also afforded speaking time in the form of single-shot monologues that ranged from humorous to chilling, sometimes simultaneously.

In the spring of 1997, Mankind took part in a series of sit-down interviews with Jim Ross that aired over the span of several weeks. To call these introspectives the most authentic work of his fifteen-month WWF tenure would be an insult to his sickening splats onto bare concrete, but they served their intended purpose of unmasking the man that donned the mask and the brown tights. Everybody already knew that he was Cactus Jack, but he was also Mick Foley, the former teenager from Long Island that leapt from the roof of his parents' house in homage to his hero, 'Superfly' Jimmy Snuka. He was the starry-eyed scamp that filmed home movies in the guise of his own wrestling avatar Dude Love, a psychedelically-urbane ladies' man that would take the wrestling world by storm, earning belts and stealing kisses with the suddenness of his rat-a-tat finger snap.

The very idea of Dude Love betrayed the unflinching masochism of both Mankind and Jack, and that irony would be employed for crowd-pleasing comic effect. On July 14, Dude Love was introduced to a live audience for the first time, foisting himself onto a bewildered Steve Austin at *Raw* in San Antonio, capturing the vacant Tag Team Titles alongside him in a win over Owen Hart and Davey Boy Smith. The response to Dude was initially enormous, particularly when Austin dropped his confused disgust long enough to wilfully tag Dude into the match. With this alter ego, for the first time ever Foley was portraying a character that could be loved without the precedent of irony or pity. In the role of Mankind at the 1997 *SummerSlam*, Foley dialled another call-back to his youthful whimsy, leaping off of a blue-barred steel cage onto a prone Helmsley as his tribute to Snuka's own famous leap. While it lacked Snuka's grace, it had sentiment and heart behind it. That sentiment and heart were the qualities many fans were beginning to identify Foley by, instead of solely viewing him as a pincushion with a toothless grin.

While the idea of Foley hamming it up in tie-dye and powder-blue tights held novel potential (and provided Foley a reprieve from taking the residual bumps expected of his other characters), some crowds loathed Dude Love, particularly in the ECW-heavy northeast. The sadists behind the rail would be thrown a bone on September 22, when *Raw* came to Madison Square Garden for the first time ever.

The scheduled match was stipulated as 'Falls Count Anywhere', and Dude would be facing Triple H. Dude's upbeat theme music played to a mild reaction, but instead of making his entrance, Dude appeared on the Titan Tron, jovially backing out of the brawl for reasons of pacifism. This led to a split-screen segment where Dude delegated the match to Mankind, who appeared in the same frame as Dude to the sound of some murmuring chuckles. Mankind also passed up on the match, excitedly handing it off to none other than Cactus Jack, 'appearing' with his kinfolk while brandishing a trash can. Helmsley sold unconstrained disbelief in the ring, while the Garden fans collectively exploded with glee. "When I emerged through the curtain, it was the loudest reaction I've ever been a part of," Foley claimed.

The opportunity to shuffle between three distinct identities afforded Foley instant freshness if required. The chance to dust off the jet-black Cactus garb or the flower child hues of the organically-endearing Dude Love also allowed him to employ a weapon far sharper than his trusty barbed-wire baseball bat: his voice. After all, it's easier to search for inspiration when the character you play is closer to your heart.

ANOTHER WRESTLER whose life was about to veer toward the vivid was twenty-eight-year-old Brian James, a fast-talking ex-Marine, and the youngest son of jaw-cracking good ol' boy 'Bullet' Bob Armstrong. The elder Armstrong was a colourful and decorated champion throughout south-eastern NWA territories. Like Foley, Armstrong too experienced a character duality, albeit out of necessity following a horrific accident. In the early-eighties, Armstrong's face was crushed and his nose was severed during a bizarre weight-lifting accident, and required extensive plastic surgery to reconstruct his features. During the time of his slow-healing disfigurement, Armstrong worked under a mask as 'The Bullet' in the Tennessee-based Continental Championship Wrestling. Instead of being hampered by the unfortunate circumstances, the scrappy Armstrong kept his career going with a heroic twist on *The Phantom of the Opera*, doing away with the gimmick after he had fully healed.

Meanwhile, his youngest son had yet to gain traction with one role, let alone two. For the previous year, James had languished at the bottom of the WWF ladder as 'The Real Double J' Jesse James. Previously, James worked as The Roadie, an unimaginatively-named gofer for Jeff Jarrett, who was in the midst of a viable run as a pompous country singer. Jarrett and James left WWF in July 1995 following various disputes, but James would be brought back in the fall of 1996, and given the 'Real Double J' moniker as an affront to Jarrett. Their 1995 story was to have revealed that Jarrett's first single, '*With My Baby Tonight*', was merely him taking credit for vocals laid down by the more melodious James, wrestling's answer to the Milli Vanilli scandal. The storyline was unearthed as Jarrett headed for WCW, 'exposing' the now-rival talent as fraudulent.

The revelation failed to make James look gallant, nor did fans particularly care as James, no matter how gifted a voice, crooned '*With My Baby Tonight*' on the way down the aisle before his matches. Even if agreeable fans in southern towns were kinder to the act, it had little chance of success in Titan's core cities, where alternative, hip-hop, and metal were the flavours of choice.

On the night of the Kansas City *Raw* tapings, a few hours after Vince McMahon's meeting with his talent roster, James embarked on a new role that more than adequately displayed his considerable gift of gab. During filming of the secondary *Shotgun* program, fellow wheel-spinning midcarder Monty Sopp had just gotten done putting over Flash Funk in what was outwardly another pointless filler match for low-impact weekend viewing. Sopp's four-and-a-half-year WWF run could have skinnied as, "productive but without flourish." As grinning cowboy Billy Gunn, he and kayfabe brother Bart populated the midcard ranks as The Smoking Gunns, holding the WWF Tag Team Championship on three occasions from January 1995 to September 1996. The Gunns were only as flashy as their well-coordinated double-team manoeuvres, and both wrestlers would have been adrift if not for a sustained push.

When the Gunns split in late 1996, Sopp treaded water up until April 1997, when he was repackaged as Rockabilly, a rhinestone-wearing protégé of The Honky Tonk Man that thudded with a boom, doomed on its arrival at the *In Your House: Revenge of the Taker* pay-per-view in Rochester. To demonstrate how little faith the company had in Sopp's makeover, Rockabilly lost his debut match - to the equally uninteresting James.

Six months later, Rockabilly's loss to Funk marked the dissolution of the unsuccessful partnership with Honky. While both heels played up disgust over the miscue that cost Billy the match, James emerged from the dressing room curtain, dressed with a white doo-rag, mirrored sunglasses, and a uniquely-designed vest with the word "ROADDOG" emblazoned across the shoulder blades. Although no longer playing a character anywhere near the realm of heroic, James was here to rescue Rockabilly from lower card obscurity.

"Me and you have been curtain jerkers since day one," barked James, who wove reality with story when he claimed that the reason Billy lost on secondary programming every single week was because of the Honky Tonk Man. While Honky wasn't politically holding Billy down, the staleness of his act was binding to thirty-three-year-old Sopp, whose leaping ability and athletic build promised better. James noted the mouldiness of the Honky character when he grunted that Honky was so old, "...Elvis Presley stole *his* gimmick!"

The segment ended with Rockabilly smashing Honky in the head with his own trademark guitar, officially forming the duo with James known as The New Age Outlaws. While the Kansas City audience initially interpreted the new team to be babyfaces, they were anything but, as their act entailed swindling victories in unrepentant fashion. Despite playing unapologetic heels, the rechristened Road Dogg and 'Badd Ass' Billy Gunn were finding it hard to not draw cheers for their irreverence, whether it was for stealing Los Boricuas' clothing, or whacking Phineas Godwinn with a stuffed pig that had been pre-loaded with a brick. Initially, the two did not even have theme music, instead walking down the aisle to the sounds of nothing but Road Dogg's confident boasts and taunts, while Gunn would usually ham it up through gestures. The fact that the two often wore licensed *South Park* t-shirts to the ring, the same attire as many high school students of the day, spoke to a clearer understanding of the fan base's preferences.

Fans quickly caught on to the freshness of the Outlaws, who went over on the once-transcendent Legion of Doom on November 24 to become WWF Tag Team Champions. There was an underlying message in the title switch: face-painted ogres of the eighties are out, and underhandedness-with-a-smile was in. Animal and Hawk would never regain the belts, falling short of dethroning the Outlaws through the spring of 1998, around which time James and Gunn officially turned babyface in correlation with the stronger reactions their act was receiving.

ONE PERFORMER'S late-1997 redesign pitted him squarely as a villain, and was more meticulously planned in the Titan lab. Tall and burly Glenn Jacobs had spent his two-year WWF life adding little oomph to two detestable, oft-ridiculed ideas: rot-mouthed dentist Dr. Isaac Yankem, DDS, and lifeless clone of former WWF Champion Diesel, donning the leather and sunglasses after Kevin Nash bolted for WCW. Despite the relative grace Jacobs demonstrated for a near-seven-foot goliath, his willingness to get better in the ring took a backseat to shoddy ideas that no fan could seriously get behind.

That would all change beginning with the June 30 *Raw* in Des Moines, in which Paul Bearer spun the strands of an outlandish storyline that claimed The Undertaker, as a child, accidentally burned down the mortuary owned by his parents, killing them and, he assumed, his previously-unmentioned younger brother Kane. Bearer, when attacked by Undertaker that night, screeched in the voice of a dastardly Tennessee Williams character that Kane was still alive, implying that vengeance was imminent. When dirt sheets claimed that Jacobs, the man behind Yankem and the impostor Diesel, would be revealed as Kane, the story was met with little enthusiasm, such was the case of many previous Undertaker feuds with towering oafs. Just another lummox to be snuffed out by 'The Phenom', thought fans.

The day of Pillman's death, the WWF would ironically present a story of retribution from nearly beyond the grave. This unseen Kane had mostly gone unmentioned through the remainder of the summer and into the fall as Undertaker shifted his focus to a feud with Michaels, stemming from Michaels' heel turn that began at *SummerSlam*. The blowoff to the story took place inside a sixteen-foot high steel cage with a roof that WWF would debut the night of October 5. Dubbed "Hell in a Cell", the cage would gain notoriety as a fearsome structure that would confine the boiling anger of near-immortals, as well as the blood they spilled. The first Hell in a Cell match was also quite possibly the best, with Michaels affording fans a look at him as a blood-soaked ragdoll, enduring chair shots, as well as tumbles off the side of the cage, and through the announcer's table.

In the final stage, The Undertaker signalled for the finish, when the lights inside the Kiel Center turned black. An ominous-sounding instrumental of guitars and organs heralded the unveiling of Kane, a stalking leviathan in a red and black bodysuit, with a matching leather mask that concealed the near unanimity of his face. Flanked by Bearer, Kane was far removed from the cartoonish hues of Yankem and Diesel. He was a legitimate monster, aided by The Undertaker freezing out of a combination of shock, confusion, and terror at the sight of a character carefully written as his vindictive brother. The Undertaker had never been unnerved by any wrestler, or even group of wrestlers, in his seven years of portraying Titan's grim reaper. His blatant apprehension did as much to make Kane a star as all of the ambiance and accessories.

"When I was originally told about the Kane character, I was elated, of course, because I was going to have the chance to work with The Undertaker," said Jacobs. "One of the things that was executed very, very well about this particular story was the fact that Paul Bearer brings up Kane and you plant that seed and it's a big deal for a while, but then it sort of goes away and you get lost in the Undertaker/Shawn Michaels story. Then wham, there's Kane at the pay-per-view. I think that just tremendously helped everything."

"There was a lot of pressure on me, I'm not going to lie about that, because this was a make-or-break deal for me," admitted Jacobs. "At the time, we didn't know what Hell in a Cell would go into, would grow into. Nevertheless, I'm in there against two Hall of Famers…two of the greatest names in the history of our business, and I'm the guy getting the spotlight for that night. Because at the end of the night, the match is going to be awesome, but as is so often the case in our business, it's going to be the finish of the match that everybody remembers. So I had some pressure on me that night because I wanted to make sure that I didn't mess it up, and of course to live up to all of the expectations, and not to let guys like Undertaker and Shawn down, because they were investing their trust in me."

Kane's reign of terror began exceptionally, Tombstone piledriving his brother with ease, which demonstrated to astonished viewers the power and size of the muted beast. He was presented as an absolute equal to Undertaker, a quality never before afforded to any of Undertaker's foes. In the ensuing weeks, Kane would dramatically commit random acts of violence, assaulting everyone from squash match fodder to The Headbangers to even Mick Foley, presenting Kane as something akin to Michael Myers - a force of evil that cannot be reasoned or reckoned with.

WHILE JACOBS' new role called for incorporating elements out of the realm of horror movies and comic books, Dwayne Johnson would be turning up the volume with little more than his own humanity. Ever since he had debuted as a cheerful namby-pamby late in 1996, the wrestler known as Rocky Maivia failed to juice his way through a disconnect with the fans. His Intercontinental Title push earlier in the year was an abject failure, earning him more criticism than acclaim for his outdated good-guy shtick.

Perhaps it was divine timing when Johnson took several months off to nurse a knee injury in May 1997, allowing time to power wash the fetid stench of his sugary character out of the product. When Johnson re-emerged on the August 11 episode of *Raw*, it was with a pronounced sneer on his face. The moniker of The Rock took precedent over Rocky Maivia once Johnson planted Brian 'Chainz' Lee with his side uranage slam, branded the "Rock Bottom". Rock's heel turn coincided with his joining of The Nation of Domination, although he did not wear the red, yellow, and green-on-black garb bestowed upon the other Nation members. By this time, the militant overtones of the group had begun to slowly peter out, replaced with little more than garden-variety anger from four men that happened to be black (or in Johnson's case, half-black, half-Samoan).

Slowly but surely, The Rock's innate charisma and timing began to manifest in his limited microphone time. As a heel, he was allowed to acknowledge the many "Rocky Sucks" chants that filled arenas, and he could explore a range of responsive tics to show his displeasure at the lack of respect. Not long after the October 6 seminar, The Rock would be put in position to show off his confident speaking abilities even more in a program with Austin.

The infusion of new blood had always been necessary, even in times where the main event ruling class was deeply affirmed. While on the surface, the WWF main event scene in the autumn of 1997 looked to be an air-tight starting line-up, circumstances both conspiratorial and incidental would call upon those fresh new voices to mature at a hastened clip.

NINE

ON JULY 14, BRET HART and Shawn Michaels came face to face for the first time since their brawl in Hartford, prior to a live edition of *Raw* from Michaels' hometown of San Antonio. The pair had both resolved to put their issues behind them for the good of the company and were surprisingly cordial towards each other. While neither man apologised for their part in the fight, nor shook hands, both at least offered vague assurances they would refrain from talking about each other, onscreen or off from that point onwards.

They had no choice but to learn to get along, because they were about to embark upon a storyline together at annual summer supershow *SummerSlam*. While Michaels was not yet returning to the ring, he had been shoehorned into Hart's program with WWF Champion The Undertaker, given the role as special guest referee for the title match. The storyline stipulations attached to his involvement stated that if he did not call the bout down the middle then he would not be allowed to wrestle in the United States ever again. Hart had already made the same vow if he failed to bring home the gold, so for the viewing audience there was plenty at stake.

Hart, while willing to work with Shawn, remained cautious that his involvement would be to the detriment to his own character's development. On August 3, the day of the event, he shared his reservations with chief agent Pat Patterson.

"I'm still kinda worried about this thing with Shawn. I'm not gonna lose all my heat to him am I?" he pondered.

"I don't think... do you have any idea what kinda finish you're gonna do?" offered Patterson in response.

"All I know is that Shawn's gonna cost 'Taker the match... Is Shawn gonna be a heel then?" asked Hart, worried that with both he and Shawn playing on the same side of the spectrum there was potentially a conflict of interest.

"That's what I understand," confirmed Patterson.

"Yeah," replied Hart, unhappy with the development, "It's almost like he's gonna be scooping my heat."

When Bret, Shawn and Undertaker discussed the contest backstage they threw various ideas around about the best way to achieve the match's ultimate goal: Bret winning the title with Shawn forced to reluctantly make the count. It was Michaels who came up with the solution. His idea was for Hart to spit at him, for which Shawn would attempt to retaliate with a steel chair, only for Bret to duck and the chair to hit Undertaker instead.

Bret and Undertaker approved, and Bret promised Shawn that he would aim for his shirt with the spit. After almost thirty minutes of rewarding action, it came time for the spot. Hart - in character - visibly mouthed, "fuck you," to Shawn before he launched his spit at him. What he had not accounted for was dry mouth due to the exertion of wrestling the match, and in hocking up the saliva he produced a large gob of phlegmy spit, which when launched unintentionally bounced up off Shawn's chest and hit him in the face. It was an accident, but given their recent history Bret was sure Shawn would take it personally and accuse him of doing it on purpose. Nevertheless, Michaels counted the three as planned then immediately rolled out of the ring and skulked backstage.

At approximately 10:45 p.m., Hart stood in the middle of the ring at the Continental Airlines Arena in East Rutherford, New Jersey and surveyed his surroundings. He had just won the WWF Championship for a record-equalling fifth time, tying him with Hulk Hogan. He thought back to the first time he had won the title with a victory over Ric Flair in Saskatchewan five years prior, noting the marked contrast between the euphoric response he had been met with on that night compared to the rain of boos, paper cups, and garbage he was on the receiving end of now. Hart had once been a hero to all, now he was the most hated man in the company. He watched as Michaels and Undertaker disappeared down the aisle, leaving him free to celebrate his triumph in the ring alone, king of the mountain once more. It had been nearly a year in the making, but Hart was now finally convinced that Vince McMahon still believed in him as his main draw, after months of uncertainty in their relationship. He smiled to himself, satisfied at the thought.

As his Hart Foundation teammates hit the ring and draped him in the Canadian Maple Leaf, Hart cast his mind back to the spitting incident with Shawn. He decided that the best course of action to avoid yet another misunderstanding, or the perception from Shawn that their flimsy pact had been violated, was to apologise immediately. To Bret's pleasant surprise, Shawn was forgiving. He simply thanked Hart for the match and the pair shook hands for the first time in months. Hart was comforted by that. It seemed, for now at least, that he and Shawn were finally on the same page again.

UPON WINNING the WWF Championship Hart was expecting to take up permanent residence in pay-per-view main events, so he was somewhat perplexed that he was immediately shunted into the midcard for a program with WWF newcomer Del 'The Patriot' Wilkes. Hart grumbled that Wilkes had no heat, believing him to be a solid worker, but little more than a cartoon character due to him working in an American flag mask and tights. Hart preferred an opponent who could better sell the drama of a contest by generating sympathy through pained facial grimaces. That Patriot could not do that irritated Hart no end. He was even more put out when he saw Michaels and Undertaker taking centre stage at the top of the card, with their program clearly the focus of Vince's attention ahead of anything he was doing. Of late he had noticed that Michaels and his running buddy Triple H were holding far more sway over McMahon than he felt was healthy for the business.

It was no coincidence that McMahon was subtly reducing the profile of Hart, despite his position as WWF Champion. He had recently met with a Manhattan investment house for early talks about the possibility of taking the WWF public, a move he felt would help boost the company's coffers and allow them to compete on a more even playing field with Turner. During the meeting, McMahon had been advised to limit or, if he could, remove any long-term obligations so as to make the company appear more profitable to potential investors. It was the same book-cooking tactic he had so vociferously accused Ted Turner of employing in early 1996 when attempting to sabotage his rival's AOL Time Warner merger.

As McMahon sat and pored over the figures he kept coming back to the twenty-year contract he had given Bret Hart under duress the previous October. From the moment he had signed off on the deal he had regretted it. He had been conflicted ever since, between wanting to keep one of his top stars and most loyal servants and being apprehensive about the huge sum of money he had been forced to commit to do so. McMahon did not want Hart that badly; he simply did not want WCW to have him even worse. Now, almost a year later, McMahon realised that he had made the wrong call. Hart had not moved numbers anywhere near as much as he had hoped, with *Nitro* still handily beating *Raw* in the weekly ratings battle, and pay-per-view buys stagnating.

In addition, the recent problems between Hart and Shawn Michaels had become a headache that Vince did not want to continually deal with. While they had been tolerating each other recently, he knew that another major blow up was only one badly taken comment away. The issues between them were still there, they had simply been temporarily buried. It was a distraction, petty quibbling between two grown men who should know better, keeping him from his real work of trying to turn the WWF's fortunes around. In July, when McMahon met with Michaels to discuss his return to work following the

Hartford locker room bust up with Hart, the miserable wrestler had begged McMahon to let him leave for WCW so that he could be back with his friends Kevin Nash, Scott Hall and Sean Waltman. He wanted to enjoy wrestling again, away from a locker room that despised him and specifically away from Bret Hart.

"Please Vince, just let me go," he pleaded, "I am miserable. I am making everyone else miserable." McMahon was starting to realise that one of the two would ultimately have to depart. They were so diametrically opposed that locker room harmony was impossible with both of them around. With Hart forty-years-old and vocally opposed to the WWF's edgy direction, at thirty-two and one of those at the forefront of the New WWF movement, Michaels was the logical choice to keep as far as Vince was concerned.

In addition to the ever-present tension between Michaels and Hart causing problem after problem, McMahon reasoned that if he did not let Bret go then it would not be long before the rest of his top stars, the likes of Austin and Undertaker, would all expect contract parity with him. That would ruin him. Michaels had already complained about Hart's contract to McMahon, grumbling that he could not comprehend how a performer he felt he was better than was earning double the money. Choosing Shawn at half the price would also remove the issue of Austin and Undertaker complaining about the disparity in pay, killing two birds with one stone.

Partly in an attempt to placate Shawn, but also because it was beginning to dawn on him that he needed to restructure Hart's contract or let him go, McMahon confided to Michaels that he had only signed Hart's deal in the first place because he felt he had to. Everyone had told him it would kill the WWF to lose Bret, but the figures were telling him otherwise and he no longer felt Hart was worth the investment. "I don't think Bret is going to last his contract," McMahon admitted. "Don't worry, Shawn, we will make wrestling fun again for you," he assured.

A few weeks later McMahon met with Hart in Cincinnati prior to an episode of *Raw* and told him point blank that he wanted to cut his regular salary of $30,000 per week in half and instead pay him the balance towards the end of his contract when the company was more profitable. It was the same topic the two had discussed in Hartford back in June, only this time McMahon was far more direct. Hart refused the request. He had no intention of letting McMahon back out of the contract because he did not trust him to live up to his end of the bargain once he was no longer wrestling.

The financial peril that McMahon was claiming to Hart as the reason for cutting his pay was far from the truth. Back in June that had been the case, but since then McMahon had increased the price of his monthly pay-per-view events from $19.95 to $29.95, which was set to make the WWF $6 million per annum better off. Buy rates had not dropped at all due to the price hike – if anything they had actually gone up – and the cries of destitution were merely an excuse. McMahon was laying the groundwork, preparing to make his move towards driving Hart away and freeing him of the twenty-year commitment, or forcing Bret to renegotiate his contract so that he could keep him for far less money.

For the first time since the aborted *King of the Ring* match in June, McMahon also discussed with Hart the possibility of him working a singles match with Shawn Michaels on pay-per-view, their first since *WrestleMania XII* in April 1996. Bret was not keen on the idea at all. Even though relations had been cordial between Shawn and himself for the past two months, Hart suggested working with him would be a problem because Michaels had not satisfactorily apologised for his "Sunny days" comments. "I am not sure if I can trust him in the ring," he told McMahon, "And if you ask Shawn, he will probably say the same thing about me." Michaels had already said as much, refusing to work with any members of the Hart Foundation other than Davey Boy Smith due to the ongoing tensions between he and Bret.

It was Smith whom Michaels was set to wrestle on the WWF's UK-exclusive pay-per-view *One Night Only* held in Birmingham, England on September 20. Smith – who was a hero in England – would be putting his European Championship belt was on the line in the show's main event. Because McMahon had told Smith weeks earlier that he was winning the match, the Brit was confident the result was set in stone and told the local press that he was dedicating the match to his sister Tracy, who was dying, ravaged by cancer aged only twenty-six. Smith should have known better than to take a promoter's word as gospel, because hours before the match McMahon found him and revealed he was changing the finish. Instead of Davey winning, Shawn would now be going over for the title.

"It was a shock," said Smith's wife Diana, "I thought, 'You bastards! Why are they doing this to him in England? Where does that leave him?' There was something in the works then and we didn't know it."

McMahon explained to Smith how he wanted to build towards a rematch when the WWF toured England again in April the following year, and he felt Shawn winning the title would be a more emotive story than Smith simply retaining his gold. Smith had no choice but to comply with McMahon's orders, but he was unable to pass the news on to his family. Tracy was so upset by the shock of her brother's defeat that she burst into a flood of tears, which devastated the rest of the family. Smith was hurt the most by her reaction, unable to forgive himself for failing to live up to his promise.

Reaction amongst the wrestlers was typically knee-jerk. Adversaries of Michaels - and there were many - were convinced that he had politicked McMahon to change the finish to stick it to the Hart Foundation and show Bret Hart who was boss. That the result happened to change around the same time

Michaels had vowed to a stunned locker room that he was no longer willing to do jobs for any of them, served as irrefutable evidence to some. But the changed finish had little to do with Michaels; it was a McMahon judgment call. He was preparing to tell Bret Hart that he wanted to cut him loose or reduce his contract, a discussion he suspected was not going to go well. McMahon decided to double down on Shawn Michaels in case the fallout from the Hart contract discussions ultimately led to Smith leaving the WWF too. He was systematically immobilising the Hart Foundation, weakening their presence to ensure the likely loss of Hart would have as minimal an impact on his company as possible.

SURE ENOUGH, two days after *One Night Only* McMahon met with Hart in Madison Square Garden prior to that evening's *Raw* taping and told him that he planned to intentionally breach his contract. It was the same scenario that McMahon had presented at the beginning of the month whereby Hart would receive every penny he was owed at the back end of his deal. Vince pleaded poverty, claiming that because of the pressures exerted on his company by Ted Turner he could no longer afford Hart's contract. McMahon explained to the stunned and dubious wrestler that he was planning on downsizing the WWF into a northeast regional promotion and would be letting a lot of his high-earning talent leave. Because of Hart's loyalty to him over the years, Vince said he had no problem with him talking to WCW to see if he could get the same multi-million dollar deal he had been offered in 1996.

"I realised that I had made a bad deal," said McMahon, "I met with Bret and said, 'I can't pay you this'. I didn't want to pay him that because I didn't think he was worth it. '[I told him] A deal is a deal and I will live up to it, but what I would prefer to do is engineer a way in which you will be 'stolen' and Turner's group will pay you a lot more money.'"

Hart could barely believe what he was hearing. Not only was McMahon trying to force him out of the door, but he actually had the gall to frame it as if he was doing him a favour. According to McMahon, he was giving Hart the first opportunity to talk with WCW before any of the WWF's other high earners, ensuring he would get the best deal possible. McMahon even offered to give Hart written permission to begin negotiating with WCW prior to a window in his contract that would have otherwise allowed him to do so. "You would be doing me a favour," he told Hart, "You don't even have to drop the belt if you don't want to. You hold all the cards."

Hart was overcome with a surge of emotions. He did not want to go to WCW, he had never wanted to leave the WWF. He was worried that he might have to sue McMahon for the money he owed him – which he felt was akin to suing his own father – and that if he left the WWF there was a chance WCW would not even want him anymore.

Due to the bombshell that had been dropped on him, Hart could barely concentrate on that evening's *Raw* broadcast from the famous New York arena, nor the following night's taping in Albany. By Wednesday he was unable to keep the news to himself any longer. On the drive to a house show in Toledo he unburdened himself, telling his brother Owen everything. Owen listened quietly while Bret confessed concerns that his relationship with Vince was going to get ugly due to money, sensing that the whole ordeal was going to leave him bitter, with ill-feeling towards McMahon and the WWF. Having thought it over for a minute Owen succinctly surmised, "You will probably have to sue him."

It was another two weeks before Hart was able to track down Eric Bischoff for a face to face meeting. Much like how the pair had first met almost a year to the day earlier, Hart was filming for a TV show in Los Angeles when the call came that Bischoff was in town and wanted to talk. To avoid Bischoff realising that McMahon had authorised the meeting, thus potentially reducing the offer he would receive, Hart said his availability was down to an escape clause he had managed to work into his contract the previous year, using the WWF's new direction as an excuse for why he wanted to leave. Bischoff was interested but said he was unable to negotiate properly until he received written clearance from the WWF. He and WCW were still tied up in legal wrangles stemming from the departures of Kevin Nash and Scott Hall from Titan to Turner in 1996 (the WWF were claiming tortuous interference) and the incident on *Nitro* in December 1995 when Debra Miceli threw a WWF title belt into a trash can, breaching intellectual property trademarks. The last thing he needed on his plate was another lawsuit.

When the clearance came through Bischoff set about putting together the most enticing deal possible for Hart. He had recently been given the green light to launch a new Thursday night prime time television show on Tuner's network called *Thunder*. To avoid overexposing his current roster he felt new talent, especially someone the stature of Bret Hart, was necessary for the show to succeed. He came back to Hart with an offer of $1.8 million per year, only $300,000 more than what he was making with McMahon. Because Hart did not want to leave the WWF he turned it down, telling Bischoff he wanted the same $2.8 million deal he had offered him in 1996 or he was not interested. Bischoff needed authorisation from higher-ups to commit to that sort of money and told Hart he would get back to him.

In the meantime, McMahon was getting cold feet at the prospect of sending his reigning WWF Champion into the welcoming arms of his fierce rivals. Second-guessing his decision to allow Hart to leave, McMahon took him into his makeshift office at a house show in Long Island and told him his money problems were now solved. He could afford to keep Hart after all. Even though he was taken aback by the unexpected news, Hart's first reaction was relief. He did not want to leave the WWF anyway, plus he had been trying to call Bischoff for three days with no success, so figured he was ignoring him because he had no interest in meeting the $2.8 million asking price. Hart told McMahon that he would still leave his options open until the November 1 negotiation deadline in case Bischoff came back to him with an offer too good to turn down, but in his heart he knew that regardless of what Bischoff came back with he was going to stay in the WWF. When he boarded a plane the next day for a brief tour of the Middle East he was at ease for the first time in over a month. The WWF had been his home for the past thirteen years; he had never wanted to leave.

When Hart returned to his Calgary home on Halloween night he had barely closed the door behind him when the phone rang. It was Bischoff, finally getting him back to him with a new offer on the eve of his deadline. The contract was for $2.5 million per annum over three years, and only 125 dates per year, which covered WCW for both of its television shows and monthly pay-per-views with little left in change. It was significantly fewer dates for Hart than the 275 he was contractually obliged to in his WWF contract. Hart realised that at forty-years-old his time left as an active wrestler was dwindling and the lighter schedule would theoretically elongate his career, which combined with the "Hogan money" he would be earning meant it was almost too good to turn down. Conflicted, Hart told Bischoff he would sleep on it. As soon as he put the phone down he called his lawyer, who whistled with surprise when he heard the offer and told Hart excitedly, "We have a sweetie of a deal here. A real sweetie of a deal."

The next morning Hart remained unsure about what to do, but he was leaning towards staying with the WWF. "I was going to turn down double the money again because I didn't want to go there," he remembered. Bret called Vince and told him what Bischoff had offered, admitting he was seriously considering taking the deal, and reminding McMahon that he had until midnight to make a decision. He reiterated that he wanted to stay with the WWF and did not need more money; he was happy with the deal they had, rather he was looking for some assurances from Vince about future plans for him. "Just give me a reason to stay," Hart probed, to which McMahon said he would think on it and call him back within the hour.

When McMahon had not called back four hours later, Bret grew impatient and called his cell phone. McMahon was sat in a barber's chair getting his pompadour styled at his favourite Manhattan salon when he took the call. "Vince, I only have until midnight," Hart reminded him, to which McMahon was casually dismissive. "Don't worry about deadlines," he chuckled, "Call me tomorrow and we will talk." Suspecting that Vince's word over the phone meant nothing legally, Hart called his lawyer for advice and had his suspicions confirmed: McMahon's verbal extension meant nothing in the eyes of the law and they needed to stick to the written midnight deadline.

In the meantime, Bischoff called Hart again. Suspecting that since he had not heard from Hart he was on the verge of losing his man, Eric wanted to sweeten the deal and convince Hart that WCW was the right choice for him. "What else do you want?" he asked jovially, "Whatever it is that you want you had better say it now!" Hart asked for permission to arrive late at shows and for full injury insurance, requests which Bischoff granted immediately. He was happy to move Heaven and Earth to accommodate the WWF Champion, one of Vince's biggest stars. He knew that for all Hart was valuable to him, equally significant would be the hole in the WWF that his departure left. With Bischoff willing to do anything to sign him and McMahon appearing aloof and uninterested, Hart reluctantly told the WCW Vice President they had a deal.

As he was waiting for the contract to come through on his fax machine, Hart tried to call McMahon again to tell him that he was about to sign with WCW. McMahon did not answer, so Hart left a message. Bret was studying his as yet unsigned WCW contract when McMahon finally called him back with only minutes left of the deadline. Nudging him out of the door with a smile, the first thing he told Hart was that he should think with his head and not his heart. Bret asked McMahon if he had come up with anything relating to their conversation earlier, to which McMahon confirmed that he had. He then offered three months' worth of booking that would see Hart lose three times in four matches with Shawn Michaels before putting over Steve Austin for the title at *WrestleMania*.

Hart was almost at a loss for words. He had asked McMahon to give him a reason to stay by presenting him with future plans that he could get excited about, whereas McMahon had given him the opposite. He started to suspect that was the intention, with McMahon wanting out of their deal but unwilling to directly tell Hart that he did not want him around anymore due to his status as WWF Champion. "You've got to be kidding me?" Hart exclaimed, "I thought you were going to come up with something to make me stay?" Losing patience, McMahon fired back, "Well you tell me. What do you want to do?"

Suddenly everything was crystal clear for Hart. Over the past year McMahon had beaten him frequently on television, cast him as an unlikeable whiner, jabbed at him with digs about his age, had him alienate his American fan base to turn heel, and then gave his heel spot to Shawn Michaels. As Hart saw it, McMahon had calculatedly weakened and destroyed the 'Hitman' character over the course of the year, right under his nose. "Hell Vince, I don't know," stammered Hart, "I don't even know what to do with me." Vince reiterated that Hart should think with his head. "Take the WCW offer," he advised, before hanging up the phone.

Reluctantly, Hart picked up two pieces of paper, one his WWF resignation and the other his WCW contract offer, and signed them both. With tears in his eyes, he watched alone in the dark as his letter of resignation disappeared into the fax machine, thirteen years of hard work, toil, sweat, broken bones, and blood all gone in a fleeting moment. He was wrestling internally with all manner of emotions, feeling betrayed by McMahon and worried about WCW's intentions for him. "The day I signed with WCW was one of the lousiest days of my life," remembered Hart, "I knew nothing was ever going to be the same."

FROM THAT moment on, Hart was working his one-month notice with the WWF, which activated a unique clause in his contract that President of WWF Canada Carl DeMarco had negotiated for him. The clause gave him "reasonable creative control" for the final thirty days he was under contract, meaning he could veto any suggestions that he felt were unreasonable, or that he was not comfortable with participating in. Hart had seen McMahon bury wrestlers who were on their way out and he had no intention of letting the same thing happen to him.

When Hart called McMahon the morning after his resignation McMahon assured Hart he had done the right thing, then talk quickly turned to *Survivor Series* and Hart's upcoming match with Shawn Michaels. Both had finally agreed to work together for the good of the company, but now fresh problems between the pair were brewing over who would lie down and do the job. "Talk about the Middle East peace crisis, try working that fucking finish out," exclaimed Jim Cornette.

The latest issues between the two had started less than a month earlier on October 12 in San Jose. Hart had just worked a three-way match with Triple H and Ken Shamrock which had featured involvement from the Hart Foundation and D-Generation X, and afterwards the participants were all in the same dressing room getting changed. As Hart was unlacing his boots he turned to Michaels and said, "Shawn, I just want you to know that despite any differences we've had this past year, I have no problem working with you. You can trust me in every way to be a professional. I want you to know that you are not in any danger and that I have no problem dropping the belt to you if that's what Vince wants." This respectful act of generosity from the departing champion should have signalled the end to any remaining animosity between the two, but Michaels decided to play it a different way. He looked Bret right in the eye and declared cockily, "I appreciate that, but I want you to know that I'm not willing to do the same for you." He then stood up and stormed off, leaving Hart, Jim Neidhart and Ken Shamrock reeling with shock. It was Neidhart who spoke first. "I can't believe he just said that," he gasped, echoing the thoughts of everyone else in the room who had heard Michaels' comments.

"Bret took it seriously, he took it to heart" said WWF producer Bruce Prichard, "But that was just locker room bravado." Nevertheless, Hart did take Michaels' insult seriously and it caused a conflict between the pair for which there was no hope of resolution. "There was no way I could ever drop the belt to him now," grouched Hart. "He'd just showed complete disrespect not only to me, but to the position of champion, which was an affront to old-school traditions and a betrayal of each and every wrestler who ever looked to me as a leader in the dressing room, or who had been a leader himself. What kind of arrogant little prick would say that to a champion offering to put him over?" Bret reasoned that he would get through the match with Michaels at *Survivor Series* and then, since his contract afforded him creative control (which would be active by the time of the bout), he would drop the title to Steve Austin instead.

Little over a week later during a *Raw* taping in Tulsa on October 21, Vince and Bret met to discuss the *Survivor Series* finish. Even though Hart was still a WWF contracted wrestler at that point and had not signed with WCW, McMahon wanted him to put Michaels over for the title and then win it back from him on the December 7 pay-per-view in Springfield. Given what Shawn had said in San Jose, and with no apology forthcoming, Hart refused. "I'm not putting him over, not now," said Hart, "He doesn't have enough respect for me. He doesn't deserve it." McMahon's face turned scarlet red as Hart explained exactly what Michaels had said, then asked him if he would not mind repeating everything he had told him in front of Shawn.

McMahon was determined to soothe tensions between the two grapplers before their rivalry spiralled out of hand again, because he already realised that he was going to have issues coming up with a finish that placated both parties. He sensed that he was going to face resistance from Michaels about putting over Hart, and Bret had already quite bluntly expressed to him his feelings about laying down for Shawn. He gathered the two of them together in his office and rather than fan the flames with confrontation, he decided to ignore what Hart had told him and tell Shawn he was winning the title at *Survivor Series*.

Overcome with emotion, Michaels tearfully told Hart how much he respected him and how grateful he was that he would do the honours for him. Bret was not so quick to return the affirmation. He was stunned that McMahon had not called out Michaels for disrespecting him, so he decided to bring it up himself. When he reminded Shawn about San Jose, the would-be champion was all apologies, telling Hart, "Sometimes I say the stupidest things. I always put my foot in my own mouth." Hart was not convinced by Michaels' act; he had seen him cry crocodile tears one too many times and was still smarting about the public manner in which Michaels had insulted him. "I'm not agreeing to anything right now," groused Hart, "We'll see where all of this is going, and, Vince, you know what I'm talking about."

Hart was refusing to budge on McMahon's request for him to put over Michaels. He knew that if he did sign with WCW then he would have his thirty-day creative control clause to protect him, so until Michaels apologised in front of the locker room for disrespecting him and agreed to put him over first, he had no intention of letting Michaels beat him. Most of the boys took Hart's side, even though they were well aware that he may be on his way out of the WWF. He was a leader in the dressing room and someone they looked up to, as opposed to Michaels who had nothing but heat with nearly everyone.

"I understand why Bret was reluctant to lay down for Shawn," said Tom Prichard, the WWF's then-head trainer. "There was a real intense dislike there between the two of them. With Bret growing up the way he did born into the business, for a guy like Shawn to say, 'I'm not gonna put you over no matter where it is, fuck you,' well, those are fighting words. Especially when Bret had already put him over in their previous high profile match at *WrestleMania XII*. I can see why Bret would say no after that. Perhaps Bret could be accused of taking himself a little too seriously sometimes, but then again, Lou Thesz took himself seriously, so did Steve Austin. Those guys had to take themselves seriously to become those guys in the first place."

On November 2, the day after Bret officially resigned from the WWF, McMahon again told Hart that he wanted him to put Shawn over in Montreal. Now that he knew Hart was leaving for definite he wanted to take no chances. Even though all parties involved in Hart's departure had agreed to keep it a secret, McMahon did not trust Bischoff one bit. He saw *Survivor Series* as the last chance he had to get the belt off Hart before Bischoff appeared on *Nitro* and announced he had signed the WWF Champion, and he was determined not to let that happen. He could not let Eric Bischoff get one over on him like that.

"I want you to put Shawn over next week at *Survivor Series*," McMahon told Hart again, but the 'Hitman' refused to budge on his stance. "I'm sorry Vince, I've always done everything you've asked but I can't do that. I will put over anyone else on the roster, anyone you want, I will even put over the Brooklyn Brawler[16] in the Garden, but I cannot, under any circumstances, put over Shawn Michaels." Dropping the belt was not Bret's issue – it was who he had to lose it to. He even had his lawyer write a letter to McMahon informing him that, among other things, "Bret will gladly lose to Steve Austin. He wants to lose to Steve Austin before he leaves the World Wrestling Federation." That was not what McMahon wanted. He had grander plans for Austin's ascension to the WWF throne culminating at *WrestleMania* the following March, so he ignored the request.

McMahon's brittle patience was beginning to crack. He despised being dictated to about who his WWF Champion could be by someone who was leaving the company in a few weeks. He warned Hart that he might have to sue him if he refused to comply. To counter that Hart reminded McMahon of the reasonable control clause built into his contract, but McMahon was dismissive.

---

[16] Steve 'The Brooklyn Brawler' Lombardi was a long-time jobber who rarely won a match. By saying he would willingly put Brawler over, Hart was making it clear that he had no problem doing jobs for anyone in the territory. The only exception was Michaels.

"We could tie our assholes up in court for years over this," he grumbled. Hart repeated the same sentiments that he had expressed prior, telling McMahon he would be happy to put Shawn over if he did the same for him first, but not in Montreal. Hart felt that such was the strength of feeling about the US vs. Canada program that his character absolutely could not lose in his home country to a man who had picked his nose with the Canadian flag, especially on Memorial Day weekend. However, that was only a minor part of it. Hart's biggest problem was and always had been putting over a man who did not respect him.

"I have been in positions where I didn't wanna put someone over because I felt they wouldn't want to do the same for me," said Ken Shamrock, "But it's a business we are in. The bottom line is, you are looking at a company that's been around many years before you came along and will be around long after you. If they ask you to do something, you do it. That's the business we got into. Whether you like it or not, that's what we signed up for."

In McMahon's eyes, Hart's refusal to lose to one of his top stars was not a "reasonable" request whatsoever. The clause had been designed to protect Hart from having his character sullied and devalued on his way out or forced into scenarios he was not comfortable with – all old McMahon tricks – it did not give him the right to refuse to lose the WWF Championship to a performer billed on an equal if not higher standing that he was. Vince also did not agree with Hart's stance on losing in Canada. Hart may well have been a Canadian hero, but he had lost in the country plenty of times before and it had not hurt his standing there. He felt Hart was taking himself far too seriously and had become consumed by his 'Hitman' character. What McMahon did not realise was that Hart's reluctance to lose in Canada stemmed from his and Eric Bischoff's plans to foray into the lucrative market north of the border with WCW. By not losing to Shawn in Canada he felt he was protecting his image in the country, keeping him hot for when WCW began running there.[17]

Both Hart and McMahon remained stubborn and stuck steadfast to their positions, with the discussion continuing throughout the day and well into the night. Finally, after hours of wrangling, they agreed to the compromise of a disqualification finish at *Survivor Series* where Hart would go over. Hart – assuming he could get a one-week extension on his WWF deal authorised by Bischoff – would then drop the strap at the December 7 pay-per-view in a four-way match in which he would not be the one defeated by Shawn. The next day on *Raw* he would give a farewell speech and leave with his head held high. Both men were satisfied with the shaky compromise. Hart got hold of Bischoff two

---

[17] WCW never did capitalise on Hart's popularity in Canada. They ran occasional events there, but the WWF had a stronghold on the territory and WCW were unable to gain much traction North of the border.

days later and asked if his WCW contract, which was supposed to commence on December 1, could be delayed for one week so he could leave the WWF on his own terms without any bad blood. Bischoff granted the request, telling Hart to do what he needed to do and to leave on good terms, but also advised that any changes to the plan within that week needed to be approved by him first. Finally, after weeks of going back and forth, the finish for *Survivor Series* seemed to have been agreed.

On Wednesday November 5, McMahon was sat by the pool of his luxurious Connecticut mansion with creative team members Jim Cornette and Vince Russo when he excused himself to go and take a call. It was Shawn Michaels, calling to discuss the *Survivor Series* finish. McMahon had already told him the plan and Shawn was calling back to offer up his opinion. He had been musing it over and was unsure whether to agree, so he asked his ever-present sounding board Helmsley what he thought. Hunter was furious when Shawn told him McMahon's proposed finish, adamant that since Hart was leaving and McMahon wanted the belt on Michaels, that Hart should do the right thing and put him over on his way out. "He's leaving and you're staying, you do not put him over on the way out before he leaves!" he ranted.

Michaels trusted Hunter more than anyone and agreed with his opinion. He told McMahon, "I'm not doing that, Vince, no way! Do you want me to do that? Do you really want me to put over a guy who is leaving to go to WCW? If you really want me to do that I will do it, but I think it is fucking stupid." According to Michaels, his refusal to go along with the plan was what McMahon wanted to hear because he did not want to kowtow to Hart's whims and do the cheap DQ finish either. It was Shawn's belief that McMahon wanted him to say no to the idea so he could go back to Hart and tell him they needed to come up with an alternative where Shawn would go over.

McMahon did exactly that. His ears on the ground had informed him that news of Bret's departure was now out everywhere in the dirt sheets and the mainstream media, and that two days earlier Eric Bischoff had promised a "huge announcement" on the following week's *Nitro*. McMahon was certain that Bischoff – who at Hart's request had agreed not to mention his signing on air prior to *Survivor Series* in order to protect the pay-per-view – was going to brag about Bret's imminent arrival in WCW the night after the show. Once that announcement was made he would be left with a lame duck champion and a dead title belt, so he decided to go back on his agreed compromise with Hart and was once again determined to get the title off him before Monday.

"It wasn't that Vince didn't trust Bret Hart," said Jim Cornette, "Nobody thought he was going to show up on *Nitro* the day following *Survivor Series*, or that he would ever turn up on WCW television with the belt. Bret had given his word to Vince, and Vince actually believed him. I did too, because Bret was a man of his word. But the thought was that it was entirely possible Bischoff would come out and say he had signed the WWF Champion. Taking the belt off Bret was Vince's way of getting the one-up on Bischoff so he couldn't say that the WWF Champion was coming in."

McMahon called Hart as soon as he came off the phone with Michaels and told him that Shawn had nixed the idea of the DQ. He told him they needed to come up with a new plan in which Hart would drop the title before Monday, be it at *Survivor Series* or otherwise. McMahon suggested that Hart could lose the belt on a Detroit house show the day before, but Hart rejected the idea because he thought it would make the pay-per-view anticlimactic. He wanted to go into Montreal as the champion because he felt he was a Canadian hero and did not want to disappoint his fans by showing up without the belt. Hart told McMahon again that he would drop the belt to anyone except Shawn any place, any time, but after the *Raw* from Ottawa, once they were out of Canada. He suggested they could switch the belt at Madison Square Garden – Vince's biggest market – on the Saturday following *Survivor Series* and film it for future airing.

That was not good enough for Vince. For one thing it cost the WWF $40,000 to film at the Garden, but more importantly it was after the Bischoff announcement. McMahon told Hart that too many people knew he was leaving now and he could not have Bischoff announcing him as having signed with WCW while he was still wearing the WWF Championship belt. Hart told McMahon that he would ask Bischoff to postpone the announcement, but McMahon was rightly sceptical. He had no reason to trust that Bischoff would do anything to protect the reputation of the WWF Championship, considering everything he had done to try to harm the company over the past two years. He was not willing to take that chance and have the WWF's image tarnished beyond repair to appease Hart. Bret told Vince to let him talk to Bischoff first, which he attempted to do, but Bischoff was not available when he tried to call him.

They had reached a stalemate. McMahon needed the belt off Hart prior to Ottawa, but Hart was refusing to lose it until afterwards. McMahon again insisted that he needed the change to come before then, so Hart suggested dropping the belt in the first match at Ottawa *Raw* to Shawn, providing Michaels put him over first at *Survivor Series* to prove he had respect for him. That did not work for McMahon either, because he was sure Bischoff's announcement would come at the top of the show before they had chance to do the switch. He was also not keen on putting Hart over one of his top stars on his way out, and he was sure Shawn would not do it anyway after their earlier conversation. McMahon tried again to convince Hart to lose to Shawn in Montreal, but the answer remained a firm no. Weary with the back and forth, Hart suggested they keep the DQ finish and that he would vacate the title at the beginning of *Raw* the next night, before Bischoff had chance to announce anything. McMahon was not sold on that idea at all, but he agreed to it because he felt like he had little choice. Hart was holding a proverbial gun to his head and holding the WWF Title to ransom. He held all of the cards.

"Goddamn it," cussed McMahon after finishing the call with Hart, in earshot of Cornette and Russo. He told them the current status of the finish, how they were still no closer to a resolution, and Cornette sighed. By now he was fed up of hearing about the never-ending bickering between two pouting millionaires who were, as far as he was concerned, acting like silly little children. Alongside Russo and other members of the team, Cornette had been racking his brain for weeks trying to help Vince come up with a solution that was to the satisfaction of both Bret and Shawn, and in the best interests of the company. It was proving to be an impossible task. Every idea imaginable had been pitched, and each one had been rejected out of hand by either Shawn, Bret, or Vince.

At the end of his tether, Cornette grumbled to McMahon, "Why didn't you think to take the belt off him before you freed him up to negotiate with Bischoff?" McMahon had no answers. Cornette was so sick of dealing with the problem finish that he blurted out, "Goddamn Vince, it's your fucking belt. Book him with goddamn Shamrock, he'll drop the belt then. Just double-cross him."

It was an extreme suggestion. A double-cross belonged in the days of carnival promoters and legitimate shooters. It was a way of getting the belt off the champion by beating him for real without anyone watching knowing any different. Though fairly common in the 1920s and 1930s, the double-cross had all but disappeared from the wrestling playbook by 1997.

Shamrock, for his part, said he would have refused to comply had he been asked to do that. "I trained with Bret, he helped me get into the business. He helped me develop my skill set to get into pro wrestling. I appreciated that. If they had asked me to do that I would have said no. I've worked too hard to gain people's trust in the ring to go in there and shoot on someone. Even if my job was on the line, I would not do that. That goes beyond my job description."

McMahon, however, was no stranger to the act. In 1985 he had done the same thing to reigning WWF Women's Champion Wendi Richter – one of the spearheads of the Rock 'n' Wrestling era – in Madison Square Garden. Frustrated with Richter's dalliance over a new contract and feeling the sudden stardom her status as a pop culture idol was affording her had gone to her head, McMahon instructed veteran Lillian 'The Fabulous Moolah' Ellison to shoot on her in the ring and pin her for the title. Moolah, working under a mask as the anonymous Spider Lady, complied. McMahon had his title back and afterwards Richter walked straight through the dressing room, out of the door and out of the WWF for good.

When Cornette suggested the idea, Vince's expression shifted from irritated to intrigued, and he mumbled, "Oh, well, do you think?" Sensing his boss wanted to hear more, Cornette continued, "It will have to be inventive," he warned, "Because if it doesn't work it's not gonna be like Moolah and Wendi where Moolah could beat her up anyway. If Shawn tries to cinch up on a small package and Bret kicks out, Bret will beat the fuck out of him right there on live television." Vince was non-committal, listening intently but not giving any indication one way or another about whether he would actually consider going to such extreme measures. A double-cross was his absolute last resort. It was a move he would only make if all other scenarios had been exhausted and he was left with no choice to protect his company, because it would irreparably damage his relationship with Hart. However, it was dawning on him that there appeared to be no other way of getting Bret to acquiesce to his requests. It was at that moment, four days prior to the show, that McMahon began to seriously consider pulling a double-cross as a real possibility.

"I never dreamed Vince would take that offhand suggestion and morph it into what he did. It took on a life of its own," said Cornette. "If I planted the seed then I take responsibility, but it wasn't like anyone who had been in the wrestling business for any amount of time wouldn't have said the same goddamn thing. Vince even had a precedent of doing that before. I do remember saying to Vince, 'Well, what's Bret gonna say or do about it?' because I never dreamed that Bret Hart, of all people, would expose the business afterwards like he did. Ultimately it was Vince's decision. It came out of his mind to do it, I just planted the seed."

McMahon knew that executing a double-cross would not be easy. For it to work he would need Hart's opponent Shawn Michaels on board. If Shawn was not willing to go through with it, then it was off the table. As it happened, Michaels and McMahon had a private conference call each Wednesday to discuss booking ideas and any concerns he had. That night was no different. Shawn called from his hotel room and placed McMahon on speakerphone, with Helmsley sitting right there by his side. "So, did you talk to Bret?" Shawn asked, curious about how the conversation between them had gone following his own earlier phone call with Vince. McMahon decided to keep the double-cross idea close to his chest. It was not something he felt comfortable bringing up casually to Shawn. "Yes, he still won't budge. He said he is not going to do it," replied McMahon truthfully, "Barring some miraculous change this weekend, I guess we are going to have to work a DQ. He wants to walk out on TV the next night and hand the belt over. I guess that's what we are going to have to do."

McMahon was keen to make it clear that he was not comfortable with the scenario and was still exploring other options, half hoping that Michaels would make a similar suggestion to the one Cornette had made earlier. That way, he would know he was onside with the idea should it have to happen. There was a long, uncomfortable silence, with everyone thinking the same thing but nobody willing to say it. Michaels broke it. "I will do whatever you want me to do," he assured his stressed boss. Helmsley was far less vague. "Maybe I'm not supposed to be talking here and maybe I'm out of line, but fuck that! What kind of business is that? Who in the world says, 'I don't want to drop the belt?' If he doesn't wanna do business then we need to do business for him" McMahon was taken aback at Hunter's bluntness, but more surprised that he had implied the exact same solution as the one Cornette had mentioned earlier. For the same idea to come from two such diametrically opposed characters did not go unnoticed by him.

McMahon still decided to play it cool and act like he did not fully know what was being suggested, beating around the bush before asking, "Well, what are we talking about here?" Michaels, realising where the conversation was going and suspecting McMahon needed more assurances, told him, "Whatever it takes. I will do whatever you want me to do. We'll just take it off him. I'll swerve him or whatever I have to. If we have to fast count or get him in a hold and tell someone to ring the bell, so be it. You tell me what needs to get done. My loyalty is here with you; I'll do whatever you tell me to."

Now that Shawn had come out and openly expressed his willingness to cooperate in a double-cross, McMahon dropped the façade. "Alright, I think I know what we are talking about here," he told the pair, "That's pretty serious stuff. That has to be a last resort. We've still got until Saturday to try and talk to Bret to convince him to do the right thing, but that may have to be a real option. This cannot be discussed with anyone. Pat [Patterson] cannot know, he is too close to Bret. Nobody can know about this except the three of us. It's something we will have to talk about in a few days."

After the call ended, Michaels and Helmsley discussed the conversation that had just transpired. They both felt that McMahon had been leading them in the direction of a double-cross and had already made up his mind to do it, but that he felt uncomfortable coming out and saying it directly. "Vince felt like he was in a corner," said Michaels, "Nobody was really saying anything but we knew what he wanted. But I don't think Vince felt comfortable coming out and saying that, he felt he needed me to volunteer first." For his part, Michaels did not exactly relish giving his detractors yet more ammunition to use against him, but by this point he hardly cared anymore. He was already public enemy number one amongst the boys, what difference did a little more heat make?

According to Michaels, when they talked again, McMahon realised he was putting Shawn in a difficult position and tried to assure him. "Don't worry, I will take the heat," he told him, but Michaels was realistic. "Dude, you can take whatever you want but the heat is gonna go on me," said Michaels, "You're the boss. How mad can they possibly get with you? The shit rolls downhill, it's gonna go on me." As they talked further, McMahon made Michaels and Hunter swear not to speak a word of the plan to anyone. It was a delicate situation and strictly need-to-know only. If too many others found out, then it was sure to get back to Hart. McMahon had to pick his soldiers carefully, because he realised that even some of his closest confidantes would be unhappy with what he was contemplating.

McMahon had finally found his elusive finish. With a willing assassin in the form of Shawn Michaels, he had come up with something that would give him exactly what he wanted. It meant the belt would go to the person he wanted to hold it and, most importantly, it snared the title away from Hart prior to Bischoff's announcement on Monday. On a personal level McMahon was not thrilled at the prospect of ending his long relationship with Hart on such a sour note, but he firmly believed it was the right thing to do for his business. And after all, this was all about business for him. Taking the title back forcibly put the power back in McMahon's hands. McMahon justified it to himself as the only choice he had because Hart had him by the balls and was refusing to do the right thing by the WWF. His mind was made up: if Bret would not agree to put Shawn over in Montreal then he was going to screw him.

TEN

NEWS OF BRET HART'S DEPARTURE had spread throughout the wrestling fraternity, with the consensus amongst the WWF fan base that Hart was being forced out of the door due to his outspoken views on the New WWF direction of which he did not approve. The fans were in no doubt about who was responsible; they blamed Shawn Michaels and Vince McMahon. Some were so vocal in their disapproval of the WWF's treatment of Hart that they bombarded the WWF's website with complaints and angry comments, causing it to temporarily shut down. Feeling the need to respond and right the perceived wrongs, two days before *Survivor Series* McMahon penned a letter to his audience that read:

> Over the past few days I have read certain comments on the Internet concerning Bret Hart and his "alleged" reasons for wanting to pursue other avenues than the World Wrestling Federation to earn his livelihood. While I respect the "opinions" of others, as owner of the World Wrestling Federation I felt that it was time to set the record straight. As it has been reported recently online, part of Bret Hart's decision to pursue other options is "allegedly due to his concern with the "direction" of the World Wrestling Federation. Whereby each and every individual is entitled to his, or her, opinion, I take great offence when the issue of the direction of the World Wrestling Federation is raised. In this age of sports-entertainment, the World Wrestling Federation REFUSES to insult its audience in terms of "Baby Faces" and "Heels." In 1997, how many people do you truly know who are strictly "good" guys or "bad" guys? World Wrestling Federation programming reflects more of a reality-based product in which life, as well as World Wrestling Federation superstars, are portrayed as they truly are: in shades of grey, not black or white. From what I am reading, it has been reported that Bret may be concerned about the morality issues in the World

Wrestling Federation. Questionable language. Questionable gestures. Questionable sexuality. Questionable racial issues. Questionable? All of the issues mentioned above are issues that every human being must deal with every day of their lives. Also, with that in mind, please be aware that Bret Hart had been cautioned on "numerous" occasions to alter his language, by not using expletives or God's name in vain. He was also told on numerous occasions not to use certain hand gestures some might find offensive. My point is, regardless of what some are reporting, Bret's decision to pursue other career options IS NOT genuinely a Shawn Michaels direction issue, as they would like you to believe! In the personification of D-Generation X, Shawn Michaels' character is EXPECTED to be living on the edge--which, I might add, Mr. Michaels portrays extremely well. The issue here is that the "direction" of the World Wrestling Federation is not determined by Shawn Michaels, OR Bret Hart for that matter. It is determined by you--the fans of the World Wrestling Federation! You DEMAND a more sophisticated approach! You DEMAND to be intellectually challenged! You DEMAND a product with ATTITUDE, and as owner of this company--it is my responsibility to give you exactly what you want! Personally, I regret the animosity that has built up between Shawn Michaels and Bret Hart, but in the end, it is the World Wrestling Federation that is solely responsible for the content of this product--NOT Bret Hart--NOT Shawn Michaels--NOT Vince McMahon, for that matter. May the best man win at the *Survivor Series*!

THE NIGHT before *Survivor Series*, Bret Hart was wrestling what would turn out be his final WWF match on American soil[18], teaming with his brothers in law Jim Neidhart and Davey Boy Smith opposite Steve Austin, Undertaker, and Mankind in a six-man tag match. Meanwhile, six-hundred miles away in Montreal, Vince McMahon and his team were putting the final touches on the *Survivor Series* card in their typical pre-pay-per-view production meeting at the Montreal Marriott Hotel. In attendance were Jim Cornette, Bruce Prichard, Jim Ross, Gerald Brisco, Vince Russo, Sgt Slaughter, Kevin Dunn, and some of the production crew. It was a long meeting, with every intricate detail of the card micromanaged by McMahon, from the order the wrestlers entered the ring to who was going over. The exception was the Hart-Michaels main event, for which the finish was not discussed.

After hours holed up in the meeting, Jim Ross and the other smokers in the room were desperate to get outside for a cigarette, something strictly forbidden in the presence of McMahon, who loathed the habit. Their rapid departure led

---

[18] Hart returned to the company in 2010, but it was now known as WWE. He was also not an active wrestler; rather he worked limited, one-off matches because he was unable to bump as a result of a stroke he had suffered following a bicycle crash.

to many believing they too were privy to the screwjob ploy. Cornette was equally eager to depart, but before he did he took McMahon aside and whispered, "Vince, you don't have to tell me what it is, but do you have a finish for the main event yet?" McMahon told him that he did, but did not elaborate. "Good, that's all I need to know," said Cornette. Everybody left the room except for Bruce Prichard, Kevin Dunn, and Gerald Brisco, who McMahon asked to stay behind. When the rest of the assembled throng had departed he let them in on the secret he had been keeping to himself for the past three days. McMahon trusted the three more than anyone else. They were his most loyal soldiers, guaranteed to side with him no matter what they personally thought about the idea. He told them that the plan could never leave the room and they all nodded in agreement, understanding the magnitude of the situation.

McMahon explained to Dunn that he would need him to have Shawn's music ready to be cued immediately after the double-cross occurred, warned him to be prepared to go to long shots if scenes became ugly and Hart tried to attack him or Shawn, and that the show would likely finish earlier than scheduled due to the truncating of the main event. Dunn nodded that he understood and was excused so he could get back to his pre-show checks, leaving McMahon, Prichard, and Brisco. Vince informed them that Michaels and Helmsley already knew about what was being discussed, but that he did not want to tell anyone else because he was worried word would get out and Hart would learn of the plan. If that happened then Hart would likely take such offence that he would walk out, taking the WWF Championship belt with him.

It was for that reason, explained McMahon, that he did not want to tell Pat Patterson or Jim Ross, two men he would usually trust with just about anything. Vince felt that Patterson was too close to Hart. He did not like confrontation and would likely try to talk with Bret and search for a compromise that McMahon already knew could not be reached. He figured Ross would likely spend the day trying to talk him out of it and searching for alternative solutions, but he was past the point of wanting further distractions; his mind was made up. McMahon also reasoned that given Ross and Patterson's respective positions as Head of Talent Relations and Head Road Agent, both roles that called for absolute trust in them from the boys, it was better for them not to know. It gave them plausible deniability rather than having to lie about something they were uncomfortable with for the remainder of their careers.

The trio decided to pay Michaels and Helmsley a visit to confirm to them that the double-cross was no longer merely an idea being floated around; it was the concrete plan. When they reached the room McMahon informed Michaels, "Bret still won't bend. Are you willing to do what we discussed?" Shawn had expected this conversation was coming and was ready with an answer. "Yeah, I'm willing to do whatever it takes," he told his relieved boss. McMahon told Michaels that he was going to make one last ditch effort tomorrow to make

Hart change his mind and do the finish the way he wanted it done, but if not, then the double-cross was happening. "This is serious," he told him, "But as of right now, this thing is actually going to happen."

Worried about how Hart would react when the deed was done, McMahon told Brisco to show Shawn some holds to defend himself with in case Bret tried to attack him. "Vince asked me to work out several different scenarios to go into the finish situation that we were going to ring the bell on," said Brisco, "And to go over some protection holds in case Bret grabbed Shawn and tried to physically hurt him." Shawn was no stranger to people wanting to kick his ass and was blasé about the prospect, realising that he had Hunter and Brisco there to watch his back should anything happen.

McMahon reiterated the same sentiments he had expressed to Michaels and Helmsley when the double-cross was first broached on Wednesday evening, again telling them that he wanted to take full responsibility for what was going to happen. Shawn might have been the bullet, but he was the one pulling the trigger. "I don't want you telling anyone about this," he warned, "When it happens, you deny you knew anything about it until the end. This is my decision, but I physically can't do it. I don't want the heat going on you. Some is going to go on you inevitably because of your history with Bret and because you are the guy doing it, but this is my decision. I don't want you telling anyone. If anyone asks you, you did not know anything about it. When it is over with it is over with. Bret's going to be hot. You have to put the heat on me. He needs to be mad at me. He's going to be mad at me and he's going to want to hit me. I'm going to let him. I owe Bret that much."

While the details of how they were going to pull off the double-cross remained sketchy, the deal was done. They were actually going to screw Bret and forcibly take the WWF Championship away from him in Canada, impelling him to leave the company under a cloud of bitterness and anger. It was exactly as Hart had predicted it would end when he talked to Owen six weeks earlier. As Brisco was leaving Shawn's room he placed a fatherly hand on his shoulder and told him encouragingly, "Shawn, I'll be in the Gorilla position if anything goes down. I'll get down there, but I'm not as fast as I used to be." Helmsley looked at his slightly anxious friend and similarly reassured him, "I'll be there for you too Shawn, no matter what happens."

MEANWHILE, OVER in Detroit, Bret Hart was beginning to get an uneasy feeling about the following night's show. He could not quite put his finger on it, but he sensed something was amiss. Word had got out around the boys that Hart was refusing to put Shawn over in Montreal and most were supportive of his decision. Even the agents appeared to be on his side, with Jack Lanza telling him, "You are doing the right thing. I wouldn't drop the belt to that little motherfucker either."

Even with the support of his peers, something still did not sit right with Hart. He decided his jitters were likely being caused by talk from some of the more paranoid members of the dressing room such as Davey Boy Smith and Vader, who kept warning him about the possibility of a double-cross. Hart was dismissive. "I was almost sure they were gonna try and pull something like that," he admitted, "But I was also sure that it wasn't gonna happen." Little did Hart realise that across the Great Lakes of Ontario and Erie, McMahon and his cronies were conspiring to do exactly that.

To cover himself in the event, Hart sought out referee Earl Hebner, whom he assumed would be officiating the bout with Shawn due to his status as the WWF's head referee. Bret considered Earl to be more than merely another in a long list of wrestling acquaintances, he viewed him as a genuine friend. He was the one member of the office that Hart knew for certain that he could trust. Whispering, Hart told Hebner, "Earl, tomorrow I think they're going to ask you to fuck me." Looking shocked, Hebner told Hart, "I swear on my kids' heads Bret, I will never do it no matter what they say to me. I would quit my job before double-crossing you. If they ask me to do that I will tell them to go fuck themselves, I swear!" Hebner's outraged response filled Hart with confidence and he began to relax a little more knowing that Earl was on his side. Nevertheless, he wanted to make sure he and Earl were on the same page so told him, "Earl all you gotta do is tell me the plan if they ask you to do it. I will take care of the rest."

Hart felt he had all of his bases covered. He knew he would cream Michaels in a real fight if it came down to it; after all, he already had earlier in the year, and that was with a bad knee. He also now had Earl's sworn promise that he would not double-cross him, so even if McMahon did try something he had established his defences in readiness for that. Despite these reassurances, Hart still spent the night tossing and turning. His attempts at catching some rest before the big pay-per-view match were proving futile, as worries about what fate awaited him less than twenty-four hours later in Montreal kept him awake all night.

AS SOON as Hart arrived in Montreal he began to get suspicious that something sinister was in the works. "I remember someone came to Bret and told him they'd seen Shawn getting into an elevator with Vince in his hotel, and that kinda got Bret a little worried," remembered his then-wife Julie Hart. "Bret said he had to go talk to our lawyer, who was in town with us as well. After he had been told what had happened Bret really started getting nervous."

In the Molson Centre, Vince McMahon and his crew were gathered for yet another production meeting, and there was a strange edginess in the room. As Gerald Brisco remembered, "A lot of people were very uneasy that day. You could feel a tension in the air." Even McMahon was unusually nervous. "I was troubled and anxious all day," he later admitted, "There's a certain angst when you have to make a decision and it is going to be an unpopular one because you know somebody is going to get hurt." The previous night's production meeting had occurred prior to the double-cross plan being fully formulated, and the finish was not discussed. It was now, with McMahon telling the assembled throng the cover story that they were running a DQ, followed by Hart vacating the title on *Raw* the next day. Afterwards, Jim Cornette expressed his opinion about that scenario to McMahon in no uncertain terms. "Why don't you just lay down and let him piss in your mouth while he does that?" he ranted. "You may be right there, pal," replied Vince, but, of course, he secretly knew that Hart vacating the belt was not on the cards.

After the meeting, McMahon met with Michaels in private to discuss the specifics of the finish. "Have you thought about it? Do you have any ideas?" he asked. Michaels had spent the previous evening contemplating how he might execute the swerve, so he was ready with a plan. "Yeah, I have. Usually when I wrestle Bret I throw the figure-four on. If I did that I don't think he would suspect anything. Maybe we can ring the bell real quick and say he gave up? Or maybe we can work a spot where I hit him with the superkick and I will cover him and hold him as hard as I can for a quick count." McMahon considered the options, but with Hart not yet in the building Michaels had been unable to talk through the match with him. Without any spots agreed upon by Hart, Michaels and McMahon were unable to say with any finality which hold could be employed to commit the deed. "As soon as you know what you are doing, you have to tell me, then we need to get Earl on board," Vince told him.

"It really started to become fascinating in a weird, nerve-wracking sort of way," remembered Michaels, "A lot of things get talked about and are never done, but we were actually going to do this. I was excited and scared. My adrenaline was pumping."

Pat Patterson had been appointed as the road agent for the match, because even though he did not know anything about the planned double-cross, Vince knew that Hart trusted him and would be more likely to leave himself open to ideas where they could execute the finish than if he was assigned to someone else. Likewise, Hart would have expected Patterson as his agent; if it was anyone else then his suspicions would likely be aroused. Patterson was excited about the contest because he loved seeing Shawn and Bret work together, and he was eager to plan the match with them. He repeatedly asked Shawn what the layout was, but Michaels told them he did not know anything until he talked to Bret.

SHAWN WOULD have to wait a little longer. When Hart finally arrived around 5 p.m. he headed straight for McMahon's office for a final crunch meeting. Both parties headed into the discussion hoping the other would finally see sense, but neither was willing to back down from their own respective stances. "Vince and I were eyeball to eyeball and nobody was blinking," remembered Hart. Bret spoke first. "This Canadian angle has really painted me into a corner," he grumbled to McMahon, reminding him of his position. "It would be hard to come up short as a hero today." Hart asked Vince what he wanted to do for a finish, and McMahon suggested that at December's pay-per-view, instead of dropping the belt in a four-way and not losing directly to Michaels as they had previous discussed, he wanted Bret to put Shawn over in a singles contest. Hart did not flat out refuse the request this time, but his hands were tied by the agreement with Bischoff that any changes to the plans after December 1 had to be okayed by him. He was unable to agree to anything until he had spoken with Bischoff.

Unhappy that his championship, his company's most prized asset, was being controlled by the whims of Bischoff, McMahon angrily snarled, "What do you want me to do? You've got me by the balls." Bret told him that all he had ever wanted was to leave the building with his head held high, reminding McMahon that in previous conversations he had made it clear he could leave in any way he wanted. Hart again suggested a scenario he thought they had already agreed on, whereby they would do a DQ finish that night and he would vacate the title the next night on *Raw*. "Let me hand you the belt on *Raw*," he requested, "Everyone already knows that I am leaving anyway. I would like to tell the truth on Monday." As Hart would later firmly state, "It was a suggestion, not a demand." McMahon still had no interest in going with that scenario, paranoid about Bischoff's impending announcement the following evening, and asked Bret, "Can you assure me that's not gonna happen?" Hart was honest with McMahon and told him that he could not promise anything because he could not get hold of Bischoff, who had failed to return his calls.

McMahon realised they were not going to reach a satisfactory solution. He was dead-set on Hart dropping the belt in Montreal, and for that the double-cross remained his only option. He decided to humour Hart and make him feel at ease, hoping he would not suspect anything untoward later in the evening. He agreed with Hart that forfeiting the title was the right thing to do, telling him, "I am determined for this to end the right way." The sentence had a double meaning. Hart believed McMahon was giving him his word, but in fact the boss was actually intimating that he wanted the evening to end the right way for him and his company. He was willing to agree with everything Bret said and accommodate him in any way so that he would be caught completely unawares by the double-cross.

McMahon knew that he would need to orchestrate the swerve from ringside and be present to deflect any heat from Michaels onto him. He needed a way of working that into the conversation, because if he simply showed up out of the blue then Hart would have immediately known something was up. When Bret pushed to know the finish of the match McMahon saw his chance to suggest his presence without causing Hart to get suspicious. "We will do a schmazz," McMahon told him. "I won't be doing commentary tonight, so when things get out of hand I can come to ringside with other officials and we can make the thing look like a shoot."

Hart nodded in agreement at the plan and did not suspect a thing. If anything, he was relieved that Vince was finally seeing his side of the situation. He was confident that his thirteen years of loyal service and his track record for delivering world class performances would prevent Vince from screwing him on the way out. "Bret was tense that day, but when he came out of the meeting with Vince he was elated," noted Paul Jay, who was filming Hart's behind-the-scenes documentary-drama *Wrestling With Shadows* that night. "He didn't want to have a big fight with Vince. He wanted things to end with a handshake."

Hart was hoping for a similar parting truce with Michaels. When the two met privately backstage in a final attempt to put everything behind them, they engaged in the friendliest conversation they had managed in years. "Part of me feels that this is a big work on the part of the office. They made it worse," began Hart. "They knew we didn't want to work together and they kept adding fuel to the fire. It's not about you, I just can't do it here in Canada, I am a hero here. They don't understand how Canada is; it's different here, it's not like the States. Don't take it personally, it's no reflection on you. Everyone will make it out to be because of you, but that's not why. And I didn't want to leave, but I'll tell you, Vince is sort of forcing me out. Yeah, I got a good deal in WCW, but I'd rather stay here."

The two expressed their respect for each other, then when Bret asked Michaels point blank if he could trust him, there was nothing Shawn could say except, "Yes". He was beginning to feel increasingly guilty with each word that Hart spoke. His bitter rival was opening his heart to him and trying to make peace before he departed, yet he knew that in a few hours he was going to be involved in something that would damage their relationship for good. "We had done this several times before, but it felt genuine this time because Bret was getting shown the door," said Shawn, "There was a trace of humility on his part. Vince was pushing him out, not me."

Hart left the conversation feeling comfortable and relaxed about the forthcoming match, delighted that he and Shawn had finally been able to work out their differences and put months of ill-feeling behind them. Conversely, Michaels left feeling like the biggest asshole in the world. "Despite all of our problems, I felt really bad for him because I knew this was the end and he had no idea what was coming," he recalled. Following the talk, Michaels sought out his sounding board Helmsley and told him about his recent conversation with Bret, complaining ruefully, "I am going to look like the biggest heel in the world." It was an event Shawn could never forgive himself for, later admitting, "It was not fun being that guy. To this day it gets me emotional."

WITH HIS defences lowered, Hart was now far more open to suggestions which potentially left him vulnerable to a double-cross than he might have been had he not spoken with Hebner, Michaels, and McMahon. He believed he had all three on his side, and was looking forward to putting on a match that would tear the house down one final time. With road agent Pat Patterson in tow, Hart threw some ideas out, and Michaels – who Hart later described as visibly nervous – was receptive to all of them. Bret put that down to the hasty truce they had made earlier in the locker room, but it was more down to Michaels' desire to keep Hart friendly with him so he could execute McMahon's plan with no roadblocks.

Soon, Hart and Patterson lost themselves in the match, and as the ideas flowed they began to get excited. Michaels, who was part of the conversation in body but not in mind, listened intently, waiting for a spot that he could take back to Vince as the gift-wrapped murder weapon needed to execute the double-cross. Attempting to come up with a fresh idea, Patterson suggested, "I was thinking about doing this spot, I don't know if we can do it. Is there any way that you could, like, reverse the Sharpshooter?" Hart had been warned to avoid letting himself get put in false finishes or holds due to the possibility of a swerve, but with his guard down he was receptive to the idea and explained how it could be done. Michaels would put the hold on first, then Bret would grab his ankle and turn it into a Sharpshooter of his own.[19]

Michaels' ears pricked up at the mention of him doing a Sharpshooter. That was the spot. He tuned out the rest of the discussion about what would follow, because he knew it was now irrelevant. By consenting to the Sharpshooter, Hart was Caesar, passing off his knife to the conspiring Brutus. "Once Bret and I figured out what we were going to do, then, and only then, could Vince and I decide how it would go down," said Shawn. With his mind and his heart both racing, Michaels circled the building, taking a scenic trip around the backstage area that led him to Vince's office. "You're never gonna believe this," he exclaimed breathlessly, "Bret came up with a spot where I get the Sharpshooter on him and then he's supposed to reverse it by pulling my leg. When I put him in it, when I turn him over, we can ring the bell right there." McMahon agreed immediately. "That's it, that's the one!" he concurred, before telling Shawn to leave the rest to him.

The next step in ensuring the plan was executed correctly was informing Earl Hebner, a job McMahon delineated to Gerald Brisco. McMahon had no knowledge of Hebner's conversation with Hart the night before, but even so he

---

[19] Hart would later claim Patterson knew about the double-cross because he was the one who suggested the Sharpshooter. It was a coincidence. Pat came up with the spot because he thought it would look good; he had no idea Michaels would take it to McMahon as the spot to ring the bell on.

knew a hard-line approach was required. He was not giving Earl the option to comply, he was demanding that he did. Brisco cornered Hebner mere moments before the match started, telling him, "When Shawn gets Bret in the Sharpshooter, wait a few seconds then ring the bell." Hebner's heart sank. He was being asked to do the one thing he had promised Hart he would never do. "I can't do it!" he stammered. "What do you mean you can't do it?" fired back Brisco impatiently. "I promised him I wouldn't count him out," Hebner pleaded. Brisco leaned close and warned Hebner that if he did not do what he was told then he need not bother coming into work the next day, or any day after that. He reminded Earl that he was mic'd, and that he would personally be in the Gorilla position so could hear every word he said in case he was thinking of telling Hart. Hebner told Brisco that he did not know what he was going to do, and set off on the long fifty-foot walk to the ring. He was in shock, with dozens of contrasting thoughts running through his head. On the way he found his twin brother Dave and hurriedly told him, "Get ready to go and get out of here because I don't know what is going on right now." He had no time to explain, but Dave knew enough that it was something serious. As a fellow referee with years of experience, he immediately had his suspicions. As he remembered it, "I thought, 'Holy Christ man, this ain't happening is it?"

As Hebner was contemplating the reality of what he had been instructed to do, Bret Hart was going through his final pre-match preparations when Vader sidled up beside him. "Be careful out there brother," he whispered, "Vince is known for fucking people in these kinds of situations." Bret lowered his voice and told him he had it covered, but even so Vader advised him not to leave himself in any compromising positions, nor allow himself to be put in any holds, and to kick out of all pinfall attempts at one rather than two. Hart appreciated the concern but he was not worried. He was confident that Earl would never do that to him. He still suspected Shawn might try to throw in a sucker punch or two and they would get into a shoot live on pay-per-view, though his worry was not that he would be hurt, but rather how it would ruin the quality of the match. He threw on his trademark leather jacket, grabbed a Canadian flag, and began his march to the ring for what would turn out to be the most infamous match in wrestling history.

JIM ROSS and Jerry Lawler set the stage for the emotional crunch, the camera trained on the veteran announcers in the standard ringside two-shot. Patriarchal Ross underscored the friction between Bret Hart and Shawn Michaels, openly promising a match where punches would not be pulled. In wrestling, the scripted conflict is generally sold as being 'real' in the first place, so Ross' declaration that the forthcoming bout was, "gonna be stiff," promised a match that was somehow more 'real' than the realness that Titan and others had forever merchandised. Ross had inadvertently cast everything prior to the main event as fiction by comparison. In the moment, he had no idea how astute he really was.

Earl Hebner was first to the ring, internal lava spilling into the widening pit of his stomach. He had sworn loyalty to Hart, a man with whom his shared match history numbered well into the hundreds, perhaps even the thousands. He had no choice but to comply with the treacherous orders. On what would have happened if Hebner had found a way to discreetly tip McMahon's hand in Hart's direction, Hart said, "I would have choked Shawn out in the middle of the ring. I would have front-face locked him and ended the match."

After the standard pre-match hype video co-opting every bit of televised angst between the two professional rivals over the previous two years, the camera faded into something a bit different from the norm. For the first time outside of televised Madison Square Garden events, viewers were able to see both performers not only make their ring entrances, but actually walk from their dressing rooms to the curtain, over the top of a music bed pulsing with tantalising bass, the heavy juts of an intensifying heartbeat. Chyna and Rick Rude stood guard outside a door labelled 'D-X', which Helmsley opened to fetch Michaels. The challenger emerged, showing no signs of the astriction coursing his veins. Instead, he twisted his face into a Robert De Niro-esque sneer, deflecting the boos from the Montreal crowd viewing him on the big screens. The entourage's endless walk through the corridor was a tracking shot worthy of Martin Scorsese, a director of many stories featuring powerful, paranoid men, ones not realising their fate was at hand until it was too late.

The scene in the arena was already caustic, even before the grinding guitars of Shawn's '*Sexy Boy*' theme song blared throughout the Molson Centre. Michaels strode up the aisle alone, his D-Generation X cohorts not there to shield him from the cascade of a flung beverage raining over him, in response to snatching a fan's Canadian flag. Shaking off the drops like a disaffected mutt, Michaels continued his antagonistic strut inside the ring, making a show of wiping his ass with the flag, blowing his nose into it, and ultimately humping it as it lay prone on the canvas. Michaels claimed that Hart had suggested taking up these coarse theatrics, weeks after Michaels used another Canadian flag to pick his nose with during an episode of *Raw*. "You got a ton of heat up in Canada. I'm telling you they were just livid," Michaels said Hart told him, suggesting another go at provocation.

"Everyone made a big deal about me jerking around the Canadian flag, but like the Sharpshooter, it was his idea," Michaels noted. Hart's account fails to verify Michaels' claims, and instead suggests that his elderly father Stu, "took very real offence to Shawn's actions, as did everyone in the building and all across Canada."

Hart made the long backstage stroll second, acutely aware that he was walking his 'green mile' as a WWF performer. Following in Hart's wake were brothers-in-law Davey Boy Smith and Jim Neidhart, while seven-year-old son Blade brought up the rear brandishing an untarnished Canadian flag. Hart has since written many words about Smith and Neidhart's gradual deterioration through poor life choices and the grappler's grind, but on this night, his faith in them as confidantes was never higher. Trust was a scarce currency for Hart that day, though he also had it in long-time friend Rick Rude. When the two noticed that Helmsley was not standing by the curtain for his planned eventual run-in, a wary Rude told Hart, "I'll watch your back in case they try to jump you or pull anything funny on you out there."

Anxiously anticipating their hero, Montreal quickly parroted the high-pitched shriek of the guitar lick that signalled the WWF Champion's arrival. Hart's face showed worrisome slack as he tagged hands with the aisle-way devotees, fully understanding that even with the match outcome he had agreed to, things were never going to be the way they used to be. Through blinded apprehension, Hart was stepping through a doorway to elsewhere.

Beneath dimmed house lights, Hart made his trademark open-armed appeals to the crowd, where fans held up signs that read 'GOOD LUCK IN WCW BRET' and 'WHERE BRET GOES WE GO.' Contrasting them were indiscreet placards bearing such witticisms as, 'ASS 3:16' and 'RICK RUDE WOULD RATHER BE IN CHYNA', the sort of juvenile sludge he lamented watching his long-time employer roll around in. Ross turned to his refined role as human encyclopaedia, firing out Hart's career credentials like a gun turret. "This match is a long journey in itself," Ross informed the home viewer. "It took eighteen months to get it done. And the smart money is that you will never, ever see it again."

"Possibly the two biggest egos in all of wrestling are about to collide," Lawler hissed a short time after, a veiled post-script to Ross' comment about the time it took to secure the rematch. Earl Hebner held Hart's belt aloft following Lawler's unfeigned decree to Ross that it was, "all about the power. You know it. I know it. Let's not kid ourselves."

Per the recently-laid plans, Michaels attacked Hart before the bell could sound, only to be bounced around by Hart to the delight of the Canadian audience. Michaels took some of his patented superball flops about ringside off Hart's strikes, and was dumped like refuse into the first row of the braying mob at ringside. Hart joined Michaels on the other side of the railing, where an immediate swarm of officials burst onto the scene to try restoring order. Mike Chioda and his fellow referees beat building security to the punch in keeping the stimulated onlookers away from the two performers. McMahon was soon on the scene with his cadre of company officers, including Sgt Slaughter, Pat Patterson, Gerald Brisco, and Tony Garea. Their duty, particularly McMahon and Brisco's, was to make sure that Hart and Michaels made it back to the ring.

"I was sat next to Vince, but I didn't know what was going on," Slaughter recalled. "Before the match he said, 'Sarge, I want you to come and sit with me.'"

The presence of so many suits apparently did not jostle Hart's security any, because he felt the story of two mad-as-hell competitors teeing off on each other was strutted by the futile attempts at restoration. Michaels took control of the fracas, sending Hart into the French announcer's table as Ross bristled, "All kinds of speculation regarding Bret Hart and his future. Everybody's got the answer. Everybody knows the story," working to plant the idea that the finish of the match was not as concrete as gossip-breathers may have been thinking. The bewildered crowd began booing harshly as Michaels wrapped an American flag bandana around Hart's throat, garrotting him in front of the broadcast desks. "There has been a lot of speculation that if Bret Hart loses this match, that this will be his last match in the WWF," Ross tacked onto his earlier point, while Michaels flung Hart into the front row on the opposite side of the ring. The amoebic horde of McMahon and his court filed over to the action once more, with Lawler noting that the match had not even officially begun.

Michaels was backdropped over the railing and onto the ringside mats when Hart reversed his attempt at a piledriver. McMahon audibly yelled "Look out!" when Michaels took the front-flip bump onto a lower back that had endured countless. Brisco could be seen gesturing angrily toward the ring in an order for Hart to continue the match there, an overt coax entirely in character, but with tinges of a secondary meaning. Instead, Hart took Michaels back to the aisleway for further extra-curricular activity, all of which was making for captivating television.

Michaels endured more spine-rattling thuds on the floor of the entrance aisle, one the result of a vertical suplex. Michaels crashed down flat, crushing a cardboard beverage carrier littered by some careless fan. On wobbly legs that were showman-like in their transference of jolts of pain, Michaels decked Pat Patterson as a means of further highlighting the turbulence of the brawl. In the famed Iron Man Match from one year earlier, where both men played it congenially competitive, ring attendant Tony Chimel was laid out with an errant Michaels superkick. The prolonged story that dragged each man's innermost resentment and ego into a work of fiction now featured once-dignified athletes taking down officials as collateral damage, before shrugging disaffectedly.

Even those on the other side of the glass could not help but get involved, for the ground covered by the melee extended beyond partition. A long-haired youngster clad in a leather jacket reached out over the guardrail and hooked Hart's arm as the champion worked in some wind-up punches on Michaels. It had been a full year-and-a-half since Michaels and his Kliq spit-brothers pulled back the curtain in a farewell that stomped out any remaining vestiges that suggested wrestling was real. When the internet-wired world learned that Hart was leaving and that he and Michaels legitimately hated each other's guts, it was hard not to get wrapped up in a scuffle mere inches from their seats. Most overzealous fans such as this one are chided for not knowing that it is all fake. The injection of dirty truth in this story made it harder to tell the difference.

Hart sent Michaels careening into a neutral area back by the entrance curtain, before using a fire extinguisher to lightly batter his opponent. Here, Hart had a brief encounter with McMahon, in which the boss pleaded in a nasally grunt to get Michaels back into the ring. Hart decked referee Jack Doan during his turn in the game of strike-the-official. McMahon continued his kayfabe commands, to which Hart acknowledged him with a prolonged glare, akin to Michael Myers tilting his head eerily at sister Laurie Strode. "Oh ho, don't push your luck, McMahon!" chortled a caffeinated Lawler at ringside.

Following ten minutes of this bruising guided tour, Hart dragged Michaels by his golden mane back to the ring, where the bell finally chimed to signal the official beginning of the match. Before the clang even finished echoing, Hart took to choking Michaels with a blue and white Quebec flag. In any other context, lifting your nemesis up and dropping their groin across your knee is hardly 'proper', but Hart's inverted atomic drop was the first legitimate wrestling move seen from either technician to this point.

The balance swung the other way with Michaels taking over on offence, prolonging the brawl with a lifting kick to a downed Hart's face, before strangling Hart with the Quebec flag. Hart contorted his face into a strained death mask to sell the loss of air, and a quick glimpse of his left hand showed a clearly bloody knuckle from the extended fight around the arena. "Michaels may have more cardiovascular conditioning here," observed Ross, one of several instances during the match in which the veteran announcer painted Hart as being outclassed by Michaels' comparative youth, speed, and endurance. This was not at all dissimilar to Ross and McMahon's ageist needles toward Hart at *Survivor Series* one year earlier, but without McMahon in any position on this night to goad Ross verbally, it seemed the comments were a preordained directive to further soften the blow of Hart's exit.

Outside the ring, Hart took an exotic bump from a gourdbuster suplex across a halved section of the metal ring steps. That was followed by even more grandstanding with native symbols as Michaels broke the splintery pole of Hart's flag across his knee, using the baton-like stick as a weapon. This time, the desecration of a sacred flag drew only moderate reprisal from the Montreal fans. In effect, it was the last gasp for a year's booking filled with patriotic pride, and the scorn of jingoism. It was no longer about Canada vs. the United States. That dead horse had been beaten into glue.

Michaels clocked Hart with fists at ringside in the heel's promenade of offence, prompting Ross to sharply quip, "No doubt a closed fist there, but who's counting?" If the two landed some intended/unintended stiff shots during their *WrestleMania XII* Iron Man Match, the skull-rattlers on display at *Survivor Series* were followed with silence instead of insincere apologies. The safest bet is that Hart's first couple of punches were not the ones that split the skin of his hand.

In a moment of jarring awkwardness, Michaels wound up for a left-handed strike, and instead snared Hart's neck with the arm, grounding him with a front-face lock. Obscured by Michaels' arm, Hart muttered the next set of instructions, few of which Michaels would seriously take on board. Hart was accustomed to having free reign over in-ring editing, and was unaware that his best laid plans were blindly weaving toward a dead end.

Hart took over once more on offence, escaping the face lock with a visually beautiful throw that spiked the crowd. From there, Hart began laying the seeds of a potential finish, working over Michaels' legs with kicks and elbows prior to wrapping them like a twist-tie around the ring post, applying a figure-four leglock outside of the ring. Hart had previously noted Michaels' cooperation with the hold during an instance back in March, his professional rival bracing Hart's foot so that Hart would not whack his head on the cement floor. Here, the care was no different, with Michaels locking Hart's leg in place during the move's execution, to which he writhed with clenched exaggeration, acting as though he was being ripped open with a rusty hook.

The onslaught continued with Hart lifting Michaels out of his boots with corner right hands. From there, it was into Hart's time-forged landing sequence, consisting of a Russian leg sweep and a side backbreaker. Anyone who's seen more than five Bret Hart matches knows his closing number as well as he did. If Hart's matches had not generally been the best or second-best performances at any given WWF event, these moves would be the cue for the audience to wake up and anticipate the finish. As per the high expectations of any of Hart's matches, nobody would've been lulled by this point, although it was time for Hebner to catch a quick catnap.

Hebner took his scripted bump off of a Hart sledge from the ropes, with Michaels pulling Hebner into the path of the oncoming 'Hitman'. All three bodies lay on the canvas to build tension for what lay ahead. In the coming years, referee bumps would become so commonplace that desensitised fans would crane their necks toward the entrance stage to see who the first run-in was going to be. There was to have been an entire stampede of interfering Hart Foundation and D-Generation X allies storming the ring to facilitate the agreed-upon schmazz finish. Referee Mike Chioda was also to have hit the ring at one juncture to take over officiating duties from dazed Hebner, and was waiting in the wings for his cue to run out, as were Hart's brother Owen and brother-in-law Smith.

Sweat-stained, Michaels rolled onto to his belly and shot a conscious glance in the direction of McMahon, who was situated by the timekeeper's table, entirely off-camera, ever since the point where the match finally made it back into the ring. He and Hart staggered to their feet, at which time Hart was grounded again after Michaels raked his eyes. Michaels snatched Hart by the ankles, by which point Hebner was into a crawling position. Backstage, Bruce Prichard acted as though he was apoplectic at Hebner's premature recovery. A confused Chioda was also panicked, overhearing director Kevin Dunn in his headset order Hebner to his feet just as Michaels began to cross Hart's legs for the Sharpshooter. Hart, unaware that Hebner was standing on faux-jelly legs eight feet behind his head, quietly notified Michaels that he was wrapping the legs incorrectly. The WWF Champion was unjamming the gun for his own execution.

The plan was for Hart to sweep Michaels' legs while trapped deep in the trenches of the hold, cross Michaels' legs, and stand up with his own application of the Sharpshooter, all the while Hebner counted the lights. Then the barrage of run-ins would begin, so that Hebner would eventually wake up to an impromptu prison riot. "I remember looking at Earl and saying, 'Here we go,'" Michaels recalled.

Michaels correctly twisted the legs and flipped Hart over onto his stomach, with Hart by now seeing a fully vertical Hebner standing before him. His relatives and Chioda could only watch in horror from behind the curtain as Hebner made deking gestures with his hands while speaking toward Hart in a frenzied snap. Hebner turned and loudly called for the bell as duped Hart grabbed at Michaels' left ankle, trying to put an end to the ruse seconds too late. Michaels clung to Hart's legs with a death grip, doing all he could to carry out his end of the secret plot.

"I saw Earl for a split second motioning with his fingers and Vince, strangely, standing at the ring apron wearing an angry scowl," Hart rued. "Then he screamed at the bell ringer, Mark Yeaton, 'Ring the bell! Ring the fucking bell!' Vince snapped hard at Yeaton - and the bell clanged, over and over."

Once again denying all advance knowledge of what was about to transpire, Jim Ross said, "I thought at the beginning that the bell ring was an inadvertent mistake and they were gonna restart the match. Sometimes it happens - but no."

"Bret was on the floor, in a hold, but he hadn't submitted. 'Holy shit, that's not supposed to happen!' I exclaimed," remembered Bret's first wife, Julie, stupefied as she watched the incident from her vantage point amongst the throng. "'No, it's not,' our lawyer said, equally astonished at what had just transpired in the ring."

"Nobody knew what was happening when it happened, we just all thought it was part of the work," remembered Ken Shamrock, "It was only later that we found out that Bret didn't know anything about it."

History captured Hart's immediate reaction under the echoes of Michaels' theme music as wide-eyed, but externally placid. "Before I went in the ring, I told myself I'd never let them put a submission hold on me," Hart explained, "But because I had Earl as the referee, and I trusted that he wouldn't screw me, I wasn't too worried about that any more. That was my big mistake."

At the time, Hart was not in the mood for rationalising everyone's justifications. The deposed champion regained his vertical base while besieged with a calm, trembling anger, that white hot rage that precedes a full blown emotional hurricane. Michaels put on a perplexed face, quizzically staring down McMahon from a seated position by the ropes. Hart glared down at McMahon, who was joined at the hip by Slaughter, from his standing position inside the ring. In as understated a manner as possible under the circumstances, Hart unleashed a golf ball-sized loogie into the face of a barely-startled McMahon.

"All hell broke loose, and I had no idea what was going on," Slaughter claimed. "I saw the look on Shawn's face and he goes, 'No not like this, not like this', and Vince says, 'Take the belt, get out of here.'"

Michaels, by now flanked by Helmsley in this acting charade, demanded answers from McMahon. "I heard Vince yell, 'Give him the belt!' I rolled out of the ring and grabbed the championship belt," remembered Michaels. "Jerry [Brisco] and Hunter had run down to the ring and Jerry started walking me back to the curtain. Right before I ducked behind the curtain, I raised the belt high up in the air as a heel would do to incite the crowd. Part of me was thinking, 'Just get out of there!' My business side thought, 'Something is going on here, but I've got to act like whatever happened was supposed to happen.'"

"I was telling Shawn to stick close to me, that he did a great job, not to stop and say anything to anybody no matter what derogatory comments people made," Brisco said of the long march into the unknown.

"They rushed us to the back and the Harris brothers came to us and said, 'We don't know what just happened but we are on your side,'" Helmsley claimed. "They walked us back to the locker room and they sat with us. Bret asked us, we said we had no idea, which is what we were supposed to do."

"Wow, you talk about controversy," groaned Ross back at the announce desk, understanding full well what had transpired. "Michaels, with the Sharpshooter, has become the WWF Champion, and Bret Hart is standing in disbelief!" Barely seven seconds after Ross sounded out the final syllable of 'disbelief', the pay-per-view coldly faded to black. Then the real show began.

Michaels disowned the belt as soon as he pushed through the curtain, putting on an act for any doubting eyes and slacked jaws in the vicinity. While the new champion pretended, a disconsolate Hart faced the ugly reality of the situation. Gasping for air, Hart tried to remain calm while his infuriated fan base waited to see what would happen next.

"I fought the tears that were swimming in my eyes and thought, 'Don't you dare give these backstabbers the satisfaction of seeing you cry over any of this!'"

Hart remembered. "I worked so hard for Vince. Fourteen years. All I wanted was my dignity."

Soon joined by Owen, Smith, and Neidhart, Hart's emotions began to get the best of him. The cameras picked up Hart drawing the letters, "WCW" in the air with his index finger, mouthing the name of his new employer that had yet to give him any sort of indignity, let alone any of this magnitude.

"I was devastated. I can't even put it into words," recollected Hart. "I loved the company and I felt so betrayed by Vince, more so than by Shawn. There was nothing they could have ever said or done to get me to do that, I was one of the boys first before I was a company guy. Even though Shawn and I had a lot of issues, I always respected him."

Struggling harder than ever to fight off the brimming tears, Hart leapt outside the ring and transformed from humble Paul Simon to hell-bent Keith Moon in a matter of seconds. Grabbing the rectangular television monitors that dotted the announcer's tables, Hart began spiking them like footballs as an outlet for his righteous anger. Hart was well past the 275 obligated work dates in his contract, so it would have been a minor stretch to call any of this 'insubordination' in the first place. Nobody dared get between Hart and the equipment he was pulverising, probably because nobody knew to what depths the ordinarily mild-mannered Hart was capable of plunging.

The world would soon find out. With steely focus, scorned Hart was making his way back up the aisle, and behind the curtain, where most prying eyes would have given a year's salary to be a fly on the wall for what happened next.

ELEVEN

THE SCENE BACKSTAGE WAS ONE of utter chaos. At first, shocked wrestlers stood around in silence, others were unsure whether to riot or walk out. Agents and officials who had not been privy to the plan worried about the repercussions, while those who were in on the ruse slipped into kayfabe mode and denied all knowledge. Within moments, some of the boys were so furious that there was already talk of insurrection, whereas others could not contain their anger and threw garbage cans and punched walls. "I was backstage with Undertaker. It was like a movie. We both looked at each other like, 'What happened?'" remembered former President of WWF Canada Carl DeMarco, "Suddenly, everyone went from shock to anger. I have never seen it like that backstage to this day. I thought it was going to be a real close call."

Mankind, a fourteen-year veteran who had spent the majority of his career outside of the WWF and had made his name in bloody death matches in Japan, was so angry with what had transpired that he was seriously contemplating breaching the lucrative six-figure contract he had worked so hard to earn. "I was really upset by what I had just seen," he recalled, "All I could say for minutes was, 'You just don't do that to a guy like Bret Hart.' I began to get angrier as time went by." Foley was so furious that he barked to a teary-eyed Pat Patterson, "How can they expect me to work here after this?" Patterson was equally dejected, sobbing, "I know, I know. I can't believe it myself." At that moment, Foley had no intention of ever speaking to McMahon again, so asked Patterson to pass on the message that he would not be coming to work the next day.[20]

---

[20] Foley followed through with his threat and did not show up at television the following day. Jim Cornette and Jim Ross eventually convinced him to come back. Cornette recalled that Foley holding out for "moral turpitude" being offended that a promoter screwed one of the boys was like being upset that porn star Jenna Jameson, "took one in the ass". Foley stated he agreed to return for the sake of his family, and that when he realised that Hart would be fine in WCW with his fat contract, the incident was

As a veteran of the business for over fifteen years, Jim Cornette recognised that there was going to be an unpleasant situation, and he had no interest in sticking around to see it play out. As soon as McMahon rang the bell on Hart he told those around him, "Okay, I'll see you guys later," then grabbed his bags and left. Another who had no intention of facing the repercussions of what had transpired was Earl Hebner, who after flying backstage found his brother Dave and yelled, "We gotta get out of here!" immediately following him to the building's parking lot where their car was ready to go. Dave later spoke of his concern for he and his brother's safety. "With it being the last match, I figured the fans would go around the back and turn the car over. We could have been killed," he mused.

Even though he had nothing to do with what had happened to Bret, Jim Ross too had a sense that he might be in danger. McMahon believed the boys would naturally assume Ross was in on it all along due to his position as Head of Talent Relations. Concerned that Ross might get punched out by one of the Harts, McMahon had one of his security personnel instruct Ross to go straight to his office and not leave. "I stayed in Vince's office under lock and key, wondering what had happened," remembered Ross. "I knew that I had to deal with all the talent and they were hot. I was on the phone with guys all that night." When Ross talked to McMahon about why he was left out of the loop, he was told, "I wanted to keep you clean of this matter. You have to continue to communicate and support the talent roster and they have to trust you. You knew nothing on purpose because you can honestly tell each and every one of them how you feel about what went down, and be honest with them that you did not know. Your role in restoring a productive and professional locker room is going to be a challenge we have to meet."

After wiping Bret's spittle from his face, McMahon stormed backstage with Sgt Slaughter and was soon surrounded by his son Shane, agent Tony Garea, Gerald Brisco, and Bruce Prichard. They made a beeline for Vince's office, with Slaughter making sure to rip down any signs pointing towards its location on the way. He knew Hart was still in the ring destroying everything he could get his hands on, and he was sure his anger would not dissipate once he walked through the curtain. Loyal to the core, Slaughter was trying to look out for his boss. Once they made it to the office McMahon locked the door behind him, then explained to those who were previously unaware why he had made the decision to do what he did. They sat and watched the monitor in near-silence and witnessed Hart pitching a fit at ringside, trashing expensive equipment and hurling around anything he could find that was not nailed down. McMahon did not say a word; he simply watched.

---

not worth him ending up homeless and starving over.

SLAUGHTER'S ATTEMPTS to shield McMahon's whereabouts from the rampant Hart were to no avail. Bret already knew where his office was and charged down the hallway towards it, attempting to smash the door down so he could take all his anger out on McMahon. He soon realised it was a steel door that was bolted to the ground and any attempts at breaking it were futile, so he decided to go and confront Michaels instead to find out whether he knew about the double-cross. "It was pure chaos," remembered Julie Hart, "Bret was walking at top speed down the hallway to the dressing room and was in such a zone. I tried to talk to him, but he just kept marching towards the dressing room." When Hart stepped foot inside the full locker room, the first sight he was greeted with was Shawn sat on a bench with his head in his hands, and the WWF Championship belt nowhere to be seen about his person.

Hart sat down on the opposite side of the room and calmly called over, "Shawn, you weren't in on that?" Having been told by McMahon to deny everything to the end, Michaels put on a show for the whole room. "I had no place [in that], with God as my witness," he whined, his words muffled by crocodile tears. "My hands are clean of this one I swear to God. He kept yelling at me out there, I gave him the belt when I got back here. I won't have any part of this." Hart told Shawn firmly, "I will judge you by what you do tomorrow on TV." Michaels would later admit, "Bret was beyond furious when he asked me if I knew anything about it. I lied, plain and simple. As a Christian now, I wouldn't say that, but I am not going to pretend that I didn't." Hart did not believe a word that was coming out of Shawn's mouth. "I knew he wasn't innocent, but I was pretty calm by then," he remembered.

Hart stood up and addressed the open-mouthed locker room, "You're all the next Bret Harts. If they can do this to me they can do this to anyone. Remember that," he warned, before jumping in the shower to freshen up. "After I tried to knock Vince's door down, I calmed down," he recalled, "The show was over and the fans were leaving, there was nothing else I could do about it. I thought I would never see Vince McMahon again."

Others were not so calm. In particular, The Undertaker was furious and was unable to restrain himself any longer. "Fuck!" he bellowed as he shot to his feet, "I'm gonna bring Vince's ass down here. I want him to explain himself to me, you, and everyone else!" With that he flung open the dressing room door and angrily stomped down the hall to find McMahon. Taker pounded on the locked door until Brisco answered, assuming it was Hart coming to exact his revenge. Taker looked right past him and bellowed towards McMahon, "You need to go apologise. Now! The boys are ready to riot." Ordinarily McMahon would not take kindly to being spoken to in such a manner, but he was aware that Undertaker was right. "Bret was hurt, there's no question about that," he later stated, "And as a result of that I felt a sense of responsibility to Bret, so I decided to go over and let him get his free shot in. I felt like I owed that to Bret."

"Vince is the kind of guy who is going to face you," said Bruce Prichard, "He's going to take whatever consequences there are and do what's right for business. Just running and hiding, what does that accomplish? He wanted to explain his side and face Bret like a man." Gerald Brisco agreed that Vince should try to smooth things over with Hart, so with his army of Prichard, Slaughter, Garea, Shane, and Brisco alongside him, McMahon set off to face the music. There was a hushed silence when McMahon entered the dressing room, with the boys realising they were about to witness something significant. They were just unsure how it would all pan out.

Hart's allies Davey Boy Smith and Rick Rude both poked their head into the showers to tell Hart the news that 'Taker had managed to get Vince out of his office, and he was in the dressing room waiting for him. "He says he wants to talk to you," informed Rude, a smirk etched on his face. "Tell him to leave me alone," yelled back Hart, "Tell him this is not a safe environment for him." Rude relayed the message with little success. Vince had made up his mind to face Hart man to man and would not be convinced otherwise. Rude and Smith traipsed back and forth between Hart and McMahon, whose respective messages remained the same. "He says he ain't leaving until he's talked to you," informed Rude, "He wants to set things straight with ya." Although Hart had a number of choice words that he wanted to voice to McMahon, he was unhappy with the development. "I was pretty angry that Vince wanted to test me out and prove something," he grumbled, "I had calmed down, I had my son in the dressing room. This was not something I had expected."

While Bret was showering, Slaughter and Brisco attempted to clear the dressing room so Hart and McMahon could talk in private. Owen motioned to leave but was stopped by Smith grabbing him firmly by the arm and hissing, "No! Don't leave. Remember what happened to Brody." Owen understood immediately and stayed where he was, as did most of the wrestlers in the room. It was a show of solidarity for Hart, who was backed up not only by Taker, Rude, and his family, but by others such as Vader, Ken Shamrock, Crush, and Savio Vega.

Hart stepped out of the shower and marched naked into the dressing room, walking right past McMahon without saying a word. As was often the case, Davey Boy had borrowed his towel without him knowing, leaving Hart without one. It was this which saved McMahon from an immediate pummelling, because as Hart put it, "The thought of me getting into a scrap with him while naked seemed ridiculous." Instead Hart found a damp towel on the floor and sat down to dry himself. Owen, Davey Boy, Rude, and Jim Neidhart all stood to his left with their arms folded, acting as his bodyguards. Undertaker was on

Hart's right, while further down the room to his right, Michaels remained a forlorn figure, sat with his head in his hands and tears rolling down his cheeks.

McMahon, who was stood up and flanked closely by his posse, began to apologise, telling Hart he could not take the chance of Bischoff announcing him the next night, or that he might go to WCW without giving the belt back. Hart, who had carried on getting dressed, acting like he was not listening while McMahon was talking, looked up and fired back, "I never had any problem losing the belt. That was never the issue." McMahon tried to placate Hart. "This is the first time I ever had to lie to one of my talents..." Hart could not believe what he was hearing. "Who are you fucking kidding, you lying piece of shit?" he shouted incredulously, before flummoxing McMahon and shocking the dressing room by listing a dozen things he had lied to him about in the past year alone.

"You told me I could leave in any way I wanted. That I was the Cal Ripken of the WWF. That I was doing you a favour. That you appreciate everything I ever did. That after everything I've done there was no reason for any problems," Hart seethed. McMahon offered little in response. He knew Bret was right, though he was hardly about to admit that in front of the boys. Seeing that Hart was unlikely to understand his perspective, he instead offered, "What I did to you today won't hurt you. You'll still get all the money you're supposed to get from WCW." Hart was fed up of listening to Vince trying to justify what he had done and told him, "If you're still here after I finish getting dressed then I have no choice but to punch you out."

Hart deliberately took his time getting dressed, hoping McMahon would leave. He also knew that since he had threatened McMahon in front of the boys, he had no choice but to follow through with it should Vince not leave. "He seemed to want to prove some kind of point," recalled Hart, "The last thing I did was tied my shoelaces, and I remember thinking there was nothing else left to put on. When I stood up I started to realise that Vince had this all planned out. He wanted to put on a good showing to all of the wrestlers, showing he wasn't this conniving little chickenshit guy that everyone thought he was."

Hart had intentionally left off his shirt because he could see through Vince's bravado and knew that any altercation they had would be a pull-apart skirmish rather than a full-on fist fight. Wearing a shirt gave McMahon's hangers-on something to grab hold of to stop him from getting his shots in. He only had one opportunity to lay a good punch before they were inevitably broken up. Once his laces were tied and Hart was on his feet, he looked at the metal knee brace he was holding in his hands and contemplated whether to deck Vince with it. Sensibly, he decided against assaulting McMahon with a weapon, though he made sure to let he and everyone else know that he was contemplating it when he snarled, "Nah, I won't be needing this."

With that, Hart pounced at McMahon, who ever-full of bluster came right back at him. They locked up almost like they were in a wrestling match, and

Hart secured a vice-like grip with his left hand on the padded shoulder of Vince's suit jacket. Standing nose-to-nose like two angry bulls, each waited for the other to blink. While getting dressed Hart had run the scenario over in his mind and could envision how it was going to play out. Everyone with Vince would be expecting an overhand punch so they would be there waiting to grab his arm to prevent him from throwing it. Hart figured that picture ended with him yelling at McMahon and cussing him out with McMahon feeling like he had backed him down. If he wanted to get a shot in at Vince and make it count, he needed to get creative.

"I knew as soon as we grabbed each other that this was not going to be a long scuffle," said Hart, "Everyone in the room was ready to pounce on us. No one in the room wanted to see us fight." When McMahon barked, "If you want to take revenge on me and hit me, then hit me!" Hart took his cue and drilled Vince in the jaw with a thunderous uppercut, taking him six inches off the ground and sending him crashing to the carpeted floor in a crumpled heap. "I went down like a ton of bricks," McMahon later admitted. Hart was proud of his work. "It was the most beautiful uppercut punch you could ever imagine," he crowed, "I actually thought it would miss and go right up the side of his head, but I popped him right up like a cork was under his jaw and lifted him right off the ground. I broke my right hand just beneath the knuckle, and knocked Vince out cold. He thought he would come out of that okay, but he didn't plan on an uppercut."

"I remember seeing Vince walk towards Bret, getting in his face, almost challenging him," recalled Ken Shamrock, "I know for a fact that when Vince went into the room his whole idea was to have Bret swing at him, because then he had Bret over a barrel on assault charges. I remember telling Bret, 'Don't hit him, don't hit him. Be cool.' Unfortunately, it didn't work out like that."

Immediately following the punch everyone jumped in to break up the fracas, exactly as Hart had predicted. Shane McMahon jumped on Bret's back to try preventing him from doing any further damage to his father, but Davey Boy pulled him off both to stop Shane from getting hurt and to free Bret. Davey would later claim to have hyper-extended his already-injured knee during the fracas, although he later admitted he made up the whole thing as an excuse to get off WWF television in order to negotiate his future. Bret ended up tussling with Jerry Brisco, who was trying to prevent him from inflicting any further damage on Vince. Bret did not take kindly to that, warning Brisco that if he lay another finger on him he would receive the same treatment as McMahon. Brisco put his hands up and backed away towards the benches. With the two sides separated, everyone sat and stared for a minute at McMahon, sprawled unconscious on the floor in an X shape. Nobody knew what to say. The boys were not about to utter a word, whilst McMahon's aides were concerned about reigniting the powder keg by saying the wrong thing to Bret.

Hart sat down. He was content that one punch was enough, especially as it had been such a good one. He had made his point. Plus, his hand was throbbing. Shane moved first, crouching down beside his father and sitting him up, pleading with Hart to let him regain his bearings. With help from Slaughter and Brisco, Shane managed to get Vince to a bench on the opposite side of the room from Hart so he could recover. As they were doing so, Brisco compounded McMahon's misery by accidentally treading on his ankle. "Gerald stood on my ankle and broke it," recalled McMahon, "It was like a comedy looking back on it."

Bret yelled at the McMahon loyalists to get Vince out of the room, picking up his knee brace as he did and threatening to finish McMahon off with it if they refused to comply. Hart motioned towards them so they did as they were told, slowly carting the woozy chairman out of the door. McMahon had come around by now and heard Bret yell as he was leaving, "Are you going to screw me out of all the money you owe me too?" Groggily, McMahon managed to utter the word, "No," as he limped uncertainly out of the door.

With McMahon gone and the dressing room too stunned by what they had witnessed to speak, Bret turned his attention to the still-crying Michaels. Hart knew that Shawn was guilty and did not believe a word he said, nor did he buy the sob show he was putting on, nevertheless he wanted to find out for sure before acting upon those instincts. "I would have hated to have reacted on Shawn and later found out that he didn't do anything," reasoned Hart, "I would have felt terrible for the rest of my life." Hart stared over at Michaels, who was now on his knees, bent over with his head still firmly buried in his hands. He so desperately wanted to run over and kick him as if his head were a football and he was trying to split the uprights with a fifty-yard field goal. As he had proven in Hartford five months earlier, he would have no trouble in a real fight with Shawn, broken hand or otherwise. Jim Cornette felt the same way. "In a real fight, Bret and the Harts would have killed Shawn and Hunter," he theorised, "One night in a hotel learning holds from Brisco wasn't going to be enough to save him from getting his ass whupped."

However, Hart's professionalism and the minute nagging doubt that he could be wrong about Shawn's involvement overwhelmed his desire to maim him. He walked over to Michaels and tapped him on the shoulder, prompting Helmsley to sit forward in his seat, anticipating a problem. Shawn stared up at Hart like a frightened deer. Instead of verbal or physical confrontation, Hart classily offered his hand and calmly said, "Thanks for the match, Shawn," then left the room as Michaels burst into floods of tears.

Hart left the arena and headed for his hotel with his family, then spent the night talking with the media and telling the world that he had been screwed, the one thing Jim Cornette thought he would never do. "I'm on my way home and the WWF can go to hell," he told the *Calgary Sun* newspaper, "This is the ultimate, final slap in the face. I'm washing my hands of the whole damned organisation. Vince gave me his word that there would be no chicanery, then he ordered his timekeeper to ring the bell on me." Hart flew home with his family to Calgary the following afternoon with his fist propping up his chin and tears rolling down his face. In the cold light of day, the pain of McMahon's betrayal was even harder to stomach. Hart was dejected. He felt like a piece of him had died in Montreal.

IN THE Molson Centre, Michaels remained in the dressing room with Helmsley and Chyna long after the show had ended and everyone else had left. He did not shower or even get changed out of his gear; he simply sat there and contemplated his actions. He realised that it had been a lucky escape not getting into a fight with Hart as McMahon had, though he admired Vince for keeping to his word and taking all the heat – and the punches. The next thing to negotiate was a city full of angry Montrealers. Shawn was acutely aware that he was deep inside enemy territory, and that avoiding a scuffle with Hart was only half the battle. His fears were realised when the trio made it to the hotel and were greeted with the sight of a large mob congregated outside of the front door. They ran inside, trying to do their best to conceal their identities, however they were still easily recognised and had to fight their way through a torrent of abuse, spit, and threats. Helmsley was even punched in the face by an irate female fan. There was no respite inside the lobby, so the three terrified performers ran for the elevator and eventually managed to make it to their room largely unscathed.

"We did it, didn't we?" panted Shawn, relieved to have made it into the room alive. "You did what you had to do, Shawn," replied Hunter. Despite his friend's reassurances, Michaels began to panic. Anxiety was taking over and he was worried about how the boys would react once the dust had settled the next night in Ottawa. "There are few things more dangerous than giving a bunch of wrestlers time to talk about something," he worried. Helmsley again tried to keep him grounded and calm. "It may take time, but people are going to realise that you did the right thing," he told him, "Shawn, *you* have to know that you did the right thing."

"It was a gutsy thing for Shawn to do," Vince McMahon later concurred, "I knew that by asking Shawn to participate in that I could have been compromising his values. I wasn't, because my interpretation was that Shawn thought it was absolutely the right thing to do. Shawn is a great solider and would do anything for the sake of the business." McMahon's right-hand man throughout the ordeal, Jerry Brisco, was similarly full of praise for Michaels. "That one night, Shawn Michaels became a real man and a real stand-up person in my mind. I think it took a lot of courage to do what Shawn Michaels did that night. He put himself in a position where he could have been injured, he could have been beaten up, he could have been knifed, or he could have been shot. That's one of the things that I will always respect about Shawn; he put himself in danger – he didn't have to – but deep down he was a professional and he did what he had to do."

At the hotel, Helmsley and Chyna retreated to their own room for the night and left Shawn to do some soul-searching. He was alone for the first time, able to reflect on everything that had happened in a whirlwind night. He thought about how the rest of the boys perceived him, how he was largely despised in the locker room. Now that would be greatly intensified and deep down he wished it was not the case. He longed to be liked, accepted. As he thought deeper, he realised he had done the two things everyone always accused him of: he had swerved someone, and he was a liar. He had openly lied to the face of Hart and everyone else, and he felt dirty about it. Michaels started to softly sob once again, wondering why he could never just be a wrestler. Why, with him, did it always have to be something else?

ELSEWHERE, EARL Hebner was doing some reflecting of his own. On the car ride to the hotel, he had filled in brother Dave on the details of the double-cross, and now he was beginning to worry about the consequences. Like Michaels, he was fearful that his decision to comply with the double-cross would lead to him becoming a locker-room exile. Those fears were hardly assuaged when one of the wrestlers confronted him and demanded to know how he could willingly do that to one of his best friends. Hebner saw no sense in having a confrontation over something he little choice in, so he decided to lie. "I knew nothing about it," he protested, "I am going to quit over this." Jack Lanza, a close friend of the Hebners who by now had been clued in on the whole thing, publicly talked the brothers out of leaving their jobs. It was all a sham. The Hebners had never intended to quit, they had simply liaised with Lanza to save face. All the co-conspirators of what was already being referred to as the 'Montreal Screwjob' were – under orders from McMahon – running the same play: denial, denial, denial.

Earl would later justify to himself his betrayal of Bret by refusing to accept responsibility for his actions. "Earl Hebner did not screw Bret Hart," he averred, "Vince screwed Bret. I was just a pawn. My boss asked me to do a job and I went out there and did it. I'm not proud of it, but I don't let it define my career. The one person who could have changed that was Bret Hart, by doing the thing we are supposed to do and doing what the boss says. The truth is, once Shawn got Bret in that Sharpshooter it was over. They were going to ring the bell whether I was involved or not. Sometimes I wish I hadn't done it. Sometimes I wonder why I did do it. It didn't really help me. It hurt me more than it helped me."

Even though Hart was crushed at the time by his friend's treachery, he would eventually come to terms with it, realising that Earl had been left with no choice. "I always felt bad for Earl," defended Hart. "I think in his heart he would have told me, but when they cornered him he rolled over. I would have shit my pants too if I had been Earl and I would have done exactly what Earl did. It's hard to watch the match because of the spot they put Earl in – he's terrified." Hebner's referee colleague Jimmy Korderas expressed the same sentiments. "Had I been in his position would I have done the same thing? Probably," he admitted. "You don't have time to think, and it's either this or you lose your job. A big contract waited for Bret, not the referee."

The Hebner twins made sure to leave Montreal early the following morning, catching a 5:30 a.m. flight to Ottawa to avoid a busy airport and a potential scene. There were other wrestlers on the plane with them and they expected a rough trip full of accusatory comments, but to their relief it was relatively placid. When Earl reached the Corel Centre for that evening's *Monday Night Raw* taping, he was starting to regret the part he had played in ousting Hart from the WWF, confessing his distress to the other referees. He told them how terrible he felt about his involvement, because he felt like he had betrayed Hart, and that he was considering quitting the company because of it. Several members of the roster and office staff overheard this, and one by one they took Earl to one side and tried to reassure him, telling him they did not blame him for what happened and they knew he was just following Vince's orders. "Undertaker was the first person I talked to," recalled Hebner, "He said, 'Don't feel bad for what you did. You supported the boys, and all of the boys have support for you.'"

HEBNER WAS not the only person who sought out The Undertaker for a heart to heart that night. As soon as Shawn Michaels reached the building he expected heat from the boys; he had been awake fretting about it all night. However, he knew that 'Taker was both the dressing room barometer and policeman. If he was okay with him, then the rest of the wrestlers would fall into line behind him. Shawn's relationship with Undertaker had always been strained, to the point that the latter formed a locker room faction called the Bone Street Krew, designed to monitor Shawn and his Kliq associates in order to keep their political machinations in check. However, a rewarding recent top-line program between the two had given both a newfound respect and grudging admiration for one another, meaning Undertaker had far more time for Michaels than he might have had a few months earlier.

When Michaels asked for a private word, Undertaker knew immediately what he wanted to talk about. Before Shawn could say anything he cut in. "I had a long talk with Vince and he explained everything to me. Everything's cool." Michaels almost did not believe him. "Is it?" he inquired, "Because I need it to be that way with us." "It is, don't worry. Everything's cool," Taker reaffirmed.

Shawn felt a wave of relief wash over him. If Taker was on his side, then he knew he was safe. What he did not know was that Undertaker had called Bret after talking with Vince and said, "I got it right from Vince. That little cunt Shawn, he was in on the whole thing." True to form, 'Taker was playing it cool with Michaels. Knowing the truth allowed him to keep his guard up, whilst the opposite was true for Shawn.

After the discussion with 'Taker, Michaels sought out McMahon for their first conversation about the previous night's events. Something Undertaker said had made Shawn become anxious: *"He explained everything to me."* Michaels wondered exactly what that meant. Had McMahon told Taker that he had been in on the whole thing? Did 'Taker know that his performance in the dressing room at the Molson Centre had been nothing more than an elaborate act? Vince was vague with the details and he simply reiterated what 'Taker had already told Shawn. Michaels decided not to ask any further questions about what exactly that meant. He figured that if he did not know the answers to people's questions then he did not have to lie about them.

Later that night, Vince gathered his troops for a meeting prior to the beginning of the taping. Despite talk amongst the boys of a full-scale walkout in a show of solidarity with Hart, only three faces were missing from the assembled throng: Mick Foley, Owen Hart, and Davey Boy Smith. Many had talked to Hart the night before and expressed their reluctance to work for McMahon again, but Hart advised them all to attend the show, not breach their contracts and potentially lose their livelihoods on his account. Needless to say the mood was fractious as McMahon took to the proverbial podium and outlined his stance. The story he weaved for his troupe was far from reality, rather the version of events that he wanted his roster to hear. He blamed Hart, saying that he was leaving for WCW the next night yet did not want to drop the title on his way out, and the only thing he would agree to was vacating it on *Raw* after Eric Bischoff had already announced his signing.[21]

Those close to Hart did not believe a word of it. However, enough of the boys bought it – or were able to convince themselves that McMahon was telling the truth so they could justify continuing to work for him – that over time McMahon's version of events became everybody's version of events. Years later, many who were in attendance at that meeting would criticise Hart for refusing to lose the title on his final night with the company, despite it being far from the truth. Hart's contract expired on December 1; it was impossible for him to begin working for WCW before then. Even if he and Bischoff had both

---

[21] This version of events was repeated so often that the boys who were present for the meeting started to believe it as the years went on. Even Shane McMahon, Vince's own son, believed the half-truths he had been fed. As is often the case in life, when the lie is repeated so often, it becomes the accepted lore.

wanted it, Time Warner would never have permitted it due to the certain lawsuit that would have followed.

The other claim made by McMahon was that Bret had flat-out refused to lose in Canada – another fallacy that was oft-parroted as a means to criticise Hart. While it was true that Hart did not want to lose to Michaels in Canada, he also did not want to lose anywhere else to him either until Shawn had paid off the debt of respect he owed for his comments at the October 12 house show in San Jose. Had Hart been asked to put over Steve Austin at *Survivor Series*, he would have done so in a heartbeat.

After thoroughly running Hart down, McMahon addressed the elephant in the room; the unrest that his decision had caused. "If you don't do things the way I want or if you don't understand why I did what I did, you can leave," he hissed. Most of the boys were too job-scared to utter a word back. As Bob Holly remembered it, "Nobody wanted to get heat for voicing an opinion too loudly." The exception to the rule was Rick Rude. A close friend of Hart's, Rude was incensed by McMahon's actions in Montreal, and his burial of Bret to the boys made him sick to his stomach. However, he knew he would have the last laugh. Rude was working on a handshake deal with the WWF and had not signed any official contract papers, meaning he was free to leave the company without any notice should he wish to.

Unbeknownst to anyone in the WWF, Rude had called Eric Bischoff from his hotel room the night before and told the shocked WCW executive everything that had gone down in Montreal, from the double-cross to Bret Hart connecting with an uppercut on Vince McMahon's chiselled jaw. As Bischoff remembered it, "I was sitting at home with my wife watching TV and the phone rang. It was Rick Rude. And Rick was fucking *livid*. He was pissed. He said, 'I'm coming back!' Not, 'Can I come back?', but 'I'm coming back!'" Because Rude had sued Turner in 1994 after suffering a career-ending injury, Bischoff needed to clear his return with company brass first, which meant Rude was unable to hop on the first flight to Memphis for *Nitro*. However, Bischoff was keen to bring Rude back into the fold, even if only to make the WWF look like a sinking ship who's despairing crew were deserting.

Instead, Rude opened that night's *Raw* alone in the ring, finding himself in the unusual and awkward position of standing firmly in the Bret Hart camp but having to publicly side with Shawn Michaels. As Rude began his speech designed to introduce Michaels, the hostile crowd peppered him with angry chants of "Bullshit!", clearly furious about what had happened the night before. There was much intrigue in the dressing room about how Michaels would handle the situation, and three thousand miles away over in Calgary, Bret Hart was especially interested in what Shawn would have to say. Michaels, with Triple H and Chyna in tow, danced to the ring as cocky as ever, showing little visible remorse for the part he had played in the previous night's ordeal.

As Michaels traversed the entrance ramp, Jim Ross on commentary informed the world that Hart had wrestled his final WWF match, for which he blamed Michaels, advising viewers to stay tuned because more would be revealed later about Hart's departure. To Bret, it was clear that Vince was showing no remorse at all for his actions at *Survivor Series*, evidently more than happy to milk the ending of the main event for all it was worth. When Michaels began his promo, it was clear to Hart and everyone else watching that he too was unrepentant, exactly as Bret had suspected. Quite the opposite, he was positively braggadocious. Almost drowned out by angry, vociferous chants of "We want Bret!", and with Rude wearing a grimaced expression of unhidden disgust behind him, Michaels snarled:

> I thought about coming out here and being politically correct, but seeing as somebody else drew first blood, the Heartbreak Kid is now gonna unload on everybody. Now, for all you people that are chanting, "We want Bret", well, I got news for ya; you can sing it, but the fact of the matter is, the Heartbreak Kid Shawn Michaels beat Bret Hart in his home country in his own finishing hold, and the Heartbreak Kid is now the new World Wrestling Federation champion. And if you thought that DX was hell to deal with before, you have seen absolutely nothing yet. The World Wrestling Federation was not big enough for the Heartbreak Kid and Shawn Michaels (sic), so what I did was put his Sharpshooter on him in Montreal, Quebec, I listened to him squeal and say I give up, then I ran his ass down south with the rest of those dinosaurs. And Hitman, the gentlemen who are not dinosaurs down there are my friends, and they are gonna beat the hell out of you one day whether you like it or not. You see, the Heartbreak Kid is the only man in this business that will ever be on top, that will ever be number one, that will ever be the true icon, and it is this simple. Not Bret Hart, not Hulk Hogan, not Randy Savage. Not anybody has the will to be the best, and Shawn Michaels will out-will every one of them because I have something the rest of you will never, ever have, and that is God-given, pure, natural talent.

As Ken Shamrock's music hit signalling the arrival of Shawn's first challenger, the new champion looked directly into the camera and broke away from the script, getting in one final parting shot at Hart with the words, "I wanna make one thing perfectly clear: the Heartbreak Kid would never, ever beat up a fifty-two-year old man." It was an obvious reference to Hart's physical altercation with McMahon the night before. To most, it was a clear sign that Michaels was firmly on the side of the WWF Chairman, and completely backed the way he had handled the Montreal situation. Vince himself abstained from appearing on the broadcast, partly due to the bruised face and injured ankle the dressing room confrontation with Hart had caused, though more because he did not feel he had to. The way he saw it, he did not owe anybody an explanation.

Over on *Nitro* the focus was heavily centred around Bret Hart too. The show opened with Eric Bischoff and his onscreen band of rebels the nWo walking to the ring for their promised huge announcement. Each member was carrying the Canadian flag, leaving little mystery about their breaking news. Even so, announcers Tony Schiavone and Larry Zbyszko played dumb, with the latter wondering out loud if the faction had somehow purchased Canada. At first they pulled a swerve and announced the return of Kevin Nash after a few weeks away having knee surgery, before Bischoff revealed what the whole world already knew: Bret Hart was on his way into the company. With a Cheshire cat grin permanently etched on his face, Bischoff bragged about his ability to spend a billionaire's money with impunity to surround himself with the biggest names in wrestling. He then dropped Bret Hart's name casually into the conversation, referring to him as a, "knock out kinda guy," in an obvious allusion to the punch Hart had delivered to McMahon, something which Bischoff had taken great pleasure in learning about. Hogan quipped that Hart had, "passed the initiation", then the group sang an intentionally terrible rendition of Canadian national anthem '*O Canada*' in a mocking, almost dismissive tone. All told, it was a fairly unspectacular way to champion the signing of the WWF's top star, especially following on from the most notorious night in the history of modern professional wrestling. As Dave Meltzer put it in his *Wrestling Observer Newsletter*:

> WCW announcers Tony Schiavone, Mike Tenay and Larry Zbyszko talked for most of the first hour about the announcement, with Schiavone and Tenay, likely on orders from Bischoff, acting stunned, describing Hart as a second generation wrestler who stands for tradition. In other words, positioning him as another Curt Hennig or Jeff Jarrett, rather than the level of a Hulk Hogan to justify a nearly $3 million per year salary.

The next night the WWF taped an episode of *Raw* in Cornwall, Ontario to be aired the following Monday, after which Rick Rude called Eric Bischoff again looking to reach an agreement. It was decided that Rude would return to WCW on the November 17 episode of *Nitro*, opposite the taped *Raw* that he was featured heavily on. When Rude stepped through the curtain in the opening segment of *Nitro* as yet another member of the nWo, he became the first person to ever appear on both rival shows in the same night. To further stick it to McMahon, Rude shaved his beard to make it abundantly clear to everyone watching that *Nitro* was live and *Raw* was taped, embarrassing the WWF and making a mockery of their claims to be live. Bischoff allowed him the forum to vent, always thrilled to have a recent ex-WWF performer bury their former employers:

Oh, what a difference a day makes. Twenty-four little hours. You know, we all have our fifteen minutes of fame and I'd like to take a couple of my fifteen minutes to talk about the rights and the wrongs in the world of professional wrestling. What's wrong in the world of professional wrestling is Shawn Michaels claiming to be World Champion when he never beat Bret Hart. What's wrong with the world of professional wrestling is for Vince McMahon to instruct a referee to ring the bell in order to rob Bret Hart of his title. But, on the other hand, what's right in the world of professional wrestling is for Bret Hart to abandon the Titanic and swim to the refuge of the nWo.

THAT SAME night on *Raw*, Vince McMahon spoke publicly for the first time about the Montreal Screwjob and offered his own well-rehearsed take on what had happened in a piece called '*Why Bret, Why? – The Untold Story.*' McMahon had been surprised at how fans and industry commentators were perceiving the incident. He had expected to be painted as the good guy of the piece for standing up for his company and what he felt was right in the face of a mercenary who was leaving for financial prosperity with his bitter rivals. Few saw it that way. To most, McMahon was the definite villain, the evil promoter who had forced out one of his most popular stars to make room for someone else (Shawn Michaels), someone who had callously stabbed Hart in the back and robbed him of his chance of a proper WWF send off. McMahon heard it in the arenas with loud "We want Bret" chants, so he wanted to put his version of the truth out into the open with the hope of shifting perception to make he and his company look like the victims of the piece.

In a darkly lit room, McMahon sat with interviewer Jim Ross, made up like a mannequin with the faint vestige of a healing bruise hanging like a dark raincloud beneath his left eye, and a picture of Hart in all his pomp hanging in the background. Vince wore a melancholy expression, with the look of brash determination etched on his face betrayed by the sorrow evident in his eyes. Throughout the interview, McMahon flitted back and forth between stances, sometimes showing regret for his actions and wishing Hart had never left, then at other times scathing and ruthless in his insistence that he was right.

[Jim Ross:] Let's cut right to the chase. Seven days ago at the *Survivor Series*, did you or did you not screw Bret Hart?

[Vince McMahon:] Some would say I screwed Bret Hart. Bret Hart would definitely tell you I screwed him. I look at it from a different standpoint. I look at it from the standpoint of the referee did not screw Bret Hart. Shawn Michaels certainly did not screw Bret Hart. Nor did Vince McMahon screw

Bret Hart. I truly believe that Bret Hart screwed Bret Hart. And he can look in the mirror and know that.

[Jim Ross:] I'm sure in some parts of the country right now there's a collective groan that you are not accepting responsibility. That you orchestrated the situation. The fact is that people are not going to understand what you mean by "Bret Hart screwed Bret Hart", so what do you mean by that?

[Vince McMahon:] I will certainly take responsibility for any decision I ever made, I never had a problem doing that. Not all of my decisions are accurate, they're not. But when I make a bad decision I'm not above saying that I'm sorry and trying to do the best about it that I can. Hopefully the batting average is pretty good. I make more good decisions than I do bad decisions. And as far as screwing Bret Hart is concerned, there's a time honoured tradition in the wrestling business that when someone is leaving they show the right amount of respect to the WWF superstars – in this case – who helped make you that superstar. You show the proper respect to the organisation that helped you become who you are today. It's a time honoured tradition, and Bret Hart didn't want to honour that tradition. And that's something I would have never ever expected from Bret, because he is known somewhat as a traditionalist in this business. It would have never crossed my mind that Bret would not have wanted to show the right amount of respect to the superstars who helped make him and the organisation who helped make him what he is today. Nonetheless, that was Bret's decision. Bret screwed Bret.

[Jim Ross:] Some folks along the internet know that in 1996 Bret signed a twenty-year contract with the WWF. And I'm sure there's some at home now saying, 'He has eighteen years left on his contract. How can he leave?' Did Bret Hart ask you to leave the WWF, or did you ask him to leave the WWF?

[Vince McMahon:] This was a joint decision and it vacillated somewhat as well when we were making the decision. It was a joint decision from both Bret and me. What happened is the two of us got together and orchestrated the opportunity for Ted Turner's wrestling organisation to "steal" Bret. I felt for business reasons that Bret Hart and the salary that we were paying him was not justified. And Bret felt for creative reasons and the fact that he had sort of become second banana in his own mind to Shawn Michaels who had "stolen his spot". So for financial reasons on my part and creative reasons on Bret Hart's part, the two of us got together and decided, 'Okay, let's do the very best we can for you, Bret.' So the two of us orchestrated Bret Hart receiving a three-year deal in which he is paid $3 million per year, which I believe is the richest deal in all of professional wrestling. And that's working 125 days per year. So I felt from a personal standpoint that Bret wasn't a great investment any longer for the WWF – although I really didn't want him to go – but the least I could do for Bret was to help him help himself. I told Bret, 'If in fact you do get this deal from Turner, I'm gonna be the very first person, personally to congratulate you.' And I was. From a business standpoint I didn't really wanna lose Bret, he wasn't paying off from a financial standpoint, but nonetheless, I didn't really wanna lose Bret.

[Jim Ross:] The bitterness of the loss at *Survivor Series* could never be more prevalent. He stands in the ring and spits in your face. Shortly thereafter he destroys WWF television equipment. Were you prepared for what happened after the match?

[Vince McMahon:] I was disappointed in Bret when he hit me, very disappointed. I sustained a concussion as a result of it, I have vision problems to this day. I'll get over it. I didn't think it was the right thing to do. Bret seems to be crowing about that, that I've read, where he feels proud of striking me. And it wasn't a question of a confrontation, because even at fifty-two-years-old I dare say that perhaps things would have been a little different if there had been a confrontation. I allowed Bret to strike me. I had hoped that he wouldn't. I had hoped that we could sit down and try and work things out as gentlemen. That's what I really hoped for, but that's not what happened.

[Jim Ross:] Have you considered pressing charges or pursuing legal remedies for that situation in his locker room?

[Vince McMahon:] I have considered it. I think those options are still available. I'm not pursuing it at the moment. I guess maybe it all depends on Bret as to whether or not I do.

[Jim Ross:] If you were only a story writer and this was the final chapter in the life story of Bret Hart: The WWF Years, how would you have preferred to write the final chapter?

[Vince McMahon:] As a storyteller I would have hoped that Bret's story would have been a dramatic one. I would hope that Bret's story would be one that would give him dignity, would give him the poise to state that he was maybe the greatest WWF superstar ever, in terms of his departure. And one way of being able to give back to the company, being able to give back to those individuals, those superstars who helped you achieve the level of success that you had, when you know you are leaving – in the time honoured tradition – might have been for argument's sake that after the most gruelling match that Bret ever had in his life, if Bret was pinned. But, in that small moment of defeat Bret would have stood straight up and showed the whole world what a true champion both as a human being and as a wrestling persona he really is. If I had been Bret, if I were writing the story, I can see Bret after a 1-2-3 simply saying, 'Okay,' to his opponent, 'You got the best of me, I wanna congratulate you, I wanna stick my hand out to congratulate you. And furthermore, I want everyone in the whole locker room to watch my match so that I can show those who follow in my footsteps the way – in a time honoured tradition – this is to be done. To show every individual, every secretary, everyone in Titan Sports, the World Wrestling Federation, who counts on me to do the right thing, that I was there. That I was a superstar – maybe the greatest ever – and I went out the way a true champion would go out.'

[Jim Ross:] Are you able to step back and objectively look at this thing and evaluate your friend, perhaps former friend, Bret Hart the human being, and have sympathy for this man?

[Vince McMahon:] Sympathy? I have no sympathy for Bret whatsoever. None. I have no sympathy for someone who is supposed to be a wrestling traditionalist not doing the right thing for the business that made him. Not doing the right thing for the fans, performers, organisation who helped make him what he is today. Bret made a very, very selfish decision. Bret is going to have to live with that for the rest of his life. I have no sympathy whatsoever for Bret.

[Jim Ross:] Erm, this is a crazy question: would you welcome Bret Hart back if he said, 'Vince, I've changed my mind. Can I come back?' Would you allow him to return to the WWF? I mean he spit in your face, notwithstanding destroying television monitors and equipment, certainly notwithstanding the fact that he punched you, would you allow him to ever come back to the WWF if that was an option?

[Vince McMahon:] This is a strange business, and yes, I would. We would have to have a real frank understanding. I would want to hear Bret say, 'Vince, I'm sorry. I didn't mean to be selfish, I just kinda lost it there for a while.' And I have no problem saying, 'Bret, geez I'm sorry that I had to do what I had to do as well.' Would I welcome him back? I would also tell Bret,

"No more free shots!" That strictly from a man's standpoint I would want him to know that. And that in the future if we are gonna have problems along the lines in the locker room or anywhere else that, okay were gonna have 'em, but no more free shots. But yeah, if Bret could tear up his contract with the other guys right now and return, I would welcome Bret Hart back under those conditions.

[Jim Ross:] Was his motivation... Do you believe his motivation primarily... He said he didn't leave for the money.

[Vince McMahon:] There were signs in the arena following *Survivor Series*: "Bret sold out". Bret seems to be sensitive to that subject, that he doesn't want to be known as someone who sold out. I'm proud of the fact that I helped Bret sell out. And that's what Bret did, he sold out. And it's not a big deal because I helped him do it! So do I think that Bret left for the money? I think that when you're making $3 million a year and working 125 days of that year, I think Bret sold out, and I don't blame him for selling out. I helped him sell out. Matter of fact, I would suggest there's gonna be a long line outside the next locker room of wrestlers begging me, 'Vince, help me sell out!' So do I think he sold out? Yeah, and I think every time Bret says, 'No, I didn't do it for the money,' I think that Bret loses credibility every time he says that.

[Jim Ross:] Did this whole ugly ordeal with Bret Hart affect you more professionally, the businessman side of Vince McMahon, or the personal side of Vince McMahon?

[Vince McMahon:] From a business side, the WWF will go on beyond Bret Hart. From a personal side, it definitely has affected me. I think that Bret and I... you can't end a fourteen-year relationship like ours ended without having feelings. I regret that I felt I was forced into making the decision that I made. I regret that Bret didn't do the right thing for the business or himself, because it wouldn't have cost him one dollar less on his deal with Turner. I regret that his fans – if there is such a thing separate from the WWF fans – are in any way hurt from this. I regret that his family is having to endure this tirade that Bret seems to be on. I regret that a member of my family – my son – had to witness some of this, especially in the locker room. I regret all of this from a personal standpoint, yet remain steadfast that I made a tough decision that was the right decision for the WWF fans and superstars that remain here with us.

[Jim Ross:] If you had the opportunity to speak with Bret – and now's not a bad opportunity because you know he is watching, everyone who was involved with this situation is watching – what would you say to him now?

[Vince McMahon:] Probably what I said to him in the locker room. And that is that he made a mistake that I believe he will regret from a professional standpoint. It had to be made that way. I felt I had to do what I had to do for my company, and our fans, and our superstars that remain here. And I'm unwavering in that point of view. And perhaps Bret is unwavering in his point of view. I don't know that we will ever get together. I hope we will one day. It's too bad that a fourteen-year relationship was destroyed because one member of that relationship forgot that we are in the sports entertainment business. Forgot where he came from.

[Jim Ross:] When will you be over this?

[Vince McMahon:] I'm over it now. At the same time, Bret has been such a part of the WWF. A part of Bret will always be here in the World Wrestling Federation. I'm gonna remember the good times. I'm gonna remember all the things we did with Bret where he performed to the greatest degree possible and told those wonderful stories. I'm gonna remember him as the Excellence of Execution. It's just too damn bad that in the end Bret really wasn't the best there is, the best there was and the best there ever will be. And he had the opportunity to live up to that in his final match with the WWF, and he failed.

Critics and those who knew the real story behind Bret's departure were quick to point out the numerous inconsistencies and half-truths peppered throughout McMahon's piece. During the course of one interview McMahon had contradicted himself numerous times. Regarding the locker room fracas with Hart, he first claimed he had given the jilted former champion a free shot by intentionally allowing Hart to strike him, and cockily extolled the virtues of his own fighting prowess. Then, in the next sentence, he threatened the possibility of legal action. He also made outright false claims that Hart's move to WCW had been a mutual decision, trying to paint himself as the hero of the hour for helping facilitate Hart earning more money for Turner, and branding Hart a sell-out. But Hart had never wanted to leave the WWF, something he repeatedly told McMahon during their September and October discourse. It was McMahon who came to Hart and informed him of his decision to terminate their deal; Bret was simply forced to go along with it because he had no other choice.

McMahon made straw-man arguments about Hart's motivations to justify his own manufactured points, wilfully lying to discredit Hart's position over the stance he had taken in refusing to lay down for Michaels. He framed Hart's refusal to lose as being due to the concern that his image would be somehow damaged and thus he would lose out on his WCW contract, which even the most ardent WWF apologist could see was nonsense. Hart's WCW deal was signed and sealed, in no way would his earning ability be predicated on whether he had his hand raised against Shawn Michaels. For McMahon to frame it that way undermined everything else he said.

It was obvious that McMahon was conflicted throughout the interview. One moment he would coldly express that he had no sympathy whatsoever for Hart's plight, then the next minute he would express regret that he was forced to take such extreme measures against him. He ranged from furious with Bret to visibly upset about his decision, openly longing for the old days and for the "right" end to the Bret Hart story, but at the same time refusing to take ownership of his role in Hart's unsavoury departure with his ludicrous claims that "Bret screwed Bret". It was full-on damage control mode from a battered organisation and its hurting captain. For many fans, the "Bret screwed Bret" sound bite alone was enough to forever cement McMahon as the villain of the Montreal Screwjob. To them, he was the man who had shafted their hero and driven him out of the organisation for his own selfish gains.

To McMahon's surprise, during subsequent television appearances he began to hear loud, hate-filled boos and venom-laced insults directed his way, in addition to a barrage of anger volleyed at him online. Far from being the babyface he had expected to be, McMahon was suddenly the biggest heel in the entire company. According to Bruce Prichard, "I guarantee you Vince didn't know things were going to click the way they did. He thought he was going to be the babyface. Vince was smart enough after a few weeks of people going, 'No, fuck you, you fucking asshole, you're the boss and you stole this guy's belt and screwed him around,' he said, 'Maybe I oughta go with this,' and Mr. McMahon was born. The character that evolved out of that was never, ever on the table. It was never on the books. It was just one of those magic moments that evolved. To convince Vince that people viewed him in another light to how he perceived himself – as a faceless announcer and the voice of the company – was a tough sell."

Without realising it or planning it in advance, McMahon had managed to turn himself into the final piece of the puzzle that was needed in the ascension of 'Stone Cold' Steve Austin. A corrupt and authoritarian corporate foil to Austin's blue-collar everyman. In screwing Bret, McMahon had lucked into the formula that would ultimately reshape his company and turn the WWF's fortunes around.

TWELVE

IN MID-AUGUST, Eric Bischoff was on his way to Wyoming for a much-needed vacation with his family, when he received a phone call from Harvey Schiller, one of WCW's chief bean-counters. It was a call Bischoff had been dreading for months, because he knew exactly what it was regarding. Sure enough, Schiller informed Bischoff that he had just come out of a meeting with Ted Turner, who had issued a directive: due to the success of *Nitro*, he wanted to launch a new prime-time WCW show on TBS which would commence at the beginning of 1998, only four months from then.

A second prime time show was hardly a new concept. Back in February, TBS executives had first broached the subject during meetings with Bischoff, but he had strongly opposed the idea, arguing that WCW did not have the talent pool, time, or staff resources to support what amounted to a second *Nitro*. Nevertheless, he had known this day was inevitable for some time. Turner Broadcasting was a corporation first and foremost, full of self-important suits and pushy executives obsessed with EBITDA[22] figures and the bottom line. Everything they could see, looking purely at hard numbers, suggested WCW could and should be even more profitable than it was. Bischoff thought that was ridiculous; WCW had made more money in 1997 than at any other period in their history, generating more revenue in one year than the previously money-losing company had lost in the entirety of Turner's spell at the helm. Still, this was corporate America, and any chance to wring a successful entity for every penny was going to be taken by the ill-informed fat cats at the wheel.

Bischoff was profoundly concerned by Schiller's news. He had already been working around the clock to keep WCW ticking along as it was, and his overworked staff were pushed to the limit. He feared adding a second show would stretch them to breaking point. What made the situation worse was the

---

[22] Earnings before interest, taxes, depreciation and amortisation.

way the TBS infrastructure had changed since the Time Warner merger. Previously, Ted Turner would make declarations and his team of aides would work to make sure they were actioned, irrespective of cost or what branch of the corporation they were funded by. Now, all departments were highly scrutinised and under constant pressure to balance their books.

Bischoff would need to hire staff to work in production, but a company-wide hire freeze meant he could only use employees from within TBS, and he had no idea where to find them. Or indeed, how to pay for them. It was a similar story with talent, bookers, agents, and writers. Bischoff needed them all, but he was not given a budget with which to bring any in. The show, which would eventually be named *Thunder*, was going to generate significant revenue for Time Warner. However, it was also going to cost $15 million per year for WCW to produce, and no one within the corporation seemed willing to fund it.

"I knew we couldn't do it, we couldn't pull it off," said Bischoff. "We were at capacity. It was everything we could do to be good at what we were doing, from an infrastructure point of view. The additional production expense in running another show was huge. Another *Nitro*-like show would call for another forty or fifty people. I'd have to hire fifteen to twenty new production people alone. And then there was the talent. If I just used the wrestlers I already had in another two-hour show, I'd overexpose them. To double our capacity without doubling the infrastructure was too much, and I knew it."

There was also morale to consider. Bischoff's wrestlers were content with their cushy deals which allowed them to work a limited schedule for high guaranteed contracts. Now he had the unenviable task of asking them to work an extra fifty-two dates per year for no extra money. Few, if any, were going to comply. The only thing he could do to keep them happy was up their guarantees, and if he did that for one then he would have to do it for all, certainly at the top of the card. It would cost WCW millions.

Bischoff was in a predicament. He knew that the new prime time show would harm WCW more than it would help, but because it was a directive straight from Turner he felt he did not have the power to tell him no. Other office staff realised it was a bad idea too, with TNT's Executive Vice President Brad Siegel imploring Bischoff, "This is a mistake. Don't walk the plank on this one. Don't step out there if you are not one hundred percent sure."

In an attempt to show his locker room that he was on their side, playing good cop to TBS's bad cop, Bischoff publicly stated that he would resist *Thunder* until he was ordered directly by Ted Turner himself to produce it. It was all situational bluster to save face, because memos had already been distributed around the company and meetings were taking place between high ranking TBS officials discussing the logistics of adding the two hour broadcast to the schedule. Realising he was powerless to resist the inevitable, Bischoff had little choice but to jump on board with *Thunder*.

Industry analysts warned that wrestling was in real danger of reaching a saturation point and strangling itself with too much content, though the same had been said two years prior when WCW and the WWF significantly increased their pay-per-view schedules and eventually began running monthly. However, rather than killing the market, both groups saw buy rates remain steady, and in some cases increase, even after price hikes across the board. When WCW launched *Nitro* in direct competition with *Raw*, the naysayers were out in full force again, suggesting that the split audience would damage both promotions. In actuality, the opposite happened. To the surprise of the industry, the core WCW audience was not the same as the core WWF audience, they were an almost entirely different demographic. What resulted was a battle for supremacy that captured the imagination of fans on both sides, and the total audience watching wrestling was soon at the highest it had been for a decade.

There were further doubts cast when ECW entered the pay-per-view market with *Barely Legal*, and again they were proved unfounded. There was room at the table for all three companies, and there seemed to be no sign of wrestling slowing down.[23] In 1997 alone, there were twenty-seven pay-per-views (twelve each from the WWF and WCW, and three from ECW), by some distance the highest amount ever presented in a single year. The number had almost doubled in the two years since the onset of the Monday Night War. Dave Meltzer in *The Wrestling Observer Newsletter* offered his take on what the forthcoming *Thunder* show would likely mean for WCW, writing:

> As has been historically the case with wrestling, every boom period more television is added until it chokes itself through decreased ratings. But at the same time, there is no evidence whatsoever based on falling ratings - if anything the opposite looks to be the case - that pro wrestling as it stands right now is overexposed. The ability to add another live show without a creative drain on those writing the shows (not to mention the problems because of the top guys rewriting their own storylines) not to mention the physical drain and increased injury rate from the wrestlers who will have to carry the bulk of the time through their ringwork, is just another item to consider.

---

[23] It was actually just getting warmed up. WCW would soon add a third hour to *Nitro*, giving them five hours of live television each week, in addition to their traditional taped Saturday shows. The WWF added *Sunday Night Heat* in August 1998, a sometimes-live Sunday evening broadcast aired on the USA Network. The following year they added *SmackDown* to the schedule on Thursday nights, which aired directly opposite *Thunder* on UPN. By then, the WWF was trouncing WCW with such regularity and ease that WCW was forced to move *Thunder* to Wednesday nights to keep its ratings in the 2s rather than the 1s.

Bischoff began planning for the format of the new show and came up with an idea that proved he had learned nothing from the *Souled Out* debacle in January: he would turn the Monday night TNT show into *nWo Nitro*, and the new Thursday night broadcast on TBS would become *WCW Thunder*. It was the brand split he had craved all along. Bischoff felt confident that such was the company's dominance in the ratings war, that WCW and the nWo would become the top two organisations in professional wrestling, leaving the WWF in a distant third place. In mid-December, Bischoff decided to give the concept a test run on the final hour of *Nitro* to see if the landscape had changed since *Souled Out*, theorising that since the company was bigger and hotter now, the New World Order as the driving force behind that should be too. With a fancy new set, banners, and a flashy introduction video to support it, it was clear that the presentation was far more than a dry run. Bischoff had made up his mind that *Nitro* would belong to the nWo.

The next day when the ratings came in, Bischoff made a sharp about-turn. *nWo Nitro* had dropped almost one full ratings point from the yearly average, the most significant drop the show had suffered. While it still beat *Raw*, it was the tightest head-to-head in all of 1997, with *Nitro* pulling a 3.3 to *Raw's* 3.15.[24] Those margins were far too close for Bischoff to risk, and the number served as a wake-up call that the nWo concept was simply not sustainable as a standalone entity on Monday nights. "It was one of those things where we thought just taking it over would be enough," said Kevin Nash, "But I don't think enough thought was put into the concept of the show."

With mere weeks left until the launch of *Thunder*, Bischoff decided to change tact and hand the new broadcast over to the New World Order instead, where there was less pressure on the show to succeed. Failing on Monday nights and the potential of the unthinkable – getting beat by the WWF – gave the perception that WCW was losing the war, but struggling on Thursdays meant nothing because there was no precedent set.

IN THE meantime, Bischoff was distracted by two other notable happenings: WCW's forthcoming pay-per-view *Starrcade*, which was set to be the biggest in company history due to a long-awaited dream match pitting Hulk Hogan against Sting, and the arrival of Bret Hart fresh from the Montreal Screwjob. Originally, Bischoff intended to hold off on debuting Hart until *Starrcade*, but the WWF

---

[24] The episode of *Raw* in question was filmed eleven days in advance, on Thursday, December 11, to air against the go-home *Nitro* on December 22. The fact that *Raw* was up over sixteen percent in the ratings from another taped show the previous week (going from 2.71 to 3.15) is quite indicative of how poorly received the nWo reconfiguration was to the audience. Aside from Helmsley "pinning" Michaels to "win" the European Championship, nothing presented on the lame-duck pre-Christmas broadcast was exactly must-see television. Fans flipped over to the USA Network less out of WWF interest than they did out of WCW boredom.

had been doing such a good job keeping his name at the front and centre of its own television that Bischoff felt compelled to use him sooner.

On December 15, little over a month following the events in Montreal, Hart was introduced on *Nitro* by on-screen commissioner J.J. Dillon, who announced him as the guest referee for Bischoff's *Starrcade* clash with announcer Larry Zbyszko for control of *Nitro*. Hart received a warm response from the Charlotte crowd, despite being ambiguously positioned (at this stage it was unclear if he would be fighting for WCW or yet another recruit for the nWo) and in the underwhelming role of a referee. Hart smiled pensively on his way to the ring, determined to put the emotional trauma of the past month behind him and make the best he could of his situation by embracing his new position.

After the familiar face of former WWF announcer 'Mean' Gene Okerlund welcomed Hart to *Nitro*, 'the Hitman' cut a brief promo declaring how pleased he was to be there, seeking fan approval by noting he was happy to be in, "Flair country". Bischoff quickly offered Hart a spot in the ever-expanding New World Order, promising him, "seven million a year and weekends off." Hart, to retain an element of mystery over how he would act at *Starrcade*, kept his intentions close to his chest and refused to accept or refuse the offer, but did note that Bischoff was on his own, because, "nobody knows like I do what it is like to get screwed over by a referee."

And that was it. That was Bret Hart's grand entrance into WCW. Few could comprehend the way WCW had handled the debut of Hart. He was the hottest name in wrestling, the man everyone was talking about, and he had come off perhaps the most infamous match of all time. Now he was positioned as a bit-part player in a rivalry pitting his cocksure new boss against an announcer who had not wrestled in years. He was nothing more than yet another pawn in the increasingly-tiresome WCW vs. nWo saga.

Hart himself was hardly bowled over by WCW's immediate creative plans for him either. "Personally I thought that appearing as a referee would be a lacklustre debut, but what did I know? What did I care? I wanted to comply, to do whatever they asked to the best of my ability – win lose or draw – then pick up my cheque and then come home safe. Nobody would accuse me of taking the business too seriously again," he huffed.

The match at *Starrcade* was a mess, with Zbyszko struggling to believably sell for the untrained and much smaller Bischoff. Hart played his role adequately but seemed unmotivated, hinting briefly at a heel turn before decking Bischoff – a clear reference to Hart punching out McMahon at the Molson Centre – then locking the interfering Scott Hall in the Sharpshooter. There was not even a legitimate finish, with Hart simply raising Zbyszko's hand after he had choked out Bischoff with his own karate black belt. On an event that was supposed to serve as the grand comeuppance for the New World Order, the ultimate revenge show where WCW would best the invaders and finally gain some traction in the civil war, they lost in almost every match. Zbyszko's "victory" was only the second time the home company won against the renegade faction all night.

BUT NONE of that really even mattered. Everyone inside Washington DC's MCI Center was only there to see one thing; they were there to witness Sting conquer the nWo's Hulk Hogan and bring the WCW World Heavyweight Championship home. It was a match WCW had been building towards for over a year. It all started back in 1996 shortly after the formation of the nWo, when Sting went rogue, refusing to pick a side in the war that was sweeping through the company. Under the advice of Scott Hall, Sting updated his look from the bleached blonde surfer he had been playing for nearly a decade, to a much darker character, designed to resemble Brandon Lee's memorable portrayal of Eric Draven in *The Crow*. He took to sitting in the rafters and silently brooding, observing, and contemplating what was going on in the ring below him. At *Uncensored '97* in March, Sting finally made his intentions clear, showing his true colours by laying waste to the New World Order then pointing his trusty baseball bat in the direction of Hogan, signifying his desire for a match-up with the faction's kingpin. For the next nine months, Sting dropped in from the ceiling to fight the nWo, acting as an almost-spectral one-man avenger. Via this one repeated, unannounced act, he got over as an all-conquering babyface hero and was soon far more popular than anyone else on the roster. Each time Sting came to save the day, his actions served as silent lobbying for a match with Hogan, which was finally signed for *Starrcade* in December.

Anticipation was at fever pitch. It was the match any wrestling fan worth their salt simply *had* to see. While the nWo had undoubtedly helped WCW take the lead over the WWF in the ratings battle, the angle had been running for eighteen-months and some were tiring of it. The group had been running roughshod over everybody on the roster, be it the cruiserweights on the undercard or the top guys who were not adorned in black and white shirts. A shakeup of the status quo was required, and Sting was viewed as the saviour. He was the man who would restore parity and bring about the beginning of the end for the Order. All great stories need a happy ending eventually. It was a lock that Sting would be defeating Hogan at *Starrcade*; everybody knew the outcome, but they still wanted to see it regardless.

The only person in the world not sold on a scenario that would see Sting winning cleanly and lifting the WCW World Heavyweight Championship was his opponent, Hulk Hogan. Upon seeing Sting arrive at the building looking pale and in poor shape, Hogan hurriedly grabbed Eric Bischoff and took him into a private dressing room to talk. While he did not implicitly state his exact reasons to Bischoff, Hogan was furious with Sting. He felt Sting had not taken the biggest match in WCW history seriously, and he expressed to the stressed VP that he had no intention of putting him over as a result.

By now, Bischoff was familiar with Hogan's frequent last-minute political manoeuvrings and remained unflustered, though at the same time he was also well aware that Hogan held the power of veto over his storylines. If he did not want to do the job, then there was nothing Eric could do about it. Bischoff decided to go for the softly-softly approach and second-guess Hogan's reasoning. Instead of engaging in a protracted argument that might turn Hogan off the idea of losing the bout at all, Bischoff decided to appease him, changing the finish from Sting winning clean to a screwy ending.

"Hogan takes the heat for this. [People say to him], 'You changed the finish! You didn't want to do it!' Bullshit. That was my call. Right or wrong, it was my call," admitted Bischoff. "Sting wasn't engaged. Up until that time he could get away with that. He'd show up at the arena and do his thing – he'd do it very well, it was great – then he'd get on a plane the next morning and disappear, and we wouldn't see him for a week. Our expectations, mine and Hogan's, was that this was Sting's time and he had an entire year to prepare for that moment. By the time we got to *Starrcade* it was clear that Sting had not only not worked out in an extended period of time, but he didn't look like we hoped he would. He came in with no intensity or energy. From my perspective, something was missing."

Sting's lack of motivation was down to struggles in his personal life. His marriage was failing, destroyed like so many others in wrestling by a life on the road. To cope with being away from his family, Sting fell into the same trap that would ultimately take the lives of so many wrestlers: he turned to drugs. "I was losing control over every part of my life," he later admitted, "I was taking prescription drugs, I was taking pain killers, I was taking muscle relaxers, and I was drinking alcohol."

He finally broke down and confessed everything to his wife, admitting it had been going on for years. She implored him to check into rehab, but he refused, claiming he did not need it. He was in denial, like so many of his peers, and he was on the road to ruin. He tried to kick the habit without outside assistance, but he was unable to do so. He spiralled further and further down the rabbit hole, unable to beat the demons that were beginning to destroy both his personal and professional lives.

Dealing with those problems on top of the back-biting political shark tank of the WCW locker room became almost too much for him to bear. "That was a really weird time," he said, "I felt the tension of WCW, the whole company, there was huge tension. Everyone's motives…the creative juices weren't flowing as they should because everyone was worried about themselves."

Come *Starrcade,* Sting was left completely in the dark about what Hogan's issue was and why it was proving so difficult to do business. "Hulk was struggling with how he wanted to do it., how he wanted to put me over," he remembered. "There were a lot of closed-door meetings with him and Eric right until we made it to the ring. I kept asking Eric, 'Does he not want to put me over? Does he not want me to win?' I just wanted to know. Eric would try and be reassuring, but he would talk to Hulk, then talk to me, then talk to Hulk, then talk to me. I was like, 'Can't we just sit and talk about this all together and just do business? Whatever the business is gonna be, let's just come up with an answer and do it.' I wondered why it couldn't just be how it was before: easy and fun."

Unlike many others in the dressing room, Sting was not the sort inclined to play the political game, even less so when Hogan was involved. Sting had too much respect for how Hogan had shifted WCW's fortunes around that he felt it was not his place to go against him. His reverence for Hogan stemmed from a NAPTE conference some years earlier while Hogan was still the king of the World Wrestling Federation. Both the WWF and WCW had booths at the convention, and Sting could not help but notice the huge difference in their respective presentations. While WCW had a modest booth without any razzmatazz or bluster, the WWF had an all-singing, all-dancing display, with Hogan as the focal point of it. Sting saw how everyone in attendance was flocking to Hogan's magnetism, which starkly outlined to him the huge disparity between the two organisations in terms of mainstream appeal. By 1997, the fact that WCW was not only matching the WWF but was actually surpassing it, was astonishing to Sting. He was able to look beyond the political scheming of Hogan because as far as he was concerned, he had a right to be that way. He had earned it. And without him, WCW would still be running small-time shows in sparsely-attended armouries. Thus at *Starrcade*, he was content to let Bischoff and Hogan engage in their protracted game of grandstanding and one-upmanship, and wait to see where the cards lay when they were finished.

After all the talking was said and done and a mutually agreed plan was put into place, it was time for the match to commence. Hogan made his way to the ring with his usual pomp and swagger, the picture of confidence who looked every bit the megastar that he undoubtedly was. By contrast, Sting's expected grand entrance was decidedly ordinary. Instead of rappelling from the rafters or storming down the aisle with purpose, he merely walked to the ring looking mildly uninterested. It was not the great unveiling fans had been expecting. As Sting was casually wandering to the ring, Hogan took match referee Nick Patrick to one side and the two engaged in a private conversation. Patrick had been instructed by Bischoff to deliver a fast count on Sting at the finish of the match, giving cause for Bret Hart to come out and demand justice, overturn the decision, then restart the match and eventually award Sting the victory. Hogan was still smarting about having to do the job, so going into business for himself, he quietly told Patrick to ensure the planned fast count was not fast at all. He wanted to deviate from the script and beat Sting first before he lay down for him, and he wanted the world to see him do it.

Patrick had not been told anything like that by Bischoff, his boss, but he understood the stroke that Hogan held within the company. In that split second he realised it was smarter to go against what Bischoff had said than what Hogan had told him. He was fully aware where the power in WCW really lay. Plus, for all he knew, Hogan and Bischoff had concocted the plan together and Hogan was simply relaying the information to him. He was not going to risk refusing to comply. In many ways it was similar to the position Earl Hebner had found himself in at *Survivor Series* a month earlier, the only difference being that the man getting "screwed" would ultimately get his hand raised at the end regardless, even if his legs were figuratively cut off in the process.

Ironically, the referee gig was originally intended for one of the Hebners, with Bischoff having approached both of the twins with job offers, looking to capitalise on their notoriety by using their role in Montreal as an angle. If it was Hebner who 'screwed' Sting, then Hart seeking retribution would be all the more pertinent. However, it was not to be. The Hebners had no intention of leaving the WWF, especially for an angle involving Hart – who in their minds may have been looking to exact revenge.

Once the bell rang, the action was disappointing, so much so that within two minutes, sections of the crowd turned on the match and were chanting "boring" as Hogan grinded away at a headlock. The way the bout was structured called for Hogan to dominate. If he was losing, screwy ending or not, he was determined that he would look as strong as possible before doing the job. It all served to make Sting look weak and second-rate, full of brine and bluster with apparently no substance to back it up. Fans, who had witnessed nWo dominance all night started to lose faith. Some were so shocked by Sting's unimpressive appearance and lack of fight that they suspected it was not the real Sting in the match at all, but rather an impostor. WCW had pulled that trick before, throwing face-paint and a trench coat on journeyman wrestler Jeff Farmer and dubbing him 'nWo Sting'. The real deal was so unconvincing that many in Washington, DC believed it had happened again. A significant percentage of the audience expected the "real" Sting to eventually come from the ceiling to expose the ruse and win the match. Unfortunately, this time it was not an impostor – it *was* the real Sting, and he was dying out there.

Then it happened. Hogan connected with his trademark match-ending combo – a big boot to the face followed by a legdrop – and pinned Sting, one-two-three. There was no fast count. Patrick had gone through with Hogan's instructions and delivered a regular count as he had been told to. As he would later reveal, "I got conflicting stories about what they wanted me to do. I had one faction telling me they wanted one thing from me, I had another faction telling me they wanted another thing from me, so I kind of split it down the middle." When Patrick's hand slapped the mat for a third time, the collective air left the building. The Washington, DC fans looked on aghast; their great conqueror had failed in his epic quest, he was seemingly yet another name on a never-ending list of Hogan and nWo victims. The announcers tried to cover for the botched finish by claiming a fast count, but it was abundantly clear to everyone watching that there had been no such thing.

Sting would later question what had transpired, wondering, "Did the referee get paid off, or what? I don't wanna believe that happened, but at the time your mind just goes everywhere." For his part, Bischoff pleaded ignorance, putting it down to an honest mistake by Patrick made under pressure, declaring, "I didn't think he had done it on purpose. I would have fired him on the spot if he had." It was abundantly clear that Hogan was the perpetrator, even Bischoff knew it, but he was hardly about to reprimand Hogan and risk driving him off to McMahon, so nothing more was ever said about it. It was this sort of flagrant indiscipline that ran rife throughout WCW which never would have been tolerated on McMahon's watch. The inmates were running the asylum, and they were bringing it down from the inside brick by brick.

Even though the count was anything but quick, WCW pressed ahead with the intended finish and sent Bret Hart marching to the ring. Hart mumbled something indecipherable on the microphone that alluded to Montreal and, "not letting it happen to him again," before walloping Patrick and restarting the match. Nobody in the building or watching in record numbers on pay-per-view at home had a clue what was going on. A few moments later, Sting locked Hogan in the Scorpion Deathlock, his original version of Bret Hart's Sharpshooter. Hogan – master game player until the end – refused to tap or give any signal that he was crying uncle, instead forcing Hart to simply call for the bell and award the title to Sting. Whether by design by Hogan or otherwise, when the dust settled Hart had technically screwed Hogan out of a perfectly legitimate victory, weakening his uppity stance as a moral beacon. Hogan with his scheming had remarkably managed to kill the momentum of two birds using only one stone. Now Hart looked like a bitter whining hypocrite, and Sting a choker who failed to get the job done alone, much to the satisfaction of the egotistical 'Hulkster'.

Sting's failure to win decisively and bring an end to the nWo's omnipotence - the only logical conclusion - left many fans sour on WCW. They had blown the biggest match they had due to petty political machinations and incoherent storytelling. Fans saw the WCW loyalists as nothing more than a bunch of no-hopers and losers. The feeling was that the New World Order was going to be around forever, dominant and unrelenting. Fans were beginning to realise that it was futile cheering for the WCW wrestlers in that fight, because they were never going to win it. Dave Meltzer summed up the disappointment in his *Wrestling Observer Newsletter*, writing:

It would turn a great phrase to say that sixteen months of work was exposed about halfway through Sting's walk down the aisle and before he ever got in the ring. The mythical superhero turned human right before the fans' very eyes. It wasn't as if it was a bad wrestling match that did it, although the match itself was bad. But you could see the big initial pop after all the hype and special effects didn't even last until Sting made it to the ring. The match itself was a struggle. The finish was totally botched up. Sting did leave as champion, but after WCW's most successful quarter in history, the record-breaking show raised more questions about the future than answers the record revenue will provide.

DESPITE BEING critically panned, *Starrcade* was a smash hit at the box office. WCW broke its gate record, drawing 17,500 fans (16,052 paid) paying a total of $543,000, almost $150,000 more than the record set by *World War 3* a month prior. Merchandise sales were the highest they had ever been, with over $161,000 coming in through the tills. On pay-per-view *Starrcade* pulled an astronomical 1.9 buy rate, which translated to 650,000 buys – easily a company record – smashing anything else on pay-per-view since the WWF's *WrestleMania V* in 1989.

Starrcade was WCW's peak, and one they would never come close to matching again. While on the surface the show was a resounding success, the failure to woo the record audience by presenting a strong card with a decisive finish in the most anticipated main event in WCW history was the beginning of a snowball effect that could not be reversed.

The next night on *Nitro*, WCW attempted to capitalise on the *Starrcade* main event controversy by presenting a Sting-Hogan rematch in the main event. Little over five minutes into the contest, referee Randy Anderson was accidentally bumped in the corner and the broadcast went off the air. The intention was to hype the forthcoming *Thunder* debut by airing the final few minutes on the new show, but it turned out to be another colossal error in judgment from WCW. Turner switchboards immediately lit up with complaints, furious that *Nitro* – which had always promised to stick with main events until they were finished – had gone off the air early during the middle of a bout, especially one that was a rematch of a contest they had been ripped off by the night before.

Fewer than two weeks later, *Thunder* finally debuted with a three hour special, on which footage of the Sting-Hogan bouts from *Starrcade* and *Nitro* both aired, leading to the title being held up. It was completely deflating for Sting, the final act in a three-week spell that had humanised and significantly devalued a performer who had become the most over wrestler in the world with just run-ins alone, sans actual wrestling or in-ring promos. *Thunder* proved to be a resource drain that WCW could not handle, exactly as Bischoff had expected.

While it would be wrong to say that its advent killed WCW, or that the mess the company made with Sting and *Starrcade* would cause their eventual demise, there is little argument that all played a part. As with *Souled Out* at the turn of the year, they were increasingly deep papercuts, small and insignificant alone but ultimately fatal over time when combined. Though they did not realise it yet, WCW was on the road to ruin.

THIRTEEN

ALMOST A FULL GENERATION HAD passed since Titan's ascent into gaudy pop culture lore. The grunt-and-groan circus preyed on last-dollar marks with the same enthusiasm as it had managed to appeal to upscale Bohemia, thrusting the World Wrestling Federation into the trendy forefront. Even though Hulk Hogan turning back various foreign menaces with showman-like right hands was not as progressive as David Bowie or Joan Jett, the McMahon formula of campiness amongst carnage nestled firmly into the spiking throes of the MTV uprising. McMahon's national revolution would indeed be televised. That was the stated agenda, anyhow.

Hogan was McMahon's skeleton key into the many doors of mainstream acceptance. Through his swaggering bombast and his rippled physique, Hogan was comic book hero, mega-athlete, charismatic talk show guest, and credible ambassador all rolled into one. Despite these qualities that any sensible wrestling promoter would covet, McMahon still needed an outside trump card to augment his wrestling. Hogan's humorous tussle with Sylvester Stallone in *Rocky III* could only carry so much weight. To make the leap onto Madison Avenue, stars of neighbouring galaxies would have to align.

The inaugural *WrestleMania* did not so much feature celebrity guests as it was infested by iconography. While living monuments such as boxing deity Muhammad Ali and flamboyant pianist Liberace leant a passing flair to the proceedings, it was square-jawed roughneck Mr. T that intertwined most tightly with The Hulkster. The two spent the weeks before *WrestleMania* lighting up the media circuit, which included dual hosting duties of the institutional *Saturday Night Live* the night before working *WrestleMania's* main event. If Hogan was the most far-reaching access pass McMahon had ever wielded, Mr. T opened the doors that Hogan, at that point, could not. It also did not hurt that Cyndi Lauper, whose 1983 album *'She's So Unusual'* spawned four top-five singles in the United States, seconded Wendi Richter in her quest to regain the WWF

Women's Championship at the same event (the album's first single, *'Girls Just Want to Have Fun'*, was appropriately Richter's theme music).

Celebrity rubs were McMahon's favourite ordnance. *WrestleMania* in its ensuing incarnations did not hesitate to roll out the red carpet for visitors from planet Hollywood, from Ray Charles to Regis Philbin to Vanna White. In the fallout of McMahon's image-bruising 1994 trial for steroid distribution, the efforts to reform Titan's public profile with positive superstar interaction only ramped up. Following McMahon's acquittal, *SummerSlam '94* featured deadpan actor Leslie Nielsen and legendary Chicago Bears running back Walter Payton in prominent roles. For *Survivor Series* that fall, death-proof martial arts guru Chuck Norris presided as a guest enforcer to ensure an interference-free main event. That was followed up by a star-studded January, as McMahon kicked off 1995 with William Shatner, Pamela Anderson, and Lawrence Taylor as his choice of billboards that mingled with his stars, ostensibly sprinkling some of their Hollywood pixie dust into the mix.

The experiment with matching up punishing linebacker Taylor with agile beast Bam Bam Bigelow at *WrestleMania XI*, while lauded as one of the better-looking matches featuring a barely-trained celebrity, was a financial disappointment. The pay-per-view only pulled in 340,000 buys, down over nineteen percent from the previous year's *WrestleMania X*. Despite the heavy mainstream interest in Taylor's squared circle foray, it did not cleanse the WWF of the acquired stink from its litany of scandals.

The new direction that McMahon was leading Titan into required more than just internal controversy, such as that of Montreal. The eyes of the juiced-in wrestling world were already aware of the WWF's explicit shift across moral lines, that it was no longer sugary pap approved for Saturday morning consumption. He needed to get the word out beyond his despotic borders.

If mephitic Austin was the cracked funhouse mirror image of virtuous Hogan, then McMahon figured he was a chain-link away from revolution revitalised. All he needed was an unwholesome Mr. T to compliment Austin's unwholesome Hulkster.

A LITTLE more than four months before McMahon would sever ties with Bret Hart following the very public betrayal, a severed chunk of the right ear of WBA Heavyweight Champion Evander Holyfield lay on a boxing ring canvas in Las Vegas. In the third round of a highly-anticipated rematch with the irascible 'Iron' Mike Tyson, the challenger engaged Holyfield in a clinch, and then chomped on the appendage, lobbing off a piece from the top part of Holyfield's ear that barely measured an inch-long.

In the previous round, Holyfield, in avoiding a punch from Tyson, leaned into his opponent, knocking heads with him and abrasing Tyson above his right eye. When the fight went into the third round, a vengeful Tyson initially exited his corner without his mouthpiece concealing his teeth. Gravelly-voiced referee Mills Lane ordered him to go back and have it put in. Tyson would claim years later that the bite was retaliation for what he thought was an intentional headbutt. There's little reason to believe that answering the bell for the third round with his fangs bared was simply out of forgetfulness.

Tyson was disqualified at the conclusion of the third round following the discovery of a second bite, as Lane had deducted two points and warned Tyson after the initial infraction. The ensuing penalty would be far more dire: the Nevada State Athletic Commission revoked Tyson's boxing licence, and fined him more than $3 million. Not being able to exchange blows in Las Vegas rings would diminish Tyson's chances at future paydays. Other states were likely to adhere to Nevada's ruling, effectively barring Tyson from boxing in the United States during an indefinite period of suspension.

Tyson was originally set for a surprise appearance on the June 30, 1997 episode of WCW *Monday Nitro*, held in Las Vegas two days after the Holyfield fight, but Turner officials quickly nixed those plans in the wake of Tyson's cannibalistic actions.

If the first half of Tyson's nineties were marred by a 1992 rape conviction for which he would be paroled after three years, the latter half of the decade dealt him a serious one-two combo in the form of his revoked licence and heavy debt. By early 1998, the former heavyweight champion was an estimated $11 million in the red, owed both to the extravagant, free-spending lifestyle that a number of fiscally-irresponsible celebrities fall into, and what Tyson would soon chalk up to financial mismanagement from his boisterous then-promoter, the charismatic Don King. *The New York Times* reported that in February 1998, Tyson owed between $7 million and $12 million to the Internal Revenue Service. In the wake of this distress, Tyson terminated his relationship with King, claiming that the flamboyant promoter was just as complicit in the burning of the boxer's fortune as he was with his spending habits. On March 5 of that year, Tyson would file a $100 million lawsuit against King, claiming the promoter had fraudulently conned him out of tens of millions of his own dollars.

IN ONE of the final united efforts between Tyson and King, the shock-topped advocate filmed a head-on speech for WWF television at the onset of 1998, confirming what Jim Ross had announced to the audience at the end of 1997: Tyson and the WWF were working on a deal for the pugilist to appear at *WrestleMania XIV* that March in Boston. "Yes, we've gotta dot a few I's, cross a few T's," King projected in his urgent squawk, "But when we get it together, Vince McMahon and I are gonna bring to you one of the greatest shows on Earth. *WrestleMania* and Mike Tyson, March 29!"

The groundwork for Tyson's WWF appearances was laid in November 1997, when Marc Ratner, executive director of the Nevada State Athletic Commission and a noted wrestling fan, fielded an inquiring phone call from Titan. If there were any chance that Tyson's reinstatement bid in Nevada would be irrevocably harmed by his taking part in a professional wrestling publicity stunt, they knew there would be no way Tyson or King would play ball. Ratner gave a vote of confidence for Tyson to work for McMahon, succinctly saying, "We can't tell him he can't wrestle. We cannot tell someone what he can or cannot do." Dr. Elias Ghanem, the chairman of the commission that Tyson would be applying for reinstatement to in July 1998, added, "We cannot stop somebody from making a living."

Ratner, for his part, urged McMahon to do his best to portray Tyson with some modicum of dignity. Any comical allusions to the Holyfield fight were out the window. If Tyson were to bite the ear of a WWF performer, even with the zaniest of jest, it would demonstrate to the commission that Tyson was not taking his revocation all that seriously. "I just hope it will be in good taste," Ratner said to the WWF Chairman.

"Vince's strategy was, 'They will pay to see Mike Tyson on pay-per-view,' asserted Vince Russo. "They can't see him in the boxing arena; they will pay to see him in a wrestling ring.' He was absolutely dead-on."

"I was the one who actually started the whole thing by challenging him," noted Ken Shamrock, recalling an angle from the April 21, 1997 edition of *Raw* in which he publicly challenged pre-bite Tyson, while also unflinchingly bringing up Tyson's rape conviction. "I think what they wanted to do was get his attention. And once they got his attention, they moved me out and moved Shawn and Steve in. That didn't bother me, they were the veterans. But when I challenged him I was thinking I was going to get the opportunity to go at him, then I saw him there and nothing was said to me whatsoever."

For taking part in a ten-week arc that would span from the *Royal Rumble* in San Jose through *WrestleMania*, Tyson would pocket $3 million, a curious number when one remembers that McMahon claimed financial straits to Hart in the fall of 1997 when he informed his then-WWF Champion of his intent to breach Hart's twenty-year contract. Any monetary peril that McMahon was in, fabricated or not, paled to Tyson's situation, because it was apparently Vince's son Shane that made Tyson fully aware of the unreasonable grip King held on the boxer.

According to a *New York Times* report published May 24, 1998, the younger McMahon had reportedly spoken with Tyson in regards to a potential action figure through WWF's Jakks Pacific line that was sure to fly off of shelves as a collector's item. Tyson was reportedly giving $300,000 of his WWF deal to King for use of his own likeness, which King owned the rights to. Tyson came to grips with the reality that for the WWF to market an action figure of his likeness, he would have to do it through King, who held all the cards.

In the *Times* article, Shane McMahon was quoted as saying, "I said, 'Mike, you are the hottest property in sports.' The next thing I knew, he started to sever his relationship with Don."

Tyson's laments carried over to a meeting in late January 1998 with Jeff Wald, Los Angeles-based talent manager, and long-time acquaintance of both Tyson and King. Tyson spoke to Wald of his annoyance with King's residual entitlement to a piece of the pie. A suspicious Wald then requested a look at Tyson's financial records, which Wald would later grumble were nothing more than, "Just numbers typed on pieces of paper." Tyson was then recommended to Hollywood-based attorney John G. Branca, who became miffed by the imbalance in Tyson's contracts. With this information, Tyson not only cast out King, but also co-managers John Horne and Rory Holloway, both of whom Tyson would claim had not acted in his best interests in matters involving King in a separate lawsuit filed that year.

The morning after Branca helped Tyson fire Horne and Holloway, King flew from Tampa to Los Angeles, where he and Horne confronted Tyson outside the posh Bel Air Hotel on Stone Canyon Road. The *Times* claimed the altercation degenerated into a, "shoving-and-shouting match," between King and Tyson, while Horne was said to be, "running for his life," in the words of rival boxing impresario Bob Arum to *New York Daily News*.

The clouds of controversy continued pissing down rain in every direction that Tyson walked. It was this sort of ugly public tumult that Vince McMahon was hoping would steer eyes and wallets in his direction.

COME JANUARY 18, the only contempt pouring down on Tyson in San Jose was the desired kind. In a quick establishing shot before the annual *Royal Rumble* match, the thirty-one-year-old exiled fighter was seated with Shane inside a luxury box overlooking the San Jose Arena. In less than two weeks' time, he would be verbally spitting fire at King. In the moment, he was a well-dressed picture of giddy serenity, enjoying a wrestling show latently similar to the WWWF wrestling he watched on television as a young child in Brooklyn. His hero was virtuous Italian strongman Bruno Sammartino, who turned back all comers with his might and grit. While Tyson remained captivated by the art of staged combat, Sammartino had begun staunchly disavowing Titan and McMahon a decade earlier, owing to what he perceived to be the rise of illegal steroid use and other illicit goings-on. It was probably safe to assume that Sammartino would not have approved of WWF's three-ring media circus with a convicted felon as its centrepiece, even if that felon idolised Sammartino as a little boy.

The image of Tyson excitedly conversing with Shane drew a deafening chorus of jeers from the 18,000-plus fans on hand. Noise was being made, and with an incredible $414,373 paid at the box office (more than double the northern California record of $192,000 set the previous year by WCW's *SuperBrawl VII* in San Francisco), McMahon's new direction was coming up aces in both the departments of energy and commerce.

As for the Rumble match itself, the idea of anyone except Austin coming out victorious was flatly absurd. Entering the thirty-man fray from the number twenty-four position, Austin back-jumped a ring full of wrestlers by sneaking in from the crowd side opposite the entrance curtain. The story was that Austin had been committing random acts of violence against his Rumble opposition for weeks leading up to the match, and once the sound of breaking glass blared to herald his arrival, more than a dozen participants halted their skirmishes and faced the entrance curtain, practically smacking their hands fist-to-palm in anticipation. It was Austin vs. the world, and in effect, Austin above the din.

Austin's trek to the *WrestleMania* title match lasted not even sixteen minutes, culminating with the elimination of twenty-five-year-old Dwayne Johnson, who had further proved his value by hunkering down for over fifty-one minutes as the gauntlet's duration king. Tyson joined the capacity crowd in cheering and clapping for the victor. "Cold Stone is my man!" a supercharged Tyson erroneously shrieked to interviewer Michael Cole in the match's aftermath, mirroring the energy WWF hoped to convey with their new direction. When the celebrity guest is happier to be there than perhaps even some of the wrestlers, the show feels like a happening place to be.

Tyson's fast-spoken emotion in the San Jose skybox was genuine, no polish necessary. Awestruck as Tyson may have been, the following night, he was going to have to kayfabe just enough to make good on his hefty price tag. There was a *WrestleMania* to sell.

THE FOLLOWING day, the Titan troupe made the 150-mile journey east to Fresno for that evening's *Raw is War*. It was still unclear what Tyson's official role would be come *WrestleMania XIV*, at least to the public eye. What was known was that Austin's WWF Championship bout would come against ailing Michaels, who had whacked the small of his back on the creased edge of a coffin the previous night in a match against The Undertaker. Instead of immediately putting Austin and Michaels in each other's faces to sell the *WrestleMania* main event, Austin's employment on *Raw* would be to captivate those whose eyes were not already glued to Monday night madness.

The main event segment was not a match, though it may as well have been. Before going into the final commercial break, Jim Ross narrated a teaser in triplicate, consecutively promising comments from *Royal Rumble* winner Austin (over a still promo shot of 'Stone Cold'), advertising a live appearance from

Tyson (shown calmly standing before *Raw's* backstage interview set), and acknowledging that McMahon was walking down the entrance ramp, all the while being booed out of the building. In an era where matches were shortened to comfort diminishing attention spans, the rotation of images was akin to sensory overload.

"Ladies and gentlemen, in just a moment, we will make the biggest announcement ever in World Wrestling Federation history," declared McMahon following the commercials. In his phlegmy bark, McMahon gave a stirring introduction for Tyson, excitedly referring to him as, "The Baddest Man on the Planet." Flanked by five imposing men in track attire, the immaculately-dressed Tyson made an otherwise understated entrance, graciously putting his arm around McMahon and shaking his hand. It was not long before McMahon began to make the big *WrestleMania*-related announcement, only to be cut off by Austin's signature shattering glass. "Mike Tyson is standing in Stone Cold's ring!" Jim Ross soberly affirmed. The Fresno fans gave Austin a hero's welcome, heatedly roaring for his turnbuckle appeals.

To add to the 'unscripted' feeling of uneasiness, a flock of suited officials, including the likes of Shane, Sgt Slaughter, and Pat Patterson, swarmed to the ring to prevent a melee. This was not Peter McNeeley's entourage hitting the ring to save 'The Hurricane' from being beaten unconscious by 'Iron Mike', but it could only add to the headlines if there was a hint of spontaneous frenzy.

Keeping with the plan, Austin took control of the microphone, blowing off a conciliatory Tyson's efforts at peace. When Austin informed Tyson as to who the wrestling ring belonged to, over 7,300 fans backed their black-shirted idol. McMahon's eyes bulged as he stood between the pair, the incredulous mediator to an apparently-unwanted dispute. "I want a piece of Mike Tyson's ass!" growled Austin to the delight of those same fans. To explain his presence, Austin claimed his umbrage was with McMahon accolading Tyson with the "Baddest Man" moniker. "Do I think you can beat my ass? Hell no! Do I think I can beat your ass? Why, hell yeah!" Austin boomed in his Texas drawl, the fans parroting his last two words with aplomb.

Like with any good wrestling match, there was a scintillating finish. "I don't know how good your hearing is, but if you don't understand what I'm saying, I always got a little bit of sign language, so here's to ya!" With that, Austin turned up the world's most famous pair of middle fingers in the face of the previously-docile Tyson, who responded with a violent shove that sent the entire ring full of astonished onlookers into pull-apart mode. "Tyson and Austin! Tyson and Austin! All hell has broken loose!" Ross cried urgently over the searing tidal wave of fan response. Neither man could afford to come out looking weak, thus after the initial skirmish, Austin focused his aggression on one downed member of Tyson's human shield while the boxer looked on. Adding more venom to the gnash was McMahon, playing the part of irate businessman to a fault. "You ruined it! You ruined it, damn it!" he screamed at a restrained 'Stone Cold', who calmly put his right middle finger into the boss' face. After one final commercial break, the broadcast went off the air following a brief denouement scene, in which the Tyson and McMahon cliques were converged backstage, the fighter infuriated and the boss trying to employ diplomacy. Within fifteen seconds before fading to black, Tyson squawked for someone to bring "faggot-ass" Austin to him.

"I didn't want it to ever stop," Tyson said of that landmark night. "I was living the lifestyle. I was living the dream. You're talking crap to the bad guys and doing whatever you want. I never wanted it to stop."

"I have never experienced anything quite like the night that Stone Cold and Mike Tyson confronted each other in Fresno, California, on *Raw*," Ross would say years later. "It was magic - animalistic magic that I had never felt before sitting at ringside. I will always feel that night was a real launching pad for our company, and did it ever get folks talking!"

The mainstream media, from ESPN's *SportsCenter* to NBC's *Today Show*, pounced on the story featuring two walking scarlet letters in Tyson and McMahon, and reported on it largely without negative editorialising, instead treating it with chucklesome human interest story voices. McMahon even spoke to the Associated Press after *Raw's* conclusion, using kayfabe to heighten the turbulent aura by claiming that Tyson wanted to actually fight Austin at *WrestleMania* instead of acting in his officially-unannounced guest referee capacity. "Mike is refusing to guest referee," McMahon told the AP with feigned sedation. "Austin embarrassed Mike Tyson and the WWF with his remarks. It was uncalled for and very unprofessional. Mike is now saying he wants Stone Cold Steve Austin."

"I think at the time, Vince had ulterior motives," Russo believed. "I think Vince was interested in managing the career of Mike Tyson. Shane was with Tyson 24/7, so I think with the situation Tyson was in at the time with boxing, I think in Vince's mind the wheels were turning. Not only would this be a great coup for the WWF, but maybe once Tyson sees what McMahon did for him here... maybe McMahon could take this to the next level."

The Tyson impact was instant: *Raw* drew a 4.0 TV rating, their highest since the dawn of the Monday Night Wars without *Nitro* being pre-empted. *Nitro* narrowly won the night with a 4.44 rating, but *Raw* spiked with a 4.7 (3.38 million homes in 1998 numbers) for the Austin/Tyson confrontation.

Through the veil of story, Austin and Tyson were sworn enemies, the diametric opposite of barbell-buddies Hogan and Mr. T. But the similarities were there: Titan was given newfound access to MTV through Austin's appearances on a new hit show, the claymation *Celebrity Deathmatch*, and he and Tyson were story fodder for outlets beyond sport. Calling it something hokey and derivative like "The Box and Wrestling Connection" would have missed the point of the modern WWF paradox: urbane, though irreverent. Instead of clinging to pop culture with a Pepsodent smile, the WWF knew they were cool, and that it would be uncool to express that sentiment openly. The rebel need not brag.

ON THURSDAY, February 5, Tyson's *WrestleMania* role would be made official: he was to be the outside-the-ring 'guest enforcer' that would stem any chicanery that might mar the Michaels-Austin title bout. The visible position was not all that different from the role Chuck Norris played at the 1994 *Survivor Series*; the only difference was in the ethos of the men. Ageless hero Norris was every bit the moral, do-the-right-thing crusader that viewers reckoned Tyson was not. With Montreal a fresh memory, the seed sown in the minds of Austin's constituency was that 'Stone Cold's' jaunt up wrestling's Denali might be compromised by unscrupulous 'officiating'.

The announcement was made at New York City's All-Star Café, during a press conference with Austin, Tyson, Michaels, and McMahon all present. The quartet sat at a long, black-skirted table, each afforded hand microphones and tented name cards that spruced up Titan's pillars with accessories out of a congressional hearing. More than one hundred reporters and several dozen television cameras were on hand to witness the mostly-benign proceedings, secretly hoping to catch another Tyson outburst in its glossy posterity.

"I don't know if I'm in a position to disqualify anybody," Tyson offered the assembled press, somewhat meekly unsure of his vested power. "But I'm in a good position to kick some ass if necessary."

The *WrestleMania* logo was splashed in conspicuous places in front of the conference table, in between square-shaped placards promoting the All-Star Café itself. The majority of media interest, however, honed in on Tyson, whose acrimonious split from King was not even a week old. McMahon understood that Tyson's controversial celebrity and public life might take precedent over what was to be a launching pad for restoring *WrestleMania* to its former halcyon glory. "We're here to talk about *WrestleMania* and not Mike's involvement in any other aspect," McMahon markedly noted at the onset of the media summit. Regardless, questions were still levied about Tyson's financial situation, to which a calmly-defiant Tyson at one juncture quipped to the gathered media, "Regardless of the situation I may be into, I have a lot more money than you'll see in a lifetime."

Finally, the press conference found its way back on track with Austin and Michaels laying in their menacing talking points, but not at one another. The goateed challenger roared that Tyson, "...won't ever want to get in the ring again," following a thrashing at his hands. Michaels echoed Austin's showman threats to Tyson, seething, "If you do anything to Shawn Michaels, I'm going to knock your teeth out and, by the looks of things, you can't afford it."

In the case of the WWF Champion, these were fairly emboldened words from an individual who would soon find himself in the worst pain he had experienced in his thirty-two-years on Earth.

THE FLIPPING bump sustained by Michaels during the *Royal Rumble* casket match, onto the casket's lid, apparently did not have any adverse effects on the flamboyant titleholder in the moment. Some time thereafter, a 'stabbing pain' developed in his lower back, first noticed while taping *Raw* two nights later in Davis, CA. *The Pro Wrestling Torch* reported that on the evening of February 11, six days after his face time before the media in New York, Michaels was working out in his San Antonio home when the pain became beyond unbearable. The man whose sinewy body had defied physics and astounded fans under the Titan banner for close to a decade was suddenly sprawled out, hardly able to drag his body across the floor. Michaels was finding it near hopeless to even reach up and pull his telephone toward him.

"It felt like there was a hot searing knife tearing through my back. I had never felt that much pain in my entire life," Michaels said of the agony. Finally able to secure the phone, Michaels pressed the buttons and placed a panicked call to his parents, who in turn called for paramedics to rush to his home.

The MRI results were grim: three damaged disks, two herniated and one crushed. Michaels' doctors provided the WWF with a lengthy injury list which included misalignment of both hips, a bruised kidney, and worsening knee injuries to go along with the dire vertebrae problems. The man whose professional life was predicated on his ability to fling his body in spirals and tumbles around the ring seemingly had few bumps left to give. Whereas a seemingly-random knee injury one year earlier left industry peers and commentators sceptical due to its timing, the longer list of Michaels' ailments this time around did not sound like a boy crying wolf, even if Michaels' credibility had been shattered by conveniently-timed excuses before then. "And speaking of Michaels, he wouldn't be in line to do a job on PPV without an injury cropping up, now would he?" huffed Dave Meltzer.

"There were many people that believed that Shawn was working it," Russo stated. "There was nuclear heat at the time between Shawn and Vince. The reason why I know that is because I was the liaison, right smack in the middle. Vince was not talking to Shawn, Shawn was not talking to Vince. Shawn would tell me what to tell Vince. I'd go tell Vince. Vince would tell me what to go tell Shawn, so I was smack in the middle of it."

Michaels was pulled from the February pay-per-view, *No Way Out of Texas*, which took place in Houston a scant three hours from his home. Michaels received cortisone shots in an attempt to allay the pain, with the hope that surgery would not be necessary. He was also advised to do as little as possible for about a week to let the inflammation diminish. This necessitated missing

Raw tapings in Dallas and Waco following the Houston pay-per-view. If the shots did not make any difference, there was a real possibility that Michaels would need surgery as soon as possible. The championship match at *WrestleMania* was in serious jeopardy.

"I was in constant pain," recounted Michaels. "It didn't matter whether I was lying down, standing up, or sitting. I just couldn't get comfortable. The pain would start in my back and shoot down my left leg."

For the WWF's part, the promotion quickly made it clear on their hotline that Michaels was likely to miss the Houston telecast, bowing out of headlining an eight-man tag that would have featured him, Triple H, and The New Age Outlaws against their respective *WrestleMania* opponents in Austin, Owen Hart, and the rambunctious tandem of Cactus Jack and Terry 'Chainsaw Charlie' Funk. Savio Vega, by this time bumping his head on the low beams of the cavernous undercard as leader of the directionless Los Boricuas faction, would be recruited to fill Michaels' spot, but was not revealed until the ring introductions for the match. By promoting the eighth spot as a 'mystery partner' in an era where wrestlers switched employers with more and more frequency, the appearance of Vega instead of some paid WCW or ECW mercenary proved wildly disappointing. The crowd at the Compaq Center collectively groaned at the let-down.

The eight-man tag, with its hastily tacked-on 'non-sanctioned' modifier, rollicked early to make up for what had been a flavourless, lacklustre pay-per-view beforehand. Without Michaels in the building to build heat for the *WrestleMania* match, the brawl was instead a showcase for Austin to stand tall above the lot, similar to his *Royal Rumble* victory that not only rubber-stamped his WWF Championship match, but placed him on a pedestal above the rest of the locker room, paralleling what the fans already knew. By obvious design, Austin shined the brightest in the frenzy, flinging a trash can like a Donkey Kong barrel into Billy Gunn's face, and scoring the winning pinfall following a Stone Cold Stunner on Road Dogg. In the aftermath, the brawny Chyna stood up to Austin, shoving him several times, only for Austin to receipt her with an emphatic Stunner of her own. Violence against women? Well, she started it, seemed to be the consensus. The attack was well-received by a capacity crowd that spent $241,992 for entry, and a whopping $166,343 on merchandise once inside the venue. Even if the first two and a half hours were so hideous that much of it could, in the word of *The Wrestling Observer*, "be saved on tape and used by future societies to torture war criminals and interns into making confessions," Austin clearly held the unimpeded power to drive home runs in the ninth inning.

The World Wrestling Federation was trucking along at an industrious speed, scurrying hard and fast into the future with the same vigour that led mobs of arena-goers to line up and purchase licensed Austin apparel, from t-shirts to the charming (and inevitable) novelty foam middle-fingers. Meanwhile, pained Michaels could only lament from afar that the operation was beaming its brand of verve worldwide, doing so without his help. "The company as a whole was on a roll. Now it was all over for me," he reflected. "Everyone in the company was looking to the future, and that meant they concentrated their time and efforts on Steve Austin. I was looking for a pat on the back, some acknowledgement that I was doing something courageous for the company, but none came. I felt neglected. It hadn't been that long ago when everything was about me, and I was resentful."

In one of his limited appearances en route to *WrestleMania*, Michaels made the journey to Cleveland for the March 2 edition of *Raw*, where he would take part in a viewership landmark for the program. At the top of the 10 p.m. hour, Michaels confronted the supposedly-impartial Tyson, teasing that he wanted to duke it out with the stone-fisted slugger right then and there. The ring cleared of Tyson's posse and Michaels' D-Generation X acolytes, while home viewers began flipping to the USA Network en masse, calling up their friends and imploring them to do the same. Tyson and Michaels circled each other like the sneering alpha males each was used to playing, only for the WWF Champion to lurch forward and rip off Tyson's t-shirt, exposing an official DX shirt underneath. The story had come upon an unexpected fork in the road: Tyson was on Michaels' payroll. As the pair yukked up their conspiracy with Triple H, Austin fans now had to wonder how he was going to win the gold against unfair odds, the lone wrench in the works of 'the inevitable'.

Raw only finished with a 3.8 rating for the night, some way behind the 4.81 rating for *Nitro*. However, when one looks more closely at the numbers, the Tyson-Michaels skirmish drew a 4.5 rating for *Raw*, putting them in a dead heat with *Nitro*, which drew the same number for the segment. Another look down into the microscope shows that in that quarter of an hour from 10 to 10:15 p.m., *Nitro* barely held off *Raw* by 8,000 households, winning the frame by a narrow score of 3,267,000 to 3,259,000 homes. The combined rating of over 6.5 million households was a new record for wrestling on Monday nights. The heavy dose of reality-based storytelling was the antithesis of the warmed-over taped show from Germany that aired one year earlier, doubling that pitiful 1.9 rating with two-fisted gusto.

TELEVISION NUMBERS were not the only measurables on the rise. In the run-up to *WrestleMania XIV*, house show attendance put to shame the meagre totals of the dreadful recent past. The average arena attendance for the WWF in February 1998 was 9,464, more than double the median 4,633 from the same month in 1997. Their take at the gate had accordingly multiplied, going from an average of $70,305 in February 1997, to $151,189 a year later.

Nine days before the Austin-Michaels showdown in Boston, the WWF drew 12,476 for a Friday night show at Pittsburgh's Civic Arena, up over 5,000 tickets sold from a Sunday matinee at the same venue in mid-January. The following night, Chicago's Rosemont Horizon was packed to the rafters with 17,273 paid, more than double a Saturday night taping in the same building weeks following the 1997 *SummerSlam*. The hat-trick of successful houses was completed Sunday night at New York's Madison Square Garden, where the WWF managed to sell more than 15,000 tickets for the third consecutive time at the historic venue. With freebies accounted for, 18,199 witnessed the last stop on what would become known as "The Road to WrestleMania", in company vernacular.

On all three cards, Austin was the undisputed headliner, decisively winning non-title matches over now-European Champion Triple H. With Michaels out of action, and only working *WrestleMania* before a period of indefinite hiatus, Helmsley was suddenly thrust harder into the spotlight. The spry member of the Kliq was left without anyone to look after, no one to prop up with an aiding arm. The question remained whether or not he could succeed at a level beyond second-banana to the era's most remarkable in-ring performer. Once out of the shadow, would Triple H sink or swim?

"When Shawn decided he needed to take time off physically, and walk away, there was a big opportunity there," Helmsley would say years later. "I don't know that a lot of people thought I could do it. You know, I think there was a lot of detractors, probably, in the room when they were discussing that, saying like, 'We should just drop the whole thing. It's never going to be as good as it was. He's not Shawn.' But then again, at that level, I'd never been given the ball and given that opportunity."

"We knew that it was only going to be a matter of time before Shawn Michaels was going to be put on the shelf," remembered Vince Russo. "We didn't know exactly when, but we knew that the time may come, so we might have to have a backup plan. If you go back and you look at all of those Attitude Era shows, you will see how slowly but surely in the background we were building Triple H. We would give Triple H the mic. Triple H would talk before Shawn spoke. We were getting Triple H over. We were grooming Triple H to take the place of Shawn whenever he was going to leave. Hunter was ready, willing, and able, but man, he could have fallen flat on his face, because Shawn was just a mega-star."

It had been a year since Helmsley was linked up with fellow Killer Kowalski protégé Chyna. The double-act had proven effective in the new ground it had been covering. For all of the coarse fan signage that preyed on the low-hanging fruit of Chyna's androgynous physique, there was a real guilty pleasure in watching her deck Sgt Slaughter with forearm dekes, and fling the near 300-pound Mick Foley into the metal ring steps. Her imposing iciness was a personality cult unto itself, making her the most effective ringside second since the days of verbose managers. Instead of hooking an opponent's leg, Chyna was more akin to throwing a right hook at their head. If Michaels was Helmsley's meal ticket for patronage at the dance, Chyna provided him more lasting power as a top-shelf act.

Functionally, Triple H was the Fabio-haired Arn Anderson to Shawn Michaels' toxic rock star take on Ric Flair. The trope had already been done, debatably better. There existed no such precedent of the partnership Triple H and Chyna had spent a year perfecting, and with Helmsley as the only vocalist of the duo, his stock had more room to grow in the absence of Michaels.

WHILE HELMSLEY was preparing to snatch the D-Generation X mantle from Michaels' weakening grasp, The Rock's preordained path to greatness was primed for resumption, after a good many detours. Like Helmsley, Dwayne Johnson came in with limitless potential and a keen eye for the wrestling business, something that was readily apparent to an all-too-eager office. The translation from marketing-to-consumer did not take initially, and a change in attitude was required to produce the desired spark. If Triple H found his voice in the stead of a proven veteran like Michaels, The Rock's search would conclude in the presence of two other experienced pros.

"I was able to help The Rock get over on the mic, to help him with his personality, with some of his catchphrases," claimed Ron Simmons, at the time playing the role of Rock's Nation of Domination superior, Faarooq. "He got a lot of this from me and I was glad to help give him an identity."

Simmons has later claimed that in his days as an unquestionable elder of the locker room, he would command those he worked with, in a quasi-light-hearted manner, to "know their role" once they were out performing. Simmons credits Johnson as being astute enough to take that specific phraseology and turn it into a million-dollar catchphrase.

"They wanted him to find his own identity and be himself," Simmons added. "And that's when he took off. It makes me feel good I had a little to do in this."

Simmons also provided immense help on camera for Rock, playing something of a disgusted straight-man to the youngster's suddenly-egocentric musings. By this point in time, the Rocky Maivia moniker had been left for dead in the same roadside ditch as the family-oriented creative mind-set that spawned the Maivia persona in the first place. In its place, Johnson was simply "The Rock", and only to be called by that name. To reinforce that point, he made sure to speak solely in the third-person, decreasing the amount of eye contact he made behind his rimless pairs of Ray Ban sunglasses.

On December 7, 1997, at the anaemic *In Your House: D-Generation X* pay-per-view in Springfield, MA, Austin retained the Intercontinental belt in an abbreviated five-minute brawl with Rock, once more accommodating Austin's still-precarious spinal condition. In this instance, the terseness of the brawl was made up for with ferocity. Austin drove his jet-black pickup truck down to the ring, all the while receiving the loudest reaction from the mostly-tranquil crowd. Austin brawled with Rock's Nation mates to make up for any in-ring limitations, famously backdropping henchman D-Lo Brown onto the truck's windshield, before hitting his patented Stunner on the roof of the vehicle.

Twenty-four hours later, the enticing bait designed to hook fans through the two-hour broadcast was an Austin-Rock rematch. Throughout the night, hints both subtle and broad pointed toward McMahon conspiring to unfairly wrest the belt from Austin's possession in favour of Rock, whom McMahon had termed, "The People's Champion". It was only twenty-nine days removed from the public execution of a time-forged 'Hitman', and the fans were quick to connect the dots. The notoriety of Montreal had thrust McMahon into the spotlight in unintended fashion, and now he was cribbing the accidental formula into *Raw's* script. Austin, still restricting physical activity in real life, chose to coolly hand the belt over in storyline instead of being subjected to the pillaging of dignity that had befallen Hart. In one fell swoop, Austin freed himself up of a secondary belt, gave it to a rising star that needed one, and did so without taking any sort of damaging, needless loss. It was here that Rock put forth one of his earliest attempts at illeism, with McMahon as an audience.

Prior to the non-match, when Austin informed McMahon of his intent to sit out, he menacingly asked what the consequences would be. "Are you gonna fire me?" Austin spat with a hint of malice, to which Rock quickly pulled McMahon's microphone his way and half-deadpanned, "Vince, The Rock thinks you should fire him." The smattering of legitimate chuckles from the crowd in Portland, ME was possibly the most favourable reaction the third-generation wrestler had garnered throughout all of 1997.

Johnson had found the silver bullet: effortless wit. By casually referring to himself by his own name, and coldly giving his frank opinion, he was doing precisely the opposite of what he had spent the first six months of his Titan life doing: trying too hard. Suddenly, the Nation of Domination had within its ranks a performer that not only surpassed the lifeless pantomimes of half-baked stereotype, but did so without playing to a type. The Rock was not a black militant, nor was he a milk-and-cookies white meat babyface. He was The Rock, and he was beginning to shed labels, defying bland definition. His act was impossible to sum up in two brief sentences, yet simple enough to catch on.

Just as Paul Levesque abandoned his snooty aristocrat caricature in becoming Triple H, and Steve Austin shouted down his early positioning as a soft-spoken mechanic, Johnson was owning the screen with his base instincts and the baring of *duende*. One element of his demonstrably-individual fingerprint was "The People's Elbow", a garden-variety elbow drop preceded by theatrical showboating and over-the-top posturing. As WCW's Cruiserweights took the air with complex nips and tucks to get a rise out of the crowd, Johnson found a way to impart sizzle with low bodily risk.

"The People's Elbow was something that Rock started doing because we were trying to make 'Taker laugh at live events," claimed Helmsley. "We were all trying to come up with the goofiest stuff we could to make him break character. I think it was Mick Foley at TV one night who dared Rock to do it live."

Rock's Nation teammate D-Lo Brown recalled that it was a tough sell on the fans early on, claiming, "I was there when you could hear crickets making love in the background when he'd [thrust his arms] the first few times. Me and Godfather would laugh our asses off." This assertion was backed up by Johnson landing the elbow on Brown during the 1998 *Royal Rumble* match, to precisely zero fanfare.

Nonetheless, Johnson pushed ahead, developing more and more confidence in his turn as a self-absorbed upper-cruster, no longer trying to make good on his advanced athletic genes, but instead openly flaunting the high dividends he was earning from them. In a perfect comic tribute to The Rock's half-aloofness/half-spitefulness, one skit taped for *Raw* the night after *No Way Out of Texas* saw Rock hand out gifts to his Nation teammates. For Brown, The Godfather, and Mark Henry, Rock gave each a solid-gold Rolex watch. For Faarooq, whose position as Nation foreman was not-so-subtly being undermined by Rock, his 'gift' was a portrait of Rock posed, holding his Intercontinental belt. Naturally, Faarooq was incensed, throwing down the blown-up image while Rock conveyed befuddled innocence.

In one year's time, Johnson had gone from being an inauthentic babyface that fans booed, to a heel that fans could naturally boo, to a heel with one-of-a-kind charisma and potential that was only beginning to be mined. In that third role, slivers of cheers were found woven into the waves of the standard boos he would receive at arenas across North America. It was the crystallising of McMahon's desired outcome for Johnson, but not down the path his old way of thinking could have imagined.

JOHNSON WOULD later claim that the entire idea of his 1997 heel turn was pitched by McMahon, who reportedly said to him, "When you come back, we could continue to shove you down people's throats, or we could turn you heel, because they want to boo you anyway." McMahon knew all too well that he could no longer portray himself as the benevolent chairman after his "Bret Screwed Bret" pulpit had misfired. Thrusting himself into the public eye behind a skin-tight carny smile was not going to fool anybody.

On that fateful *Raw* in which Austin handed over the Intercontinental strap to The Rock at McMahon's behest, the boss took to embracing the inevitable jeers. He also set himself up for a wicked pratfall at the end of the broadcast, following Austin's predictable, yet entirely welcome, Stunner strike on Rock following the handover. An annoyed McMahon stood on the apron of the ring, only to be jolted off and to the floor once Austin 'accidentally' flung himself into the ring ropes. Austin mockingly feigned innocence as McMahon blew a mini-gasket, violently pivoting his head and neck in a rage after regaining his vertical base. He was not playing the innocent victim of an assault by a wrestler he would once have regarded as an ornery heel. This was McMahon, as Rock would say using words generously borrowed from Simmons, 'knowing his role'.

One week later, McMahon stepped back from full-fledged acknowledgement of his presumed villainous leanings to play salesman for his product. It was one thing for McMahon to play a nefarious schemer in the context of giving Austin a formidable, and unique, foe. It was another to have the public voting no-confidence on WWF viewership were they to believe the company were run by a nefarious schemer in real life. That was why McMahon filmed a pre-recorded speech with a lone camera trained on him, enthusiastically selling the changes in Titan's product, justifying the darker shifts:

> It has been said that anything can happen here in the World Wrestling Federation, but now more than ever, truer words have never been spoken. This is a conscious effort on our part to "open the creative envelope", so to speak, in order to entertain you in a more contemporary manner. Even though we call ourselves "sports entertainment" because of the athleticism involved, the keyword in that phrase is "entertainment." The WWF extends far beyond the strict confines of sports presentation into the wide open environment of broad based entertainment. We borrow from such program niches like soap-operas, like *The Days of Our Lives*, or music videos such as those on MTV, daytime talk-shows like Jerry Springer and others, cartoons like *King of The Hill* on FOX, sitcoms like *Seinfeld*, and other widely accepted forms of television entertainment. We, in the WWF, think that you, the audience, are quite frankly tired of having your intelligence insulted. We also think that you're tired of the same old simplistic theory of "good guys vs. bad guys." Surely the era of the superhero [that would] urge you to say your prayers and take your vitamins is definitely passé. Therefore, we've embarked on a far more innovative and contemporary creative campaign, that is far more invigorating and extemporaneous than ever before. However, due to the live nature of *Raw* and *War Zone*, we encourage some degree of parental discretion, as relates to the younger audience allowed to stay up late. Other WWF programs on USA, such as the Saturday morning *LiveWire*, and Sunday morning *Superstars*, where there's a forty percent increase in the younger audience obviously, however, need no such discretion. We are responsible television producers who work hard to bring you this outrageous, wacky, wonderful world known as the WWF. Through

some fifty years the World Wrestling Federation has been an entertainment mainstay here in North America, and all over the world. One of the reasons for that longevity is [that] as the times have changed, so have we. I'm happy to say that this new vibrant creative direction has resulted in a huge increase in television viewership, for which we thank the USA Network and TSN for allowing us to have the creative freedom. But most especially, we would like to thank you, for watching. *Raw* and the *War Zone* are definitely the cure for the common show.

OVER THE next few months, McMahon would appear sparingly on camera, surfacing only for ceremonial endeavours like the Austin-Tyson skirmish. That low profile came with a curious duplicity: his absence shifted the focus away from his somewhat-tarnished image, but when he did appear, his tarnished image was suddenly intriguing, and far less repellent. A scant two weeks before *WrestleMania XIV*, McMahon popped up at the live *Raw* from Phoenix, once more beneath a torrent of boos, and chants for Austin. The crux of his appearance was to take part in an interview with announcer Kevin Kelly, during which McMahon was confronted with footage from the prior edition of *Raw*, in which Austin explicitly flipped him off, and later ripped the breast pocket from McMahon's designer jacket. Despite Kelly's prodding and questioning, McMahon maintained the put-on 'professionalism' that would define him as both a long-time broadcaster, and a public figure that needed to play nice with sceptics.

Gradually, McMahon made a wolfman-like transformation from benign businessman to spiteful mongrel before the eyes of the audience, pausing midway to let out a goading remark. Fingers firmly embedded into the pulse of the audience as though the groove were laughably easy to find, McMahon responded to Kelly's questions as to why he did not strike Austin when 'Stone Cold' prompted him. McMahon at first blurted out that he was 'saving' the main event of *WrestleMania*. When Kelly asked for clarification, McMahon declared audaciously, "How could 'Stone Cold' Steve Austin compete against Shawn Michaels for the WWF Title at *WrestleMania* with a broken jaw?", pompously smirking in time with disbelieving catcalls from the fans on hand.

Masterfully, McMahon re-established his phony politician candour, claiming he did what he did, "for all of the WWF fans all over the world," as though he were Dr. Banner fighting like hell to stave off the greening of his skin. Kelly then echoed a question posed by Austin the previous week, unanswered by McMahon, in which the Chairman was asked if he wanted to see Austin as WWF Champion. "Yes or no? What's the answer?" demanded Kelly, while McMahon wore a lemon-wedge smile. "Well, it really doesn't matter what *I* think; it matters what all of you, the WWF fans, think," McMahon hollowly offered. A second prompting from Kelly earned a plain-spoken response from

McMahon, declaring that if Austin would, "listen to reason," reshaping himself as a respectable role model as opposed to the reckless hell raiser that he unabashedly was, then that would be fine. Still not satisfied, Kelly firmly asked for a succinct answer. Wearing a narrow-eyed grimace, McMahon gave in, throwing out all pretences of modesty for good by heartily declaring, "It's not just a 'no', it's an, 'Oh, HELL no!'"

The resounding boos for placid McMahon laid the groundwork for the plugged-in fans' soggiest dream, of repeated beatings for the haughty tyrant at the hands of Austin, the chafed voice (and fists) of the people. Austin's career culmination in thirteen nights was as assured as sunrise, to the point where *WrestleMania* was already taking a backseat to the yet-to-occur fallout. Few would have imagined that Austin could have a stronger foe than the coddled, oft-injured WWF Champion, or a polarising, headline-grabbing heavyweight boxer, but there was fifty-two-year-old McMahon, sowing the seeds for the feud that everybody truly wanted to see. His ear-to-ear shark's grin was more than just character posturing; it was the exultant smirk of a man that at long last had found the winning flavour.

FOURTEEN

"OH SAY, CAN YOU SEE..." wretched twenty-nine-year-old Long Island-born Chris Warren, the lyrical Zack de la Rocha doppelgänger that headed up the official DX Band. Tent pole-thin with a Jim Morrison screech that could blow over a mobile home, Warren and his bandmates were the opening act for *WrestleMania XIV* at Boston's Fleet Center, filled to the brim with 19,028 in capacity (15,681 paid), netting the company just shy of a staggering $1.03 million at the gate, and an equally-astounding $273,000 in merchandise sales.

Warren jerked his body as though he was being overtaken by serpentine forces, drinking in the annoyed reaction to his melancholy delivery of *'The Star-Spangled Banner'*, although "mangled" is a bit more apt than "spangled". His understated approach crescendoed at the delivery of the word "gleaming", piercing ears with his high-pitched shout of, "Whose broad stripes and bright stars." This was not de la Rocha verbally shoving the powers-that-be with a refrain of, "Fuck you, I won't do what you tell me," but it was served at the same counter-striking volume. In the second part of the plausibly-patriotic medley, Warren transmitted his spin on *'America the Beautiful'*, just as cacophonous with shrieks of, "UH-MAR-I-CUH" over the twangy bass plucks. Not even a hint of applause could be found among the white squall of derision. "Only in the USA, in the WWF, can there be this type of freedom of expression," professed Jim Ross to the home audience, wooden as the bandstand itself.

"After we were done, everyone's booing and we were all psyched because we were just on TV," Warren recalled years later. "We're like high-fiving each other in the back, and people are going, 'You suck!' It was this really surreal thing."

"We went backstage and everybody was looking at us with grimaces and frowns," added bass player Drew Stiles. "I liked playing the part of the bad guy when everybody started yelling at us. I thought it was funny because people actually take the whole thing seriously."

Warren claimed that one person in particular approached to offer commendation for the unorthodox performance: the boss himself. "McMahon comes up and goes, 'That was beautiful! That was great, we love it,'" claimed the vocalist. It certainly corresponds with the suggestion that Warren and his bandmates were instructed to perform in that helter-skelter fashion to better generate instant heat for Shawn Michaels and Triple H's entrances that night, since the band would be playing out each DX member live.

Even if it worked as prescribed, the performance never made it to subsequent home video releases of *WrestleMania XIV*. Ray Charles' stirring rendition of *'America the Beautiful'* at *WrestleMania II* it was not. Nor, apparently, was it supposed to have been. "This is *WrestleMania XIV!*" proclaimed Ross, both justifying the performance, and properly setting the stage for a supercard like none before it.

A HEFTY sum of thirty wrestlers would open up the *WrestleMania* telecast, in the confines of a fifteen-team battle royal, where the winner would earn a WWF Tag Team Championship match at a later date. It was not that Titan boasted fifteen legitimate duos, but rather some pairings were hastily cobbled together from undercard wanderers that would otherwise have no *WrestleMania* potential. Some authentic duos like Henry and Phineas Godwinn, as well as the Headbangers, were obvious choices for the match. In other cases, stables like the Nation of Domination and Los Boricuas were split into pairs for purposes of the fray, a testament to how hard the entire 'Gang Warz' concept that had dominated 1997 had crashed onto the bedrock.

Inadvertently giving the impression that the roster suffered from bothersome bloat, the broadcast virtually opened up cold – no pyro, nor a widened pan over the crowd expanse, but rather a shot of Nation members Faarooq and Kama Mustafa making their bare-bones entrance. The ring was as overcrowded as the roster at the time, in desperate need of a clear-out. By the time of *WrestleMania XV* a year later, twelve of the thirty participants would be gone from the company, while a thirteenth, Barry 'Recon' Buchanan, would spend two years retooling his work in developmental before a 2000 return to the main roster. In a mark of how little momentum would be afforded most of the match participants, at that same *WrestleMania XV* in 1999, out of the eighteen performers still with the WWF, twelve of them would be thrown into another uninteresting battle royal for a Tag Team Championship match. Making matters worse, this battle royal was relegated to the *Sunday Night Heat* pre-game show. D-Lo Brown, Bob Holly, and Bart Gunn were the only entrants in the 1998 version of the match to participate on *WrestleMania XV*'s main show one year later.

The final tandem due for introduction was an unannounced surprise, and a welcome one judging by the initial cheer for the sound of Michael Hegstrand's "What a Rush" vocal cue. From the entranceway emerged Hawk and Animal, now bedecked in motorcycle helmets with snaggletooth airbrushing, and their spiked shoulder-pads matched the eye-catching design. Joining them was the voluptuously-sleek Tamara 'Sunny' Sytch, dressed in a skimpy warrior-goddess outfit with tassels and boots. This was not merely the Legion of Doom, but instead LOD 2000, an ostensibly Y2K-compliant version of the battle-worn Road Warriors. If the aging duo was going to be sticking around for the Attitude Era, they definitely needed a new paint job and some re-spackling.

Joe 'Animal' Laurinaitis was unimpressed with the overhaul, calling the helmets "ridiculous". "I remember thinking, 'What the hell happened to the Road Warriors?'" he recalled. "We were getting further and further away from our roots, which was the worst thing that could've happened to us."

For the previous month, Animal and Hawk had been absent from the wrestling eye, which Laurinaitis claimed was due to yet another failed drug test for his partner. "When Hawk came up positive for whatever (just pick one substance) at the end of February, we sat out for thirty days while Vince and his team of creative writers literally planned the rest of our miserable fate in the WWF," grumbled the powerhouse.

Their last appearance before *WrestleMania* came in defeat to the Tag Team Champions, the New Age Outlaws, on an episode of *Raw* aired on February 23. Following the brief match, Animal and Hawk erupted in a brawl amongst themselves, seemingly spelling the end of the partnership. Instead, they were afforded one last kick at the can with the new look, and the hope that the old Road Warriors magic could still be conjured up. As Vince Russo tells it, the repackaging had as much to do with freshening up one unhappy female performer.

"Sunny was so jealous of Sable, and was like the biggest headache at the time," Russo contended. "If you go back and look at these shows, you can clearly see every week we're trying to find something for Sunny to do.... because God forbid we put Sable out there and we didn't put Sunny out, we had to hear it until the cows come home. So LOD 2000, a big part of that was, 'What do we do with Sunny?'"

While much of the battle royal consisted of primitive punching and kicking due to the claustrophobia-inducing mass of bodies on hand, the ending was an amiable one, with Animal and Hawk clotheslining Holly and Gunn out of the ring for the victory to respectable cheers. Holly and Gunn had by this time been re-costumed as The New Midnight Express, a lifeless take on a well-versed heel act of the 1980s south-eastern territories that rotated through several pairings, almost always managed by Jim Cornette. The idea had no legs, and was an instant flop. "Throwing Bart and me together and hoping we'd immediately develop what took Dennis Condrey and Bobby Eaton years to get was plain stupid," Holly griped.

A decade or so earlier, the idea of a Road Warriors-Original Midnight Express match-up would send fans of Jim Crockett's wrestling into an excitable tizzy. In 1998, Animal and Hawk trying to appear hip and millennial against two unenthused stand-ins for 'Loverboy Dennis' and 'Beautiful Bobby' was, at the very least, a quizzical choice to lead off the Attitude Era's rendition of Woodstock.

A TOTAL of sixteen wrestlers took part in the evening's final six matches, which included four singles contests, a standard tag team bout (as standard as a 'Dumpster Match' could possibly be), and a mixed tag team match of male-female pairings. Of that sixteen, only three of them were over the age of thirty-five: veteran female bruiser Gertrude 'Luna' Vachon (36), former high flier-turned-midcard chauvinist Marc Mero (37), and ageless, endtimes-resistant Terry Funk (53). Although each still had something to offer a WWF product that feasted on colourful variety, none of them were figured into the long-term plans of the promotion. Both Funk and Mero would be out of sight by the end of 1998, while Vachon would sit out much of 1999, suspended long-term after a backstage scuffle with Sable.

Sable was part of that remaining thirteen that would help comprise the upper crust of the Attitude Era, the core group that would monopolise the World Wrestling Federation's penthouse tier for much of the next three years, give or take the occasional opening in the cracks for a WCW defector or two. Of those thirteen individuals, six of them would hold the WWF Championship at some point over the ensuing three years. Five of them (Steve Austin, The Rock, Kane, Mick Foley, and Triple H) would all be given a run with said championship for the first time in their careers. Four other wrestlers from that group (Road Dogg, Billy Gunn, Ken Shamrock, and Goldust) would at least reign as WWF Intercontinental Champion during the same stretch.

In all, 1,099 days passed between *WrestleMania XIV* in 1998 and *WrestleMania X-Seven* in 2001, the latter being by consensus the apex for Attitude's run. For 868 of those days, a wrestler that participated in a notable match at *WrestleMania XIV* held the WWF Championship, or 79 percent of the time. The only exceptions were Vince McMahon (a joke six-day reign in September 1999), Paul 'The Big Show' Wight (seven weeks around the turn of the millennium), and Kurt Angle (around four months in late 2000-early 2001, a near-eternity given the frequency of title changes in those frenetic times). The belt was also vacated for seven weeks from September through November 1998 for storyline purposes, a gap that transitioned the gold from Austin's second reign into The Rock's first.

In other words, in the matches that mattered most, the puppeteers of *WrestleMania XIV* were about to properly position the future of professional wrestling.

WHEN THE babyface wins at *WrestleMania*, it's the vanquishing of a fiend, the righting of a wrong, or the attaining of long-elusive rewards. When the heel is victorious, he's denying comeuppance, turning back valiance. Triple H and The Rock were the only villains that had their hands raised come *WrestleMania* Sunday in 1998, but their respective wins hardly felt like the deflation of high hopes.

For Triple H, his European Championship defence against previous titleholder Owen Hart felt like a safe bet for a token heel win. The youngest Hart sibling's role in the fallout of Montreal was to act as steely-eyed avenger for his deposed brother, laying low for one month before targeting D-Generation X for their treachery. While a pay-per-view match with Michaels for his brother's belt seemed like a slam dunk, the only high-profile match between the two came on the final *Raw* of 1997, with Hart winning on a disqualification after interference from Triple H.

In truth, Hart had completely soured on being part of the WWF. It's an easy position to understand, given the ignominy bestowed upon his brother after more than thirteen years of undying loyalty and body-breaking service. Brothers-in-law Davey Boy Smith and Jim Neidhart found their way out of the company to follow Bret into WCW, though Smith had to buy out his WWF deal with the forfeiture of $150,000. That left Owen as the only remaining Hart family member under McMahon rule, and that was not about to change.

"Owen had asked to be released, but Vince refused to let him out of his contract," insisted Bret. "When I approached Eric Bischoff about my brother, he was interested, but he didn't want to pay Owen the same money he was making with Vince."

'The Hitman' also recalled taking up his brother's cause with Vince Russo, noting to the company scribe that McMahon, "...wasn't good for his word and that it was impossible for Owen to trust anything he ever said again."

"Willing to forego a contract that was to pay close to $300,000 (US) each of the next three years, Owen felt he simply could no longer work for a man he couldn't trust," confirmed Hart's widow, Martha. "However, McMahon refused to let Owen out of his contract."

Had Owen gotten his way, he would have been free to do as he pleased, sometime in 1998, anyway. According to Martha, her husband was approached with a five-year contract offer from Titan in 1996 that provided the security of $300,000 a year ($250,000 plus $50,000 in merchandising), though Owen was disinclined over the length. "What Owen really wanted was to sign on for two years and then retire from wrestling altogether," claimed Martha. "He had ideas of moving onto other interests, like running a bike shop, after he retired. However, McMahon wouldn't budge so Owen signed a contract that wouldn't release him until he was thirty-six years-old. It was then [that] we finally had to accept wrestling was his career, like it or not."

Hart had other pains weighing him down, in the form of an ankle injury sustained during a *Raw* taping four weeks before *WrestleMania*. Hart only had his cast removed the day of the pay-per-view, and was working the match at less than optimum strength. Threading the match was the story of Chyna, whose dauntless manhandling of company males was having an interesting effect. Her brassy attitude was finding increasing praise in an era of femme fatales like Xena: Warrior Princess and Lara Croft of *Tomb Raider* fame. She was to be handcuffed to the increasingly-bumbling company commissioner Sgt Slaughter at ringside, to prevent her from interfering in the match. Already an anachronism in 1991, the balding Sarge was even more out of place among wrestling's Generation X. When Slaughter attempted to fasten one cuff around her wrist, Chyna forcibly shoved him to an electric response, an obvious sign of the changing times. This certainly was not the Boston Garden crowd of June 1984 that cheered Slaughter on as he whipped The Iron Sheik in a 'boot camp' match.

Hart walked with an obvious limp toward the ring, but still managed to mete out his half of a strong wrestling match with the improving Triple H, who was at least justifying his elevated position on the card with quality performances. Highlighting the designed ineffectiveness of Slaughter, as well as Chyna's guile, the chiselled valet still managed to free her charge from Hart's Sharpshooter with her one free hand, dragging Hunter (and actually, Hart too) to the bottom rope, despite Slaughter's presence. He was further rendered moot when Chyna blinded him with a handful of powder, before covertly giving Hart a low blow that allowed Triple H to win with the Pedigree. Once liberated from the handcuffs, Chyna once more provoked a roar from the Boston crowd by knocking Slaughter off his feet with an exaggerated right hook. If the criticism of the gung-ho Attitude Era was that wrestling took a back seat to character posturing, what does one say when an eleven-minute wrestling match, and a pretty good one, instantly pales to the act of an Amazonian woman cold-cocking a ghost of sports entertainment past? What was Titan's crime, if it was not giving the audience what it wanted?

CHYNA WAS not the only female presented as fearlessly inspirited that evening. Her assaults on oafish males was by then business-as-usual, but Sable was still carving out her own sanguine image. In her first two years of accompanying husband Marc Mero to ringside, and modelling licenced t-shirts before live crowds, Sable was the new millennium Miss Elizabeth, filling the niche of fair-haired damsel, albeit with the appropriate sexual voltage of the era.

After all, what was Sable, if not a leather-clad Elizabeth that busted out with comic book heroine proportions? Her parading around in high-heels while clutching a cat-o-nine-tails took plenty of focus off of her husband's performances. Once Marc returned from ACL surgery in the fall of 1997, his dazzling aerial offence was replaced by a simpler move set that offered nods to his Golden Gloves boxing past. It was just as well, since nothing he could do was going to outshine his wife once presented before the whistling 18-to-34 male demographic.

"They came up with the storyline of me being jealous of her and I'm thinking, 'Wow, what a great idea.'" claimed Marc Mero. "I know a lot of wrestlers were saying, 'That buried you, when a girl beats you up or something, you're never considered anything again,' but you know what, all of that didn't matter. They were backing up the Brinks truck to our house, so you really look at what is really important, it's entertainment, it's being an actor, and I'm being paid very well for it."

Russo added that the justification to push Sable hard grew in accordance with her increasing popularity, both in ratings numbers and arena decibels, but that her augmented role did not sit well with some performers at the head of the locker room. "I witnessed the biggest names on the roster in Vince McMahon's ear, and they did not like the fact that she was getting over," claimed the head writer. "I really didn't care, because all that mattered was how many people were watching Monday night."

Mero understood his role was to step aside and let Sable shine during their mixed tag team bout with Goldust and Luna Vachon, both deep into their roles as garishly-dressed eccentrics like Riff-Raff and Magenta from *The Rocky Horror Picture Show*, albeit more colourful than gothic. Mero and Goldust were largely inconsequential to the tale of Luna the wild aggressor and Sable the once-timid cheerleader, which morphed into Sable the fed-up ass-kicker after enough provocation. Sable began physically standing up to Luna in the lead-up to *WrestleMania*, and looked downright capable in spite of her limitations come the mixed bout. Everything Sable did (squeezed like sausage into a vinyl vest and matching shorts) drew incredulous "oohs" and "aahs", from a clearly-cooperative powerbomb on the helpful Vachon, to borrowing her husband's 'TKO' fireman-carry cutter for the finish.

Vachon had done an admirable job making Sable look like a world-beater, and would later insist that she had to be extremely careful in her handling of the novice performer, for her spot within WWF apparently depended on it. "Sable has this preconception that she didn't have to learn how to take bumps," Vachon said. "If there ever was anytime when a match that I was involved in would be called 'choreographed', it would have to be that match with Sable. Her not wanting even to learn how to take bumps and me getting the warning that if you scratch or bruise her, you're gonna lose your job. This is wrestling, and for a woman not knowing how to protect herself, how to distribute her weight properly, and take bumps, you're asking a whole lot of their opponent to make them look good, or for her to try to make me look good."

Vachon recalled there being little praise for her carry job, except for one notable moment of graciousness. "I walked though what's considered the Gorilla Position and (didn't receive) a thank you or a second look," Vachon recalled, "and you're kinda not sure under these conditions whether you have done an okay job or not. Nobody said anything. Nobody pulled me aside, and [then] Owen pulled me behind the big makeup box and he said, 'Thank you. You did great.'"

VACHON WORKED hard in defeat to hold Sable to the light as a superior fighter. The following match would require a bit more intricate storytelling, to cast the loser of the bout as somehow fierce and unbreakable, while sacrificing a winner that was beginning to show signs of a smudge-proof exterior.

Before his planned Intercontinental Title match against Ken Shamrock, The Rock was afforded an extra session of character shaping earlier in the telecast, with the help of a rather schismatic celebrity. Gennifer Flowers had come forward during the 1992 Presidential campaign of Arkansas Governor Bill Clinton, claiming that she and Clinton had carried on a discreet twelve-year affair in the wake of the Monica Lewinsky scandal. Flowers, a folksy ex-model from Oklahoma, took to the tabloid circuit with her claims, including a notable December 1996 appearance on the syndicated *Richard Bey Show* to discuss the alleged affair. The show was cancelled one day later despite reportedly favourable ratings.

In a January 1998 deposition, Clinton, now in his second term as US President, admitted to a sexual encounter with Flowers, after having previously denied the story. Weeks after the revelation, it would be announced that Flowers would attend *WrestleMania* as a celebrity guest, completing a curious trifecta with Tyson and banished baseball icon Pete Rose. While Flowers had not served prison time like the other two had (Rose pled guilty in 1990 to tax evasion, and spent several months behind bars), her biggest claim to fame was not exactly something to be proud of. Given the tone of the era, the trio of Tyson, Rose, and Flowers (and the shameless DX Band, if one considers them celebrities) came with an unmistakable message from Titan: If you're not going to give us any good press, we'll gladly take some bad press. And there was plenty. "All this nonsense in the Fleet Center was a sports sacrilege to the cherished memory of the Boston Garden, the ancestral home of the Celtics and the Bruins just down the street," groused Dave Anderson, a Pulitzer Prize-winning sportswriter for *The New York Times*.

For Flowers, now forty-eight-years-old and looking more motherly than comely, her most significant involvement at the pay-per-view came in a recorded sit-down interview with The Rock, giving him a benign sounding board for sharpening his already-pointed comedic chops. Behind mocha-tinted sunglasses, Rock spoke with faux deliberations about the political issues Flowers was bringing up, a transparent allusion to Flowers' history with candidates on the campaign trail. Given the elements in the mix, the set piece was fertile ground for penile humour, as Rock playfully made clear his thoughts on the judicial system, noting that if he were a general jury, "...nine times out of ten, [The Rock would] be a 'hung jury', if you smell what I'm cooking." Crotch-oriented puns in a world laden with testosterone and alpha-maleism were as common as headlocks in the New WWF, but history would relegate that offhand remark behind Rock's innocuous, "smell what I'm cooking," punctuation. Dwayne Johnson's million-dollar catchphrase was born in this most inane of skits, at indoor volume, without any revellers to scream it in unison.

Johnson would play it far less suave and hep during his abbreviated match with Shamrock, in which it appeared that Shamrock had cleanly won Rock's Intercontinental Title by submission, using his trademark foot-twisting ankle lock. In the aftermath, a wound-up Shamrock fell into another one of his identifying tropes, that of the obdurate beast. Shamrock dropped Rock's Nation disciples with belly-to-belly suplexes before re-snaring Rock, who had blood cascading from his mouth, in the winning ankle lock. Rock grunted while Shamrock emitted primitive screams of aggression. When a heap of officials swarmed the ring to save the dethroned champion, Shamrock sent a handful of them flying with high-hoisting throws as well, a kick-padded bull in a China shop. By the time the bug-eyed Shamrock was brought under control, it was announced that the decision had been reversed, and Rock, now being gurneyed out of the arena in a bit of black comedy, retained the belt as a result of a disqualification.

"I felt like the way it was being done it was pretty clear that I was winning the matches, and the only way Rock could win was to cheat every single time," said Shamrock. "I felt it made me look like a stronger character because I always came in doing the ring thing, and he had to cheat."

Already, the job of protecting Shamrock without having him outwardly lose was complete, but that didn't prevent a welcome bit of overkill, in which Shamrock stormed the stretcher, flipped it over, and resumed trying to pry Rock's foot off of the bone. As Austin proved a year earlier, even in defeat a wrestler can not only maintain his credibility, but come away from a loss looking even stronger.

GRIZZLED MARAUDER Terry Funk had only re-joined the WWF three months prior to *WrestleMania*, at a point in time where the fifty-three-year-old had already been retired for over three months. Funk and retirements are an unintended, but potent, running gag throughout wrestling lore, dating back to his first exodus in 1983 at age thirty-nine. Since then, Funk performed in World Championship bouts in the WWF with Hulk Hogan and the NWA with Ric Flair, before his sentimental reign as ECW Champion that began in April 1997. In less than nine months since the title win, he had dropped the belt in a barbed wire match to Sabu, retired at a farewell event the following month in his native Amarillo, TX (in which he wrestled visiting WWF Champion Bret Hart), and made his WWF comeback on the last televised *Raw* of 1997. Upon his WWF return, the thirty-two-year veteran of seditious brawls and Japanese death matches did not exactly portray Terry Funk, despite his ubiquitous recognition with the majority of wrestling fans. For his return, in which he backed up Cactus Jack in standing up to the New Age Outlaws, Funk's face was not even visible.

"For reasons that I still don't quite understand, Terry was, at his own request, turned into Chainsaw Charlie, and the result wasn't quite what I was looking for," Foley would bemoan. The Chainsaw Charlie character consisted of a different take on Leatherface of *The Texas Chainsaw Massacre*, in which Funk wore a sheer stocking doused in baby powder over his head, along with tattered jeans, a buttoned-up industrial shirt, and suspenders, all while brandishing a whirring chainsaw with its chipper teeth removed.

The early ideas of coaxing Funk out of his all-too-recent retirement came from Foley himself, who had proposed a best-of-seven deathmatch series with the man he had infamously warred with in the mythic IWA *King of the Deathmatch* tournament final at Kawasaki Stadium in August 1995. Funk was on board with working with his brother-in-masochistic-arms once more. So too was McMahon, who Foley claimed was "intrigued" by the proposed final match for *WrestleMania*, a call-back to the no-rope, barbed-wire, exploding ring deathmatch that was their tournament final, this one potentially being filmed at Funk's Double Cross Ranch. However, plans for skin-ripping mayhem were out the window with the media eye on controversial Tyson. "McMahon didn't think that having two human beings blow each other up would be the best way to expose our product to this new audience," Foley deduced.

Instead, Foley would press forward with Funk, or rather Chainsaw Charlie, as a tag team partner that could match his charming madness. They would challenge for the Outlaws' belts at *WrestleMania*, working the first ever 'Dumpster Match' on record. The stipulation stemmed from an absurd angle on the February 2 *Raw* from Indianapolis, in which Foley and Funk faced off in a match that one could consider a 'friendly' if their appreciation for irony was deep enough. The two wound up in a rolling trash receptacle that was situated on the entrance stage. Once inside, Gunn and Road Dogg emerged, locking both men inside the container, before pushing it off the side of the stage and through some conveniently placed tables. This set off one of the most outside-the-box episodes of *Raw* to ever take place, as the Outlaws' initial joy at their actions turned to melancholy when it was revealed that Foley and Funk were "hurt". Not hurt in the manner that a babyface selling a major twist in the story is hurt, but in a way that betrays the script. Soon, Gunn and Dogg were reduced to "acting" as Monty Sopp and Brian James, now concerned they had gone too far with the angle. Jim Ross and Jerry Lawler went from hyperbolic shock to a half-mast tone in their voices, while EMTs and officials tended to the injured brawlers.

Both men were taken out in an ambulance as the show slowed to a snail's pace, with McMahon making an appearance to realistically dress down both Outlaws, while members of both sides of the locker room tried to attack them for being so careless. The most notable acting job from the abstract scene came from Sunny, who cried through her heartbreak at the condition of both men. Once back on track, the remainder of the broadcast was intentionally clouded by the appalling act of a stunt apparently gone wrong, but there would be a happy, albeit undermining, ending. Dogg's main event match with Austin was cut wildly short due to time, resulting in run-ins from Gunn, Michaels, and Triple H immediately, while the cavalry of Funk and Foley made the save, ludicrously wearing a hospital gown and dragging an attached IV pole, respectively. From dire to derpy in ninety minutes, the gamut of emotions has its own express lane. "Within an hour-and-a-half, we went from being unconscious in an ambulance to hitting the bad guys with our IV stands," Foley observed. "Terry was even wearing a hospital gown, although, mercifully, his wrinkled ass never made the air."

As for the Dumpster Match itself, in which to achieve victory, one team had to deposit both opponents into a designated dumpster at ringside and close both plastic lids, it was far less preposterous. All four men continued to usher in the uptick of weapons-based violence that Titan was game to allow, taking turns smashing their respective foes with prop cookware, and sending each other careening into the sides of the heavy receptacle. At one point, Funk took a nasty spill into the dumpster off a tandem powerbomb from the Outlaws, resulting in near-immediate discolouring on his lower back by one of his hips. "Within minutes of the fall, his back was visibly bruised, and within hours, had filled with liquid," Foley would note.

The challengers ended up winning the belts following a comical visual. After the brawl spilled into the locker room, Foley dropped both champions onto a wooden pallet that Funk would scoop up from behind the wheel of a forklift. "You don't need a crazy man driving a forklift!" shouted Ross in his trademark fire-breathing Oklahoma drawl, as Funk eased the machine toward a backstage dumpster. Foley rolled off both Gunn and Dogg into the container, closing both lids for the ostensible victory. It would be revealed the following night on *Raw* that Foley and Funk were stripped of the belts for using an 'invalid' dumpster to win. In an era with seemingly no rules, it almost figured that the only rule that stuck was as ludicrous as the rampant anarchy itself.

BY 1998, The Undertaker had already become a walking legacy, deified arguably before his prime years. In the hands of someone with even slightly less gravitas and conviction, the role of an unflinching mortician with an inhuman threshold for pain could have been a flop, a misfire ripe for howling ridicule. At the same time as Mark Calaway left WCW and emerged on the Titan scene with ghoulish eye shadow and a plodding gait, WCW was failing with their own darkened overlord characters, including the incongruous Black Scorpion angle, and a wet-behind-the-ears Kevin Nash floundering as 'Oz', a barbarous wizard based on L. Frank Baum's literary creations.

The WWF was hard at work in the nineties assembling other characters designed to strike fear into the hearts of young audiences, but the ilk of disquieting voodoo master Papa Shango and near eight-foot beast Giant Gonzalez proved to be duds, both artistically and in performance. Only The Undertaker, whose otherworldly nature was augmented by strong hits of gripping coldness, had come anywhere close to replacing the giant void, literally, left by the departing Andre the Giant in 1990. That Undertaker is viewed as a peer to the godly Andre is a tribute to his attention to detail, both minor and major. That Kane, in less than six months of life before the cameras and crowds, could be viewed as a peer of Undertaker's, a figuratively-biological peer for which Undertaker may have finally met his match, speaks to Glenn Jacobs' own effectiveness.

That isn't to say the booking was not protective. To build a monster that could stand on equal heavy-footing with Undertaker, Jacobs had to grow up quickly. Calaway had plenty of time in the slow-burning early nineties to notch his belt with memorable moments, but the breakneck speed common to the latter half of the decade meant that Kane needed to ace the accelerated course of myth-making. In little over four months' time from his debut at October's *Badd Blood*, Kane was designed to annihilate Mankind at *Survivor Series*, immolate The Undertaker alive inside a locked casket at the *Royal Rumble*, and put the monstrous Vader out of action at *No Way Out* after bashing him in the face with an enormous wrench.

"I was very proud of my match with Kane, who was in the beginning of a huge push as an unstoppable monster," Foley would assert. "I thought I had been successful in adding both to Kane's aura of a monster and my aura of never backing down."

There was less emphasis on Kane actually wrestling in matches at the time, affording him the status of 'special attraction'. The less he wrestled, the more important it was when he actually did. From a more cynical perspective, using him sparingly in the ring reduced the chances of him being exposed as a less-than-optimum worker. Over time, Jacobs would develop into a talented all-around performer for a larger wrestler, but the man who only one year earlier was performing a no-frills imitation of Kevin Nash was still in formation.

Naturally, a match between two colossuses was not going to be about the finer points of easy-flow grappling. A feud that features a wicked younger sibling not only trying to burn his zombie-like brother alive, but would later see the two take turns shooting lightning from their hands in some sort of thermodynamic pissing match, doesn't come with the expectations of hammerlock reversals. Instead, this was to be a Hulk vs. Andre for the Fangoria crowd; an over-the-top conflict with graphic novel colouring.

"I believe that the story with Undertaker and Kane was the best bit of epic storytelling that the WWF has ever done," Jacobs would later opine. "It really was something out of Greek mythology, and that was the culmination of that whole story. For that reason, it made it very special."

The critical reception for the seventeen-minute match was mixed, with Dave Meltzer noting Jacobs' limitations, writing that the bout "was pretty dull since Kane isn't at the level of being out there that long." The Undertaker sold far more than his opponent, a rarity for him, but understandable given the need to further augment Kane's character. Kane took the loss, but it took three Undertaker Tombstones to finish the job, deferring to the discarnate powers of the match's loser. As a consolation prize, Kane was scripted to take part in a high-profile encounter that spawned a droll *WrestleMania* tradition.

Pete Rose made his *WrestleMania* appearance prior to the match in a role not clearly defined, but apparently with the intent of playing guest ring announcer for the Undertaker/Kane showdown. For cheap heat, Rose, winner of three World Series championships with the Cincinnati Reds and Philadelphia Phillies, insulted the then-baseball woes of the city of Boston, gut-punching them with wound-poking references to notable Red Sox shortcomings. This segued into the entrance of Kane, who upon his arrival in the ring snatched up near-fifty-seven-year-old Rose, flipped him upside down, and deposited him with a Tombstone piledriver to wild cheers, contra to the desired reaction he had spent six months working for. If the match was not especially memorable, Rose's involvement would endure far better as a snicker-worthy flashback moment in forthcoming years. Rose would be welcomed back as a willing punching bag to cement an unusual legacy within the wrestling world. "The more money you gave Pete Rose, the more he'd do," laughed Russo. "It was literally that simple."

The days of a tuxedoed Bob Uecker conducting yuk-yuk interviews and Robert Goulet performing opening ceremonies were as old hat as Sgt Slaughter portraying any sort of respectable and commanding authority figure. The celebrities at *WrestleMania* were no longer glamorous. The only rub that could be gained from the dregs of their stardom was by striking at their cracked visages of fame.

THE STIFF, frigid breeze off the Massachusetts Bay whipped wildly the Thursday before *WrestleMania*, slightly fogging the air after a chilly morning rain. The unfavourable weather failed to chase away a sizable crowd at Boston's City Hall Plaza, with most reasonable estimates listing 10,000 on hand for what would be termed a 'public workout'. The event was a last-stop commercial for Sunday night's pay-per-view, and would feature one final conflict between Michaels and Austin, with Tyson also on hand. After arriving via limousine, the DX contingent was set to agitate a crowd already churned by the sustained winds. Michaels, however, was the one whose nerves would be jangled.

Behind weekend-biker sunglasses and a leather vest, Michaels began his heel's soliloquy, but was quickly cut off by a fan's projectile clocking him in the side of the head. Calmly, but exhaling fire from his nostrils, Michaels strode from the outdoor ring, and back up the aisle-way, leaving an awkward chasm of dead air. MC Michael 'Dok Hendrix' Hayes politely advised the crowd not to throw objects during the quiet scramble, while the WWF Champion became apoplectic away from prying eyes.

"I lost it and started cutting promos on everyone in sight," Michaels admitted. "I threatened to not show up [at *WrestleMania*] unless they provided me with personal security guards."

"Someone had thrown something at him and hit him, and he got back into the car I believe, and kinda threw a temper tantrum," added Austin, who was counting on Michaels to be present for a nugget of photogenic gold at the conclusion of the workout. Helmsley managed to pick up the pieces and carry on insulting Boston sports teams and rival WWF notables (with the help of independent wrestler and spot-on impersonator Jason Sensation) before Austin made his entrance with the help of a police escort. By the time 'Stone Cold' hit the ring, Michaels rematerialized, taking part in the group beat-down alongside Helmsley and Los Boricuas. In the end, the WWF had their desired video of seething Austin entangled in the ropes, subjected to a taunting double kiss on the head from Tyson and Michaels, to give the irascible challenger one more reason to kick the champion's ass come Sunday night. However, Michaels' state of being was becoming more of a concern than ever. He just needed to survive the weekend, and the WWF gave him a security guard for the remainder of his stay in Boston, to ensure no more freak-outs from the fragile, hair-trigger headliner. Extra special care was being taken to soothe his mangled psyche.

"When Vince came into my dressing room, he said that he appreciated my doing this," Michaels recalled, also noting that McMahon became embroiled in a verbal dust-up with his father, retired Air Force Colonel Richard Hickenbottom, who was not thrilled with the idea of his son being subjected to a potentially-gruelling match in his condition. Nonetheless, McMahon was nothing but cordial and reassuring toward the understandably-wary elder Hickenbottom.

"Vince understood that my dad was just trying to protect his son," Michaels stated. McMahon may have been midwifing Michaels through the heart of an uneasy transition, but according to Vince Russo, there was a point where McMahon's coddling of 'the Heartbreak Kid' reached a nadir.

"When Austin came along, and Austin started getting hot, I literally could see Vince McMahon kick Shawn to the curb like yesterday's news - it's time to go with the hot new toy," Russo claimed. "In my opinion, that's what Vince was doing, and that triggered Shawn's anger. In my opinion, he had every right in the world to be upset. Shawn would be the first one to tell you, 'I would have been happy to see me go,' He was not the Shawn Michaels he is today. He was under the influence of a lot of things. He was in a foul mood because of the way Vince was treating him. I think Shawn would've been happy to see Shawn go."

"Shawn wasn't in a good place physically or mentally," Austin confirmed. "He had a pretty tough attitude on him as well, and really didn't feel like dropping the strap."

"Vince was in a difficult situation," Michaels conceded. "I know he cared about me and wanted to take care of me, but the company's future was riding on Steve. He needed to put his focus there." Michaels claimed that he had no problem putting Austin over at *WrestleMania*, contrary to Austin's belief, or the belief of anyone that would assume selfishness on account of Michaels' past dealings. Also of dispute was an incident that reportedly took place prior to Michaels making his *WrestleMania* entrance, designed to ensure that he played ball.

"Undertaker taped his fists, sat right down at Gorilla position, and watched the monitor, to watch Shawn drop the title to Austin," Cornette claimed, "And provided everything went the right way, that was all that was going to happen." With the notorious Kliq fragmented through the chasing of dollars in other places, and Michaels at his most vulnerable, it made sense that the top cop from the neutralising Bone Street Krew would have a vested interest in the finish of the *WrestleMania* finale, where the right thing had to be done.

"There was a time where Undertaker was not very enamoured with Shawn Michaels the man, the person, or the wrestler," Austin remembered. "Undertaker and myself both respected Shawn's ability, his work, the talent, the things he could do in the ring because he was pretty much kinda almost unparalleled - he was that damn good. But as a person, I didn't like him. Quite frankly, I didn't like him at all."

As far as Undertaker wrapping his soup bones with tape as a method of intimidation, Austin noted, "I've always heard that rumour, and I've heard Shawn talk about it. I think I've heard Undertaker acknowledge it. I can't speak to how valid or true it was. I think it was true, it probably was a shoot."

Michaels has gone on record, stating that this was not precisely the case, but concedes that Undertaker was prepared to assert himself in the event of any funny business. "Mark went to everybody and told them, 'If this doesn't go down the way it should, I'm going to have a big problem and Shawn is going to have a big problem. I'll go over there and beat the heck out of him.' But he never had to say anything to me," Michaels asserted.

Where Michaels did take umbrage was with the planned fallout to the title switch. After referee Mike Chioda[25] would be rendered incapacitated following a designated bump, Austin was supposed to plant Michaels with the Stunner. Tyson would run in to levy the three count, a different sort of screwy-finish that would turn the tables on Michaels' involvement in Montreal. Turnabout's fair play. After some posing by the new titleholder, Austin would watch a stunned Michaels angrily confront Tyson, only for Michaels to be drilled by a pulled right-hook to further spell out the disassociation. With Michaels prone, feeling for his teeth with his tongue, Tyson would drape an 'Austin 3:16' shirt over the deposed ruler's face. For Michaels, everything up to that point was copacetic, but employment of the shirt was apparently over the line.

"I didn't want them doing that. I believed losing was enough and that covering me up with the shirt was overkill," Michaels insisted. "Pat Patterson pushed really hard for it, and I made a big stink. I told Pat, 'If you are going to do that, I'll get up and leave.'"

Prowling the corridors prior to his entrance, Austin sent the Fleet Center into a gushing frenzy solely through this image that could just as easily serve as B-roll footage. Once the familiar glass broke, the reaction grew even louder. Even with the chicanery that had riddled the main event scene across both top wrestling promotions, it was clear that Austin was winning this match. No other ending would be fathomable. In thirteen prior *WrestleManias*, the curtain dropped on a babyface victor. Just because 1998 was about a new set of rules did not mean that all traditions would be changing.

It was Austin that put together the structure of the match, keeping proceedings relatively simple for the usually-spry Michaels, whose mind was certainly elsewhere, less focused on show-stealing, meekly keen on fulfilling his duty. "I threw down four pain pills and somehow made it through the match," he would later admit. The early going saw Michaels bob and weave around Austin's lunges, striking with showman-like left hands while cackling gleefully at the ringside boxer that evidently taught him the finer points of pugilism. Between this and Michaels' overt preening, the first couple of minutes elapsed without a single taxing bump. That changed when Austin flattened Michaels with a double sledge to the face following a chase sequence, the champion thudding his sciatic region into the canvas, but springing up quickly enough.

---

[25] Chioda was refereeing the match in place of Earl Hebner, because Hebner was in hospital following a brain aneurysm. Michaels, in a rare moment of compassion, spoke directly into the camera during his ring entrance and said, "This one's for you, Earl," as a show of support for the ailing referee.

More smoke-and-mirrors as Austin tugged the seat of the tights of a fleeing Michaels, exposing his ass for a cheap thrill. "Full moon in Boston tonight," quipped Ross on the call.

A few more simple back bumps for Michaels before a truly risky one, taking a back body drop over the ropes, butt-crack semi-visible, with Helmsley attempting to break his fall. Instead, Michaels' legs slammed onto his best friend like downed power wires, while he jack-knifed to the floor, landing on the black mat with his lower back. Michaels quickly pulled himself to his feet, evading the pursuant Austin, but he was clearly in a permeating haze. "I felt like I was running in quicksand, and that made me fatigue much faster than I normally would have," Michaels remembered, explaining how several minutes of activity suddenly had him on rubber limbs.

Buying Michaels some time to catch his bearings, Helmsley assaulted Austin by sending him into the guardrail. This prompted an ejection for both him and Chyna to unanimous jubilation, with the presumed benefit of putting Michaels on offence, where he would not have to fling his body around with his usual cavalier flair. The fight spilled to the bandstand at the back of the arena, where Michaels walloped Austin with a cymbal stand. Running the gamut of physical and mental feeling, Michaels cursed at a fan before bringing the match back to the ring. Incredibly, Michaels returned to taking bumps, including a spine-rattler from an Austin Irish-whip into the corner that Michaels attempted to tuck and roll through, only to loudly whack the buckles, dangling like a parachutist in distress on the ropes.

After a Stunner tease, Michaels pushed off and ducked through the ropes to the apron, where Austin knocked him off with a charging right hand. Michaels twisted like a tornado in falling from the edge of the ring, virtually face-planting onto the front of the announcers' table. When Austin attempted to continue the motions of the match, it was clear that Michaels was in incredible pain. Instead of dragging his opponent to his feet, Austin took hold of Michaels' head and allowed him to get to his feet on his own. Seconds before, Michaels was clutching his knee while grimacing in teeth-clenching agony. Everything Michaels did from here on out would prove laborious. The greatest main-event athlete that the WWF had ever known was now reduced to intermittently leaning on the ropes and gasping in anguish between routine spots. Even sitting on Austin's chest to deliver a series of hammering punches nearly brought Michaels to tears. After a basic snap mare takeover, Michaels grabbed his lower back and squeaked out an agonised, "Ah shit!"

To this point, Tyson, in his official D-Generation X t-shirt and black cargo pants, had been nothing more than a spectator, far too subdued for critics to find fault with, aside from his mere attendance. Tyson paced ringside while Michaels began working over Austin's legs, the sudden flat-footed pacing increasing the anticipation for the other shoe dropping. When was Tyson going to get involved? After Michaels managed to throw a baseball slide at Austin on the floor, Tyson tossed the challenger back into the ring, inadvertently giving him a wedgie on one side. Between that and blindly allowing Michaels to clutch the middle rope during a figure-four leglock, the $3 million man was little more than the richest fan in the building.

"The gut check here is off the page; both these guys gotta be hurtin' like hell," Ross grunted with his rural affirmation, telling both a story and the truth simultaneously. Chioda's bump would follow, as a sleeperhold-bound Austin backed Michaels into the corner, smooshing the referee into his preordained nap. With concern, the crowd grew silent, sensing that Austin's banana peel lay in wait. Even Austin's stomps on a cornered Michaels could only draw a mild reaction, with all eyes locked on Tyson's every move. The prelude to the intricate finish was Michaels ducking a clothesline, rebounding with what would ordinarily be a gliding forearm smash, one of his signatures. Par for his current state, his soles only achieved about four inches of elevation, making for an exaggerated clothesline instead. After a spell where both men sold exhaustion, Michaels somehow managed to throw his mangled carcass to his feet, the classic kip-up of the classic Michaels.

"Watching that match, there was one specific spot where Shawn kipped up," remembered a quizzical Russo. "And I watched that and I said, 'There is no way in the world...', but then again the other side of me was like, 'Well, if your adrenaline is going a hundred miles an hour in front of a sold out *WrestleMania* crowd...'"

After a flying elbow smash, Michaels pantomimed the coup de grace, stomping his right leg of multiple surgical repairs in anticipation of Sweet Chin Music. From here, it was a literal race to the finish - Austin ducked the kick, Michaels pushed out of the Stunner, and Austin caught the foot of a second kick attempt. Spinning Michaels on his axis, Austin performed the Stunner at long last. Tyson quickly slid into the ring, and even more quickly slapped his palm on the mat three times. The accelerated cadence had more to do with Tyson's inexperience, and probably adrenaline, but could just as easily be seen as the hurried ushering of the Austin Era. The sooner, the better.

The 'gotcha' double-cross was complete, and Tyson raised Austin's hand under heavy adulation. "The Austin Era has begun! Stone Cold's eight-year journey has been culminated!" cried Ross at ringside, happy to see his real-life chum enjoy the spoils of being the man. Eight months earlier, Austin was struggling to feel his limbs after a wrestling move gone bad. Holding the classic 'winged eagle' version of the WWF Championship belt on the middle turnbuckles to adoring, exultant screams, he could feel every pulsation. This was Arcadia.

Temporarily, Austin's music stopped, the cue for Michaels to drag what was left of himself to his feet for one last fall. Accusing Tyson of treachery, Michaels took a swing and was drilled with the Tyson right. A beat earlier, Michaels snatched the 'Austin 3:16' shirt away from Tyson's hands and flung it as far out of the ring as he could. Not to worry, Austin had a back-up slung over his shoulder. Sure enough, Michaels would be literally shrouded in black against his wishes. The boyhood dream of 1996 was indifferently broken, Michaels left behind while the new flavour led himself off to a theoretical throne.

"I STARTED thinking about Tyson draping the 'Austin 3:16' shirt on me and my blood started boiling," recalled Michaels, on his decision to leave the Fleet Center in an annoyed huff. While Vince McMahon took part in a post-show presser with Austin and Tyson, Michaels was cutting a hell-bent swathe through the backstage area, and Vince's son Shane ended up in the crosshairs. "I didn't make a scene or anything, but I let him have it for a few minutes," Michaels mused. "I told him how the shirt thing was B.S. and how I deserved better after all I had done for the company."

Conversely, it was all smiles and yuks before the assembled media, with Tyson raving about the experience and proudly saying he would do it again. Considering how well-behaved Tyson had been under this particularly scrutinising microscope, the endorsement rang a few tones louder. McMahon even chimed in on Tyson's wrestling prospects, but also conceded that he did not think 'Iron Mike' was through boxing yet.

Tyson would not work with the WWF in any capacity again until long after the 'F' became an 'E', guest hosting an episode of *Raw* in early-2010. His wattage was welcome, but no longer required. An estimated 730,000 homes purchased *WrestleMania XIV*, up 208 percent from the comparatively-paltry 237,000 that witnessed Austin's blood staining the canvas in Chicago. More than triple that audience had just gotten done watching Austin stick the flag firmly into the apex. Tyson helped, but megastar 'Stone Cold' could take it from here.

There was an undeniable irony in Michaels exiting from the spotlight only five months after helping slam the door into Bret Hart's face. For the previous two years, the WWF depth chart would list Michaels and Hart as one and two in some order, or perhaps even '1a' and '1b'. A silent competition rooted in insecurity, self-worth, and the need for respect spilled over into finances, with one wrangling himself an unprecedented contract, and the other unhappy with how it dwarfed his own hard-earned dollars. Cordiality between the two degenerated into bitterness, professionalism eroding away like wave-bitten dunes. Feelings turned to words, and words turned to fists. Weary Michaels helped rid the WWF of one of the few people unafraid to go nose-to-nose with him, only for his long-aching back to collapse beneath the weight of work and worry. There would have been a time where McMahon losing both Hart and Michaels, not just one, would have been viewed as a catastrophic knockout blow to his jutting chin. As red-hot Austin returned the media's volleys with relaxed confidence, McMahon probably wondered why he ever bothered losing sleep over the pair's angst in the first place.

He could barely hide his smirk watching Austin and Tyson charm the reporters, far less biting than they had been to his company two months earlier. His pride was showing, and it had every right to - only three years earlier, *WrestleMania XI* was packed with copious celebrity involvement and had bombed on pay-per-view, the least-bought *WrestleMania* of all time until the two subsequent incarnations topped it chronologically. His big name talents had gradually defected to WCW and the lure of greener lining. One took an unprecedented contract to stay with the WWF, and ended up leaving for WCW anyway, forced out under a cloud of incredible ugliness. None of that mattered, because the pieces had fallen into place, the winning formula happened upon.

Once thought of as a wounded, decrepit general in a losing war, McMahon's WWF was thriving at the box office, the merchandise stands, on pay-per-view, and in TV ratings. *Raw* had not beaten *Nitro* in the ratings in close to two years, but the Monday Night Wars were still being decided. More than ever, McMahon had the ammunition to shoot down the opposition, and as it turned out, it would not take him much longer to snatch the clear lead. Trying like hell to pull the sword back out of the stone, the resilient McMahon had recited a spell from an entirely different book. The mojo was back, and the WWF was about to embark upon the most prosperous run in its storied history.

REFERENCES

Author Conducted Interviews

Jim Cornette

J.J. Dillon

Danny Doring

Tod Gordon

Brittany Pillman

Lanny Poffo

Tom Prichard

Ken Shamrock

Rob Van Dam

Del Wilkes

Books

Shaun Assael, Mike Mooneyham, *Sex, Lies, and Headlocks: The Real Story of Vince McMahon and World Wrestling Entertainment.* Broadway Books, 2004

Steve Austin, Dennis Brent, Jim Ross. *The Stone Cold Truth.* WWE, 2003

Eric Bischoff, Jeremy Roberts, *Controversy Creates Cash.* WWE Books, 2006.

Emma Bull, *Bone Dance, A Fantasy for Technophiles (Second Edition).* Orb Books, 2009

Graham Cawthon, Grant Sawyer, *The History of Professional Wrestling Vol. 1: WWF 1963-1989 (Volume 1),* Create Space Independent Publishing, 2013

Graham Cawthon, Grant Sawyer, *The History of Professional Wrestling Vol. 2: WWF 1990-1999 (Volume 2),* Create Space Independent Publishing, 2013

James J. Dillon, Scott Teal, Philip Varriale, *Wrestlers Are Like Seagulls: From McMahon To McMahon,* Crowbar Press, 2005

Ric Flair, Mark Madden, Keith Elliot Greenberg, *Ric Flair: To Be The Man*, WWF, 2004

Mick Foley, *Have a Nice Day: A Tale of Blood and Sweatsocks*. Harper Entertainment, 1999

Eddie Guerrero, Michael Krugman, *Cheating Death, Stealing Life: The Eddie Guerrero Story*, Gallery Books, 2006

Bret Hart, *Hitman: My Real Life in the Cartoon World of Wrestling*. Grand Central Publishing, 2008

Diana Hart, Kirstie McLellan, *Under The Mat: Inside Wrestling's Greatest Family*, Fenn Pub, 2001

Julie Hart, *Hart Strings*. Tightrope Books, Inc, 2013

Martha Hart, Eric Francis, *Broken Harts: The Life and Death of Owen Hart*. M. Evans and Company, 2004

Bob Holly, Ross Williams, *The Hardcore Truth: The Bob Holly Story*. ECW Press, 2013

Chris Jericho, Peter Thomas Fornatale, *Undisputed: How to Become the World Champion in 1,372 Easy Steps*. Grand Central Publishing, 2011

Jimmy Korderas, *Three Count: My Life In Stripes As A WWE Referee*, ECW Press, 2013

Patrick Laprade, Bertrand Hebert, *Mad Dogs, Midgets and Screw Jobs*, ECW Press, 2013

Joe Laurinaitis, Andrew William Wright, *The Road Warriors: Danger, Death, and the Rush of Wrestling*. Medallion Press, 2011

Thom Loverro, *The Rise and Fall of ECW*. WWE, 2006

Heath McCoy, *Pain and Passions: The History of Stampede Wrestling*, ECW Press, 2007

Shawn Michaels, Aaron Feigenbaum, *Heartbreak and Triumph: The Shawn Michaels Story*. WWE, 2005

Irvin Muchnick, *Chris and Nancy: The True Story of the Benoit Murder-Suicide and Pro Wrestling's Cocktail of Death*, ECW Press, 2009

R.D. Reynolds, Bryan Alvarez, *The Death of WCW*, ECW Press, 2004

Jeremy Roberts, *Rey Mysterio: Behind the Mask*, WWE, 2010

Vince Russo, *Forgiven: One Man's Journey From Self-Glorification to Sanctification*. ECW Press, 2005

Scott E. Williams, *Hardcore History: The Extremely Unauthorized Story of ECW*. Sports Publishing, 2006

DVD / Blu-Ray / Documentaries

Hitman Hart: Wrestling With Shadows. Paul Jay, Vidmark/Trimark, 1998

The Life and Death of Owen Hart. Paul Jay, J Films, 1999

Beyond the Mat. Barry Blaustein, Universal Pictures, 1999

nWo: Back In Black, WWE, 2002

The Best of WWE Confidential. WWE, 2003

Sting: Moment of Truth. Image Entertainment, 2004

The Rise and Fall of ECW, WWE, 2004

The Monday Night War, WWE, 2004

Forever Hardcore - The Documentary. Big Vision, 2005

Bret Hitman Hart: The Best There Is, The Best There Was, The Best There Ever Will Be, WWE, 2005

McMahon, WWE, 2006

Brian Pillman: Loose Cannon, WWE, 2006

The Shawn Michaels Story: Heartbreak & Triumph, WWE, 2007

The Rise & Fall of WCW. WWE, 2009

Hart & Soul: The Hart Family Anthology, WWE, 2009

Bret Hart: Survival of the Hitman. Fight Network, 2010

Greatest Rivalries – Shawn Michaels vs. Bret Hart. WWE, 2011

Shawn Michaels: My Journey, WWE, 2011

Stone Cold Steve Austin: The Bottom Line On The Most Popular Superstar Of All Time. WWE, 2011

nWo: The Revolution, WWE, 2012

Barbed Wire City, Kevin Kiernan, John Philapavage, 2013

Triple H: Thy Kingdom Come. WWE, 2013

Ladies and Gentlemen, My Name is Paul Heyman, WWE, 2014

The Kliq Rules. WWE, 2015

Online Articles

Mike Mooneyham, "Nasty Boys Living Up To Name", Mike Mooneyham, 1997
http://www.mikemooneyham.com/1997/01/19/nasty-boys-living-up-to-name/

Wresting Classics, "Ken Shamrock vs. The Nasty Boys", Frank Dusek, 1998
http://www.wrestlingclassics.com/mu/mu-st/mu-st-nastyboys.html

Biz Journals, "Wrestler Trades Body Blows With WCW", Alan Byrd, 1998
http://www.bizjournals.com/orlando/stories/1998/05/25/story4.html?page=all

New York Daily News, "WWF Offers, Tyson Bites, Nevada Grapples With Wrestlin' Mike", Michael Katz, 1998
http://www.nydailynews.com/archives/sports/wwf-offers-tyson-bites-nevada-grapples-wrestlin-mike-article-1.800958

New York Daily News, "Dumps Co-Managers as He Signs With Rival, Tyson Flees King Camp", Michael Katz, 1998
http://www.nydailynews.com/archives/sports/dumps-co-managers-signs-rival-tyson-flees-king-camp-article-1.786558

SLAM! Sports, "Mike Tyson Accepts Wrestling Challenge", 1998
http://slam.canoe.com/SlamWrestlingArchive/jan20_tys.html

New York Times, "Big Money, Big Fallout For Tyson; The Ex-Champion Blames the Promoter for Financial Problems", Barry Meier, Timothy W. Smith, 1998
http://www.nytimes.com/1998/05/24/sports/boxing-big-money-big-fallout-for-tyson-ex-champion-blames-promoter-for-financial.html?pagewanted=all

New York Times, "Sports of The Times; Tyson Is Just One of the Three Stooges", Dave Anderson, 1998
    http://www.nytimes.com/1998/02/06/sports/sports-of-the-times-tyson-is-just-one-of-the-three-stooges.html

New York Times, "Sports of The Times; In the Realm of Phantom Sport, the Best Punch Tyson Never Threw", Dave Anderson, 1998
    http://www.nytimes.com/1998/03/30/sports/sports-times-realm-phantom-sport-best-punch-tyson-never-threw.html

New York Daily News, "Wrestlers Lured To Risky Drugs", Kevin McCoy, 2000
    http://www.nydailynews.com/archives/news/wrestlers-lured-risky-drugs-ring-fan-doc-prescribed-illegally-complaint-article-1.874419

Mike Mooneyham, "'Dr. Feelgood' Facing Charges", Mike Mooneyham, 2001
    http://www.mikemooneyham.com/2001/01/27/dr-feelgood-facing-charges/

SLAM! Sports, "Killer Kowalski Slams Chyna's Book". John Powell, 2001,
    http://www.canoe.ca/SlamWrestlingBiosK/kowalski_01feb06-can.html

Los Angeles Times, "A Wrestler's Widow Remembers His Pills, Hormone Injections", Lance Pugmire, 2003
    http://articles.latimes.com/2003/mar/29/entertainment/et-pugmireside29

CBN, "'Sting' Out Of The Ring", Barbara Cornick, 2004
    http://www1.cbn.com/700club/sting-out-ring

ESPN, "Mike Tyson on WWE and Real Life Glass Joe", Jon Robinson, 2012
    http://espn.go.com/blog/playbook/tech/post/_/id/3388/mike-tyson-on-wwe-and-real-life-glass-joe

Wrestling Inc, "Sean Waltman Gives His Take On The Roddy Piper – Kevin Nash Backstage Incident In WCW", Raj Giri, 2014
    http://www.wrestlinginc.com/wi/news/2014/0420/574343/sean-waltman-gives-his-take-on-the-roddy-piper-kevin-nash/

TNA Wrestling News, "Kevin Nash: 'I Just Spoke To Roddy Piper On The Phone'", 2014
    http://www.tnawrestlingnews.com/headlines/kevin-nash-i-just-spoke-to-roddy-piper-on-the-phone/

Sports Illustrated, "Bret Hart Opens Up About The Infamous Montreal Screwjob", Justin Barrasso, 2014
    http://www.si.com/extra-mustard/2014/11/19/bret-hart-opens-about-infamous-montreal-screwjob

Pro Wrestling.Net, "Former WWE Wrestler Marc Mero On Ex-Wife Sable Becoming A Star, Recalls A Fun Arn Anderson Story, Working With A Young Triple H", Steve & The Scum, 2014,
   http://www.prowrestling.net/artman/publish/WWE/article10035074.shtml

Chinlock, "Exclusive: Jan Interviews Former WWE Canada President Carl DeMarco", Jan Murphy, 2014
   http://www.chinlock.com/2014/02/exclusive-jan-interviews-former-wwe-canada-president-carl-demarco/

Bleacher Report, "WWE Superstar Triple H Exclusive: On Arnold, Aging and Wrestling Sting", Jonathan Snowden, 2015
   http://bleacherreport.com/articles/2385233-wwe-superstar-triple-h-exclusive-on-arnold-aging-and-wrestling-sting

SLAM! Sports, "It's Damn Hard Being Ron Simmons", Patrick Laprade, 2015
   http://slam.canoe.com/Slam/Wrestling/2015/07/03/22485931.html

Fox Sports, "Good Ol' JR Takes You Inside The 'Montreal Screwjob' On Its 18th Anniversary", Jim Ross, 2015
   http://www.foxsports.com/wwe/story/jim-ross-vince-mcmahon-bret-hart-shawn-michaels-montreal-screwjob-110915

Newspapers

Dayton Daily News, March 2, 1997

Podcasts & Radio Shows

Chris Warren radio interview, 2007
   https://www.youtube.com/watch?v=g2tU9XRGrzQ

Inside The Ropes Radio, "Interview With Diana Hart-Smith", 2012
   www.insidetheropes.co.uk

Inside The Ropes Radio, "Interview With Julie Hart", 2012
   www.insidetheropes.co.uk

Inside The Ropes Radio, "Interview With Earl Hebner", 2012
   www.insidetheropes.co.uk

Place To Be Podcast. "Episode #172 – Kevin Kelly 1997 WWF" 2013
   http://placetobenation.com/place-to-be-podcast-episode-172-kevin-kelly-1997-wwf-part-one/

Steve Austin Show. "Episode #169 - WrestleMania 13" 2014, http://podcastone.com/Steve-Austin-Show

Piper's Pit With Roddy Piper. "Episode #55 – Cousin Sal", 2014 http://www.podcastone.com/pg/jsp/program/episode.jsp?programID=642&pid=500258

Sam Roberts Wrestling Podcast. "Episode 012 - Jim Ross" 2014 http://podbay.fm/show/934576040/e/1421222400

Talk Is Jericho, "Episode 116 – Shawn Michaels", 2015 http://podcastone.com/pg/jsp/program/episode.jsp?programID=593&pid=483001

Vince Russo's Nuclear Heat, "Episode 7", 2015 https://www.youtube.com/watch?v=pquwbX2-de4

The Two Man Power Trip of Wrestling - Glenn Jacobs interview, 2016 topropepress.com/features/24571/kane-wwe-exclusive-interview

Sgt. Slaughter interview with Bret Hart, https://www.youtube.com/watch?v=Jorb9VmSLAk

Steve Austin interview, 2014(?) https://www.youtube.com/watch?v=Q74m1B-DxbM (unsure of actual episode)

Steve Austin podcast, episode unknown, https://www.youtube.com/watch?v=v83u1ag0qCc

Shoot Interviews

D-Lo Brown Shoot Interview, Title Match Wrestling LLC, 2003

Luna Vachon Shoot Interview, CY Wrestling, 2003

Timeline: The History of WWE - 1997 As Told By Jim Cornette. Kayfabe Commentaries LLC, 2011

Timeline: The History of WWE - 1998 As Told By Vince Russo. Kayfabe Commentaries LLC, 2016

Timeline: The History of WCW - 1997 As Told By Kevin Nash. Kayfabe Commentaries LLC, 2016

Breaking Kayfabe: Lanny Poffo. Kayfabe Commentaries LLC, 2012

Shoot Interview With The Nasty Boys: Just Plain Nasty. RF Video

Ken Shamrock Shoot Interview. RF Video

Bruce Prichard Shoot Interview. RF Video

Interview With Ken Shamrock. Pro MMA Insider, 2012
http://proboxinginsider.com/ken-shamrock-discusses-the-ufc-nasty-boys-more/

Scott Hall Interview. In Your Head Wrestling Radio, 2010

Scott Hall Shoot Interview. RF Video

Eric Bischoff Shoot Interview. RF Video, 2014

Shawn Michaels Shoot Interview. RF Video, 2000

Bret Hart Shoot Interview. RF Video, 2000

Bam Bam Bigelow Shoot Interview, Title Match Wrestling LLC, 1998

Honky Tonk Man Shoot Interview, Great North Wrestling, 2013

Guest Booker… With Bruce Prichard: Screwing Bret. Sean Oliver. Kayfabe Commentaries

YouShoot – Jim Cornette, Sean Oliver, Kayfabe Commentaries

YouShoot – Kevin Nash, Sean Oliver, Kayfabe Commentaries

Earl Hebner Interview, WrestleTalk TV, 2015

Dave & Earl Hebner Shoot Interview, RF Video

Stone Cold Steve Austin Shoot Interview, Michael Schiavello, AXS TV The Voice, 2013

Nick Patrick Interview, World Wrestling Insanity, 2010

Sting Interview, Wrestling Epicenter, 2005

TV Shows

WWF Monday Night Raw, February 1, 1993

WWF King of the Ring, June 25, 1995

WWF In Your House: Mind Games, September 22, 1996

WWF Thursday Raw Thursday Live, February 13, 1997

WWF Monday Night Raw, February 17, 1997

WWF Monday Night Raw, February 24, 1997

WWF Raw is War, March 10, 1997

WWF Raw is War, March 17, 1997

WWF WrestleMania 13, March 23, 1997

WCW Monday Nitro, March 24, 1997

WWF Raw is War, April 7, 1997

ECW Barely Legal, April 13, 1997

WWF Raw is War, April 21, 1997

ECW Chapter 2, May 10, 1997

WWF Raw is War, May 12, 1997

WWF Raw is War, May 19, 1997

ECW Wrestlepalooza, June 7, 1997

WWF SummerSlam, August 3, 1997

ECW Hardcore TV Episode 229, September 8, 1997

WWF Raw is War, September 22, 1997

WWF Raw is War, October 6, 1997

WWF Shotgun, October 11, 1997

WWF Survivor Series, November 9, 1997

WWF Raw is War, November 10, 1997

WCW Monday Nitro, November 10, 1997

WWF Raw is War, November 17, 1997

WCW Monday Nitro, November 17, 1997

WWF Raw is War, December 8, 1997

WWF Raw is War, December 15, 1997

WCW Monday Nitro, December 15, 1997

WCW Starrcade, December 28, 1997

WWF Raw is War, January 5, 1998

WWF Royal Rumble, January 18, 1998

WWF Raw is War, January 19, 1998

WWF Raw is War, March 16, 1998

WWF WrestleMania XIV, March 29, 1998

Oprah's Master Class, "What Dwayne Johnson Learned After Being Booed by 20,000 Wrestling Fans", 2015

Off The Record With Michael Landsberg, February 25, 1998

WWE Network Specials

Legends of Wrestling – The Monday Night Wars. WWE, 2007

Legends of Wrestling - nWo. WWE, 2011

Legends of Wrestling – Rivalries. WWE, 2011

Monday Night War – The Hart Of War. WWE, 2014

Monday Night War – The Kliq. WWE, 2014

Monday Night War – The Austin Era Has Begun. WWE, 2014

All television rating data provided by Nielsen Media Research

All pay-per-view buyrate data provided by the Wrestling Observer Newsletter.

The following issues of the Wrestling Observer Newsletter (http://www.f4wonline.com/) were used for research purposes to help compile this tome.

January 6 1997, January 13 1997, January 20 1997, January 27 1997, February 3 1997, February 10 1997, February 17 1997, February 24 1997, March 3 1997, March 10 1997, March 17 1997, March 24 1997, March 31 1997, April 7 1997, April 14 1997, April 21 1997, April 28 1997, May 5 1997, May 12 1997, May 19 1997, May 26 1997, June 2 1997, June 9 1997, June 16 1997, June 23 1997, June 30 1997, July 7 1997, July 14 1997, July 21 1997, July 28 1997, August 4, August 11 1997, August 18 1997, August 25 1997, September 1 1997, September 8 1997, September 15 1997, September 22 1997, September 29 1997, October 6 1997, October 13 1997, October 20 1997, October 27 1997, November 3 1997, November 10 1997, November 17 1997, November 24 1997, December 1 1997, December 8 1997, December 15 1997, December 22 1997, December 29 1997, January 5 1998, January 12 1998, January 19 1998, January 27 1998, February 2 1998, February 9 1998, February 16 1998, February 23 1998, March 2 1998, March 9 1998, March 16 1998, March 23 1998, March 30 1998, April 6 1998

ACKNOWLEDGEMENTS

James Dixon: Thanks to the following, without whom this book would not have been possible: My wife and children for their constant support. My parents for encouraging me to pursue my various endeavours. All of the people who read and enjoyed *Titan Sinking* and *Titan Shattered* enough that I was convinced to keep writing these tomes. Benjamin Richardson for his fastidious proofing, fact-checking, reworking, and reimagining of many of the words in these pages. Not to mention the wonderful cover art. RD Reynolds for honouring us by agreeing to write the foreword, and for his inspirational work down the years. Jim Cornette, for agreeing to go over the stories from the year in fine detail, and with an enormous amount of patience. His character references and insight into the inner workings of the WWF were, as with *Titan Sinking* and *Titan Shattered*, invaluable. A big thank you to Tom Prichard, Brittany Pillman, Axl Rotten, J.J. Dillon, Lanny Poffo, Ken Shamrock, and Tracy Smothers for opening up to me in interviews about their own experiences of 1997, and their insight into the behaviour of others. Dave Meltzer, for his incredible weekly Wrestling Observer Newsletter, a vital source of information, facts and stats, not to mention being on hand to confirm facts and stories. Graham Cawthon from thehistoryofwwe.com for his celebrated work documenting the history of the WWF/WWE. His website is perhaps the finest resource on the web. Sean Oliver and the team at Kayfabe Commentaries for bring a whole new level of quality to their various wrestling interviews. Their *Timeline* series was the inspiration for these books. Chris Gilder, Lee Maughan, Drew Ortman, Jonathan Sullivan, Bob Dahlstom, and the rest of the team at *History of Wrestling* for the great work they do, especially in the times when I ask them to pick up the slack due to my absence while I am writing these books. Matt Holmes, Peter Willis, and all of the whatculture.com team, who have made me feel a welcome and valued addition to their wonderful crew. I am thrilled to be releasing this book under their brand. Kenny McIntosh for being an ear when one was needed, for sharing information from his experiences with some of the players in this book, and for his help in promoting the series. Scott Keith for his hard work over the years documenting wrestling in his own distinctive way, and for his support and championing of *Titan Sinking* and *Titan Shattered*. Matthew Gregg from *Botchamania* who was a key figure in helping my early books reach a larger audience. Alex Shane for his continued support and championing of this project. Dustin Nichols for his assistance filling in my knowledge gaps in American geographical matters. Jon Apsey for his encouragement to go ahead with this project in the first place. Without him, the Titan series may well not exist. Martin Kirby for always offering support and enthusiastic comments on these books. Findlay Martin for being an inspiration to begin writing in the first place thanks to his wonderful work with the much-missed *Power Slam* magazine. Brian Elliot and John Lister for their positivity and support of these projects over the years. Finally, thanks to Justin Henry for being such a wonderful writing partner. Without his desire to see this book become a reality I doubt I would have found the inspiration alone. It has been a pleasure to work with him over this past year, and I look forward to covering every year in WWF/WWE history with him for the foreseeable future.

Justin Henry: Thanks to the following people for their support of my work in this book, and in general. My mother and father, for encouraging my pursuit of writing and journalism, for putting up with my hefty devotion to an unorthodox hobby such as professional wrestling, and for their unwavering support and generosity throughout my entire life. This book doesn't happen without them, nor does any project I've ever undertaken. Thanks also goes to my brother Joshua, who introduced me to wrestling in 1989, and would laugh uproariously with me through Vince McMahon's phlegm-riddled screams and antics over the years. My long-time best friends Dave, Rob, Brett, Jimmy, and Aris for their like-minded companionship, and for providing a forum to share my many thoughts and ideas over the years. To every webmaster that has ever given me a forum, including Eric Gargiulo, RD Reynolds, Sean Carless, James Guttman, Ben Kerin, Kerry Byrne, Todd DeVries, Mark Whited, Matt Holmes, Scott Keith, and Matthew Gregg, thank you for believing in me to whatever degree of faith you have held. For the subjects that allowed me to interview them in conjunction with this book, including Rob Van Dam, Dan Morrison, Del Wilkes, Tod Gordon, and Jim Cornette, thank you for taking time out of your lives to patiently recall events that were upwards of two decades in the past, providing clarity for the sake of history and accuracy. Additional thanks to the oracle that is Dave Meltzer, for clarifying a few details when I needed a hand. Brian Elliott, the overworked editor of the incredible *Fighting Spirit Magazine*, for the forum to let me shape my writing acumen, and for his faith in me to write as many cover stories as I have; that kind of faith has been as encouraging as anything, and it helped lead me to this project. For all of my other friends that supported me during this long process, thank you so much. And of course, thanks to James Dixon for letting me come aboard this project, for providing many opportunities for me to succeed down this chosen path, and for his relentless patience through the long process of compiling this book. I'd do it all again. And we will!

Printed in Great Britain
by Amazon